RICHARD HOFSTADTER

Richard Hofstadter

An Intellectual Biography

DAVID S. BROWN

The University of Chicago Press CHICAGO & LONDON

David S. Brown is associate professor of
history at Elizabethtown College in Pennsylvania.

The University of Chicago Press, Chicago 60637
The University of Chicago Press, Ltd., London
© 2006 by The University of Chicago
All rights reserved. Published 2006
Printed in the United States of America

15 14 13 12 11 10 09 08 07 06   1 2 3 4 5

ISBN: 0-226-07640-7 (cloth)

Library of Congress Cataloging-in-Publication Data

Brown, David S. (David Scott), 1966– .
Richard Hofstadter : an intellectual biography / David S. Brown
p. cm.
Includes bibliographical references and index.
ISBN 0-226-07640-7 (cloth : alk. paper)
1. Hofstadter, Richard, 1916–1970. 2. Historians—United States—Biography.
I. Title
E175.5.H55B76 2006
973'.072'02—dc22

2005017592

♾ The paper used in this publication meets the minimum requirements of
the American National Standard for Information Sciences—Permanence of
Paper for Printed Library Materials, ANSI z39.48–1992.

My model of the historian engaged in the controversies of the day appears in many varieties. In his own day, and his own way, Richard Hofstadter was an exemplar of the engaged historian. Hofstadter was intensely concerned with the political issues of his time and wrote history as a contribution to contemporary political discussion. Primary research — the sine qua non of the Recovery ideal — was not his strong point nor the focus of his attention. He wanted to recover the past but that was only part of what he considered the historian's larger job: to explore how we in the present should think about the past and present and to persuasively convey those critical reflections to his readers. Some of Hofstadter's interpretations have stood up well, others not. His political passions marred some of it, but made all of it vivid and helped to break new intellectual ground. His books are still today an education and a pleasure to read. I don't know how many of us can expect to do better.

DOROTHY ROSS

Contents

Acknowledgments

The pride of authorship is, at its heart, a shared pleasure. In this particular case, the debts run especially deep. One can find at the close of this book the names of three dozen individuals who favored me with their recollections of Richard Hofstadter. Their words and letters parted many clouds, helping to illuminate a complex subject prone to counter the public demands of academic celebrity with a natural inner reserve. Closer to home, Paul Gottfried and Gabriel Ricci offered collegiality and friendship along with insightful criticisms of an early draft. What they read was largely the fruit of research that could not have been recovered without the generosity of Elizabethtown College and the Gilder Lehrman Institute of American History. I enjoyed remarkably skillful assistance from a number of archivists and librarians, but I recall with greatest pleasure the cooperation of two individuals. Fred McKitrick kindly allowed me to work in his late father's papers, and Kenneth Stampp trusted me with a splendid cache of Hofstadter letters culled from his private collection. I consider myself more than fortunate that Robert Devens edited this book. He smartly shepherded the manuscript from a rough draft through publication, improving its contents, assuaging the concerns of its author—and this with a certain editorial grace and good humor. In closing stages, James Banner, Jr., Thomas Bender, Eric Foner, Peter Gay, James Gilbert, Michael Kazin, Lawrence Levine, Jack Pole, Dorothy Ross, and the late James Shenton read all or parts of the manuscript. Their extraordinarily helpful suggestions are here acknowledged with appreciation.

Richard Hofstadter's letters and other unpublished work inform every chapter of this book. I regret, however, that the Hofstadter estate has not allowed me to quote from these materials.

Interior, Exterior

In a liberal society the historian is free to try to dissociate
myths from reality, but that same impulse to myth-making
that moves his fellow man is also at work in him.

RICHARD HOFSTADTER, 1956

There is a certain mystique to Richard Hofstadter. For nearly thirty
years, the legend goes, he wrote the best books for the best publisher,
won the best prizes, and taught in the best city, at the best school, at the
best time. Among historians, *The American Political Tradition,* House of
Knopf, Pulitzer, New York, Columbia University, and postwar America
evoke a hazy attachment to a lost world of scholarly giants confident in
the curative powers of the enlightened mind. This was a world raised in
the collective memory of the Depression thirties, tormented by the
anti-intellectualism of the McCarthy fifties, and rejected in the student
wars of the radical sixties. Along the way, American society changed and
historical writing changed, too. The older generation's preference for
exploring the politics and ideas of elite personalities yielded before a
broad canopy of studies focusing on race, class, and gender that revolutionized the academy's presentation of the past. Now, as the last great
historians of the postwar period leave the scene, it seems particularly
useful to candidly assess the greatest among them. Richard Hofstadter's
career as a professional historian paralleled the heyday of twentieth-
century liberalism (1933–68). Tracing his life reveals a complex tapestry
of internal and external motivations that merged to produce a uniquely
insightful mind, alert to the promise and perils of American democracy.

As the academy moved to the left, the nation's political culture lurched
to the right, leaving liberals clinging to an ever-shrinking center. That
Hofstadter, a symbol of the postwar consensus, is still commonly quoted
in the pages of the nation's most popular general interest and political

periodicals attests to his unusual hold on the public's imagination.[1] More than three decades after his untimely death from leukemia at the age of fifty-four, legions of journalists and Internet bloggers routinely adopt social-psychological concepts — status anxiety, paranoid style, anti-intellectualism — popularized by Hofstadter. Among professional historians, only the distinguished Progressive thinkers Frederick Jackson Turner and Charles Beard and postwar notables C. Vann Woodward and Arthur Schlesinger, Jr., made as lasting impressions on their culture. Like these men, Hofstadter exhibited an enviable ability to connect with a large, critical, and politically conscious readership. He shared further their striking intellectual charisma and penchant for producing "relevant" scholarship that both reflected and shaped the course of twentieth-century liberal thought.

More than any of his peers, Hofstadter was sensitive to the increasingly urban and ethnic character of American life. Eager to embrace the future rather than commemorate the past, he rejected the conventional signposts that had for so long given direction to American civilization — a culture of capitalism, individualism, and isolationism. These established values, he knew, had long served Americans eager to define themselves as a Protestant, farming people. But the times no longer supported this vision — nineteenth-century liberalism collapsed in the 1930s. Its failure to solve either that decade's industrial crisis or the ideological schisms that prefaced fascism's war on the West and communism's hold in the East elicited from Hofstadter a sharp intellectual response. His criticisms frequently drew blood and aroused strong opposition from both conservatives and progressives. And they had good reason to worry. Unencumbered by deep roots in the native soil of his immigrant father's adopted country, Hofstadter enlisted the past to reveal the failings of a time-worn political tradition and by inference highlight the promise of what he believed was a more humane, cosmopolitan, and pluralistic postwar liberalism. Anglo-Saxonism and agrarianism were out. Ethnic diversity and modernity were in. As the old codes gave way, America's need for fresh heroes and new perspectives encouraged Hofstadter to rewrite its history as a prelude to moving its culture.

In the pages of his most popular books, Hofstadter championed a thoughtful and pragmatic social philosophy sympathetic to the welfare state reforms initiated by the New Deal. To describe his views as essentially relativistic, however, is to miss the point. Hofstadter respected history, took it on its own terms, and according to the merits of evidence, demonstrated an admirable responsiveness to rethinking earlier positions and revising earlier statements. His controversial experimentation with the social sciences in the 1950s came from an urgent desire to understand the past more fully and accurately, to expand historical inquiry beyond the economic interpretations favored by the previous generation in order to entertain a broader and yet more subtle scope of human activity. In tracing the psychology and emotional needs of his subjects, Hofstadter hoped to make history at once more complex and more clear. Above all, he delighted in lucid, unsentimental thinking and solid argumentation; indeed, they formed the foundations of his own work.

Social environment inevitably intrudes upon historical analysis, however, and so we must appreciate not simply the author's work, but also the public and personal circumstances that sustained and gave meaning to his efforts. "Before you study the history," one commentator advised, "study the historian. . . . The historian, being an individual, is also a product of history, and of society; and it is in this twofold light that the student of history must learn to regard him." Hofstadter referred to this paradox as the historian engagé — the participation of a scholar in the events he recorded. Involvement, no doubt, sacrificed a scientific pose, yet, as he knew from firsthand experience, it also provided the writer with a surfeit of fresh insights and new perspectives.[2]

Upheaval too, can abet the imagination. Hofstadter's formative years were witness to the abrupt failure of long-established moral, intellectual, and political currents in American life. The fragility of the times undoubtedly shaped its survivors. Two world wars, the Great Depression, Nazi-Soviet pact, Holocaust, and early stirrings of the cold war served as the somber context for Hofstadter's first three decades. These turbulent days drew him into a deep and meaningful engagement with a radically altered postwar world. As the old liberalism expired in the twin failures of Hooverism and isolationism, he felt free to challenge the dominant outline of American history.

Identity played a vital and no less significant role in contextualizing Hofstadter's scholarship. Half Jewish, he was part of the first wave of intellectuals to incorporate secular, cosmopolitan, and universalist perspectives into his work; as such, he served as a thoughtful agent of change in a nation rapidly moving away from its Protestant moorings. And this required a rather explicit break from the way American historians customarily handled their subject. Hofstadter found in earlier schools of historical writing a Wasp bias that favored Anglo-Saxon preferences over more nuanced and culturally diverse narratives. His rebellion against the dominant trends of prewar historiography occurred as others close to him remained committed to the inherited past. In 1942 Hofstadter's most influential graduate teacher, Merle Curti, announced his departure from Columbia's Teachers College to accept a position at the University of Wisconsin. Illinois native and Columbia colleague Allan Nevins regretted his friend's impending absence, but still congratulated Curti on a kind of moral upgrade of station by moving to the nation's heartland. He warmly extolled the virtues of Madison: "Your children will have a better community to grow up in than any in or near New York. The Middle West is our authentic America." Hofstadter never shared this opinion or the nostalgia that lay behind it. He came from Buffalo, an ethnically mixed city lacking a dominant identity, his sense of ambiguous geographical origins further sharpened by the fact that American historians traditionally came from New England or the Midwest. And this fueled his creativity. "I can never wholly identify with any collectivity," he remarked late in life. "This kind of marginality is by now a more general American experience; so today I am not an unrepresentative American."[3]

Hofstadter's identification (and fascination) with the odd edges of his society merged with a heightened awareness of human weakness — including his own. A hypochondriac, Hofstadter, his son Dan recalls, was "a cheerful melancholic. What I mean is that he was not what is commonly known as a manic-depressive, but rather that his cheerfulness held his melancholia in solution, as salt may be dissolved in water." According to Columbia historian Walter Metzger, Hofstadter's temperamental divide informed his published work. "There was," he insisted, "a manic, slightly manic, slightly depressive quality in his writing style." Even a cursory reading of Hofstadter's books reveals that he frequently — and sometimes carelessly — overplayed his findings. This was in part a literary tactic designed to draw attention to his scholarship by garnishing it with a rhetorical bite that made it impossible to ignore. At a deeper level, however, it touched upon certain internal concerns that enlivened his work but chipped away at the scholar's quest for balance. In weak moments he lost sight of the American stage altogether and projected the great evil of his day — fascism — across the national landscape. His critical (and funny) portrait of Theodore Roosevelt in *The American Political Tradition* made TR into a kind of Mussolini lite. In *The Age of Reform* he accentuated with too few qualifications the anti-Semitic side of midwestern Populism, and in 1964 described the *uber* conservative Barry Goldwater's winning of the Republican Party nomination in language that evoked the coming to power of Adolf Hitler: it "gives him a strong position from which to form a new kind of political union, which will be based on jingoism, economic ultra-conservatism, and racial animosity."[4] These examples — and there are many more — make it hard to escape the impression that beyond the playfulness there was a slightly erratic and perhaps slightly paranoid side of Richard Hofstadter that surfaced in his work.

The historian H. Stuart Hughes believed that Hofstadter's apparent premonition of an early death explained his anxieties. "One has the impression that there are some people who have a pessimistic attitude towards life and their own health that suggests that they are destined to die young, and I think this was true in Dick's case. There was a very deep running pessimism in his attitude." Dan Hofstadter adds that "the death of his mother and then of my mother, left him in a state, I believe, of unresolved discomforts, none of which were imagined — he was simply aware of his bad heredity and bad luck. He seemed at times to feel dogged by a malign providence." And this doubt spilled over into his scholarship. Reading Hofstadter, one quickly notes his lack of faith in the public's commitment to political pluralism and intellectual freedom. It was an astute rather than crippling judgment that aligned with his way of looking at the world. "Dick had a strong sense of human limitations and was not at all sentimental about human fate," noted William Leuchtenburg. "One day he and I were walking across the Columbia campus on 116th Street. I was talking enthusiastically about how psychotherapy can change people for the better, and Dick shook his head and cited [the psychoanalyst Otto] Fenichel to me as demonstrating how our lives are irrevocably shaped by the cards we are dealt in infancy."[5]

Hofstadter's cultivated, necessary detachment found an important counterbalance in his scholarly vocation. "He was a very fragile, not very brave person, who became brave in his work," Dan Hofstadter maintains. "He struck a workable truce with his fears." The juxtaposition between interior and exterior could be confusing. "When you met him," one Hofstadter student remembered, "you didn't have a sense that this was Richard Hofstadter. You didn't have the sense that you were in the presence of a distinctive mind whose work had really changed the face of American historiography." In fact, he played different roles before different audiences. A talented mimic, he entertained brilliantly at intimate social settings, impersonating comedians, politicians, and the more starchy historians he encountered at professional gatherings. This was neither a precious nor private talent. Hofstadter openly communicated a genius for fearless exposure, perceptive play, and bold commentary through his scholarship. A quiet and in some ways distant man, he came alive in the motion of performance, and this included the liberating freedom of the open page.[6]

*   *   *

This biography is naturally an extended conversation with the formal writings of Richard Hofstadter. It is also attentive, however, to the personal and private circumstances that shaped his work. An exploration of Hofstadter's inner life provides an indispensable tool for evaluating his scholarship and politics within the context of his sense of identity. If we approach Hofstadter only through his books and reputation, we are in danger of leaving much out; of forgetting that this quintessential "New York Jewish intellectual" was actually christened in his mother's Lutheran faith, and absorbed a host of cultural references rooted in the rhythms and traditions of the nation's interior. His background, in other words, had deep and important connections with the Protestant, property-rights tradition that he wrote against. When Hofstadter arrived in Manhattan in the autumn of 1936, his western New York origins yielded a wonderful sense of perspective that he always cherished. It protected him (though less than he imagined) from the incestuous academic circles, stale debates, and provincial attitudes that sometimes constricted intellectual life in the East. In a letter to David Riesman written in the fifties, Hofstadter suggested that New York intellectuals were out of touch with American life and culture West of the Hudson. They would benefit, he continued, tongue not completely in cheek, from long sabbaticals in Kansas, North Dakota, Utah — or Buffalo.[7]

People — like places — also influenced Hofstadter. His first wife, the novelist Felice Swados, played an instrumental role helping her husband forge a relationship with the Left. Her death in 1945 — the year the Second World War ended and the reforms of the New Deal expired — coincided with Hofstadter's growing disenchantment with the political radicalism that he first discovered at the University of Buffalo. Eighteen months after Felice's death, he married Beatrice Kevitt, an editor who proved immensely helpful "turning a good writer into a masterful writer."[8] She further arranged her family's physical settings with an eye toward encouraging Hofstadter's scholarly routine. Productive working summers on Cape Cod complemented a home on the Upper West Side receptive to the comings and goings of her husband's friends, colleagues, and graduate students.

As Hofstadter's private affairs stabilized, so did his professional fortunes. In 1945 he was teaching at the University of Maryland—then considered something of an academic backwater—for a paltry salary, and his one book to date, *Social Darwinism in American Thought,* had earned good reviews but seemed destined to be read by only a limited, academic audience. He was, moreover, struggling with a terrible private crisis as a widower separated from his infant son, then being cared for by family in Buffalo. Facing an uncertain future, he considered leaving the academy for a career in journalism. Within a year and a half, however, his circumstances changed dramatically. Remarriage allowed Hofstadter to bring Dan to New York, where he had accepted a position at Columbia University. In time, financial success — trips to Europe, private schools for his two children (a daughter, Sarah, was born in 1952), the Cape home — followed and he fell into a comfortable role as one of America's most popular historians. These personal and professional relationships were the touchstones of Hofstadter's adulthood. And when the accolades began to pile up he took them in stride, bemused but not overly impressed. "Dick," wrote the cultural critic Irving Howe, "became for me a model of what the scholar-intellectual ought to be, and I tried to learn from him. . . . He worked hard and wanted to write good books, but he was wonderfully free of that grating aggression which is so frequently declared the spring of American success. Modest and humane, but above all without the need to impose himself that seems a special curse of intellectuals, Dick Hofstadter set an example that might yield a moral education. There was profit even in his silence."[9]

The modesty and humane sensitivity referred to by Howe underscores a paradoxical trait in Hofstadter: he combined a deferential exterior with opinionated and fiercely independent judgments in his professional work. A highly evolved sense of humor linked the two qualities together. "He was basically a quite proper, even conventional person," Dan Hofstadter recalls. "His humor was contagious and I believe it sprang largely from irreverence." Readers familiar with the sharply drawn portraits of politicians in *The American Political Tradition* will recognize the accuracy of Dan's observation that among family and friends his father "had a sly way of diminishing public figures by mimicking certain silly signature phrases of theirs." Hofstadter's imitation of FDR was so dead-on that his first wife encouraged him to perform at comedy clubs.[10]

* * *

Richard Hofstadter did not live a long life — he was born in 1916 and died in 1970 — and he devoted little of it to self-promotion. "There was a delicacy that prevented [his] making of personal claims upon others," wrote two of his students, "and that excluded any sense of proprietorship over their work. It was the work itself that mattered, not his relationship to it. Discipleship was a thing he never asked for, probably because it never occurred to him."[11] Accordingly, there is no Hofstadter school. Moreover, the years have taken their toll and most historians today know Hofstadter through his books rather than by personal contact. Their memories are of publications, not of a man, and one must have some insight into both to appreciate what Hofstadter was trying to accomplish with his scholarship. For as my research led me beyond secondary sources and into first Hofstadter's private papers and later the homes of those who knew him best, it became clear that his published work reflected the personal interests and ideological concerns of their author. Each affirmed and gave coherence to the other.

More than a historian, Hofstadter was a product of his times, and the life he led offers valuable commentary on a number of salient topics that continue to shape our lives: the impact of eastern European immigration; the rise and fall of the American Left; the emergence of McCarthyism and the "radical" Sun Belt Right; the spectacular growth of higher education that culminated in the student movement of the sixties; and a fleeting but influential Upper West Side world anchored at Columbia University. Hofstadter was, Daniel Bell reminds us, "*the* historian of [the postwar] generation." And the passage of time has done little to detract from his importance as a leading interpreter of American liberalism. Considering that Hofstadter wrote history with such consummate attention to his own age provides an opportunity to explore not merely the scholarly and literary value of his writings, but also the hopes and frustrations of these fascinating and critical years.[12]

By the end of the great twenties bull market, immigrant America had found its first voices in politics (Al Smith), law (Felix Frankfurter), and aesthetics (Meyer Schapiro). But it was still searching for someone to write its history. Ideas moved Hofstadter more than demography, and the diversity of thought represented by this population proved crucial in forming his historical judgments. And these were original ideas that broke abruptly from the nation's long-standing prejudice against urban life. Thomas Jefferson's famous mandate that "the mobs of great cities add just so much to the support of pure government, as sores do to the strength of the human body" still resonated powerfully in a country that celebrated Frederick Jackson Turner's loving tribute to the land — the Frontier Thesis. In his famous 1893 address, "The Significance of the Frontier in American History," Turner stated that American democracy was a product of frontier individualism. Like Jefferson, he favored the western farmer over the eastern — and increasingly immigrant — factory worker. In the twentieth century, however, the city stood poised to claim a more significant role in public affairs, even as its expanding influence aroused the resentment of traditional ethnic groups. Concerned that a resurgent Right menaced the fresh but fragile gains carved out by the new liberalism, Hofstadter's criticism of McCarthyism — populistic, paranoid — captured the tension of the two Americas and made him an urbane critic of the masses to some, and a prickly opponent of democracy and public protest to others.

Some commentators have asserted that Hofstadter did not really understand conservatism, or its true place in the panorama of American politics. *The American Political Tradition* let the eccentric John Calhoun carry the case for nineteenth-century conservatism — a telling selection in a book that found no place for Alexander Hamilton, Henry Clay, Charles Evans Hughes, or Henry Stimson. In retrospect it seems clear that Hofstadter's work on the political Right revealed as much about the insecurities of the liberal center as the ideological extremism of its opponents. The issues that galvanized many of the constituencies designated by Hofstadter as "anti-intellectual" — the Korean War, concern for individual rights in an age of burgeoning government power, fear of nuclear annihilation — are absent in his scholarship, lost in the struggle to place history on the side of the postwar consensus.

Hofstadter's devotion to the new liberalism was not unique among cold war historians. Profoundly influenced by FDR's successful crusades against economic depression at home and Nazi tyranny abroad, Arthur Schlesinger, Jr.'s influential *The Age of Jackson* (1945) and Eric Goldman's acclaimed *Rendezvous with Destiny* (1952) emphasized the efficacy of vigorous executive authority in the American past. Though important distinctions separate Hofstadter and these men — Schlesinger and Goldman served as special advisors to presidents, an unthinkable situation for the power-wary Hofstadter — they collectively popularized postwar liberalism in their books. But Hofstadter never excused the country's internal defects. His criticism of racial segregation and the Vietnam War are matters of public record and, unlike Schlesinger, he respected but never revered Roosevelts or Kennedys. Yet, his confidence in liberalism to both perpetuate the reforms of the thirties and fend off the Far Right clearly made its way into his scholarship. And there was a cost. Nation-building, abuse of the national security state, and imperial presidencies crippled the liberal experiment and produced in its path a sharp and still ongoing reaction.

The long-term prospects of the New Deal order, Hofstadter knew, were more tentative and less secure than many suspected. While the Columbia literary critic Lionel Trilling announced in 1950 that "nowadays there are no conservative or reactionary ideas in general circulation," Hofstadter strongly dissented. The global catastrophes of the thirties and forties had, he believed, stirred up powerful feelings of discontent in America to be felt for years to come. While the consumer paradise of the twenties offered an artificial sense of calm, he wrote in the introduction to *The American Political Tradition,* the cumulative impact of unemployment and war resulted in a curious mixture of nostalgia, insecurity, and pessimism. Where did this leave liberalism? Memories of Europe's turn toward totalitarianism were painfully fresh, and in the psychological anguish of the American mass mind, Hofstadter felt, lay the seeds of reaction, repression, and red-baiting.[13]

Postwar liberalism was by no means perfect, but its defenders would hasten to point up its more constructive contributions and ask if political attitudes since 1968 have advanced equally inclusive and pragmatic visions of American life. The patient containment of cold war tensions — no Far Left appeasement, no Far Right rollback — appears in light of the early 1990s implosion of the USSR, a safe and successful end to the great ideological split between communism and capitalism. In domestic politics liberals regularly operated as the party in power and sought a consensus or (to use Hofstadter's term) "comity" that recognized the good will and loyal opposition of its partisan rivals. Though his work routinely questioned the attitudes and motives of American conservatives, Hofstadter embraced the two-party system as a valuable hedge against political extremism. When Barry Goldwater's Sun Belt Right surrendered to Johnson liberals and their centrist allies in the 1964 election, he felt the system had worked. But then came Vietnam, Watergate, and twenty-four-hour cable news. The slash-and-burn campaigns that pass as political discourse in our own times would have offended and depressed Hofstadter, for they emphasize what divides rather than unites Americans. The festishization of conflict has obscured the value of consensus.

Historical circumstances aside, any formal evaluation of Richard Hofstadter must come to terms with his rare gift for literary expression. Rather than churn out highly specialized monographs read by graduate students and warehoused in academic libraries, he expected his books to ripple through the culture. Their popularity and influence were signs of the times and reflected Hofstadter's ability to engage a wide range of feelings, prejudices, and emotions from both liberals and nonliberals. He recognized that the older Jeffersonianism was rapidly giving ground to a modern Rooseveltian state that prized secularism, cooperation, and cosmopolitanism. Some changes, of course, proved more permanent than others. To look back upon Hofstadter's lost world of liberalism today — from the vista, that is, of a conservative age — is to recall its surprising fragility. To understand its weaknesses as well as its strengths we must appreciate the ideas and politics — and history — that it produced.

PART I

Education, 1916–1950

What started me off as an historian was a sense of engagement with contemporary problems. As one who matured in the 1930's, my interest has centered mainly on politics. The events of those years no doubt also influenced my views on the past.

RICHARD HOFSTADTER, 1960

* 1 *
Radical Roots

We had been formed by the Great Depression, but Hofstadter was a secret conservative in a radical period. The times
caught up with him.

ALFRED KAZIN, 1978

The uprooting of global populations is by its nature a violent, unsettling act. During the half-century industrial renaissance running from the peace of Appomattox to the First World War, more than twenty million immigrants arrived on American shores in a remarkable exchange of human talents and customs. Their collective contributions in art, politics, education, law, and criticism broke cleanly from long-established cultural preferences that were rooted in the Wasp past. While the pioneer theme evoked by the newcomers appealed to native traditions as old as the country itself, the eclectic geographic and ethnic diversity of the current crossings — more eastern than northern European, more Catholic and Jewish than Protestant — differed dramatically from previous migrations. This complex, vibrant, and vulnerable population challenged the authority of the established caste, inciting a variety of tensions not to be easily negotiated nor reconciled. Among the more extreme responses, literary expatriates Henry Adams, Ezra Pound, Henry James, and T. S. Eliot rejected the reconfigured American scene and sought solace in the cultural heritage of the Old World. "My country in 1900," Adams sighed, "is something totally different from my own country of 1860. I am wholly a stranger in it."[1]

Born in the immigrant city of Buffalo in 1916 to a Jewish Polish father and his German Lutheran wife, Richard Hofstadter grew up in a nation on the threshold of momentous and irreversible change. A resplendent rural, Protestant tradition still collected upon the sympathies of old-stock Americans. But its days were numbered. The twentieth century became the American century. And New York City became the world's city. Along the way, Americans fought hot and cold wars, built a huge social welfare state, and created the most diverse nation in history. Positioned perfectly by the circumstances of birth to comment on this stirring transformation, Hofstadter matured with the new cosmopolitanism, probed its strengths and weaknesses, and proved to be an astute commentator of its impressive but imperfect progress.[2]

The cyclical lag that divided Adams and Hofstadter—the first a canny defender of Wasp privileges, the second a beneficiary of the new pluralism—is marked by a host of culturally charged tensions. The great historian of the American West Frederick Jackson Turner lamented the passing of the democratic frontier, and the anxious pitch of his scholarship betrayed the old order's profound unease with recent demographic trends. "Tides of alien immigrants," he gloomily recorded, "were surging into the country to replace the old American stock in the labor market, to lower the standard of living and to increase the pressure of population upon the land." While the idea of America as a frontier of freedom found expression "in the dull brains of great masses of unfortunates from southern and eastern Europe," Turner continued, many others rejected capitalism's promise of social mobility in favor of the European radical exotica of socialism and syndicalism.[3] As a contemporary document, Turner's devotion to agrarian individualism impressed many of the newcomers as hopelessly out of tune with the times. In a country historically dependent upon the economic and political leadership of the East, the call of the frontier had lost much of its charm. The midwestern ascendancy trumpeted by Turner was over. And with it the Wasp imperium.

Following the Civil War, the rapid flow of immigration into America combined with fresh economic opportunities in the trans-Mississippi West and the New South to produce a nation in flux. Corporate leviathans, including Carnegie Steel and Standard Oil, quickly grew into industrial empires, colonizing under the direction of the titans as aggressively as any sovereign power. The sprawling enterprises spilled across time zones, employed millions of laborers, and were acutely sensitive to fluctuations in both domestic and international markets. Too great for a single hand to command, the day-to-day operations of the barons' businesses were given up to small armies of managers. This profitable shift to standardization encouraged scores of institutions to jettison the "unscientific" conventions associated with preindustrial culture, and among its many devotees, the cult of professionalization bit deep into academia, forever changing the way that higher education operated. During the second half of the nineteenth century, some 200 scholarly organizations were founded, including the American Historical Association in 1884.[4]

In the days before professional training, antiquarians and well-heeled patrician writers dominated historical writing in America. George Bancroft and Francis Parkman captured the thematic convictions of the period in a series of celebrated studies that emphasized the nation's postfeudal roots and pointed to a brilliant future of Protestant liberalism. In the ten-volume *History of the United States from the Discovery of the American Continent,* Bancroft portrayed his countrymen as a providential people building a progressive civilization destined to stand as a moral force to the rest of the world. Parkman was equally attuned to the stylistic expectations and cultural values of his readers. In both *The Oregon Trail* and his masterpiece, the multivolume history *France and England in North America,* he composed heroic tales of Protestant pioneers claiming the American wilderness and vanquishing the Indian and French presence from the forest primeval. Like Bancroft, his books were meant to be instructive — a demonstration of the Anglo-Saxon's inevitable conquest of the New World.

In the postpatrician era, universities emerged as the primary gatekeepers of the historical profession. Trained in Europe or influenced at home under the Germanic "stress on the history of institutions, constitutions, social organizations, legal history, public law, administration and government," Herbert Baxter Adams of Johns Hopkins, Edward Channing of Harvard, and John W. Burgess of Columbia made objective historical analysis the academy's abiding article of faith.[5] To ensure a uniformity of purpose, training, and perspective, scientific historians offered graduate school instruction, established trade journals, and conferred (or denied) a kind of organizational imprimatur through control of the academic job market.

In the wake of the professionalization movement, the authority of patrician historiography and its touchstone principles of progress and providence collapsed in favor of a history that was thought to portray the past, in the words of Leopold von Ranke, "as it really was." In spite of its brilliant promise and claims to methodological sophistication, however, the new scholarship looked a lot like the old scholarship. It adopted conventional prejudices, substituting science for providence by couching Anglo-American exceptionalism in the imposing language of evolutionary biology and racial hierarchies. In sum, the profession readily accepted patrician claims that the Protestant, property-rights tradition bestowed uniquely favorable advantages upon Western nations and reflected the moral and material superiority of the Anglo-Saxon peoples.

As a product of an intellectually turbulent period, the scientific school could not survive the circumstances that created it. The crushing inequalities of Gilded Age America inspired a determined reaction to traditional models of social organization, evident in a series of brutal labor strikes, radical farmer movements, and consumer outcry for public regulation. As the academy's uncritical acceptance of the new industrial regime gave way to activism, a cluster of functional ideas including the social gospel, literary realism, and philosophical pragmatism merged to advance "progressive" insights designed to engage a politically conscious readership.[6] Liberal writers emphasized the social utility of history and read into the past an endless cycle of violent struggles between capital and labor. Rather than serve as apologists for the business class, they critically scrutinized the titans whose advantages, they insisted, were unmerited and fundamentally at odds with the nation's preference for political equality and social mobility. In their rebellion against the intellectual complacency of the scientific historians, Progressives emphasized the prevalence of conflict rather than continuity—democracy versus aristocracy, industry versus agrarianism, producers versus consumers. They rejected the bleak philosophy of historical inevitability (at least when tilted in favor of unrepentant capitalists) and portrayed the past as a series of hotly contested episodes that directly impacted upon the freedoms that most Americans believed to be their birthright.

In truth, the "new history" pioneered by Progressives shared important points of connection with both the scientific and patrician schools. Turner, Charles Beard, and Vernon Parrington were products of the Midwest, where the dominance of Anglo-American thought and culture mirrored that of the Brahmin East. Turner's democratic frontier was populated exclusively by traditional ethnic stocks, while Parrington declared the main currents of American thought to be of English and French origin, inferring that the intellectual traditions of nonwestern Europeans exerted little influence upon the nation. As Hofstadter and his peers matured and matriculated into the schools, the cumulative impact of Progressive historiography struck the more curious among them as fundamentally false. Their references — ethnic, metropolitan, and sensitive to clashing cultural (rather than economic) traditions — emphasized the importance of pluralism among first- and second-generation immigrant populations eager to project their own aesthetic, historical, and social values.

* * *

As the product of a complex family history composed of Jews and Gentiles, eastern and western Europeans, Richard Hofstadter was intuitively sensitive to the extraordinary diversity that underlay American life. His maternal lineage arrived in the United States around 1850 from the Rhineland principality of Hesse-Darmstadt, economic expatriates possibly spurred on by the political uncertainty that accompanied Europe's midcentury revolutions. His grandparents, Mary Newman and Richard Hill, met and married in Buffalo, a manufacturing and shipping city with sizeable German and German-Jewish populations. Their union produced five children, including the historian's mother, Katherine Hill. The Hofstadter line is first recognized in Wisnicz-Nowy (New Cherry Orchard), a small town in Galicia near Krakow on the northern fringe of the Austrian-Hungarian Empire.[7] From its advantageous position in Central Europe, the Hapsburgs ruled over a highly complex multiethnic state embracing Jews, Croats, Serbs, Czechs, Romanians, Moravians, Poles, Ruthenians, and South Slavs. By the late nineteenth century the United States had replaced imperial Austria as the principle haven for Europe's minority peoples, and interior cities like Buffalo were attracting thousands of immigrants.

According to the jurist Samuel Hofstadter, the Hofstadters were noted intellectuals in the empire's major cities, earning distinction as "sages, scholars and saints" in Krakow, Lemberg, Tarnow, Vienna, and Warsaw. The subsequent success of related Hofstadters in America — a New York State supreme court justice (Samuel), a Nobel physicist (Robert), a Pulitzer Prize–winning cognitive scientist (Douglas), and a twice-awarded Pulitzer historian (Richard) — suggests a family of unusual enterprise and genius perhaps limited in Hapsburg lands by racial prejudice, economic inertia, or the unwelcomed encroachment of Russian power in the region. In 1896 eight-year-old Emil Hofstadter, the historian's father, abandoned Krakow with his parents, Meyer and Emma, for a three-year relocation in London followed by a more permanent removal to New York's Lower East Side. While still in his teens Emil left his family, a youthful reaction to the strict devotion of religious orthodoxy expected in the home. Sibling jealousy may have also played a role.

While Meyer expected Emil to follow him into the furrier trade, younger sons Samuel, William, and Benjamin received formal educations and matriculated into the professions. Emil's movements during his young manhood are undocumented, though it is known that he returned to Europe for a brief period before resettling in America, this time bypassing the Jewish East Side to make his home in Buffalo. For his historian son it was important that this provincial city shared neither the nostalgia of the frontier that shaped the Progressive generation, nor the smart cosmopolitanism that bred its own exclusive traditions. Buffalo, observed Peter Gay, "gave Hofstadter something a little wider than the City College milieu."[8]

Easily in reach of Europe by an all-water route (Atlantic Ocean, St. Lawrence River, Lakes Ontario and Erie), Buffalo has a rich history of commercial and industrial development that attracted a substantial migrant peopling. At the time of the Hill family's arrival, over 60 percent of the city's population was foreign-born — mostly German and Irish. Wasps retained power and privilege in Buffalo by dominating city government and the professions of law, medicine, and real estate. On the cultural front, they organized crusades for temperance and sabbatarianism. The public school system was decidedly anti-Catholic. "Sensing that they were in the crest of a last wave," Buffalo historian Mark Goldman wrote, "the WASP gentry strove consciously to define and to strengthen their identity and their legacies as the bearers of a noble, yet clearly threatened New England Tradition."[9] The rapid pace of industrialization and immigration, however, undermined the city fathers' traditional authority and tensions were inevitable. Bloody railroad strikes in 1877 and 1892 were notable examples of the fierce conflicts that accompanied the transition from old Buffalo to new.

The ethnic composition of the city continued to change in the 1890s with the influx of Italians, Poles, and eastern European Jews. Their combined presence broke down the culturally consistent quota of Buffalo Germans, Protestant Americans, Canadians, and Britons and pressured the city to contend with a larger and more conspicuously ethnic population. At the time of Emil's arrival, Buffalo's Jewish neighborhoods prospered in traditional immigrant merchant activities, including the clothing and retail dry goods business and the wholesale jewelry trade. Upward social mobility softened the assimilation process and Buffalo proved to be immune from the ethnic baiting that arose in many American cities during the First World War. Still, Goldman reminds us, "it was not easy to be Jewish in Buffalo in the early twentieth century. Unlike in

New York, Philadelphia, or Chicago, where Jews through sheer force of numbers had begun to play an important role in the cities' civic life, in Buffalo Jews, vastly outnumbered, were far less visible." As their population increased (to 13,000 in 1920), Buffalo's Jews carved out a dominant presence on the city's East Side — "a half-way house between the culture of the eastern European village and the mainstream of American life." In this community Emil chose the outward symbols of ethnic identity he wished to retain — he enjoyed lox and herring and frequently took his children to the city's delicatessens — and those, including strict observance of orthodox religious practices, he thought best to relinquish.[10]

The social and educational freedom enjoyed by Buffalo minorities made the city a remarkably supportive haven for gifted Jewish minds. "Buffalo," H. Stuart Hughes wrote with only a trace of hyperbole, "seemed to export intellectuals on a scale surpassed only by Budapest."[11] The catalogue of Jews born in Buffalo between 1900 and 1920 is brightened by an impressive array of scholars, artists, and architects that place Richard Hofstadter in the midst of an improbable renaissance of imaginative thinkers collected along the east shore of Lake Erie. They include Stanford physicist Marvin Chodorow, the talented leftist novelist (and Hofstadter's future brother-in-law) Harvey Swados, philosopher of phenomenology Marvin Farber, European historian Solomon Katz, artist and pioneer of "time painting" Lewis Rubenstein, and architect Gordon Bunshaft, the designer of the Hirshhorn Museum and Sculpture Garden in Washington, D.C., and Yale's Beinecke Library.

The Hofstadters — Emil, Katherine, Richard, and his younger sister Betty — lived on the top floor of a modest two-family home on Welmont Place, a lower-middle-class German American neighborhood located just east of the city center. While Katherine oversaw her children's early spiritual life — the blue-eyed, towheaded Richard was christened in his mother's Lutheran faith and sang in the church choir — Emil emerged as the dominant parent. "He always seemed rather more forceful and pungent than my father," Dan Hofstadter recalls. "He was coarse, irreverent, perhaps communicating this spirit to my father." Emil demanded academic excellence, organized memorable summer excursions to Grand Island, and introduced his children to New York City on rare cross-state trips to visit their uncles. His presence in Richard's life was magnified after Katherine's 1926 death following a brief battle with intestinal cancer. Richard's Grandmother Hill moved in to keep house while Betty was separated from her father and brother, crossing the street to live with her Aunt Gertrude, an Episcopalian who had her deceased sister's children confirmed in her church.[12] On matters of religion, however, Richard took after his father and stopped attending services in his early teens.

Two brief remarks on Hofstadter's early life suggest the depth of his reaction to Katherine's death. An interviewer recorded in 1969 that after the loss of his mother "childhood became so difficult that Hofstadter no longer remembers, or cares to remember, much before his high school years." In an unpublished essay, the historian's first wife, Felice Swados, described a quiet, self-contained adolescence: as a boy, she wrote, Hofstadter spent much of his time alone walking the city, fishing for pike and perch in Lake Erie, prowling the aisles of the Buffalo Public Library, and haunting the piers as seamen unloaded ships in the evening.[13]

In the fall of 1929 — three years after Katherine's death — Hofstadter enrolled in Fosdick-Masten Park High School where he quickly asserted himself as an active and popular student. In the first term of his freshman year the stock market smashed and industrial Buffalo was devastated. Despite the economic downturn, Emil's furrier shop continued to show a steady profit and his family managed to avoid the kind of desperate poverty typically associated with the era. Emil "annually traveled to Florida for the horse races," Hofstadter's first biographer wrote. "He was able to present his son a car upon graduation from high school, and . . . he put both children through college without help. In the 1920s and 1930s, in any city of the United States, these were marks of middle-class status."[14]

Fosdick-Masten Park enjoyed a reputation as one of Buffalo's best high schools. Hofstadter excelled there, completing a demanding curriculum that included credits in English, Latin, German, geometry, and ancient and American history. He joined the Delta Gamma Lambda fraternity, worked on the yearbook, and participated on the forensics (debate) team. During his senior year, the school paper ran a spoof edition dated twenty years in the future announcing Hofstadter's election to the presidency of the United States — a sign of his popularity, sense of humor, and academic accomplishments. He reaped several honors at Fosdick-Masten Park, including class president, valedictorian, and the Dartmouth Award for outstanding scholarship, character, and achievement.[15] The prize capped a notably successful period in Hofstadter's life. The loss of his mother might have prefaced a retreat from the public pressures of competition, but instead his natural talents and emotional resources proved stronger than the childhood trauma of his personal tragedy.

The University of Buffalo recognized Hofstadter's promise with a $100 tuition waiver, and in the autumn of 1933 he began taking courses on the urban campus. Founded as a medical school in the 1840s, Buffalo did not create a college of arts and sciences until 1913; its pretensions to academic excellence were further compromised by the outside pressures upon a largely commuting clientele. The intellectual pace of the university picked up as the sons and daughters of first-generation immigrants pressed upon the school's resources and reshaped its mission from practical medical training to an institution capable of generating serious theoretical work. Hofstadter did not regret having gone there. "Everybody wants to go to a great university," he once told his son, "but I went to the University of Buffalo and got a very good education."[16]

During Hofstadter's years at Buffalo, socialist and Communist student organizations were an active and intellectually important part of the campus scene. The Student League for Industrial Democracy (SLID) and the National Student League (NSL) captured the interest of left-leaning undergraduates or those simply interested in the milieu of critical theory. Like many Americans who grew up in the Depression, Hofstadter identified capitalism as the enemy. In 1935, he published a letter in the campus newspaper blaming the nation's economic system for creating an impoverished underclass — and he advised his peers at Buffalo to offer compassion rather than cynicism for recipients of government aid. As both the resident of a city overwhelmed by industrial layoffs and a student receptive to the fresh social and intellectual opportunities encouraged by university life, it is not surprising that Hofstadter gravitated to Marxist politics in his youth. Over time, however, he came to understand that a less rigid ideological impulse governed his behavior. "He never struck me as a reformed radical, the way so many of that generation went," Peter Gay adds. "Hofstadter was a liberal of a very skeptical kind. He did not like pieties for their own sake. He had trouble with automatic liberalism along with automatic anything else."[17]

During his sophomore year at Buffalo, Hofstadter met Felice Swados, a driven and intellectually serious senior philosophy major. Her grandfather, Israel Swados, immigrated from Lithuania and taught briefly at the Buffalo Beth El before becoming "the virtual dictator" of the Talmud Torah, a Hebrew school that opened in 1904. Israel's first marriage produced a son, Aaron, who took a medical degree at the University of Buffalo and married Rebecca (Rivie) Bluestone, "a singer, pianist, and painter," of a prominent New York medical family. Rivie's father, Joseph Isaac Bluestone, emigrated from Kalvarija, Lithuania, in the 1880s and became an active Zionist in America. His maternal grandmother's surname was Trilling, and his second cousin, the eminent literary critic Lionel Trilling—a socially and intellectually influential friend of Richard Hofstadter—became the first Jewish scholar to receive tenure in Columbia University's English department. The union between Aaron and Rivie produced Felice, born in 1915, and Harvey five years later. Contrary to Emil's secular preferences, Aaron maintained an active presence in William Street's Jewish activities. Through his association with Felice, Hofstadter may have unconsciously followed in his father's footsteps by selectively exploring the cultural side of a spiritual system he could never fully embrace. "He came slowly to Judaism," Columbia sociologist Daniel Bell noted. "I think that when he met Felice and that whole Buffalo crowd he became more involved in that milieu. Judaism is a people and a history and Dick came to identify with that."[18]

Hofstadter's new relationship had a significant impact on his early adulthood. Possessed of a natural intellect and easy self-confidence, he was attracted to Felice's energy, charisma, and intensity. More committed to radical politics and the dream of a workers-state than her future husband, she helped initiate Hofstadter into the milieu of left-wing activism at the University of Buffalo. He was never fully immersed. Temperamentally the more careful and detached of the two, he found it impossible to suspend his critical judgment in the name of ideology. By comparison, he described Felice's politics in his correspondence as naïve and simple.[19] Hofstadter's solicitous nature and impulsive humility were in striking contrast to his first wife's self-assurance and determination to urge her views on those around her. Alfred Kazin furnishes a memorable portrait of Felice in 1937:

> I had never met anyone like her. I had never met a *woman* like her. Not so much tall as big, big with a round baby face made rounder and more unlikely by the bangs that fitted over her forehead like a visor, and from underneath which her eyes gave you a look both pert and inquisitorial, she radiated a hungry-self-confidence, an intellectual positiveness. . . . I was always to feel in Felice's presence that she was taking up more space *physically,* in any room we were in together, than she had a right to . . . nevertheless I felt happier in her presence, charged with an excitement

that I did not try to account for—Her ambition seemed to carry every-one else along.[20]

Two people as intelligent and ambitious as Richard Hofstadter and Felice Swados were bound to find each other on the small Buffalo campus. There were, however, self-inflicted obstacles. Elizabeth Early, the first wife of historian Frank Freidel, spent time with the Hofstadters at the University of Maryland in the early forties and recalls Felice's intellectual ambitions and desire "to beat Dick at his own game." Of the two, she added, "Dick was pretty easy going. . . . Felice was a . . . vivid, vibrant, competitive girl." Kazin recorded in his journal that Felice "was probably the first to recognize just how brilliant [Hofstadter] was and fought him on it."[21]

The couple's private difficulties were exasperated by Aaron's and Emil's determination that their children end their relationship. For reasons that are unclear, Emil disliked Felice, and his antipathy grew after Richard, only nineteen at the time, announced their engagement. Dr. Swados also disapproved. A stern disciplinarian, both proud and envious of his daughter, he thought Hofstadter was lazy and unfocused—certainly not a suitable match for his talented daughter. Felice probably came closer to the truth when she noted in correspondence that Aaron's hostility was rooted in jealousy.[22] Two years into the marriage, Aaron remained unreconciled with the situation. He sent a letter to Felice's work address encouraging her to leave Hofstadter—then a mere graduate student with limited career prospects living off his wife's earnings.

As a university-trained professional, Aaron occupied different physical and social spaces than Emil. The Swadoses lived in the heart of Buffalo's Jewish community, several blocks south of the working class Welmont Place neighborhood familiar to the Hofstadters. Aaron and Rivie emphasized art, literature, and music in the home—the doctor's devotion to Goethe was a source of some comedy among Richard, Felice, and Harvey. Ethnicity may have also divided the families. Emil had married a Gentile and that made his son, of course, only half Jewish. When Harvey announced in the late thirties his interest in a particular woman, Hofstadter cautioned in a lighthearted but direct manner that if parental approval was desired, the female in question must under no circumstances be a *shikseh*.[23]

More than anything, Felice wanted to be a novelist. Her only book, *House of Fury* (1941), combined the social realism of the class-conscious thirties with its author's surfacing feminism. Felice worked for *Time* magazine while she wrote the book, and despite her own rapid ascent up the Luce ladder, denounced the company caste system for relegating women to the research pool while men did the writing. The adolescent girls in *House of Fury* struggle to find a common humanity in a soul-denying prison system that embellished the racial, class, and gender roles imposed by their society. This message was lost in the sexual subtext of the novel — exploited in the 1958 film version, *Reform School Girl,* starring Edd Burns. A capable writer of the kind of short, nonfiction pieces that she routinely cranked out for *Time,* Felice exhibited little promise as a serious novelist. Her book is today considered a pulp classic.[24]

Richard and Felice studied philosophy at Buffalo under the direction of the noted phenomenologist Marvin Farber. "I think philosophy interested me a bit more" than history, Hofstadter later remarked, but pragmatic concerns won out. "I was astute enough to see I had no gifts in the field and jobs for philosophers were harder to come by." His most important undergraduate teacher was Julius Pratt, a University of Chicago Ph.D. who left Rutgers in 1926 to become the Emanuel Boasberg Professor of History at Buffalo. A specialist in American imperialism, Pratt's major works — the well-received *Expansionists of 1812* (1925) and *Expansionists of 1898* (1936) — caught Hofstadter's eye. Pratt believed that the economic model favored by Progressive writers minimized the impact of social and psychological forces on history, and his own scholarship pointed to a more complex investigation of the past. Much has been made of Hofstadter's fondness for Charles Beard, and rightly so. "Beard was really *the* exciting influence on me," he once remarked, "Beard . . . got me excited about American history."[25] But Hofstadter's respect for Beard's iconoclastic style and interpretive genius did not blind him to the fact that the once fresh field of "interest" studies favored by the Progressive generation had grown stale.

Beard and Pratt diverged most notably in their most notable books. In *The Rise of American Civilization* (1927), Charles and Mary Beard argued that big business had maneuvered the country into the Spanish-American War: "With the growing economic surplus which sustained the colorful and exuberant culture of the Gilded Age ran an increasing pressure for foreign markets and investment opportunities." In *Expansionists of 1898,* however, Pratt dismissed the corporate conspiracy thesis and declared that "business sentiment . . . was strongly anti-war, Wall Street stocks turned downward whenever the day's news seemed to presage war and climbed again with information favorable to peace."[26]

He maintained that intellectual and emotional factors — what Hofstadter would later describe in *The Age of Reform* as the "soft" side issues to differentiate from "hard" economic variables — pushed the nation to war.

Moving beyond the Beards, Pratt stressed the impact of ideas on American foreign policy. Social Darwinism, he argued, supplied convenient views of racial hierarchies that empowered expansionists. "If the survival of the fittest was the law of nature and the path of progress, surely the more gifted races need offer neither apologies nor regrets when they suppressed, supplanted, or destroyed their less talented competitors. And who could doubt that the Anglo-Saxon race, especially in its American branch, possessed those superior traits which entitled it to survive."[27]

Pratt's most original idea involved the therapeutic use of power. Colonial possessions, he noted, frequently operated as financial liabilities yet remained highly prized for their psychological value. Great nations, after all, were supposed to rule over great dominions. Americans, however, had no history of overseas colonization, and Pratt argued that internal rather than external considerations pushed the country along the path of empire. The closing of the democratic frontier and emergence of an urban, industrial, and ethnic nation seemed to presage a dawning era of decline and loss of Wasp identity. Defeating Spain allowed the country to direct its anxieties onto a feeble foe and wield imperialism as a powerful lightening rod for internal dissent.[28]

Pratt's ideas influenced Hofstadter both inside and out of the classroom. During the war-weary thirties, universities were in the forefront of exploring the possibilities for peace in a world divided between fascism, communism, and democracy. Pratt, writing as both a concerned citizen and an expert on foreign affairs, contributed polemical essays to the university newspaper, the *Buffalo Bee*, defending American neutrality and discouraging war trade, as he put it, "under any circumstances." In both his scholarship and personal convictions, in other words, Pratt was a classic interwar isolationist. As an active member of the NSL, Hofstadter accepted the Soviet position of peace through collective security and strongly endorsed Pratt's articles. He confirmed his commitment to the peace movement by taking part in the April 1935 nationwide student walkout; an exercise designed to draw attention to the youth culture's opposition to war by affirming the virtue of pacifism. Hofstadter served on the Strike Publicity Committee and encouraged Buffalo professors to dismiss their classes for the one-hour boycott.[29]

The student peace initiatives of the thirties anticipated the more contentious rebellions that rocked college campuses in the 1960s. Both movements raised serious questions about the nature of the university. Was it exclusively a house of instruction or did students have the right to pursue political agendas under its wing? One Buffalo undergraduate, hostile to the NSL strike, complained that "stirring up trouble, dissension, and other forms of rebellion" proved antithetical to the disinterested pursuit of knowledge supported by the university. Years later, as a distinguished senior professor working with students at an institution that had suffered its share of campus unrest, Hofstadter adopted this position. The disruption of classroom instruction by demonstrators, he reasoned, threatened to overturn higher education's historically fragile balance between coercion and academic freedom. He looked more favorably upon student reformers who operated within the spirit of institutional guidelines — as he himself had done. As an undergraduate, Hofstadter endorsed resolutions to make ROTC noncompulsory at Buffalo, and he backed opportunities in the curriculum for promoting international neutrality and peace. Thirty years later, he advised Columbia officials to prohibit military recruitment on campus, and supported teach-in style dialogues as an important feature of higher education in the Vietnam era.[30]

During his final year at Buffalo, Hofstadter served as president of the campus chapter of the NSL and produced an unusually capable senior thesis — "The Tariff and Homestead Issues in the Republican Campaign of 1860." The paper was modeled on Pratt's critical handling of Progressive historiography and anticipated its author's life-long dialogue with scholars of the conflict school. In their popular textbook *The Rise of American Civilization,* the Beards had defined the Civil War in starkly economic terms: "the capitalists, laborers, and farmers of the North and West drove from power . . . the planting aristocracy of the South" in order to remove barriers to commercial expansion. This iconoclastic interpretation dismissed intellectual currents, political culture, and antislavery sentiment as important sources of sectional tensions. It also encouraged Hofstadter to think more critically about the Progressive contribution to historical writing. He boldly wrote to Charles Beard and asked for assistance unraveling the financial issues faced by antebellum Americans. Beard wrote back and suggested that Hofstadter investigate the "whole history of the effort to get a new bank after 1837." Finding the advice too far removed from his topic to be useful, Hofstadter proceeded to emphasize ethnic rather than economic divisions.[31]

When Hofstadter examined the impact of the tariff and homestead issues on antebellum politics, he discovered that southern Democrats opposed homesteading — the parceling out of western lands to pioneers — because immigrants were to be among the act's chief beneficiaries. A German and Scandinavian exodus into the Northwest threatened to empower abolitionism by producing several free states. Recovering the important role antebellum immigration played in the birth of the Republican Party encouraged Hofstadter to reject the Beardian interpretation of the period. Financial issues, including homesteading, were subsumed within larger ethnocultural tensions, he argued. The Republicans championed the Homestead Bill in 1860 not to line their pockets, but rather to elect their presidential candidate. And this meant carrying the Northwest, which meant appealing to the immigrant vote.[32] Three generations later the modern Democratic Party followed a similar formula to success: abandoning the politics of provincialism and welcoming ethnic voters into the fold. It seems very likely that Hofstadter was influenced by the New Deal coalition, and that he felt his thesis recovered its roots among a complex web of native institutions and impulses. This would not be the last time that he read present politics into the past.

Hofstadter completed his work at the university in 1936 (his degree was conferred in February 1937), a necessary prelude before marrying Felice and finishing a master's degree in philosophy at Smith College. Despite Hofstadter's interest in history, Emil and Samuel were convinced that a career in the academy held little promise and pressured him to attend law school. Because of his professional success, Uncle Sam's opinion carried considerable weight among his siblings and their children. He was, Dan Hofstadter notes, "very much what the French call a vieux garçon. A handsome, fussy, pompous old bachelor, fond of his creature comforts [and] attached to a stultified, pseudo-classy version of Judaism."[33] While Emil retreated upstate to a quiet family life, Samuel worked his way through New York Law School before winning election as a Republican state assemblyman in 1925, and three years later to the state senate. It was in this body that he served as chairman of the famous Seabury Committee investigating corruption in the administration of Democratic mayor, James J. Walker.

In the summer of 1932, widely spread allegations of abuse in city government by the Tammany machine forced governor Franklin D. Roosevelt to organize hearings. To the dismay of the city bosses, these resulted in Walker's resignation. In turn, Tammany broke with Roosevelt, voting against his nomination on every ballot at that summer's Democratic convention. Looking to dodge a sticky local controversy as he campaigned for the presidency, the governor, many believed, struck a deal with Samuel Hofstadter. A cartoon in the 4 October 1932 *New York World Telegram* titled "What Price Glory?" shows Samuel sitting at a writing table before the voluminous "Report of the Hofstadter Committee." Behind him, the Tammany Tiger approaches holding up a Supreme Court justice's robe. Its eyes are closed to the implied improprieties being carried out before it. Justice Hofstadter's 1970 *New York Times* obituary fairly noted that these accusations were "never substantiated."[34]

Deferring to his uncle, Richard Hofstadter made postgraduation plans to attend law school in New York City. He informed Farber, however, that his heart was not in it and, without his family's knowledge, was soon exploring the possibility of winning an academic fellowship. Farber advised Hofstadter to follow his instincts, insisting that "the question of your own satisfaction with your work must be faced frankly. There is no question concerning your promise."[35] He anticipated Hofstadter's interest in Columbia and encouraged Felice to establish contact with Barnard College, intuiting that an academic situation anchored at Morningside Heights — an arrangement Hofstadter later shared with his second wife — would prove suitable to the temperaments and talents of the young, ambitious couple.

Before the matters of marriage and career could be confronted, however, a brief but painful crisis nearly upended Hofstadter's plans. In the spring of 1936, Felice considered a year apart from her fiancé to travel. Emil sensed an opportunity to sever the relationship and lobbied hard for a permanent break. Hofstadter briefly followed his father's advice, no doubt fortifying in the process Aaron's accusations of his unreliability. The split did not last, but it did leave a scar. In correspondence, Felice described her surprise that a man she considered generous, sympathetic, and civilized should lose his courage and abandon her in the face of parental disapproval.[36] Her fiancé's erratic behavior, however, prefaced a pattern. It was characteristic of Hofstadter to shrink from confrontation in his personal relationships, and he was always uncomfortable, even paralytic, when forced to choose sides.

*   *   *

In October 1936, Richard and Felice married and moved into a two-room flat over a bakery at 134 Montague Street in Brooklyn Heights.

He enrolled in the evening session of the New York School of Law and spent his days clerking in the law office of Irving Kauffman, a position arranged by Justice Hofstadter. Seeking "political" work, Felice was briefly employed by the National Maritime and International Ladies' Garment Workers Unions before landing a research position on the medical column at *Time* magazine. Within a few months, she took over the column and her name appeared on the publication's masthead. Despite her hunger for professional success, Felice felt guilty writing for the conservative Luce publication and, in her moral indignation denounced *Time* as a sexist, sensationalist rag that discouraged the kind of serious social commentary that interested her most. She threatened to quit several times but remained a columnist for five years until her husband secured a tenure-track position at the University of Maryland.[37]

While Felice wrestled with the perils of success, Hofstadter faced a completely different problem — bored in law school, his own work was going nowhere. He moved quickly over the Christmas holiday to alter his circumstances, dropping his legal studies and enrolling in Columbia University's graduate school. Lacking the courage to confront Aaron Swados directly with his decision, Hofstadter composed a surreal letter to the entire Swados family complete with graffiti footnotes, nonsensical Latin expressions, and exclamation points. It was a desperate performance. He communicated through comic relief, hiding nervously behind a fictional young man accused of making life impossible for his wife by infecting her sleeping quarters with a bed bug — Hofstadter's law school troubles in metaphor. Rather than poisoning the relationship, Hofstadter wrote, satirizing Aaron's accusations, the young man retained his wife's respect and affection. Hofstadter concluded by promising the Swadoses that he would finish his M.A. program at Columbia and become a historian — or perhaps a journalist.[38]

Hofstadter began taking courses at Columbia in the spring of 1937 — initiating a thirty-three-year relationship with the distinguished institution. Two evening classes prefaced a full academic schedule in the fall, including a section on "Economic and Cultural Aspects of American Civilization" taught by Harry Carman, an unpretentious and well-liked figure on the Morningside campus. A specialist in agricultural history, Carman's compassion for the rural poor and criticism of capitalism aligned comfortably with Hofstadter's own views at the time. Their initial meeting developed into a paternal friendship — Carman was known in some circles as the "Patron Saint of Lost Boys" — that proved increasingly important to the young historian over the years. As dean of the college in the late forties, Carman brought Hofstadter back to Columbia from the University of Maryland, and when some colleagues wished to deny the gifted scholar tenure in 1950 on the grounds that his work lacked primary documentation, he successfully fought them off. The dedication page to Hofstadter's 1965 book *The Paranoid Style in American Politics* reads "To the Memory of Harry J. Carman."[39]

Carman's course proved of such interest to Hofstadter that he dropped work on a dull M.A. thesis on the New York Board of Assessors in favor of a paper reviewing southern agricultural policy under the New Deal. To recover materials, he and Felice planned a summer research trip to the South, naïvely anticipating the discovery of an ideological solidarity between them and the Dixie proletariat. In a letter to Harvey Swados, Hofstadter wrote enthusiastically about reaching the Delta Cooperative in time to join the workers harvesting in the fields. It seemed the perfect opportunity to mix political and intellectual interests — sharecropping as an introduction to the science of socialism.[40]

Considering their meager finances, the Hofstadters' opportunity to travel hinged upon Richard's application for financial assistance from Columbia. With his undergraduate thesis soon to appear in the *American Historical Review*, he had reason to be optimistic. When the awards committee failed to tender a grant, the slight stung, and Hofstadter suspected anti-Semitism, a presumption that became more pronounced when he was passed over again in 1939 and 1940. Felice complained to Harvey after one such disappointment that her husband's ethnic-sounding name was the problem. She spelled out his middle name (Irving) in capital letters to draw attention to the difference between Hofstadter and the men Columbia liked to reward. The university, it is true, did retain vestiges of an old student quota system that funneled Jews to City College and Seth Low Junior College. The distinguished historian George Mosse recorded that his 1941 "application to the graduate school at Columbia University was rejected quite overtly because the Jewish quota was full." While this practice was rapidly breaking down at Morningside Heights, some quarters of the campus sustained strong Wasp preferences into the 1940s before the cumulative impact of the war, the Holocaust, and liberal hiring practices opened the university to Jewish students and faculty.[41]

Hofstadter shared his wife's belief that the awards system had worked against him and complained to Harvey Swados that his achievements at Columbia were greater than those typically awarded fellowships. Many years later Richard Kostelanetz wrote that Hofstadter was "not a particularly successful graduate student, he failed at first to receive the fellowship for which he applied (indicatively suspecting an anti-Semitism he since knows was unfounded)." Hofstadter later insisted to Kostelanetz that he could not recall discussing the matter, but the latter was sure of his source. "Let me defend the remark about anti-Semitism on the fellowship application . . . not only because you told it to me at least twice . . . but also because it indicates your conception of yourself as a Jew in a non-Jewish or discriminating society." And yet the manner in which Columbia opened up to Jewish scholars and students after the war not only turned the old discrimination on its head, but also made the institution a magnet for gifted minorities. It proved to be just the place for Hofstadter. "Dick had to learn how to balance off the conflicts of his Gentile/Jewish ethnicity," James Shenton remembered. "I think he was always uncomfortable in dealing with the fact that he was half. But at Columbia he found another identity, it was open, unlike Harvard, and a peculiar place, and Dick was comfortable with it precisely because it was peculiar."[42]

Denied a fellowship, Hofstadter completed his master's thesis in 1938 without supporting interviews or personal recollections of southern agricultural operations. He produced a scathing indictment of the New Deal's Agricultural Adjustment Act (AAA), which, he discovered, placed federal financial credits into the hands of southern conservatives who used the funds to control the region. Government payments were supposed to go to the farmers who actually cultivated crops, but in the byzantine system of liens and sharecroppings such distinctions were often difficult to ascertain and it was easy for landlords to designate themselves as the party to receive payment. "It should not be surprising to find that tenants were almost entirely excluded from the administration of the program in the South," Hofstadter wrote, and "it is clear that the provisions of the contracts and the methods of payment facilitated abuse by landlords."[43] Opposition to the land barons could be easily diffused by the oligarchs' refusal to renew tenant contracts or by removing sharecroppers from the fields.

The operations of the AAA convinced Hofstadter that the government had consciously worked in hand with southern Democrats to retain the region's autocratic heritage: "Of all the undertakings of the Roosevelt administration, the AAA cotton program was farthest from giving a fair distribution of governmental largesse to all classes. It is no accident that this occurred in the least democratic region in the United States, and one upon which the Democratic party is heavily dependent."

What was worse, he concluded, the program resulted in a vicious perpetuation of the traditional "rural unemployment" of the South backed by the "planned scarcity" of the AAA.[44] The thesis won Hofstadter his M.A., but more importantly, it introduced him to the problematic history of American liberalism.

During his first year of doctoral work, Hofstadter met the talented intellectual historian Merle Curti. The son of a Swiss immigrant, Curti was born in Papillion, Nebraska and, following stints teaching at Smith and Columbia's Teachers College, spent the balance of his academic career at the University of Wisconsin. He shared Hofstadter's skepticism of American capitalism, but regional differences produced an underlying tension in their relationship. "As a Midwesterner," one historian wrote, Curti "tended to regard the American heartland as the source of American virtue and to view the East, especially Wall Street, as the great enemy of the American dream."[45] Hofstadter could hardly have disagreed more. He thought the "heartland" a source of political reaction and organized his emotional and intellectual sympathies around a polyglot East. Curti's presence nevertheless proved crucial to Hofstadter, for his success — a 1944 Pulitzer for *The Growth of American Thought* — provided ample evidence that a leftist scholar could make it in academe.

Curti further extended to his graduate students a degree of support and personal kindness that, over the years, amounted to a lasting contribution to the historical profession. At Columbia, Curti and Henry Steele Commager each regarded the intellectually independent Hofstadter as his own protégé. Hofstadter dealt with the issue in a 1954 letter to a colleague declaring that while he was never in a Curti seminar and took only one of his lecture courses, he was nevertheless pleased to be counted among Curti's students. Curti's scholarship, he continued, introduced him to American intellectual history and his encouragement helped pull the young Hofstadter through graduate school when it appeared there were no jobs for new Ph.D.'s. A 1961 letter written to Curti by Myra Hicks, Hofstadter's Wellfleet typist, attests to the humane influence he had on his most gifted student. "While [Professor Hofstadter] was waiting for me to finish some typing, he picked up a copy of [Curti's] *Rise of the American Nation* and was most interested in it because he was once a student of yours at Columbia. He said that you had more direct influence upon him and the direction of his career than any one person he knew. . . . He said your interest in. . . . his future. . . . changed his entire attitude toward his work . . . and he would never cease to admire and respect you.[46]

Curti's course "The History of American Social Thought" made a powerful impression on Hofstadter. Aside from drafting a series of thoughtful essays for the section, he produced the gem "Physiocratic Elements in the Thought of Jefferson and Franklin," a stunning critique of the Progressive literary historian Vernon Louis Parrington. In the hugely influential *Main Currents in American Thought,* Parrington neatly divided the national experience into a spare dichotomy: Jeffersonian liberalism in tension with Hamiltonian conservatism. The Jeffersonian side of the American character celebrated intellectual freedom, religious pluralism, agrarian democracy, and personal liberty. They were the good guys. Their Hamiltonian opponents stood in a long line of capitalist killjoys that included cranky Puritans, greedy robber barons, and Jazz Age prohibitionists. They were the not so good guys. Parrington's authoritative if cartoonish sketch of the past was striking and his "discovery" of a perpetual conflict in American life between the forces of reform and reaction seemed to hold the interpretive key to the nation's history. In 1967, Hofstadter wrote Vernon Parrington, Jr.—the writer's son—that reading *Main Currents* as a graduate student had been both a pleasurable and a revelatory experience.[47]

But Parrington's spell quickly wore off. The Jeffersonian emphasis on moral regeneration through the land offended young minds shaped by the cities and intellectually weaned on the "scientific" social theory of Marxism. By challenging Parrington's interpretation of the physiocratic (that is, agrarian) influence on American life, Hofstadter hoped to shake classical liberalism's hold on the historical imagination. *Main Currents* had claimed that "the Physiocratic theory . . . sank deep into [Jefferson's] mind and creatively determined his thinking, with the result that Jeffersonian democracy as it spread through Virginia and west along the frontier assumed a pronounced Physiocratic bias." But Hofstadter flatly rejected this pleading on behalf of an agrarian renaissance that seemed nowhere in sight in the Depression thirties. Instead, he emphasized points of departure between the rural French thinking class and its putative American heirs. European Physiocrats supported a single tax on land revenue that, Hofstadter argued, ran counter to the interests of the American yeoman class. While true Physiocrats sought to preserve "the ancien regime by reforming its tax system [and] . . . shifting the burden of taxation upon the largely tax exempt feudality," this proved impossible in America, for there existed no feudal class to tax.[48]

The large differences between the aristocratic landholders in France and the small-scale agrarians in America made Republican allusions to physiocratic solidarity both grossly sentimental and impractical. As Jefferson celebrated the "warm humanitarian enthusiasm that had come down as a rich heritage of the Physiocratics school of thinkers," the nation moved rapidly toward more complex market relations. Tidewater planters, Hofstadter argued, never consistently opposed capitalism but rather responded vigorously to its requirements. "A survey of the economic thought of the Jeffersonian and Jacksonian movement," he wrote, "shows that at no time did they ever produce, even in theory, a design for American agrarianism. At best their philosophy led to a negative conclusion: abandon the national banking system, reduce expenditures, cut taxation, divorce government from finance, democratize incorporation, keep hands off."[49] Scrutinizing *Main Currents* encouraged Hofstadter to sharpen his critical reconsideration of the conflict historians. From the vantage of Depression America, Parrington's ideas, and the Progressive impulse that lay behind them, had lost all intellectual and moral power to persuade.

*   *   *

Hofstadter's decision to study history at Columbia coincided with the most politically active period of his life. He attended with Felice meetings of the Young Communist League and his correspondence during this period bears evidence that he carefully monitored the progress of the Spanish civil war. In a letter to Harvey Swados, he argued that socialism was on the rise in Spain and held out hope that Franco's army would be defeated — and along with it the power of the church, the landlords, and the capitalists. It was a rare flash of political optimism on Hofstadter's part.[50]

While Felice's commitment to party discipline led her to the edge of intellectual surrender—her letters called for a dictatorship to end American capitalism—Hofstadter's radicalism was of a more cerebral, critical, and pessimistic kind. As one colleague put it, "Dick was typical academic parlor pink. He could see the complexity of issues, but was not a real hands on radical." Hofstadter explained his October 1938 decision to enlist in the Columbia graduate unit of the CP as something of an obligation rather than a passion: after years of debating the class struggle, it was time to do something about it. Once he joined, however, his worst fears were confirmed. Deviation from the party line — Hofstadter questioned CP positions on collective security and the Moscow trials — brought condemnation and "reeducation" by section leaders.

His first skirmishes with anti-intellectualism, in other words, were fought against the Left.[51]

As Hofstadter completed his first year of doctoral training, the fate of European democracy hung in the balance. The Nazi occupation of Czechoslovakia offered a brutal lesson in power politics that stunned the young scholar and shattered his faith in the peace movement. In a letter to Harvey Swados, he expressed his disappointment at the strong support for isolationism in the country. He had believed since the Spanish civil war that collective security was the only sensible solution to military aggression. It struck him now how different most of the country—particularly midwestern isolationists—felt about America's role in the world. His half-hearted commitment to the Communist Party complicated matters. The Moscow trials were morally repugnant to Hofstadter, and in February 1939—just four months after he had joined the party and six months before the Nazi-Soviet pact—he withdrew. "As he told me," Kenneth Stampp later reported, "he couldn't stand the people." Intellectually, Hofstadter had nothing but contempt for the regimented thinking that accompanied party membership. To imagine Hofstadter writing essays on dialectical materialism, Alfred Kazin smiled, was like imagining "Pope Pius doing a striptease."[52]

The Swados Papers suggest that Felice stayed in the Communist Party for several months after her husband dropped out. Moscow's pact with Hitler, however, cast her off into a kind of political nowhere. In letters to Harvey she expressed a range of emotions—anger, confusion, alienation—and commented that aside from preserving the reforms of the New Deal, she was politically sure of nothing.[53]

Hofstadter's own political disillusionment encouraged a private rejection of both organized communism and the masses who filled the party's ranks. Forced by the fallout of the Nazi-Soviet pact to rethink his relationship to the Left, he chose separation. In letters to Harvey Swados, Hofstadter claimed that for the first time he saw clearly the gap that divided him from the party faithful. He valued intellectual autonomy, scientific inquiry, individual freedom, and cultural latitude. He knew that given the opportunity, the followers of Stalin, including the American Marxist leaders Earl Browder and Max Schachtman, would not think twice about stamping out critical thought if it furthered their agenda. Hofstadter's alienation, of course, was about more than politics. Temperamental and intellectual compatibility were important sources of happiness and creativity for him, and he confessed to Swados that neither he nor Felice had been able to conform to or connect with the values of the average CPer. Their earlier enthusiasm was an illusion, for ultimately they were ill suited to adopt party-line thinking. They were, he concluded, not workers, and could find no place and no peace among the working class.[54]

As support for the New Deal crested and European populations supported fascist and Communist regimes hostile to free inquiry, Hofstadter became increasingly convinced that labor radicalism constituted a serious threat to intellectual freedom. Never one to suffer fools gladly (graduate students, colleagues, critics, bloc ideologies) he found the Communist Party's visceral style of political expression a poor match for his own more thoughtful and reflective sensibilities. He *thought* his way into the Left but never *felt* the pang of emotional commiseration, anger, or empathy that allowed others to overlook party inconsistencies and dubious intellectual positions. In a 1940 letter to Harvey Swados, Hofstadter declared that American autoworkers were more likely to adopt fascism than socialism. If the workers actually took over, he continued, men like himself and Swados would be targeted for their intellectual habits, critical instincts, and petty bourgeois backgrounds. Popular power, he was coming to believe, stood opposite the set of values he prized for himself.[55]

Hofstadter's spirits were further dampened by a lengthy struggle to find a suitable dissertation topic. He worked briefly on a biography of the radical Reconstruction senator Benjamin Wade before casting his eye on Lincoln's secretary of war, Simon Cameron. After discovering that another scholar was busy working on a Cameron study, he had to begin anew. Columbia historian John Allen Krout suggested a biography of the revolutionary-era financier Jeremiah Wadsworth—a depressingly narrow subject ridiculed by Felice. A $1,000 research stipend offered by backers of a Wadsworth biography tempted Hofstadter to a topic that, he admitted, bored him intellectually. Fortunately for the historical profession the money did not come through and the search for a thesis continued. Influenced by Felice, then preparing a never completed study on the relationship between social Darwinism and capitalism, Hofstadter discovered a topic that captured his imagination and became his first book— *Social Darwinism in American Thought.*[56]

The discovery of a meaningful thesis lifted the young scholar's mood, as did his entry into the teaching profession. Hofstadter secured a part-time job at Brooklyn College in 1940, earning his first full-time position at the downtown branch of City College the following year. The offer came when several instructors were fired because of their alleged ties to the Communist Party. "Ironically," wrote Eric Foner, the son of Jack Foner, one of the purged professors, "Hofstadter's first full-time job resulted from the flourishing of the kind of political paranoia he would later lament in his historical writings."[57]

The City College position came at a critical time in Hofstadter's career and coincided with his earning Columbia's best graduate prize, the William Bayard Cutting Traveling Fellowship. With a job, research money, and an important dissertation topic, Hofstadter's prospects were suddenly bright. Only two years earlier, amid the dispiriting backdrop of CP anti-intellectualism and the failure of collective security, he had complained to Harvey Swados that they would benefit neither from the capitalism of the nineteenth century nor the socialism of the twentieth. History had boxed them in.[58] In fact Hofstadter's professional life was just beginning to reveal its possibilities, and from this point on the arc of its ascent would be dramatic.

* 2 *

The Twilight of Waspdom

One always has to reckon with the generation
that has gone before.

RICHARD HOFSTADTER, 1960

The New Deal changed everything. More than simply a model for economic recovery, it launched the crucial process of affirming the deep
and still controversial changes in American life triggered by modernity.
Roosevelt's reforms appealed to black and ethnic voters, celebrated the
cities, and initiated a social-welfare state more expansive than anything
imagined by either the Populists in the 1890s or the Progressives in the
1910s. A raw, anarchic enthusiasm for property rights had fueled the
swift expansion of American material progress, but the laissez-faire
state proved incapable of mastering the current crisis. Something had
to give. Among thoughtful observers, it seemed clear that the old order,
and the social, intellectual, and racial underpinnings that supported it,
were ripe for revision.

As he searched for a dissertation topic in the late Depression spring
of 1940, Richard Hofstadter sensed a fundamental shift in American
life. Waspdom was breaking up. The subject, and its extraordinary implications linking the Anglo past to the ethnic present, never ceased to
interest him. "The United States began with the heritage of slavery and
with white Anglo-Saxon Protestant domination," he wrote in a late career summing-up. "The upsurge of the new immigrants, the Catholics,
and now finally of the Negroes has made our twentieth-century history
into a story of ethnic wars of various kinds, wars incidental to trans-
forming the old America into a multi-ethnic, multi-religious urban society." As a critic of the older liberalism, a product of a mixed ethnic
parentage, and an ambitious junior scholar in search of an important

28

topic, Hofstadter knew that he had stumbled onto something special. His friends, Felice wrote Harvey, were envious and wanted a hand in the project. Hofstadter cribbed in the note's margin, however, that this was no time for generosity—the subject was all his.[1]

Social Darwinism in American Thought, 1860–1915 is much more than a review of capitalist apologia. A product of the 1930s struggle to carve out a new liberal tradition, the book responded to the political and intellectual milieu that shaped its author's youthful interaction with a tumultuous era. "Although it was meant to be a reflective study rather than a tract for its times," Hofstadter wrote in a revised edition, "it was naturally influenced by the political and moral controversy of the New Deal." It is not surprising, therefore, that more than any other Hofstadter book, *Social Darwinism* adopted a neo-Progressive perspective that emphasized, as Eric Foner has noted, "economic self-interest as the basis of political action."[2]

Hofstadter may have left the Communist Party, but his dissertation clearly showed that he had not surrendered intellectually to the capitalist system. Still disenchanted with Roosevelt, still suspicious of the New Deal, and still unreconciled to the undemocratic underpinnings of the industrial state, he laid waste to the empty idols and false gods that propped up the temple of free enterprise. Under the command of a less original thinker, *Social Darwinism* might have descended into a crude commentary on class relations—a sort of neo-Beardian "Economic Origins of Social Darwinism." But Hofstadter produced his thesis under the eye of Merle Curti, a pioneer in the emerging field of intellectual history. Liberated from the Progressive penchant for appointing heroes and villains, Hofstadter was able to merge both his politics and scholarship into a powerful critique of the great titans. So while he recognized the importance of class conflict, he was more interested in recovering the intellectual than the economic roots of that conflict. In *Social Darwinism* he argued that deeply internalized beliefs moved people, for ultimately whoever controlled the prevailing value system—defining God, morality, politics, and patriotism—won the right to apportion rewards. For a historian just beginning to cut his teeth in the fresh field of the history of ideas, social Darwinism—the grandest idea of the last eighty years—was a splendid target.

Progressive thought was an important but not exclusive source in formulating Hofstadter's ideas on the science of survivalism. Nazi racial theories claimed a certain legitimacy under the broad tent of Darwinism, while the daunting staying power of the Depression undermined conservative claims that government intervention imperiled the health of the economy and eroded public moral. While *Social Darwinism* concluded in 1915—the year before Hofstadter's birth—it bore the imprint of its author's disenchantment with the Hoover administration's resistance to government relief programs. The reputation of economic individualism had somehow survived the Progressive Era. And Hofstadter was determined to show in his dissertation why it did not deserve another chance.

*   *   *

Social Darwinism played nicely to Hofstadter's talent for using irony as a tool for insight. The plutocrats who exploited the nation's uniquely egalitarian principles to make their fortunes, he pointed out, had shown their gratitude by building an industrial regime hostile to future social mobility. Eager to attach their unsavory tactics (bribery, theft, collusion) to familiar homilies (thrift, hard work, perseverance), the titans discovered in the reinterpretation of Darwin's theory of natural selection a science of evolution congenial to economic relationships. The English social philosopher Herbert Spencer adapted survivalist etiquette to political economy, touted the virtues of social selection, and linked human progress to technological innovation. In need of an ideological umbrella to rebuff the growing demand for regulation, industrialists found Spencer's views philosophically functional and morally convenient. Darwinism, Hofstadter wrote, "was admirably suited to the American scene. . . . It had a reassuring theory of progress based upon biology and physics. It was large enough to be all things to all men, broad enough to satisfy agnostics . . . and theists. . . . It offered a comprehensive worldview, uniting under one generalization everything in nature, from protozoa to politics."[3]

The industrialists, he continued, required society's approval to carry off their work unhindered, and they were eager to make heroes of the public intellectuals who made laissez-faire a part of the natural law. Following (or so he thought) Darwin's idea of biological selection, Spencer made a virtue of aggression, arguing that the subsistence state benefited the human race as it placed "a premium upon skill, intelligence [and] self-control." The self-preservation instinct, coupled with a scarcity of resources, "had stimulated human advancement and selected the best of each generation for survival."[4] Human perfection, the new science declared, was not merely desirable, but in fact, inevitable. The industrial machine's victory over the American garden may have resulted from a particularly ferocious mixture of expansion and exploitation, competition and crisis, but social Darwinism brought an ersatz order to this chaos and offered an airtight atonement for the sins of the business class.

Amazingly, social Darwinism's impressive popularity extended even to those whom it injured. Hofstadter noted that while farmers and factory workers challenged many of the privileges assumed by the industrial state, they rarely objected to its right to accumulate wealth. And this forced the late nineteenth-century Left — Grangers, Greenbackers, Populists, socialists, and trade unionists — to accept the contradictory principal that democracy could thrive in a plutocracy. This respect for old-fashioned American individualism had long predated social Darwinism, and its deep roots in native soil made it the founding and most enduring myth of the survivalist school.

Social Darwinism's acceptance in America relied on more than popular veneration for individual rights, however, and it also tapped into the country's Protestant heritage. William Graham Sumner— the American Spencer— captured the intellectual high ground of the times, Hofstadter wrote, "because he provided his age with a synthesis of three great products of western capitalist culture: the Protestant ethic, the doctrines of classical economics, and . . . natural selection." These forces, he explained, formed a dark trinity of Calvinism, classical liberalism, and scientific rationalism supportive of Darwinian orthodoxy. Hofstadter believed Sumner's Saxon spiritual preferences revealed the fatal linkage of antinomian Christianity and economic individualism, and he went to great rhetorical lengths to emphasize this point. *Social Darwinism* described Sumner as "a great Puritan preacher," a "frugal man of the Protestant ideal," and an enthusiast of Christian laissez-faire "brought up with respect for the traditional Protestant economic values."[5]

Trained as a theologian, Sumner preached the bountiful exploits of the free market as a professor of political and social science at Yale University. Hofstadter had little sympathy for Sumner's corporate-Christian vision and described his work as a remarkable example of the regressive spirit of nineteenth-century liberal evangelicalism. *Social Darwinism* did not, however, deny the particular virtues of Christian morality. Hofstadter greatly respected those clergy in the forefront of the reform/revival movements that swept through the nation's larger cities. Influenced by the violent strikes of the 1880s and the severe economic downturn of the 1890s, well-established urban churches acknowledged their waning relevancy among working-class congregations and pursued partnerships outside the business community. "As the social gospel developed," Hofstadter noted, "it became increasingly cordial to municipal social or public regulation of basic industries."[6] Urban Protestantism thus benefited greatly, he added, from the presence of non-Wasp groups. These churches absorbed ethnic and radical traditions alien to older native spiritual systems but friendly to the material needs of the typical metropolitan parishioner. Rural Protestantism, he concluded, remained depressingly enamored with the survivalist code.

Hofstadter found a foil to Sumner's philosophy in the impressive scholarship of Lester Ward. Author of the popular text *Dynamic Sociology* (1883), Ward, a professor at Brown University, "attacked the unitary assumptions of Social Darwinism and natural-law laissez faire individualism," profitably replacing them "with a positive body of social theory adaptable to the uses of reform." Ward's pioneering ideas initially attracted little attention outside the academy. Americans accustomed to the tooth-and-claw version of civilization rejected his call for collective action, while Christian reformers were put off by his agnosticism. But Ward's claim that society could direct rather than merely respond to the laws of nature soon became the compelling opinion among opponents of social Darwinism. His struggle against the prevailing intellectual principles of his day elicited an affectionate response from Hofstadter. His assessment of Ward's reaction to the governing ideas of his profession — "[He] *felt a certain personal alienation from the dominant characters and opinions of American intellectual life*" — sums up his own diminishing confidence in the Progressive paradigm.[7]

Hofstadter's strongest sympathies in *Social Darwinism* are reserved for the men who pioneered Pragmatism as a coherent system of thought. Charles Sanders Peirce, William James, and John Dewey maintained that the "truth" of an idea could be most accurately measured by its outcome. This called for a certain intellectual flexibility, and recognition that working hypotheses were superior to rigid axioms that left little room for debate or revision. The Pragmatists "believed that since ideas are provisional responses to particular unreproducible circumstances, their survival depends not on their immutability but on their adaptability." Hofstadter sensed in this social philosophy a valuable alternative to native traditions — Anglo-Saxonism, property-rights individualism, popular democracy — which threatened the delicate ideological and ethnic equilibrium emerging in the post-Depression era. Pragmatism's patriarch, William James, impressed Hofstadter as "the first great product of the scientific education emerging in the United States," and further as a highly imaginative thinker who combined disciplined scientific training with a dose of Swedenborgian mysticism passed down from his father. James's eclectic tastes and aesthetic influences, Hofstadter argued, led him into a profitable "rebellion against all 'block-universe' philosophies, all systems which were finished and executed, impervious to change or choice."[8] In place of entrenched and decaying codes of thought, James pushed for an experimental philosophy that acknowledged the capacity of human creativity to produce a more satisfying existence.

In accord with Ward and James, a new generation of thinkers contributed to the overthrow of the old competitive tradition. Louis Brandeis "opened up new possibilities in law by drawing up for the first time a factual sociological brief in defense of a state law regulating conditions of labor in private enterprise," and Franz Boas "led a generation of anthropologists away from unilinear evolutionary theory toward cultural history and took pioneer steps in the criticism of race theory." In the field of history, Charles Beard and Frederick Jackson Turner departed from the hagiography of their patrician ancestors to pursue economic and environmental explanations for historical causation. The idiosyncratic and stunningly original Thorstein Veblen drew attention to the inconsistencies of classical economic thought and interposed a complex, anthropological interpretation of consumer habits. These important thinkers effectively deconstructed the mythology of nineteenth-century liberalism and replaced it with a more sophisticated analysis of social development that corresponded with the cultural and political needs of their day. They played a critical role as well in Hofstadter's education, helping him to clarify his recent rejection of the Communist Party as a blow for intellectual freedom. He too had once been interested in a simple, monolithic system of thought — Marxism. But studying the Pragmatists' attack on social Darwinism helped him discover why he had been uncomfortable on the left. It was another rigid philosophical system that made no room for human agency.[9]

In time, Progressive scholars created their own intellectual enclosure, complete with a reinforcing mythology that became an inviting target for Hofstadter's generation. Turner in particular was vulnerable. Despite distinguishing himself as an important critic of Brahmin historicism and an early champion of the social sciences, the Wisconsin scholar remained unequivocally committed to the familiar agrarian, Anglo-Saxon traditions. Blood, it seemed, remained thicker than professional training. Turner's stiff devotion to the politics of the "frontier" flattened out into a Progressive celebration of democracy that left a troubling legacy for postwar historians struggling to understand the popular origins of fascism in the thirties and McCarthyism in the fifties.

Progressivism itself was linked closely to the burgeoning field of scientific racism. The reformers took for granted the inferiority of blacks, embraced the eugenics movement as a way of drawing racial distinctions among Americans, and eagerly shouldered the "White Man's Burden" in foreign affairs. Despite claims that their views were informed by fresh scientific research, Progressives had merely put a new spin on an old story. Hofstadter recognized that the making of human hierarchies predated Darwin's discoveries and their application—or misapplication—by imperialists, industrialists, and intellectuals alike. The roots of the republic were nourished in the potent rhetoric of "Anglo-Saxon dogma," providing a kind of supremacist sanction to early Americans in their quest to remove native peoples, enslave Africans, and take Mexican territory. Hofstadter exposed the creaky intellectual underpinnings of genetically based theories of social development and explored the ideas behind racialism and the formidable thinkers—Henry Adams, Josiah Strong, and John Fiske—who advanced them.

These Brahmin spokesmen revered the Anglo privileges of the past and strongly dissented from the pluralist course of modern American social development, condemning in their wake "immigrants, Catholics, Mormons, saloons and tobacco, large cities [and] socialists . . . as grave menaces to the Republic." Hofstadter's rhetorical condemnation of racial Darwinism is striking and worth noting. Within the space of a few pages he used or invented more than a dozen categories to denounce the tactics favored by the Wasp hierarchy to solidify its superior position. They include: "Anglo-Saxon mystique," "Anglo-Saxon clique," "Anglo-Saxon school," "Anglo-Saxon thesis," "Anglo-Saxon liberties," "Anglo-Saxon movement," "Anglo-Saxon lineage," "Anglo-Saxon power," "Anglo-Saxon heights," "Anglo-Saxon superiority," "Anglo-Saxon cult," and the "Anglo-Saxon myth."[10]

Taken as a whole, the Brahmins' protest amounted to a strong rejection of modernity in general and post-Wasp America in particular. Hofstadter's criticism is correct—Adams, for one, never bothered to conceal his disappointment in what America had become—but it is interesting to note that the young historian's attack on the patricians softened over the years. Influenced by the red-baiting that followed the Second World War, Hofstadter no longer drew attention to the discriminatory racial practices of the elite, but rather emphasized the social-psychological hang-ups of a working class that he associated with the anticommunist crusade. Considering his sympathy for organized labor in *Social Darwinism,* this was quite an about-face.

Hofstadter's denunciation of Anglo-Saxonism in his first book was something of a personal fight over privilege. In a 1943 letter to Alfred Kazin, he hammered away at the injustice of a nation that prized Aryans over ethnics. After reading Henry Adams's letters, Hofstadter wrote Kazin that he had never realized before what a vicious anti-Semite he was. He conceded the importance of Adams's prose but argued that no one had ever bothered to analyze the ugly racism that formed his historical judgments. Remarking on Adams's famous concept of the Virgin and the Dynamo, Hofstadter insisted that if any Jewish author had written the same lines, they would have been quickly forgotten.[11]

As Hofstadter composed *Social Darwinism,* evidence of racism was striking—and close by. New York's eclectic higher education system bombarded the young teacher with daily doses of race-based animosity. He informed Harvey Swados that his Jewish students at Brooklyn College regularly outperformed their classmates—despite missing several sessions in observance of the Jewish holidays. Because he graded on a sliding scale, Hofstadter's students competed against each other—and knew it. The less talented—Italian Americans, Hofstadter generalized—resented the competition and developed hostile attitudes toward their more successful Jewish peers. This, he concluded, was anti-Semitism American-style.[12]

Only twenty-six when he completed *Social Darwinism,* Hofstadter enjoyed mostly glowing reports from critics. *New York Times* reviewer Howard Mumford Jones called the work "as excellent a study as you can hope to find," while Northwestern University historian Ray Allen Billington commended the young writer for producing an "exciting . . . important book." Darwinian scholars approached the monograph with expectations commensurate to their specialized expertise, and while judging the study a success, determined that it suffered from imprecision. Bert J. Lowenberg believed that Hofstadter had failed to distinguish Darwinism from Spencerism, while Albert Keller (William Graham Sumner's successor at Yale) correctly complained, "I find a scattering of social scientists, as contrasted with Social Darwinists on this Hofstadter roster."[13]

Despite the Progressive influence on his work, Hofstadter was further guilty of exaggerating the impact of ideas over material considerations — a point he later conceded. The criticism showed up again following the publication of *The Age of Reform,* a brilliant study that emphasized status as a powerful variable triggering political activity, but failed to account fully for the economic concerns that guided Americans. While it is true, in regard to *Social Darwinism,* that some business leaders were sympathetic to the science of survivalism, many more endorsed a traditional Christian ethical code stressing hard work, frugality, and philanthropy. It is clear today that the marriage between biology and society was a more complex union than Hofstadter realized and that most Americans adhered to a pre-Spencerian view of individualism. Nevertheless, the book's enduring success — over 200,000 copies sold in its first half century in print — attests to its author's impressive ability to communicate intellectual history to a general audience. Eric Foner concludes that "Hofstadter's central insight — that analogies with science helped to shape the way Americans perceived and interpreted issues from the differences between the races and classes to the implications of state intervention in the economy — remains the starting point for serious investigations of American thought during the Gilded Age."[14]

In light of Hofstadter's career-long defense of intellect, it is worth noting that no interest group bit more deeply into the Spencerian apple than the intellectuals. There was nothing inherent in Darwin's ideas that gave the game to the titans by default. The Left, in fact, had good reasons of its own to claim his legacy. Biological struggle could have been forcefully presented as scientifically analogous to the class struggle, while evolution in the natural world suggested that the conservative customs of the social world were equally impermanent and susceptible to change. But Hofstadter failed to ask why intellectuals like Spencer and Sumner were so quick to make Darwin's ideas heel before the industrialists. As a young scholar, he may have had difficulty understanding the degree to which public thinkers could be coopted by their society. By the end of his career, he would know better.

Finally, one must note the incredible resiliency of social Darwinism. Hofstadter presumed that his dissertation was something of a parting shot for an ideology that rightfully died on the cross of the Great Depression. Yet the controversial ideas debated by Spencer more than a century ago are with us still. Big government or small government? Regulation or free enterprise? Eugenics or right to life? The boom market of the 1990s nurtured the counterintuitive fantasy that all Americans were winners in the survivalist sweepstakes. All rich, all smart, all fittest. Hofstadter's generation carried life-long memories of the relief workers, apple salesmen, and migrant mothers who peopled the crisis thirties. It was grateful for vigorous executive leadership and congressional oversight in national and international affairs — government, if not precisely the solution, was acknowledged as a valuable counterbalance to market anarchy. At the time of Hofstadter's death in 1970, however, that trust was fast fading, and had he lived, he might have felt compelled to update *Social Darwinism* with a new chapter or fresh introduction. He would have found the survivalist ethic of our own day both fascinating and discouraging.

*   *   *

Hofstadter graduated from Columbia in the spring of 1942 and following an anxious job search ("in the mail came an unanticipated offer") accepted an assistant professorship at the University of Maryland. College Park was then in the midst of an extraordinary expansion as president Harry Clifton (Curly) Byrd, a former Terrapin football star, used his political connections in Annapolis to funnel federal money to the campus. Byrd rode the crest of "vast New Deal construction projects, war-time training programs and especially the postwar enrollment boom" to expand the university financially and physically. Between 1935 and 1954 student registrations at the College Park and Baltimore campuses rose from 3,400 to nearly 16,000, while the value of the physical plant increased from $5 million to $65 million.[15]

Unfortunately, rapid expansion encouraged aggressive administrative centralization that, in the words of one observer, led to the "treatment of faculty as hired hands." Byrd's domination of the university, coupled with his emphasis on constructing buildings and increasing enrollments rather than increasing professors' meager salaries, aroused charges of anti-intellectualism on the campus. Notwithstanding faculty grumbling, the president's actions did have certain favorable repercussions. The university's 1938 budget emphasized support for the arts and sciences in what proved to be a successful effort to expand staff, course offerings, and library resources. Full-time faculty at College Park increased from 130 in 1934 to 263 the year before Hofstadter arrived, while the number of professors holding doctorates nearly tripled over the same period. The history department benefited substantially from this upgrade, hiring Hofstadter and University of Wisconsin doctorates Kenneth Stampp and Frank Freidel. The sociologist C. Wright Mills (also a Madison product) arrived at this time as well.[16]

The Hofstadters moved into a furnished Washington basement apartment on K Street and immediately judged the war capital a dull, small southern town. Stampp complained that "the place smells, the streets are filthy, the dirty slum sections (3/4 of Washington) are grim evidence of the application of the Four Freedoms at home." The Library of Congress's rich manuscript collection might have compensated for the lack of intellectual and cultural amenities in the area, but Hofstadter seldom worked in archival materials and he rarely visited the facility. Thus began a three-year term at Maryland that Hofstadter endured as a kind of academic purgatory — farmed out to the provinces to cut his scholarly teeth and make a mark that would enable him to return to the Northeast. The parochial attitude of the upper South and the racism of the region further diminished the young historian's respect for both the campus and its environs. He wrote Harvey Swados at the end of a frustrating first year that he had no business teaching at College Park. Blacks were not permitted to take courses and faculty spouse Elizabeth Early Freidel remembered an anti-Semitic strain on the campus that reached into the history department. "They didn't like the fact that Frank [Freidel] was the sponsor of a Jewish sorority. It wasn't even supposed to be talked about that Dick was half-Jewish."[17]

Ironically, anti-Semitism helped Hofstadter get the Maryland position. "I need a man in intellectual history," department chairman Wesley Gewehr wrote at the time of Hofstadter's appointment. "I tried to take on Eric Goldman but Pres. Byrd was unwilling or at least *reluctant* to take a man dropped from Hopkins because of local rivalry. There was doubtless also a bit of anti-Semitic sentiment." Four years later, however, Gewehr noted that anti-Semitism handicapped Hofstadter on the southern job market. "You probably know by now," he informed historian Howard K. Beale, "that Vann Woodward was given an Associate Professorship at Hopkins at $5000, which he has accepted; that they looked over Hofstadter, but did not hire him — I believe because there was fear in the department that [Johns Hopkins president Isaiah] Bowman might make difficulty when he found that Hofstadter was half Jewish."[18]

Despite his grievances, Hofstadter was able to pursue areas of personal interest in his teaching, offering courses in historiography and intellectual history. University of Wisconsin historian Margaret Beattie Bogue took a seminar and lecture course under Hofstadter's direction at College Park and recalls a young professor who impressed his students with the quality of his mind. "I remember Hofstadter well, he came into class with rumpled up hair, glasses and a roundish face. He was a man of medium height, trim and looked every bit the intellectual. He was ironic, articulate, approachable — a forceful and convincing lecturer with a good voice and smooth delivery. He approached ideas in a very reasoned and logical way, developing what he was doing and where he was going by progression. I think of all my instructors — and I include Freidel and Stampp — Hofstadter was the most intellectually serious lecturer I had at College Park"[19]

Outside the classroom, Hofstadter made a favorable impression on the fresh hires in his department. Freidel praised his new colleague as "an exceptionally brilliant man" distinguished by his "charm and friendliness" as much as his mental gifts. Stampp described Hofstadter to his mentors back in the Midwest as "a *New Republic* liberal" and later recalled a brief period of initial mistrust that, in terms of recovering the ethnocultural roots of Hofstadter's work, is telling: "We had lunch at [a] drug store and sort of looked at each other suspiciously. I, coming from Wisconsin with a German background, must have belonged, as I think Hofstadter thought, at least sympathetically to the German-American Bund. . . . I remember that one of the first things I had to do was explain to Hofstadter that all Germans in Wisconsin were not Nazi sympathizers." Initial cautions aside, Hofstadter quickly formed strong and sustaining friendships with his new colleagues. His years at Maryland were not happy ("I was toiling away in the provincial dungeons . . . at my first full-time, half-paid job") and these relationships amounted to an intellectual and social oasis for the uprooted New Yorker.[20]

As Hofstadter struggled to make a successful transition from Columbia to College Park, large numbers of G.I.'s arrived at Maryland under the War Department's Army Specialized Training Program. In the spring of 1943, Hofstadter taught four classes consisting of three sections of uniformed soldiers and one of civilian engineers also in the army program. Their classroom decorum — standing at attention when their instructors entered the room — took some getting used to. Hofstadter's own draft status obviously weighed heavily on his mind. He prized structure and routine in his life and the war threatened to break up his equilibrium. There was also a question about his emotional fitness to fight. "My father once confessed to me," Dan Hofstadter notes, "that he simply wouldn't have had the courage to fight in the war," and Richard Hofstadter wrote to Harvey Swados that if he were not drafted he would under no circumstances volunteer. After receiving a 1A status (Stampp and Freidel were initially given 2A deferments because they had children; Mills avoided induction due to hypertension), he appealed to the draft board for an exemption on the grounds that instructing soldiers made him an essential civilian. In the spring of 1944, Hofstadter received a 4F deferment due, he wrote Curti, to allergies and digestive troubles. Missing out on this formative generational experience played on Hofstadter's mind, and in anxious moments he made half-hearted gestures toward entering the fight. Describing himself as tired of teaching stale history courses to soldiers as the world exploded around him, he once wrote Harvey Swados that he was on the verge of enlisting. Like his brief flirtation with the Communist Party, however, the feeling passed. After the war, Hofstadter attributed his deferment to educational rather than medical reasons, telling an interviewer in 1969 that he had "earned a military exemption for teaching soldiers."[21]

The war naturally proved a source of great interest — and anguish — among the men in Hofstadter's circle. His lunchtime conversations with Stampp, Freidel, and Mills were dominated by the group's common hostility for Roosevelt, the war, capitalism, and southerners. Stampp later recalled that the context of the times predisposed men of their background and training to view American leadership with distrust and cynicism. "All four of us having grown up in the thirties, having grown up in that disillusioned generation following World War I, none of us liked FDR, we were all hostile to him as too conservative." Despite their common complaints about Roosevelt and the war, the Maryland scholars varied in the style and intensity of their criticism. Mills was the most radical, conveying a populist suspicion of centralized power absorbed in his native Texas and given sharper focus at Madison. Stampp came from a progressive German evangelical tradition in Milwaukee opposed to war, and Freidel was a Quaker. Hofstadter, the latter remembered, "was not nearly as radical . . . as the three of us at that time. He was more thoughtful and more contemplative."[22]

Despite expanding its course offerings and hiring new faculty, the University of Maryland suffered during the war. Faculty morale plummeted following the regents' announcement that professors were henceforth expected to work a three-semester year-round schedule until the war's conclusion. For aspiring junior scholars like Hofstadter, the summer months offered the only opportunity to engage in sustained research and writing. Academic standards were also a source of concern. With students called off to war, requirements were shamefully lowered in order to fill seats — undergraduates not holding high school diplomas were admitted into the university, which found it expedient to abandon final exams. An ROTC guard posted outside the administration building drew attention to College Park's commitment to the nation's military effort, but simultaneously offended professors upset that President Byrd's "reforms" culminated in Phi Beta Kappa's refusal to establish a charter on the campus. Hofstadter and his friends were discouraged and looked to leave the institution as quickly as possible. "The University of Maryland is a sinking ship," Mills declared, "I do not believe the institution could or should be accredited."[23]

Fed up with the administration's heavy-handed tactics, Hofstadter, Stampp, Freidel, and Mills pressed the campus chapter of the American Association of University Professors (AAUP) to organize opposition to faculty cutbacks and low salaries. When President Byrd proposed an unpaid increase in the teaching load from twelve to eighteen hours in order to instruct army recruits, the four went into action, attempting to organize a faculty rebellion. While Hofstadter knew, as he wrote Swados, that their efforts were hopeless, they did enjoy taking over an AAUP meeting in which they challenged Byrd from the floor and managed to push a resolution through the faculty calling for an investigation of the army contracts obtained by the university.[24]

President Byrd's conduct and the question of the army contracts, however, were soon dwarfed by larger personal and professional developments. In December 1943, Hofstadter's first child, Dan, was born, and over the next several months he and Felice looked forward to a richer professional life beyond College Park. Columbia historian John Allen Krout informed Hofstadter in the fall of 1944 that "there are several teaching opportunities . . . in which your name has been discussed. . . . My own guess is that you will not remain long at the University of Maryland. . . . I feel sure that this Department will strongly support you for a more important place in the historical field."[25] Felice made preparations of her own to leave and mulled over an offer to return to New York and write for *Newsweek*. Whatever the future held for the Hofstadters, their prospects appeared bright.

Tragically, their plans collapsed in the spring of 1944 following a physician's diagnosis that Felice had cancer. Hofstadter, in the early stages of writing *The American Political Tradition,* was devastated, confiding to Curti that he had been unable to work for several weeks after receiving the crushing news. At the end of the school year the small family returned to Buffalo and moved in with Felice's parents. Hofstadter pecked away at his new project throughout the summer, but his time was consumed as a caregiver. The couple hoped to return to Maryland together for the start of classes in the fall, but Felice's deteriorating condition made such optimistic plans impossible. Unable financially to take the semester off, Hofstadter left his wife and baby son in Buffalo and moved into the Millses' home in the College Park suburb of Hyattsville. A few weeks into the semester, however, his friends in the history department took over his course load and, granted a paid leave by the university, he returned to his family.[26]

While in Buffalo, Hofstadter became embroiled in a political controversy with the American Historical Association (AHA) that forced him to again confront the limits of his radicalism. He learned through Stampp and Freidel that Columbia historian and former ambassador to Spain (1942–45) Carlton J. H. Hayes had received the association's presidential nomination. Hayes's supporters praised his role in preventing Spain from joining the Axis powers, but rumors circulated that while serving in Madrid, the ambassador had openly sympathized with the protofascist Franco government. Considering that the Spanish civil war remained an open sore to the American Left, Hayes's candidacy was bound to raise a few eyebrows.

Stampp and Freidel hoped to politicize the association by opposing Hayes. They knew that it was impossible to rally enough support to quash his election, but rather worked to deny him the customary pleasure afforded incoming presidents of receiving unanimous consent. In order to forward another candidate—for convenience' sake vice-presidential nominee Sidney Fay of Harvard—the young insurgents needed to collect at least twenty signatures from AHA members. Their crusade caught fire. A month before the meeting, Stampp enthusiastically reported to William Hesseltine that "our anti-Hayes movement has developed into something bigger than I ever expected it would." Historians from Michigan, Illinois, Wisconsin, and Chicago signed the protestors' petition while departments at several institutions, including Ohio State, Cal Berkeley, and Columbia refused. "No doubt Hayes will be elected," Stampp conceded, but he believed it important to counter "the tight little machine that runs this outfit." The Maryland historians, he happily reported, had "stirred up a first class revolution in the A.H.A." Hofstadter signed the petition in Buffalo and immediately regretted his actions. The refusal of several influential historians to sign bothered him. More importantly, the December (1944) *Harper's* ran a story on Hayes—"How We Dealt with Spain"—emphasizing the ambassador's criticism of both fascism and the Franco government. Hofstadter believed that the article, cowritten by Earnest P. Lindley, a journalist known and respected by Felice, had effectively put the anti-Hayes crusade out of business.[27]

In reaction to this new evidence, Hofstadter moved quickly to distance himself from the radicals. It was too late to take his name off the petition, but he informed Stampp of his second thoughts, declaring now that hostility for the Spanish government rather than specific actions carried out by Hayes had motivated the Maryland historians.[28] His friends felt betrayed. Stampp believed that he had put his career on the line over the Hayes fight and resented Hofstadter's decision. In a letter to Hesseltine, he explained the price he was paying.

> I am the first victim to suffer, and I have made the supreme sacrifice. I submitted an article to [*American Historical Review* editor Guy Stanton] Ford a week before this thing started, and at the time he was quite interested in it. I had the naïve idea that Ford, who is an employee of the Association, would not let this fight have anything to do with the consideration of papers for publication. But yesterday I had my paper fired back at me along with the most insulting letter I have ever received in my life. He told me curtly that it was the opinion of experts that my paper was no good, but he didn't give a single reason why it was no good. So I am on Ford's black list from now on. . . . Frank and I are in this thing so deep now that there is nothing for us to do but keep on fighting them. . . . Damn it, we learned all this from you. You've got to stand with us now.[29]

Believing that Hofstadter had not stood by them, Stampp and Freidel accused their colleague of opportunism, suggesting that his desire to return to Columbia (where Hayes wielded considerable influence) overshadowed his commitment to radical politics. Exasperated by the criticism of his friends and drained from caring for his infant son and sick wife, Hofstadter offered a candid response. In a letter to Stampp, he described himself as timid, conservative, and acquiescent by nature, a radical only in the sense that his critical temperament could function no other way, and not because he possessed the kind of automatic hostility to social injustice of his friends. Brushing aside the charge of opportunism, Hofstadter maintained that his actions in the Hayes case had much to do with a pervasive inner depression that, in this instance, proved paralytic.[30]

The fight over Hayes's candidacy had placed Hofstadter in a vulnerable position. He was caught in the middle between his friends (men who had taken over his teaching load so that he could secure a paid leave) and his Columbia professors (men who had trained and launched him into the profession). In debt to competing constituencies, Hofstadter found it painfully impossible to please everyone, and he simply withdrew from the field of conflict. His actions in the Hayes controversy paralleled his earlier half-hearted decisions to break with Felice and to attend law school. In each, Hofstadter demonstrated an overwhelming desire to avoid confrontation, even if his decisions committed him to actions he knew he could not carry through. He habitually demurred to forceful personalities, reserving his most arresting thoughts for intimate social gatherings or placed between the covers of his books. "The thing about Dick," James Shenton observed, "one always had the feeling that when confronted by opposition he'd retreat. There was an element in him that was not prepared to carry out an argument to its logical conclusion."[31]

In the most fractious AHA assembly to date, the business meeting opened with the insurgents' petition favoring Fay for association president. The Harvard historian did not attend, but wrote a sharp rejoinder read by Arthur Schlesinger, Sr., "deprecating the grounds on which the petitioners had acted and declining to accept, if nominated for the presidency." Wesley Gewehr, chairman of the Maryland history department, moved quickly to protect his "boys" by reading a statement elucidating their position and emphasizing their "undiminished loyalty to the Association." Hayes won the contest by 110 to 66.[32]

*   *   *

Determined to publish his way out of Maryland, Hofstadter refused to rest on the laurels of *Social Darwinism*. An important essay, "William Leggett: Spokesman of Jacksonian Democracy," appeared in the December (1943) *Political Science Quarterly* and gave a taste of the biographical critique of liberalism its author would soon perfect in *The American Political Tradition*. Leggett occupied the unofficial post of "intellectual leader of the New York Locofoco movement"—the radical offshoot of the Empire State's Jacksonian coalition. As an associate editor for the *New York Evening Post,* Leggett's columns celebrated the agrarian side of the Democratic party while denouncing its urban wing. His prosaic views on political economy, Hofstadter wrote, were the product "of a few well-hallowed elements: laissez faire liberalism, the natural rights philosophy of the Declaration of Independence, and strict construction of the Constitution."[33]

Leggett's agrarian sympathies were woefully out of touch, Hofstadter continued, with the realities of a dynamic commercial market. The age of the "common man" encouraged political ferment of a quality and scale unfamiliar to Leggett as laborers in New York City adopted an increasingly class-conscious outlook that prized government assistance as a crucial step to arresting economic decline. The symbols of undemocratic privilege in Manhattan, Hofstadter noted, included lending institutions, for they "restricted competition and often prevented new men from entering the avenues of enterprise. . . . To the ambitious craftsmen who constituted such a large part of the union membership, the banks seemed a part of a huge monopolistic conspiracy."[34] Legislatures issued bank charters to favored groups and rarely lent to workers. The New York Democratic machine enjoyed close ties to the burgeoning Manhattan financial system and refused to break up the monopolistic powers of these institutions. In protest, the left wing of the party split from the dominant Tammany faction.

The *Evening Post* served as a mouthpiece for the radicals, but Leggett's tepid response to the grievances of workers can be gleaned from his uncritical acceptance of classical economic principles. He blandly advocated "equal rights" but more earnestly discouraged "government interference in the private economic affairs of the people." Working men and women of the early republic faced real hardships — they were often paid in notes that rapidly depreciated in value — yet Leggett, their chief "spokesman," called not for reform, regulation, or protection from fiscal insecurity (as happened a century later, Hofstadter knew, in FDR's New York), but rather for the expansion of the free market system along more democratic lines. Leggett assumed that the industrial working class consisted largely of expectant capitalists and he perversely declared that the promise of political equality could be achieved only when "poor men [are] able to compete with rich in the launching of business enterprise."[35] In his devotion to the laissez-faire state, Leggett prefaced the age of Hoover.

The *Quarterly* piece anticipated a series of Hofstadter studies on the paranoid mind that became standard reading material for graduate students in the fifties and sixties. "The fatal weakness in [Leggett's] thinking," Hofstadter wrote, "was his failure to assign any of the hardships of his day to the inherent disorders of a growing economic system, his tendency to trace all difficulties to an evil conspiracy on the part of the rich and well born." Union College president and former Columbia historian Dixon Ryan Fox praised the essay, but cautioned Hofstadter in a private communication to resist linking the reform impulse (a sacred cow to Fox's generation) to paranoid fantasies. "Certainly he was not alone in his conspiracy theory of trouble. We can find that still existing on every side." Fox's gentle admonition, however, did not keep Hofstadter from drawing attention to the crank side of American reform. Nearly twenty years later, C. Vann Woodward advised Hofstadter that his work tended to give "the impression that nativism and racism are peculiarities of the unwashed and the semi-literate Populists. I think it should be pointed out," Woodward continued, "that these prejudices were rife at the time among New England patricians and intellectual elite on the East coast."[36]

A second major Hofstadter article appeared in 1944, "U. B. Phillips and the Plantation Legend." A native of the Georgia Cotton Belt and the nation's preeminent scholar of slavery, Phillips (1877–1934) devoted the better part of his career to drawing sympathetic portraits of southern history, traditions, and cultural values. *American Negro Slavery* (1918) and *Life and Labor in the Old South* (1929) secured his reputation among Progressives, but Phillips's assertion that a paternalistic system of bondage benefited innately inferior blacks infuriated younger historians.

In "U. B. Phillips and the Plantation Legend," Hofstadter accused Phillips of neglecting important source material that contradicted his approving appraisal of master-slave relations. Issues sensitive to the ruling race including miscegenation and health care went unexplored and Phillips's selective use of plantation records belied his claims of comprehensiveness. The interpretive bias that informed *American Negro Slavery* struck Hofstadter as self-evident. "The way of thinking which underlay Phillips' work needs no elaboration here," he wrote. "He was a native of Georgia, to whom the Southern past always appeared in a haze of romance. . . . His books can best be placed in the course of our intellectual history when it is realized that they represent a latter-day phase of the pro-slavery argument."[37]

Hofstadter proved a discerning student of Phillips's sectional leanings, yet his own regionalism undoubtedly played a role in his loving dismemberment of the "plantation legend." In an autobiographical work published in the 1980s, Woodward recalled that southerners of his generation routinely suffered under the critical gaze of their neighbors to the north. "Combining a literature of exposure with one of satire and ridicule, South-baiting became a Northern journalistic industry with fabulously rich resources to mine below the Potomac. . . . Its influence and productivity persisted into the 1930s and spread through the academy, especially among the social scientists. Investigators of Southern atrocities and monstrosities poured through from the North." Hofstadter's unhappy stay at Maryland reinforced his belief in the regressive nature of southern society and came through in correspondence peppered with asides condemning the region's racism, anti-intellectualism, and cultural backwardness. Still, connections were made. Despite their differences, Hofstadter and Woodward shared a long and affectionate friendship. "An improbable bond," the latter acknowledged, "this tie between the Arkansas-bred, Georgia-Carolina educated provincial and the cosmopolitan city-bred intellectual. The friendship . . . was never threatened by our differences, either of origin or of views. They were assumed rather than debated."[38]

*　　*　　*

Bombarded with medical bills and eager to write a trade press book that might lead to a more lucrative career in journalism, Hofstadter applied for a Knopf History Fellowship in the spring of 1945, submitting chapters on Lincoln and Hoover for a work titled "Men and Ideas in American Politics." The publishing firm of Reynal and Hitchcock had already turned the manuscript down, and Hofstadter informed Stampp that he entered the fellowship competition with little hope. His pessimism proved groundless. Alfred Knopf was then looking for someone to write a biography of Benjamin Sillman, the father of American scientific education. After consulting some of his friends among the Columbia historians, he asked Hofstadter if he would be interested. Hofstadter replied that he was then engaged in "Men and Ideas," but the introduction proved important. He submitted, with Alfred Knopf's blessing, two chapters of his new project to the Knopf contest.[39]

Impressed with both Hofstadter's obvious promise and the immediate merits of his project (an internal report declared "the Hoover chapter . . . a lulu"), the Knopf awards committee designated the young scholar's application "the outstanding submission of our history fellowship. Excellently written, vigorous, informed by a realistic liberal point of view based on sound scholarship. . . . It is unorthodox; it will outrage many people. . . . But no one will deny its distinction." The prize included a generous research stipend and publication of the winning entry — a point that probably kept Hofstadter from winning the contest outright. Due to the committee's resolute assumption (widely off the mark as things turned out) that a book of essays stood little chance of winning a popular audience, Knopf split the $5,000 award between Hofstadter and University of Indiana historian R. Carlyle Buley. Even more meaningful than the financial assistance, Hofstadter's publishing future was now secure. His relationship with Alfred Knopf quickly grew warm and supportive and in later years he remembered fondly how "surprised and touched" he was to receive detailed textual criticism of his early manuscripts from Knopf himself.[40]

As spring gave way to summer and the war ground to a halt, however, the fellowship provided Hofstadter little comfort. Felice's year-long illness took an inevitable psychological toll on her husband, who found peace only in his scholarship. "Hofstadter told me," Robert Dallek recalls, "that when he was writing *The American Political Tradition* and his first wife was dying, he was producing five pages a day. For him it was a kind of therapy." The length of Felice's infirmity permitted Hofstadter time to prepare himself emotionally for her death—and as that date grew near, she began to disappear from his correspondence. Leaving her husband with a one-and-a-half-year-old infant, Felice died in July 1945. Hofstadter's reply to Stampp's note of condolence gave only the sparest hint of its author's grief. A mere fifty words, it emphasized his desire to resume his work.[41]

The year's absence from College Park (1944–45) only heightened Hofstadter's desire to find another position. Since taking his doctorate, he had cultivated close ties to Columbia, spending long weekends at Morningside Heights, maintaining a study room in the Butler Library, and conscientiously sending offprints of his published work to the history faculty. In the winter of 1945, Columbia began a search, as Commager put it, for "someone who can really take hold of intellectual history and develop this place as a center for the study of American civilization." The department first approached Curti, who chose to remain at Wisconsin, before ranking Hofstadter ahead of Arthur Schlesinger, Jr., as its top candidate. After the former was hired, Harry Carman congratulated (and perhaps reassured) his colleagues—"I'm sure we chose correctly for the long run."[42]

The offer may have saved Hofstadter's career. His salary at Maryland was less than $3,000 and postwar inflation absorbed every bit of it. Hofstadter supplemented his university income by writing for several publications, including the Sunday *New York Times* and the *New Republic,* and for a time he considered dropping historical work entirely for a career in journalism. His lucid, playful writing style made a career in criticism a real possibility—"I am as much, maybe more, of an essayist than an historian" he once noted with customary insight. "I think people like Edmund Wilson had much more influence on my style than any historian."[43] With both Maryland and the ordeal of his wife's illness behind him, Hofstadter began the exhausting process of redefining his professional and personal identity. The return to New York helped immeasurably on both accounts.

In the summer of 1946, Hofstadter met Beatrice Kevitt, a Buffalo native trained in the classics at Cornell University. Six years Hofstadter's junior, Kevitt was a war widow seeking a fresh start in New York City. She planned to study journalism at Columbia in preparation for a writing career, but her place was taken by the university to make room for a returning veteran. She remained in Manhattan and worked for *Parents* magazine. Hofstadter was excited to be in a new relationship and wanted badly to put his life back together. Dan was living with Felice's parents in Buffalo and he desperately wanted to bring him to New York. In a letter to Stampp, he explained his inability to care for an infant on his own and stressed his desire to remarry. He had begun dating in Washington shortly after Felice's death and two of his closest friends — Harvey Swados and William Miller— married in 1946. Hofstadter followed suit, marrying Kevitt on 13 January 1947. Six weeks later they brought Dan to New York.

In the eighteen months following Felice's death the resonance of past places and past relationships began to grow less audible for Hofstadter. Buffalo, Montague Street, Merle Curti, *Social Darwinism,* and the leftist thirties gave way to Manhattan, Claremont Avenue, Lionel Trilling, *The Age of Reform,* and the liberal fifties. Emerging from what Curti described as "the rough times in your young manhood," Hofstadter found in Kevitt, Knopf, and Columbia new and important sources of strength. With the crystallization of these relationships and the maturing of his creative powers, he entered the most intellectually prolific period of his life.[44]

* 3 *

The New American
Political Tradition

I always thought *The American Political Tradition* was a paradoxical book. In it, Hofstadter traced a tradition that he destroyed.

JACK POLE, 2001

Richard Hofstadter's return to New York in the autumn of 1946 prefaced his greatest achievement as a historian. While peers Eric Goldman,
Arthur Schlesinger, Jr., and C. Vann Woodward prepared important
studies assaying the strengths and weaknesses of the reform tradition,
Hofstadter's work in progress, *The American Political Tradition: And the
Men Who Made It,* has earned a singular position in the annals of professional historical writing.[1] On the strength of the book's stunning popular success, Hofstadter succeeded Charles Beard as the most influential
and intellectually significant American historian of his time. The book
offered critical and provocative essays about notable public figures, but
its underlying themes were responsive to more contemporary concerns.
In an era clouded by the Taft-Hartley Act, loyalty oaths, blacklists, and
McCarthyism, *The American Political Tradition* ran against the conservative counterrevolution to the New Deal. A study ostensibly of past politics, it offered a fresh vision embraced by generations.

Hofstadter's cautious defense of New Deal liberalism earned him the
title (privately much resisted) of *consensus historian.* While the designation hints at the ideological solidarity practiced by many postwar scholars, it fails to convey the complexity of Hofstadter's private pilgrimage
from the left to the liberal center. Rather than celebrate an unusually
successful and conservative continuity in national life, *The American Political Tradition* drew attention to the rather sharp economic, political,
and cultural differences that divided Hoover's America from FDR's.

Hofstadter prized intellectual independence as the source of original scholarship and the consensus label puzzled him. It was never his intention, he repeated over the years, to produce a grand theory of American politics. The book's introduction, however, gave precisely that impression. As the manuscript underwent final revision in preparation for its fall 1948 release, Alfred Knopf pressed its author to identify a unifying theme in the work in order to make the project more marketable. "We want, as far as possible," Knopf explained to his young author, "to get away from the idea that it is just a collection of essays. . . . I feel that the introduction is . . . very important." Hofstadter's editor, Harold Strauss, played a key role recasting the manuscript along the lines emphasized by Knopf and stressed to Hofstadter the need to offer a harmonious structure. "There is no single theme which runs through the book," Strauss complained, "and that is betrayed by the present title [*Men and Ideas in American Politics*]. I have been toying with the idea of some such title as *Personality and Politics,* with the subtitle, *A Re-interpretation of American Leadership.* . . . I think that our promotion line must be the reinterpretation of 'The American Past.'"[2]

Hofstadter's brief introduction responded sympathetically to Strauss's suggestions. It described the book as a "quest for the American past," and pointed to the need for "a reinterpretation of our political traditions which emphasizes the common climate of American opinion." Knopf's promotional blurb further reinforced the consensus theme: "In this age of political extremism, this young and brilliant Columbia historian searches out the common ground among all American parties and factions. He uncovers the taproot of the political tradition which has united the nation since its birth. He shows that all great parties, even the Populists, are loyal to the twin principles of property and progress, and differ only on policies and tactics."[3] What began in 1943 as a critique of the country's commitment to property-rights liberalism evolved under commercial pressures into a sweeping judgment on the national character.

The title of the book proved as vexing as the introduction. A few months before publication, Strauss suggested changing the title from *Men and Ideas in American Politics* to *Eminent Americans: Their Growth and Political Traditions.* Hofstadter resisted. He reminded Strauss that his book did not demonstrate growth; rather it emphasized just the opposite — an absence of real development in the American political tradition. Accordingly, he requested that the word *Growth* be struck from the subtitle. Strauss searched for a compromise. "In the subtitle, I yield to your argument concerning the word growth. But it is very easy to substitute a word which will not distort your intentions without invalidating the subtitle. The words shape, pattern and force come to mind." Hofstadter accepted Strauss's recommendation and in January 1948 it appeared that the title was settled — *Eminent Americans: And the Shape of Political Traditions.*[4]

In late March, however, Hofstadter began having second thoughts about the inscription *Eminent Americans.* To complicate matters, Knopf wanted to put on the jacket of the book the separate heading *Great Men and Great Ideas in the American Past.* Again, Hofstadter rejected the house's recommendation. "*Great Men and Great Ideas,*" he explained to Strauss, violated the spirit of the book, which, after all, argued that there had been but a single idea in the first political tradition — and certainly not a great one. On the twenty-ninth — one day before the matter had to be settled — Strauss asked Hofstadter to come to his office with a fresh title and subheading if he continued to object to the house's proposal. "I've discussed your title with Alfred and he is willing to throw the matter open provided that you come back to us with a constructive suggestion. Perhaps you can develop something between the time you receive this and the time you come in tomorrow."[5] With only hours to act, Hofstadter came up with a new title. Knopf's choice: *Eminent Americans: And the Shape of Political Traditions,* with the subheading *Great Men and Great Ideas in the American Past,* had now been changed according to Hofstadter's wishes to read simply *The American Political Tradition: And the Men Who Made It.*

Hofstadter's book did not celebrate the great American postwar consensus; rather it initiated a notable departure from past historiographical practices. Progressive thinkers had taken the conflict theme as far as it could go. The old battles between capital and labor had receded as an encroaching affluence — what David Potter described as a "people of plenty"—influenced the writing of the American past.[6] Historians were now eager to emphasize the multiple roots of causation (rather than a single economic interpretation) and borrowed heavily from the social sciences to explore the moods and mentalities of their subjects. But there was more at work here than changing intellectual styles. The combination of cold war and decolonization encouraged an uncritical appreciation of the common qualities of American life. Episodes of cultural rebellion including racial violence and class conflict were deemphasized as a liberal front worked hard to bring third world nations into the Western orbit by praising the impressive continuity of the country's democratic, egalitarian institutions.

Aside from political and intellectual influences, it is evident that Hofstadter's ethnicity shaped the way he understood and wrote history. John Higham addressed the multicultural foundations of consensus historiography (and neatly summed up Hofstadter's formative experiences as the son of a Jewish immigrant) when he wrote that

> the vision of America that consensus scholars offered . . . was a picture of social diversity, not of solid uniformity. One of their objectives was to encompass within American history a greater variety of groups and impulses than could find a place in the simple dualism of the Progressive school. They proposed, therefore, that Americans were a variegated people held together by a unifying ideology or a common way of life. Many, if not most, of the leading consensus historians were secularized, highly assimilated Jews. Themselves the sons of immigrants, they belonged to the first generation of Jewish students who encountered no serious obstacles in rising into the humanistic disciplines. How could they avoid perceiving the United States as an increasingly inclusive society resting on a universalistic value system?[7]

Hofstadter's ethnicity is not easily pegged. Alfred Kazin and Daniel Bell believed that Hofstadter wrestled with his mixed identity and, in Bell's case, that he came, through the milieu of radical politics at Buffalo, two marriages, and many Upper West Side friendships, to appreciate his secular Jewish background. This view is consistent with Hofstadter's admission to an interviewer that "I spent a lot of years acquiring a Jewish identity, which is more cultural than religious." A perfect summation of Hofstadter's ambiguous ethnic status can be found in a communication between Berkeley historians John Hicks and Raymond Sontag. The issue: a 1947 opening in the University of California history department. The concern: was Hofstadter too radical? With the American Historical Association's annual meeting on the horizon, Hicks went into action, writing to Sontag, "If you attend the meeting would you take pains to see Hofstadter of Columbia and give him the careful once-over? I am not yet quite sure that he is the man we want. His point of view strikes me as rather typical of the New York Jewish intelligentsia, although I do not even know that he is a Jew."[8]

To return to Higham's statement, historians of mixed or minority backgrounds frequently emerged from political upbringings more radical than their Anglo cousins. They were receptive to incorporating the social sciences into historical analysis — a legacy of their intellectual ghettoization in economics and sociology departments — and demonstrated a commitment to civil rights and labor reform often absent from the progressive agendas of Brahmin and midwestern thinkers. Ethnic Americans, in other words, were at the forefront of expanding and redefining American liberalism. The Wasp worldview, described by Hofstadter as isolationist, individualistic, nationalistic, and capitalistic, broke before a sharp cultural realignment shaped by demographic change, depression, and war. As practiced by Hofstadter, consensus history was the product of multiple traditions.

Hofstadter intended *The American Political Tradition* to overturn the Progressive synthesis, and he steeled himself for a chilly response among colleagues. He knew he had written a good book, he informed Merle Curti, but assumed that its critical tone would alienate readers. Hofstadter's concerns illuminate the power of historical circumstances to separate the generations. Born at the tail end of the Progressive Era, Hofstadter had no personal recollections of the reformers or their crusades against the trusts. His most visceral memories were of the weaknesses and inconsistencies of the old liberalism; its failure to end the Depression, contain fascism, condemn racism, or develop a productive intellectual system to counter native veneration for the yeoman and the frontier. By the thirties, progressivism was in full retreat, a casualty of the Depression era's drift toward nostalgia. In their search for a set of sustaining values amid the dark backdrop of economic collapse and global conflict, scholars emphasized simplicity over complexity, regionalism over metropolitanism, and cultural homogeneity over cultural pluralism. The most popular historical studies of the period — Carl Van Doren's *Franklin,* Carl Sandburg's *Lincoln,* and Douglas Southall Freeman's *Lee* — presented a lack of serious ideological conflict in America that struck postwar scholars as grossly false. As progressive literature dissolved into self-congratulations and cultural nationalism. It became vulnerable to fresher and more insightful interpretations.[9]

The American Political Tradition is a striking example of revisionist history in the best sense. Rather than succumb to the temptation to render crippling judgments of the nation's heroes, it dissected the politicians without destroying them. Anyone who has read the book carefully understands that the "men who made it" were not Hofstadter's primary concern. His human subjects, rather, represented certain ironic and tragic features in the nation's past that exposed the limitations of the old system, and distinguished the divide between pre- and post-1933 philosophies. The economic crisis of the thirties and the war that followed upended illusions of American exceptionalism and produced in their wake a generation skeptical of the "self-evident" truths of the past.

As a product of the 1940s, it is worth asking how *The American Political Tradition* continues to attract twenty-first century readers. Certainly its author's aphoristic style—what Paula Fass remembers as her mentor's "desire to be epigrammatic"—goes far to explain the work's enduring interest. In Hofstadter's hand, a highly expressive sense of humor illuminated history, and he clearly owed a debt to H. L. Mencken, the most important American satirist of the American century. Their shared respect for sharp literary expression and long-standing love-hate relationships with democracy combined with superficially similar views on politics and popular culture. "No one would dream of imitating [Mencken]," Hofstadter noted in 1960, "but he awoke me to the buffoonery and playfulness one can inject into one's style. I soaked up everything of Mencken's when I was an undergraduate at the University of Buffalo."[10]

Like Mencken, Hofstadter respected clear and unsentimental thinking. Both men were offended—too offended, really—by the intellectual shortcomings of the popular mind. Christopher Lasch argued that Hofstadter

> could not conceal his disdain for the hopelessly muddled thinking of ordinary Americans, their inability to think straight about politics, their tendency to confuse images with actions, their insatiable appetite for symbolic actions that provide the illusion that something is being done when in fact nothing is happening, their absolute dedication to a kind of entrepreneurial view of life, and above all their racism, xenophobia, anti-Semitism, which in his view were never very far from the surface of American life. I've come to see Hofstadter as a latter-day version of H. L. Mencken, endlessly belaboring the "booboisie."[11]

Lasch's criticism fails, however, to account for the fact that both Mencken and Hofstadter were popular writers who produced work read mainly by what Lasch described as "ordinary Americans." In Hofstadter's case, *The American Political Tradition* proved to be a remarkable example of scholarship that appealed to both the professors and the public. How many books reviewed by the eminent Harvard literary historian Perry Miller found their ways into the nation's high schools?

The American Political Tradition's popularity can further be explained by pointing up its important role promoting the postwar search for ideological solidarity. While the New Deal failed to right the economic ship of state, its undeniable triumph over both the old Right and Left was more impressive. In an age of American and Soviet expansion, the public required confirmation that the new politics could stand up to authoritarian governments while maintaining a separate identity from conservative anticommunism at home. *The American Political Tradition* offered a tested, skeptical liberalism, averse to ideological crusades and capable of sustaining recent domestic and foreign policy initiatives. "More than the volumes by Hartz and Boorstin, such contemporaneous works as Schlesinger's *The Vital Center* and Lionel Trilling's *The Liberal Imagination* are its true bedfellows," David Greenberg wrote. "Hofstadter not only was personally close to the authors of these books but shared with them a modernist determination to position liberalism between the poles of hidebound conservatism and knee-jerk sentimentalism."[12]

It was by no means clear that the new politics could carry the day. Lewis Mumford's 1940 *New Republic* essay "The Corruption of Liberalism" commented that American social reformers were in a state of self-inflicted crisis—weakened and humiliated by their embrace of Stalin and failure to stand up to Hitler. "The record of liberalism during the last decade," Mumford admonished, "has been one of shameful evasion and inept retreat. Liberalism has compromised with despotism. . . . Liberalism has been on the side of passivism . . . it has been on the side of appeasement." In sum, liberalism lacked the courage and conviction to create a tougher and more pragmatic system of values that could punish dictators abroad while promoting democracy at home. Mumford called for a mature liberalism to counter the "incurable optimism" commonly associated with ideology. "What is demanded," he concluded, "is a recrystallization of the positive values of life, and an understanding of the basic issues of good and evil, of power and form, of force and grace, in the actual world." Shorn of progressive pieties, Hofstadter began in *The American Political Tradition* the process of reconstructing—or, as Mumford put it, recrystallizing—American liberalism.[13]

*   *   *

The founding fathers of the original American political tradition were Jefferson and Jackson. Their emergence as national heroes legitimized public power and won favorable treatment from generations of scholars sympathetic to the democratic aspirations of the "people." Hofstadter was not impressed. Urban, industrial, and ethnic, the new nation, he argued, had no practical use for Jefferson's agrarian vision. Twentieth-century liberalism expected vigorous government intervention on behalf of the indigent, he continued, but Jefferson's reflexive fear of centralized power worked against robust federal regulation and gave the game to the industrialists by default. Commitment to a stifling vision of individualism and limited government, he concluded, made the Master of Monticello's ghost the perfect spokesman for the trusts.

Jefferson's brand of democracy led to the protopopulism of Andrew Jackson, a controversial president whose deft political maneuvers and large popular following attracted considerable attention among postwar scholars. The most important of these studies, Arthur Schlesinger, Jr.'s Pulitzer Prize–winning *The Age of Jackson* (1945), argued that early-republic oligarchs came perilously close to bending the government to their will before the people — under Jackson's leadership — restored the nation to its egalitarian roots. For obvious reasons, cold warriors found this celebration of popular power a source of inspiration. One of the last major statements of Progressive historiography, *The Age of Jackson* amended the Turnerian approach to the period by stressing urban rather than rural sources of reform. "It seems clear now," Schlesinger wrote in a line memorized by a generation of graduate students, "that more can be understood about Jacksonian democracy if it is regarded as a problem not of sections but of classes."[14] Still, Schlesinger's insistence that popular democracy advanced liberal reforms (albeit in a class-conscious East rather than a frontier West) aligned snugly within the main contours of Progressive thought. In the great public crusade of the Jacksonian period, he noted, urban Democrats successfully restrained the business community by destroying the Second Bank of the United States and returning the republic to the "people."

Schlesinger's attractive thesis won the book lavish attention — some of it quite critical. Bray Hammond, an official of the Federal Reserve Board and expert on the history of American banking, complained that *The Age of Jackson* portrayed the era "as one of triumphant liberalism when it was as much or more an age of triumphant exploitation; it fosters a simplistic view of continuing problems of human welfare; and it thickens the myths around a political leader who had more capacity for action than for accomplishment." Hofstadter agreed with Bray's position, believing that *The Age of Jackson* had replaced Turner's mythical frontier with an equally improbable proletariat movement.[15]

In reply, Hofstadter turned Schlesinger's argument on its head.[16] The electorate did not fear the expansion of the market, he maintained; rather it embraced the new economy, tying its fortunes to their own. Jacksonians were dissatisfied with the slow pace of economic development and hoped to secure advantages previously reserved for commercial elites. They were not anticapitalist nor were they anticredit, they simply wanted a bigger piece of the pie. Jackson's victory over the bank, however, had unanticipated and unhappy repercussions for the country. Federal deposits formally placed in the system were now put into private "pet banks," and without a central unit to regulate the flow of capital, the nation suffered an acute and crippling bout of inflation.

Drawing attention to the deficiencies of the Jacksonian economy allowed Hofstadter to stress the precedent-breaking actions of the Roosevelt administration. Schlesinger saw the New Deal as a *continuation* of the Jacksonians' successful struggle against the business community, but Hofstadter praised the regulatory programs of the thirties as a *departure* from past political decisions. While he understood the temptation to draw parallels between the two periods, he considered such comparisons historically implausible. Jacksonianism, he noted, was an agrarian movement premised on economic opportunity, laissez-faire, and the removal of government barriers to investment among small capitalists. The New Deal, by contrast, was an urban movement that assumed that the great era of capitalist ascendancy had passed and that government regulation was needed to revitalize American markets. The New Deal, Hofstadter continued, offered a rational response to economic crisis, while Jackson's suspicion of privilege — culminating in the destruction of the "aristocratic" bank — revealed an ugly conspiratorial style of political paranoia. In years to come, Hofstadter would have much more to say about the paranoid attitudes of politicians and their followers.

The Jacksonian campaign against privilege guaranteed the party's popularity but did not combine all strands of antebellum thought. For a fuller discussion of this subject, Hofstadter turned to the spirited abolitionist Wendell Phillips, a rare example of a homegrown Yankee radical. The subject of *The American Political Tradition*'s most appreciative portrait, Phillips was an early advocate of organized labor, refreshingly critical of the American capitalist system. Most reformers, including the celebrated William Lloyd Garrison, adopted conservative responses to the labor issue, enthusiastically attacking southern lords of the lash while ignoring the exploitations of northern lords of the loom. But Phillips argued that workers of all races required protection from an exploitative free market, and he believed that the abolitionist crusade was an important but not conclusive effort in securing rights for labor.

Following the Civil War, most abolitionists retired from the field of reform, certain that their efforts on behalf of the bondsmen guaranteed a warm reception in the history books. But the desperate postslavery plight of the freedmen convinced Phillips that authentic political citizenship could not be won without economic independence — for both black and white workers. With a shrewd understanding of the limitations of the property rights system, Phillips recognized, Hofstadter wrote, that both slavery and the old liberal tradition had to surrender to a new economic arrangement that guaranteed producers ownership of production.[17]

Phillips's status as an outsider appealed to Hofstadter, but he found Abraham Lincoln a more intriguing historical figure precisely because of his reputation as the quintessential insider. Lincoln's path from the prairie to the presidency revitalized the spirit of social mobility at the precise moment when international capitalism anticipated a less egalitarian order. Farmers, artisans, and factory workers looked to his life as an affirmation of the rising-class values of education, initiative, and self-help; industrialists presented the martyred president as an opponent of organized labor and government regulation. The results were striking — and pathetic. The great barons, in their quest to build economic empires, choke competition, and turn a socially mobile working class into a subdued proletariat, manipulated Lincoln's legacy. In "victory," Hofstadter observed, Lincoln lost everything.

*   *   *

The Lincoln chapter concluded the first half of *The American Political Tradition*. The rest of the book, covering much the same chronological terrain as *Social Darwinism*, found Hofstadter working with familiar material. "Hofstadter's judgments and historical imagination are more at home in the recent past than in the pre-Civil War period," Harold Strauss wrote of an early draft. "In the later portions of the book there is independent judgment, perspicacity, a flare for irony that approaches genius, and an exciting freshness of style."[18] The freedom to burlesque the grotesque hypocrisy of New York political boss Roscoe Conkling,

the political fundamentalism of William Jennings Bryan, and the sentimental chauvinism of Theodore Roosevelt played nicely into Hofstadter's strength for satire.

As Lincoln's memory gave way to a rising industrial gentry, rural
America discovered in the Nebraska Populist William Jennings Bryan a
powerful voice for its resentments. Known in youth as the "Boy Orator"
of the free silver campaigns, Bryan emerged late in life as a potent symbol of evangelicalism's march against modernity. In return the Klan,
prohibitionists, antievolutionists, and rural Protestantism gave him
their allegiance. The influence of the small town in American politics,
however, was fast fading. At the 1924 Democratic convention, Bryan im-
plored his party to unite along the principles of midwestern morality in
opposition to the enemies of Anglo-American culture. The assemblage
replied by heckling him mercilessly. With the foot soldiers of rural reform in retreat, Bryan's political base quickly unraveled. And in a final
bid to reenergize his following, he fused the politics of provincialism to
a primitive Christian fundamentalism. During the famous Scopes trial
in Dayton, Tennessee, he attacked the academic freedom of professional educators, insisting that taxpayers rather than certified instructors enjoyed the right to determine curriculum. By what perverse measure, Hofstadter concluded, could such a view, or such a man, be
considered progressive?

Bryan held the heart of reformers for many years, but Theodore Roosevelt was the most successful and popular politician of the Progressive
Era. Hofstadter marveled at this fact — in his opinion TR's patrician instincts were paramount, his progressivism a pose. Roosevelt detested
the American Left — "Muckrakers" and "extremists," he tarred them —
and blamed their penny press exposes as key sources of public agitation
and unrest. Reform, he believed, belonged in the hands of the old elite,
and could best be accomplished through a stern dedication to nationalism, martial values, and a common spirit of racial identity and destiny.
Hofstadter saw in this conservative attitude a slight variation of the fascist politics that poisoned Europe following Roosevelt's death. A nation
agitated by industrial capitalism and unsettled by demographic trends
trumpeting the emerging power of non-Anglo-Saxon peoples, however,
embraced Roosevelt's authoritarian values.

As a moralist, TR truly shined. His bully pulpit denouncements of
the industrialists and great eastern financiers assuaged the fears of millions of Americans concerned with the problems of competition and
corporate "bigness." As an outspoken critic of the monopolies and a

conspicuous if selective opponent of trusts, Roosevelt relieved popular anxieties and happily played the role of therapist to the American masses.[19]

Hofstadter's tart appraisal of TR encouraged a sharp reaction from Roosevelt specialist Howard K. Beale. "It is obvious that you do not like Theodore Roosevelt in fact, that you have an intense hatred of him," Beale observed in a private communication. "Should that be obvious in an historical treatment of an important figure. . . . I suspect that you are just another product of the student generation of fifteen years ago when the swing of the pendulum made it fashionable to deprecate TR and to laud FDR. I hate to see you write a book for all time that is so badly dated in supporting the fashion of a particular moment." Hofstadter replied that his iconoclastic treatment of Roosevelt was the prerogative of an author writing in the journalistic-literary strain rather than offering a purely historic account. His book was not written primarily for scholars, he asserted, and thus could not be judged as if it were.[20]

Hofstadter's discontentment with Progressive leadership extended beyond Roosevelt to include Woodrow Wilson. A southern conservative devoted to the principles of Christian moral redemption, Wilson evoked the politics of the past in his unwavering dedication to the native traditions Hofstadter distrusted. At first glance, the achievements of Wilson's administration appeared substantial. It produced the first downward revision of the tariff since the Civil War, placed the nation's banking and credit system under public control, and awarded farmers badly needed government credits. But Hofstadter saw in these actions an eye on the past rather than the future. Wilson's domestic reform initiatives responded to the public's cry for a restoration of small-scale capitalism in an age of soaring industrial concentration and impressed the young historian as a misguided attempt to reprise the individualism celebrated in Jefferson's day. Like the first Roosevelt, Wilson prized competition. He hoped to restore the old politics.

The first American political tradition expired amid the colossal failure of the 1920s bull market. Herbert Hoover—an orphan cum millionaire cum president—became a fitting if tragic symbol of the self-made philosophy. Like Lincoln, Hoover embodied the qualities of individualism, opportunity, and success that captured the American imagination. In return, the nation showered its affection on him; his precrash popularity rivaled that of any contemporary save Charles Lindbergh. Hoover embraced the laissez-faire politics pioneered by Jefferson and Jackson, but the age of the expectant capitalist was over. The crash inaugurated a decade of limitations, pessimism, and a quest for regulation that called for fresh thinking and a bold break from orthodoxy. Hoover's disastrous embrace of the old conventions cast the last Progressive president as a political anachronism remarkably incapable of addressing the needs of a metropolitan nation.

Hoover's successor, the Hudson Valley patrician Franklin Roosevelt, appeared an unlikely candidate to lead the nation in a new direction. As a young radical, Hofstadter was highly critical of FDR, but the passage of time encouraged a softer evaluation. "Dick had considerable reservations as to the success of the New Deal at least in FDR's lifetime," Jack Pole remembers. "But he once remarked to me, 'The New Deal may have been a failure in the thirties but it sure is a success in the fifties!' — an irony he characteristically enjoyed." Hofstadter delighted in Roosevelt's 1932 San Francisco Commonwealth Club address, a happy eulogy read before the unmourned grave of the old politics. "Equality of opportunity as we have known it no longer exists," Roosevelt proclaimed, without a trace of sentiment. "Our industrial plant is built . . . our last frontier has long since been reached, and there is practically no more free land. More than half of our people do not live on the farms or on lands and cannot derive a living by cultivating their own property. There is no safety valve in the form of a Western prairie to which those thrown out of work by the Eastern economic machines can go for a new start. . . . Clearly this calls for a re-appraisal of values." And reappraise, Hofstadter did. "In cold terms," he concluded, "American capitalism had come of age, the great era of individualism, expansion, and opportunity was dead."[21]

*　　*　　*

The American Political Tradition sells many thousand copies each year. While scholars have long since revised the book's biographical sketches, its message, that national identity is frequently the offspring of historical mythology, remains compelling. Contemporary readers embraced the book, for their own experiences pointed to a past much more complex and ambiguous than popular historians had previously allowed. And Hofstadter's strength lay precisely in pointing out the counterintuitive. He delighted in challenging his audience with a host of ironic insights that suggested that the old historiographical tradition could no longer be relied on: the Founders resisted democracy, Lincoln was as much opportunist as emancipator, Theodore Roosevelt coddled the trusts. Lauraine Vaughn, then the wife of Alden Vaughn, a young colleague at Columbia, offered the following tribute to Richard Hofstadter's wife shortly after her husband died: "The first time I ever heard of Dick was . . . when I picked up a paperback of his American Political Tradition. . . . I devoured the book, getting angrier by the minute, at this arrogant historian who dared to say *my* Abraham Lincoln was a politician not a saint. Immediately I set out to read more to prove the author was wrong, and in this instance . . . I failed. Yet, I succeeded too; never again was I able to read history with such lofty innocence."[22]

Vaughn identified in Hofstadter's work an original approach to American institutions and ideas that both enlarged and enriched the framework available to scholars and students alike. *The American Political Tradition*'s playfully instructive chapter titles — Jefferson the egalitarian is downgraded to "The Aristocrat as Democrat," Calhoun is transformed into "The Marx of the Master Class," and the progressive Wilson is reinterpreted as "The Conservative as Liberal" — mocked the stately treatment hitherto reserved for these men. The effect, Jack Pole notes, was liberating. "Through Hofstadter's book, students discovered a new freedom to question academic authority, and to reconstruct American history for themselves." At times, however, Hofstadter strained too hard to revise the past and his devotion to irony and paradox became formulaic. One reviewer found the book's lack of gravitas annoying, complaining that "this is neither an intellectual history of basic issues nor a political analysis of pressures and operations. Inevitably, therefore, the book is superficial by serious intellectual standards, and supercilious by realistic political standards."[23]

The nation's most distinguished younger historians, however, were impressed with Hofstadter's book. "Mr. Hofstadter," C. Vann Woodward wrote, "has penetrating things to say in all of his portraits," while Arthur Schlesinger, Jr., described *The American Political Tradition* as "an important and refreshing work. It more than fulfills the high promise of Mr. Hofstadter's earlier work on Social Darwinism and signals the appearance of a new talent of first rate ability in the writing of American history."[24] The nation's leading historian of ideas, Perry Miller, lauded the book as a stimulating contribution to intellectual history — a field, he noted, only beginning to come of age under the hand of junior scholars.

A generation ago historians began to reach into literature and into what they called "intellectual history"; the pioneers of the movement, notably

Beard, assumed that they became historians of the mind by producing catalogues of names, titles, and isms, though they showed little or no aptitude for, or understanding of, the nature of thought itself. A younger group is now working within the structure, above all with the dynamic tendency, of ideas. They write from a depth and with a fluency unknown to Beard and Curti because they understand what ideas mean; they understand because they have taken the life of ideas into their own consciousness.[25]

Miller's warm review in the prestigious *Nation* delighted Hofstadter. He had worked four long years on his book, uncertain of its audience. And now that he caught sight of it he encouraged his publisher to go after it hard. He suggested to Alfred Knopf that the house's sales and publicity staffs renew their efforts to market *The American Political Tradition*. He was gratified by the reviews it had earned in professional journals, but drew Knopf's attention to the book's generous treatment in the nation's newspapers and counseled a fresh round of advertisements listing the names of journalists who had praised the work. Professors Merle Curti, Thomas C. Cochran, and Joseph Dorfman had provided promotional statements for the first printing—and not all were to the author's satisfaction. Curti's letter, though it did yield a blurb, was particularly disappointing to Hofstadter. Curti had never finished the book, and his praise was peppered with qualifications.[26]

Now, in the postpublication stage, Hofstadter advised Knopf that any further advertisements should feature quotes lifted from newspapers and popular periodicals, and he specified which ones: the *New York Times, Newsweek,* the *Nation,* the *Newark News,* the *Washington Star* and the *Toledo Blade.* With an additional boost from his publisher, Hofstadter concluded, *The American Political Tradition* might make its author a profit, perhaps even a future. He was more right than he knew.[27]

The American Political Tradition quickly became *the* history book for a generation. Rather than alienate its readers as Hofstadter imagined it might, the work announced the arrival of a modern pluralistic state that recognized both the promise and limitations of the New Deal. It captured the historical high ground for liberalism and became a symbol of the ideological status quo that distinguished the era. Its popularity, however, should not obscure the fact that the book was conceived and written from the Left. Among students of history in progressive Madison, Wisconsin, it stood as a grand achievement in the literature of radical studies. George Rawick praised it for taking a "Beardian, even Marxist approach," while James O'Brien informed Paul Buhle that "Hofstadter's *American Political Tradition,* which I've read several times, seems to me to combine an economic interpretation with numerous shrewd insights into the way historical forces influenced the people he writes about." A quarter century after the book's publication, it continued to impress and influence talented leftist scholars. *"The American Political Tradition,"* wrote Eric Foner in 1974, "remains as devastating a critique of American politics as anything yet produced by radical historians."[28]

*   *   *

The American Political Tradition has educated several generations of students in American history. Its author's record as a classroom teacher is somewhat more uneven, though it must be understood within the particular context of a large and often impersonal urban academic setting. As a rule, Hofstadter displayed little enthusiasm for classroom instruction and graduate-level advising—twin distractions that had little connection with his *real* vocation. "I'm not a teacher," he once told Foner, "I'm a writer." But this confession addressed only Hofstadter's self-image and level of interest in the lecture hall. He was a marvelous instructor in more intimate settings and, of course, through the power and example of his scholarship. Peter Gay commented that "Hofstadter taught me a lot about writing. I still at times take one of his books from the shelf and refresh myself with a paragraph or two." James Banner, Jr., echoes this sentiment: "Whenever my own writing gets sticky, I'll pick up one of his books and just read a few pages."[29]

At Morningside Heights, a widely acknowledged pecking order existed among the various institutions and schools. Columbia University tended to look down on Columbia College and neither recognized the faculties of Barnard and Teachers College as equals. Status defined this small world and shaped all that it touched. "I remember a friend of mine who taught at Columbia in 1968 speaking of the annual history dinner," James Gilbert notes. "He told me that as usual, he almost sat outside the door, because his [position] was in Teachers College. Hofstadter sat at the head of the table. And he used Hofstadter as an example of the old hierarchical ways of the department. I doubt anyone missed this."[30] The college bore its slights from the graduate programs with dignity; it embraced its mission of offering a first-class education and pointed proudly to a distinguished faculty, including Lionel Trilling in English, Moses Hadas in classics, Jacques Barzun in history, and C. Wright Mills in sociology. Hofstadter's relationship to the Columbia history curriculum was a case of half in and half out. He taught in both the university and the college, avoiding Fayerweather Hall—home of the graduate professors—for the more congenial climate of Hamilton Hall, the academic residence of several Claremont and Morningside friends.

During his years at Columbia, Hofstadter's courses frequently skimmed the cream off whatever book he was currently writing. A colloquium titled "The Problem of American Conservatism" reflected his interest in the radical Right, while a seminar called "The Early Political History of the U.S." emerged in published form as *The Idea of a Party System* (1969). James Shenton was surprised and delighted when Hofstadter offered to teach "The Progressive Historians in the U.S." to a group of undergraduates. His enthusiasm turned to curiosity when students showed up at his office late in the term, puzzled that their instructor had abruptly ended the section. Following a brief investigation, Shenton discovered that Hofstadter had read the galley proofs of his forthcoming book *The Progressive Historians* (1968) to his class each day until he had reached the end of the manuscript.[31]

Hofstadter's efforts as a graduate advisor were frequently no more energetic than his activities in the college. This was, in part, an act of self-preservation. His name and reputation attracted unusually large numbers of students seeking a distinguished sponsor for their work, and he once complained that he and colleague William Leuchtenburg typically advised as many Ph.D. candidates as all the Americanists on the Yale history faculty combined. Without a certain calculated distancing, he would not have survived. This led some students to view him as an aloof figure who worked behind a secretary and a closed door. "Most [graduate students] felt we knew Hofstadter by his published work rather than any kind of oral transmission," Dorothy Ross recalled. John Milton Cooper remembered Hofstadter as a "distant man" who called students by their last names and read his mail while conducting mentoring sessions. "Whenever you hear someone praised for letting students find their own way," Cooper added, "that usually means they just did not give very much supervision. That was Hofstadter. When I was writing my dissertation, I used to refer to him as 'Richard—send me a draft—Hofstadter.'"[32]

Hofstadter's unwillingness to compromise his time, or his selective detachment, surfaced in a personal rule to avoid providing promotional blurbs for books—and this included the books of former students. "Hofstadter liked self-directed souls," Michael Wallace observed, and

believed that the impersonal nature of Columbia encouraged independent scholarship. The neglectful attitude practiced by many Morningside professors "fit very well with the culture of Columbia at the time,"
Ross maintained. "It was a place that had very minimal standards for admission to graduate school and rigorous standards for going on. It took
in a lot of people and a lot of people fell by the wayside. Also, it is obviously a city where the faculty is dispersed and very much living their own
lives."[33]

Ann Lane's experiences at Columbia in the sixties underline the degree of separation that could exist between faculty and students. Working primarily with Brooklyn College historian John Hope Franklin on
a Hofstadter-supported doctoral thesis, she showed up for her 1968
dissertation defense seven months pregnant. "I don't think anyone on
my committee from Columbia had read my work," Lane recalled. "Hofstadter's first comment to me was 'how many weeks did we beat the
baby?' Then we had a pleasant chat and fifteen minutes later it was all
over. Now I have to tell you, I saw that man twice in all the years I
worked on my dissertation and after we finished he put his hand on my
shoulder and, I swear he meant it sincerely, except that I almost laughed,
he said, 'you passed with distinction and these are the moments that
make teaching gratifying.'"[34]

Despite indifferent efforts at formal instruction, Hofstadter exhibited certain valuable interior qualities that endeared him to students.
"He was a genuinely decent man in terms of personal relationships,"
Ross remembers, "and went out of his way to help those who were having troubles with their advisors. At a place like Columbia that was crucial and compensated for his relative disinterest in teaching." In an age
when women were just beginning to make their presence felt in the
academy's elite institutions, Hofstadter advised a number of talented
female scholars — including Ross, Lane, Linda Kerber, Regina Morantz,
and Paula Fass. "He was very fair with his women graduate students,"
Lane recalled, while Ross observed that Hofstadter "took women graduate students as seriously as he did male graduate students and at that
point in time that was by no means universal and there were other members of the department who made it very clear that women were second
class citizens and would always be second class scholars."[35]

More generally, Hofstadter bestowed tremendous occupational fa-
vors on several of his students. He helped Ross land her dissertation at
the University of Chicago Press, introduced Christopher Lasch's work
to Alfred Knopf, and placed Lawrence Levine, Robert Dallek, and

Richard Weiss — "three tall, attractive, smart Jewish intellectuals who were liberal Left but not very far Left and certainly not Right, they were sort of the image he had of himself" — at prestigious West coast universities.[36]

By far, Hofstadter's greatest service to his students was the example he set as an engaged thinker. James Shenton remembered that when he arrived at Columbia in the 1940s, men like Carlton J. H. Hayes and Allan Nevins, productive scholars but very much bound to orthodox methods and traditional insights, dominated the history department. Nevins's love for "the romantic literature of the Victorian era," his biographer wrote, made him "in many ways . . . a nineteenth-century man living out his life in the twentieth-century." Appointed to the department in 1946, Hofstadter immediately projected a fresh intellectual quality, more receptive than his colleagues to experimenting with the social sciences and completely comfortable with the playful and paradoxical sides of historical interpretation. "There was still among many historians at that point and time very much the ideal of the historian as someone who worked exclusively from primary sources," Ross observed. "The research and getting the facts was the important thing. What Hofstadter made clear to his students is how important the interpretation and the language and the presentation are and I think many of us felt this was something we might aspire to." James Banner, Jr., goes so far as to describe Hofstadter as a kind of archetype. "I think of him in the abstract, as the kind of person that all historians should strive to be. An engaged intellectual, reflecting on his society, trying by the force of ideas and their expression to change it for the better. Even without having a forceful personality, even being uninterested in teaching, Hofstadter's ideas came through in his writing and they came through in the way he carried himself."[37]

Hofstadter rarely entered the archives but directed his students to do so, for he understood that the profession expected newly minted Ph.D.'s to work primarily from original sources. In a 1960 letter to Eric McKitrick, he explained his approach to directing doctoral seminars as heretical in comparison to the rest of the department. The conventional wisdom at Columbia called for professors to train students in research methodology and then quickly launch them on to dissertations. Hofstadter preferred to have his seminars read deeply in American historical literature in preparation for their doctoral examinations. Only after passing this hurdle did he believe students were justified in moving on to dissertation work. This historiographical approach to research conformed to Hofstadter's unique way of understanding the past—reacting to historians rather than history—and allowed him to assume that formal instruction could be conveniently left to a well-conceived reading list.[38]

Hofstadter's casual pedagogical practices irritated some students, but others found his manner liberating. After earning a B.A. at Harvard, Stanley Elkins arrived at Morningside Heights determined to study both history and sociology. He appealed to Hofstadter, then in the midst of his own yielding to interdisciplinary studies, to make sociology a secondary field. This unusual entreaty (most Americanists at Columbia took complementary areas in European history) was not ignored. For his dissertation, Elkins proposed a cross-disciplinary study of slavery emphasizing the psychological impact of the peculiar institution on the African American mind. The project's reliance on intellectual and sociological insights rather than archival documentation greatly interested Hofstadter. Unfortunately, the topic's exotic interpretive angle aroused the ire of more methodologically conservative historians, and Elkins's early struggles in the profession reveal why few scholars were encouraged to imitate Hofstadter. After leaving Columbia, Elkins accepted a position at the University of Chicago, where his new colleagues were critical of the impressionistic and lightly researched quality of his work. David Herbert Donald's unsympathetic review of Elkins's published dissertation, *Slavery: A Problem in American Institutional and Intellectual Life,* included the following charge: "The reading of secondary materials, a broad-ranging interest in other disciplines, and an extended use of comparisons and analogies do not compensate for the want of basic research." Donald's statement repeated criticism endured by Hofstadter throughout his career.[39]

The 1957 dismissal of Elkins and Eric McKitrick by the University of Chicago drew attention to the fact that no single consensus had emerged in regard to how the social sciences were to be used by historians. Hofstadter's formidable reputation protected him from such head-on attacks (although the Harvard historians thought long and hard before tendering a 1958 offer that he refused), but protégés who identified too closely with his fondness for insight over research were vulnerable. McKitrick offered this wry assessment of the fate of two Columbia-trained social scientists in the Midwest:

> The grounds for the auto-da-fe were, that the type of work we did was unhistorical & the Dept. could not approve of it. The acting chairman,

in telling us these things today, was quite befuddled & I must say I felt a little sorry for him while we climbed his frame. When we pressed him, the most specific criticism that he could report on our writing was: a) that the reasoning was "a prioristic" (he wasn't entirely sure what that was but I gather they meant our formulating hypothesis & testing them, as we learned to do you know where, but which isn't kosher here); b) that we did not use "original sources.". . . It appears that there was also some mumbling about "social science" but never quite to the point (you know, like "we concede in principle the right of collective bargaining, but — "). Well, what it comes to is that a very serious judgement on our stuff has been made, by people none of whom understand it, none of whom was competent to judge it (or willing to consult anyone who was), and certain key ones of whom were simply maddened by it.[40]

Most of Hofstadter's students pursued research agendas that followed more traditional paths and, to their mentor's credit, they felt at liberty to challenge his published claims in their own work. Levine's dissertation on the late career of William Jennings Bryan is a sympathetic portrait that argued against Hofstadter's unflattering appraisal of the Commoner in *The American Political Tradition*. "I felt myself enormously free, I never worried about contradicting him," Levine recalls.[41] The story of Daniel Singal's efforts to define himself as an independent scholar working under Hofstadter's direction is worth quoting at length. He refers to his dissertation, published in 1982 as *The War Within: From Victorian to Modernist Thought in the South, 1919–1945*.

Hofstadter was generous, but also forthright and candid. When I sent him my formal prospectus for my dissertation topic, prior to submitting it to the department as a whole, he shot back a two-page, single-spaced letter telling me in no uncertain terms that I should find another topic. He said that he was always "suspicious" of topics in literary-intellectual history, and pointed out that I had not put forward an actual thesis, but rather had posed a series of questions about southern writers between the two world wars that I somehow hoped to answer. I will never forget his closing line: "My blunt but sensitive nose picks up the first faint whiff of disaster." As it happened, I felt pretty sure about my topic. Yes, I had no actual thesis yet, but I planned to fashion one as I went through the archival evidence and discovered what was lurking in it. There are plenty of prima donnas in our profession who would have been outraged by a graduate student who refused to take their unambiguous advice, but not Hofstadter. He said that if I wanted to go to the department with the prospectus he would back me. And he did. One of my great regrets is that he did not live to see the project completed. It would have vindicated his willingness to give me the leeway to write the kind of history I wanted to write. What a rare thing, I would say, for a teacher to have such confidence in a student despite his own considerable misgivings. And beyond that, what remarkable proof of Hofstadter's abiding commitment to academic freedom in the truest sense of the word.[42]

As Singal noted, Hofstadter's intellectual openness ensured that his students developed into independent scholars rather than disciples. Following his death, several of them put together a Festschrift in his honor. The unusual title — *The Hofstadter Aegis* — caused some at Knopf to pause. "Aegis," Eric McKitrick assured the house, "exactly conveys — complete with a note of intended ambiguity — the meaning we had in mind for the enterprise. He served us all as a sanction and protector for what we all did: go our separate ways."[43]

* 4 *

The Historian as
Social Scientist

Despite what is surely no more than a fragmentary and random acquaintance with the literature of the social sciences,
I have found that my interest and gratification in my own
discipline have been enormously intensified by what I have
been able to take for it from other disciplines.

RICHARD HOFSTADTER, 1960

As the Progressive influence waned, historians were intellectually free
to pursue new approaches to writing American history. The Depression
thirties pointed to a perpetual cycle of clashes between capital and
labor, but the unexpected economic boom that followed the Second
World War quickly drained interest in the class struggles that engaged
the previous generation. Postwar scholars were drawn, instead, to
a more contemporary and troubling problem: why had nineteenth-
century liberalism proven so receptive to the siren songs of twentieth-
century tyrants? The influence of dictatorships on the mass mind cried
out for investigation. And, in an age of Nazism, Stalinism, and (some on
the left insisted) McCarthyism, historians were eager to analyze the particular social conditions that gave rise to authoritarian personalities.
Richard Hofstadter's first two books, *Social Darwinism* and *The American Political Tradition,* had repeated rather than revised the main currents
of Progressive thought. At the century's midpoint, however, he discovered in the fields of sociology and psychology disciplines that encouraged a more complete recovery of the hopes, dreams, resentments, and
emotional motives of historical actors.

The Progressive historians had once led the charge to bring the social
sciences into the academy. Beard's handling of economic history and
Turner's studies on political geography are notable examples of their
generation's efforts to create a more comprehensive account of human
activity. The works of Freud, Max Weber, and Karl Mannheim, however,
were either unavailable or too novel to be adopted by Progressive minds.

Hofstadter himself avoided the techniques used in social scientific research. He remained committed to history as a literary art, and the apparatus of statistical sampling and computer-generated data never found its way into his books. Rather, in broadening the variables customarily measured by historians to include the impact of status, mobility, and occupational satisfaction, he assimilated the analytic vocabulary and interpretive structure of social theory into his scholarship. He prized their fresh focus but also recognized their limitations. The historian, Hofstadter wrote, "is engulfed in a complex web of relationships which he can hope to understand only in a limited and partial way." Even, or perhaps especially, with the aid of the social sciences, "his task has not been amplified; it has been enlarged. His work has not greater certainty, but greater range and depth."[1]

Hofstadter's development as a professional historian owed a terrific debt to Morningside Heights. This was, in every respect, a community of passionate idea men connected, Daniel Bell recalls, by "Hamilton Hall, Claremont Avenue, and Riverside Drive, what we used to call the Upper West Side Kibbutz." Bell and colleague Seymour Martin Lipset recognized in Hofstadter a kindred spirit, sympathetic to the impressive outpouring of critical studies then redefining the social sciences. All agreed that Marxism was no longer relevant to postwar thinkers. Recent assaults on rationality — there seemed no satisfying economic explanation for the Moscow trials, the Holocaust, or McCarthyism — made a powerful impact on the men in Hofstadter's circle. "We knew about the concentration camps," Bell remembers; "it was a fear of mass action, a fear of too much activism to the extent there was a political set of attitudes which shaped the way we looked at the world. It was simply a wariness of mass movements and I think this was very important to Dick."[2]

The new methodology reflected further the increasing influence of Jewish scholars in the academy. David Hollinger reminds us that prior to the Second World War "Jews were suspect in academia partly because many Anglo-Protestants thought them socially crude and aggressive, and politically radical." Jewish professors were customarily ghettoized in the social sciences and barred from the culture-transforming disciplines in the humanities. *The American Political Tradition* joined Alfred Kazin's *On Native Grounds* (1942) and Trilling's *The Liberal Imagination* (1950) as seminal works on American history, literature, and aesthetics written by Jews or half-Jews. At Columbia — where Hofstadter and Trilling taught — the sociology department included prominent Jewish scholars Bell, Lipset, Robert K. Merton (né Meyer Schkolnick), and

Paul Lazarsfeld, and quickly established itself as the American avant-garde for social scientific thought. Its search for the authoritarian roots of Wasp behavior influenced Hofstadter and encouraged his own use of the social sciences. In this case, physical environment proved critical. It is difficult to imagine the intellectual community in a Progressive bastion such as Madison, Wisconsin, providing warm support for *The Age of Reform* or *Anti-Intellectualism in American Life.* "Columbia, so long resistant to the Jewish population in the city," Hollinger writes, became in the forties and fifties "suddenly so responsive to many of the nation's most prominent Jewish scholars."[3]

The new history pioneered by Hofstadter revolutionized the academy, but it was not the first time Columbia professors had redefined the historiographical landscape. Years earlier, Morningside scholars James Harvey Robinson, Charles Beard, James T. Shotwell, and Lynn Thorndike stressed the importance of social, ideological, and economic forces over the arid political and constitutional studies of their predecessors. Their devotion to the social sciences, Dorothy Ross notes, "grew out of the Enlightenment effort to understand modernity. In their belief that the West had embarked on a novel course of historical development that was still unfolding, early social scientists shared the historicism of the eighteenth century. But unlike the historians, their focus was on the social and economic dimensions of civil society that modernity disclosed. Using analogues of scientific method, they produced social theories rather than political narratives." The new history encouraged scholars to move beyond legal documents and pursue novel strategies that placed a premium on the creative skills of the historian. Frederick Jackson Turner supported the topical recasting of his profession, advising J. Franklin Jameson that "in order to bring our work into more vital touch with current interests and needs . . . we should enter the overlapping fields more — the borderland between history in its older conception, and economics, politics, sociology, psychology, geography, etc."[4] While Hofstadter and several Columbia scholars responded favorably to Turner's example, they steered sharply from the kinds of studies anticipated by his generation. Contrasts in ethnicity (Progressive historiography was largely written by Gentiles) and perspective (Turner's peers accepted the primacy of economic issues over the nuances of psychological motives) ensured that the new history, as conceptualized in 1900, bore little resemblance to that written fifty years later.

*　　*　　*

In light of the methodological upheaval in the historical profession, Hofstadter renewed his critical dialogue with the Progressive scholars. It was a risky venture. In two separate essays on Turner and Beard, he took on the two greatest icons in the American historical profession.[5] Hofstadter recognized the genius in Beard's pathbreaking work on the economic origins of the American constitution, but his essay, "Beard and the Constitution: The History of an Idea" (1950), more heavily criticized Beard's use of the new history as a tool to push the Progressive agenda. Turner was dealt with even more sharply. The frontier idea, Hofstadter argued in "Turner and the Frontier Myth" (1949), was a major step back for scholarship in the United States. It coaxed the academy into celebrating the agrarian values that energized the Bryan campaigns and posited a national self-image of rural life that contradicted the twentieth-century reality of America as an urban nation.

In regard to both historians, however, Hofstadter's criticisms seem off the mark. Yes, Beard's scholarship supported Progressive causes, and yes, Turner's essays could be read as anti–East Coast manifestos. The real question posed by Hofstadter, however, was not whether these men produced scholarship that reflected the regional and social biases of their times (they did, of course), but rather, did they advance historical understanding through new approaches and fresh strategies — as Hofstadter himself now hoped to do. The answer to this question must be yes. Beard stressed the economic interests of historical actors with more sophistication than any previous American historian, while Turner's writing popularized the impact of environment on character and served as a powerful challenge to the views of his graduate school mentor, the venerable Johns Hopkins historian Herbert Baxter Adams.

America's uniquely free political institutions, Adams had argued, were products of a superior Anglo-Saxon civilization that genetically passed democratic instincts along the Northern European/North American lines of colonization. Adams's "*germ* theory" employed language consistent with his generation's post-Darwinian efforts to identify with contemporary trends in the hard sciences — not unlike Hofstadter's own post-Freudian turn toward the social sciences. Adams's dominance in the field soon gave way as midwestern scholars expressed interest in regional rather than racial interpretations of American identity. The residue of pioneer-like conditions — presumed to encourage democratic institutions — in Turner's Wisconsin combined with the rise of the great eastern monopolies to convince Ohio Valley historians that popular rule owed more to geography than genes. But in repealing

Adams's explicitly racial theory, Turner and his disciples replaced it with one implicitly so. The frontier thesis, by definition, authenticated the democratic credentials of the Anglo, German, and Scandinavian Americans who pushed into the nation's interior. Concurrently, it implied that immigrants settling in the East — including Slavic peoples, Italians, and Jews — were less American than those residing on the "frontier."[6]

In some quarters of the profession, Hofstadter's criticism of midwestern historiography signaled a retreat from the radical promise of his first two books. Merle Curti, the Frederick Jackson Turner Professor of American History at Wisconsin and a friend of Charles Beard, deeply regretted his former student's attack on the Progressive heritage. Hofstadter assured Curti in correspondence that whatever differences he had with his historical fathers, he respected Beard's intellectual contributions — but not Turner's. While the economic interpretation had been overemphasized, he wrote, it nevertheless represented in his opinion the most original contribution to American historical writing ever made. Its influence, he continued, was far better than that of Turner, who had simply read his personal obsession with the frontier into the nation's past. While Beard's ideas had been helpful, Turner's were retrogressive and led scholars down blind paths. Hofstadter concluded by confessing his regret that what he had published on Beard to this point in his career — an article and two reviews — did not reflect his admiration for Beard's talents.[7]

The letter did little to lighten Curti's concern that Hofstadter had abandoned the Left. Wisconsin doctoral candidate Richard Kirkendall seconded Curti's displeasure with the retreat of reform-minded historians: "Your observation about Hofstadter's relationship to neoconservatism is certainly true . . . among the younger generation liberalism is all but dead. These people share many liberal values, but liberalism to them connotes first of all naiveté — tender mindedness — a failure to recognize the 'sinfulness of men.'" These charges, Peter Gay noted, "puzzled and irritated Hofstadter," who defined himself as a liberal critical of, yet not hostile to, the Progressive achievement. The men most invested in the democratic *spirit* of Beard's and Turner's scholarship, however, saw matters much differently. They labeled Hofstadter a metropolitan outsider, unfamiliar with the Midwest and thus wary of the popular politics that energized the reform era.[8]

That is a fair assessment. Hofstadter did detect in the red-baiting fifties a tremor of the recent authoritarianism that rocked Europe, and he did turn his attention during this decade to the problematic history of popular power in America. It was not the first time he was forced to face down a political demon. In the thirties, he had written several letters to Harvey Swados declaring his contempt for both capitalism and the Communist Party. These were, however, both monolithic institutions, and in some sense abstractions to a young graduate student taking courses, preparing for exams, and settling into marriage. Now the demon was closer—and it seemed more real than abstract. "McCarthyism led Dick to distrust the mass mind," William Leuchtenburg remembered, and Frank Freidel recalled that the 1950s were "traumatic [for] Hofstadter.... All the values, everything [he had] stood for; all the groups that [he had] been involved in in the 1930s were now being attacked."[9]

Responses to the New Right varied from scholar to scholar and from institution to institution. While Columbia escaped relatively unscathed, the University of California imposed a loyalty oath during the 1949–50 academic year upon UC employees. The oath seemed to single out professors—war veterans, some of them—as particular threats to the nation's security. Several talented scholars, including refugees from Nazi Germany who felt they knew something about the grim repercussions of state power on the academy, resigned from the Berkeley and Los Angeles campuses rather than submit to a political litmus test as a condition of their employment. Like many scholars, Hofstadter opposed loyalty oaths as detrimental to the critical attitude necessary for authentic intellectual dialogue. In a 1960 letter to a Columbia student, he provided a list of objections to allegiance tests in universities: they neither proved nor inspired loyalty; they divided colleagues and students; they suggested that universities are in some sense particularly prone to subversive activities; and they encouraged anti-intellectualism by implying that those who study are uniquely susceptible to seditious behavior.[10]

The crisis in California aroused Hofstadter's indignation and in a letter to a Berkeley colleague he discussed the need for professors to organize in order to defend their rights against a creeping anti-intellectualism disguised as national security needs. Given the opportunity to act on his own—a 1950 invitation to teach at Berkeley—Hofstadter explained to its history chairman Carl Bridenbaugh that he could not consider any offer from a California system school until the state had resolved its oath problems.[11]

On the question of firing Communist professors, however, Hofstadter took a more hard-line approach. His first full-time teaching position came as a replacement for a City College historian removed for allegedly belonging to the CP, and he refused in 1949 to criticize the University of Washington for dismissing Communist instructors. All fair-minded faculty and administrators must in principal support academic freedom, he stated at the time. But he acknowledged his personal dislike for the fired Washington teachers — "Stalinists" he called them — arguing that if their kind controlled the academy, liberals themselves would be purged.[12] Clearly Hofstadter drew little distinction between the Left and the Right on the issue of academic freedom. He believed that both represented serious threats to intellectual life, equally willing to sacrifice the critical climate that sustained independent thought.

It is more difficult to assess the impact of Hofstadter's brief (and secretive) stint in the Communist Party on his thinking. James Shenton commented that "Dick was afraid at that time, McCarthyism really unsettled him. What would happen if suddenly the record of his own past were exposed? He thought of himself as an intellectual, but in a certain sense an intellectual who was not part of a certain movement. He was part of the Left defrocking itself."[13]

The style of this political "defrocking" varied greatly among former radicals. While some intellectuals, including Hofstadter, responded in very searching and private struggles to redefine their political commitments, others preferred a more visible mea culpa. Daniel J. Boorstin, for example, cooperated fully with the House Un-American Activities Committee. A CPer at Harvard in the thirties, Boorstin provided the names of three Cambridge associates while emphasizing how his scholarship — "an attempt to discover and explain to students in my teaching and in my writing, the unique virtues of American democracy" — corroborated his loyalty.[14]

*   *   *

The rise of the national security state put unique pressures on American professors — with and without radical pasts. The academy's quest for intellectual freedom contradicted the great national consensus and forced American educators to occupy the borderland between conformity and critical thought. This tension intrigued Hofstadter, for he recognized that in a democracy the fate of the university was ultimately tied to the public's opinion of its work.

A founding member of the National Academy of Education, Hofstadter produced in little more than a decade several important books on instruction. These include *The Development and Scope of Higher Education in the United States* (1952, with C. DeWitt Hardy), *The Development of Academic Freedom in the United States* (1955, with Walter Metzger), *Higher Education: A Documentary History* (1961, with Wilson Smith), and *Anti-Intellectualism in American Life* (1963). Combined, these studies praised the particular virtues of liberal education while — in Hofstadter's contributions — drawing attention to popular power's habitual suspicion of gifted minds. More than any of his coauthors, he resisted the majority's desire to dictate educational and cultural terms to a highbrow minority, and he placed McCarthyism in a long line of native movements hostile to intellect. Hofstadter was not a historian of education, but matters of curriculum reform or the evolution of pedagogical practices were not really his concerns. Rather, he wrote in defense of a separate sphere for the mind, one extending beyond the reach of government, politics, religion, economy, or even the bureaucratic structure of the university itself. He hoped to establish a new historiography, to present the educational past as indispensable to the progress of American freedoms. Wars, revolutions, puritans, and planters held the historical high ground, but some of the greatest struggles for liberty were carried off in the relative obscurity of quiet New England colleges or among the nation's major universities. Nor was this ancient history. Now that modernity had aroused the enemies of intellect, the battle was rejoined.

The Development and Scope of Higher Education is perhaps Hofstadter's least appreciated work. Sponsored by the Commission on Financing Higher Education and financially supported by the Rockefeller Foundation and the Carnegie Corporation, it responded to two critical issues then facing the universities: declining public support for professorial autonomy, and the rapid democratization of academe initiated by the GI Bill. Hofstadter's contribution — essays on the pre–Civil War college, graduate and professional training, and the weaknesses of higher learning in America — appears to break fresh ground for a scholar preeminently interested in the history of ideas. But Hofstadter saw in the broader outlines of the project the opportunity to draw distinctions between the mind and the masses. Having read little in the literature of education before working on his current book, Hofstadter wrote Merle Curti that he was struck by how much there was to be learned about intellectual life in America by studying its schools.[15] In this important respect, the work constituted its author's initial immersion into the corpus of ideas that led directly to *The Age of Reform* and its more ambitious offspring *Anti-Intellectualism in American Life.*

Americans, Hofstadter wrote in *Development and Scope,* liked to celebrate the pragmatic rather than the theoretical. The deeply imbedded egalitarian roots of the republic resented expertise, undermined serious learning, and offered few rewards for intellect. "It is fairly safe to say," he observed of the contemporary undergraduate scene, "that as the mass of students has grown larger, the proportion who come to college with genuine intellectual and cultural goals has grown smaller." Standards suffered, he continued, as publicly funded universities "admit all graduates of state high schools who have academic records that can be examined without shuddering, with the consequence that an unholy proportion of the freshman classes in these institutions consists of sheer excess baggage. This is 'democracy' with a vengeance." American students were not unusually hostile to ideas, Hofstadter added, but he felt that among his countrymen — unlike their European cousins — suspicion and contempt for intellect meshed seamlessly with the nation's egalitarian principles. "The difference between the anti-intellectualism so common among American undergraduates and the casual pose that is popular even among gifted students at Oxford and Cambridge," he wrote, "is that the English student values and shows pride in his own intellectual gifts and accomplishments but likes to imply that they have cost no great effort on his part, whereas the American philistine has a profound and entirely heartfelt suspicion of ideas."[16]

One might fairly question whether Hofstadter projected his own sense of occupational decline in *Development and Scope.* In reference to the vulnerable station of the college instructor, he wrote that "something in the cultural milieu has steadily deprived him of status gratifications." The American professor could never expect to reach the elevated rank of the mandarin, the Talmudic scholar, or the Oxford don. "All these men of knowledge," he wrote, "have been shown great deference, equal or superior to that given the richest businessmen, high political officials, and high-ranking military officers. In the United States a severely attenuated form of this respect is perhaps granted to a few eminent professors at a few great centers of learning; but even among them it is a dilute affair, and the status gratifications of the stereotyped assistant professor of English at Podunk College are negligible." Critical of the academy's egalitarian underpinnings, *Development and Scope* refused to bow to the leveling wind. If the Commission on Financing Higher Education anticipated a study promoting good will between the pedagogues and the public — essential if universities were to fend off red-baiting and defend their appeals for state funding — Hofstadter's pessimistic survey undermined that mission. "One emerges from reading this book," *New Republic* reviewer Stringfellow Barr wrote, "wondering just how the teaching profession, so weakly organized as a profession, can hope to protect itself and the American people from the know-nothing anti-intellectualism that parades for the moment as anti-Communism."[17]

Hofstadter's views on American education received their fullest airing in *The Development of Academic Freedom,* a Columbia University Press book financed by Louis Rabinowitz, a Russian emigrant made wealthy in the city's garment trade. Rabinowitz valued the free exchange of ideas and may have sensed in McCarthyism the kind of political censorship he had experienced in the land of his birth. The manuscript comprised two separate sections, "The Age of the College," written by Hofstadter, and "The Age of the University," by Walter Metzger. While the authors noted in the book's preface that "except for the fact that it contains no collaborative prose, this has been in every sense a collaborative enterprise," the tone of Metzger's contribution is decidedly more optimistic than his coauthor's.[18]

"The Age of the College" reads like a passion play between the forces of pedagogical good and evil. Hofstadter wrote with great respect for the secular curriculum, the scientific mentality, support for educational excellence among colonial elite, and a host of progressive intellectual attitudes tied closely to the Enlightenment. He revered, in other words, the legacy of the European academy. On the American side, Hofstadter found little to praise in what he described as "the great regression" of denominational colleges, nonacademic boards of regents, utilitarian curriculums, and the democratic obsession with egalitarianism. While the colonies had tried with some success to create colleges receptive to the needs of accomplished students, the emergence of a mass American democracy in the early nineteenth century, he wrote, undermined the goal of educational excellence. "To found a great many small rather than to build up a modest number of larger ones meant to fill the country with precarious little institutions, denomination ridden, poverty stricken, keeping dubious educational standards, and offering little to teachers in freedom or financial awards." It was an era of "backsliding" in the collegiate system, one regrettably distinguished by a "decline of freedom" in the troubled halls of academe.[19]

Hofstadter would have been remiss not to draw the reader's attention to the deficiencies of the antebellum curriculum. But he went too far. "The colleges were genuinely popular institutions in their localities,"

Roger Geiger reminds us. "They served as multipurpose, multilevel institutions that substantially enhanced educational opportunities. . . . The education they offered, above all, provided mobility for rural sons to pursue urban or professional careers."[20] Many of America's early colleges were creatures of a folkish, democratic, frontier culture that prized the pragmatic and utilitarian ends of intellect. They deserved to be judged on their own standards of success rather than those imposed by a twentieth-century cosmopolitan who had no real contact with or sympathy for their local missions. There is little doubt Hofstadter believed that intellect was a fragile commodity, constantly bullied in a democratic, market-driven society. And in his eagerness to protect the academy from its enemies, he went on a career-long crusade against them. Thus, his attacks on the denominational colleges in *The Development of Academic Freedom* prefaced his rejection of John Dewey in *Anti-Intellectualism in American Life* and criticism of student activism in his 1968 Columbia University commencement address. It is sobering to think that among intellect's adversaries Hofstadter included colleges, progressive educators, and students. Was this not the heart of the academy?

Hofstadter's studies on higher education were influenced by his work for the American Committee for Cultural Freedom (ACCF), a society of liberal cold warriors opposed to international communism. The committee's parental affiliate, the Congress for Cultural Freedom, enjoyed lavish funding from the CIA as part of a broadly structured effort to emphasize the West's commitment to literary, scientific, and artistic integrity. As one commentator put it, the congress hoped to "nudge the intelligentsia of Western Europe away from its lingering fascination with Marxism and Communism towards a view more accommodating of 'the American way.'"[21] It is unclear whether the CIA funded the committee, but at least two periodicals that published Hofstadter's work in the early sixties (*Daedalus* and *Encounter*) benefited from CIA largesse. Hofstadter was probably unaware of their covert affiliation—the *New York Times* broke the story in 1967—though his wry sense of humor would no doubt have appreciated the strange irony of a massive propaganda campaign to promote American intellectual freedom carried out by the nation's chief intelligence organization.

As part of the committee's efforts to defend the mind against the masses, Hofstadter and Nathan Glazer agreed in 1953 to coedit a study on intellectualism in the United States. Although the manuscript never materialized, its proposed themes—"a chapter might be done on the [anti-intellectualism] of the left and the right, or possibly a special chapter for the A-I of the 'liberals.' There might be a chapter on anti-intellectualism in business and labor. There might be a chapter on the nineteenth-century roots of anti-intellectualism. This chapter might go back to the frontier (wanted: practical men, not intellectuals). This chapter might also touch on the significance of anti-intellectuals in a popular democracy"—were developed by Hofstadter in subsequent years. ACCF members interested in the project—Hofstadter, Glazer, Bell, Sol Stein, Irwin Ross, and Melvin Arnold—considered status anxiety a critical variable in the McCarthy era's hostility to ideas. No historian had looked at it quite this way before. While scholars like Boorstin praised the pragmatic and intellectually simple roots of the republic, Hofstadter and his Cultural Freedom colleagues interpreted the American suspicion of the thinking class as a sign of psychological discomfort, "an aspect," they agreed, "of anti-Europeanism because of our inferiority complex."[22]

The social sciences enlarged the scope of historical analysis in the postwar academy, but it was really the conservative course of the country's political life in the 1950s that empowered the methodological revolution. Eisenhower's rise to the presidency, Hofstadter observed in *Anti-Intellectualism in American Life*, reflected the public's repudiation of the liberal politics favored by intellect. And nowhere was this repudiation felt more painfully than at Morningside Heights. During his tenure as president of Columbia University (May 1948–January 1953), Eisenhower cultivated a strong network of influential connections sympathetic to his political future. Following a suspension of his presidential activities to serve in Europe as NATO commander, the general retired from active duty in June 1952 and returned to the president's home at 60 Morningside. There he met with Republican leaders, including isolationists William Jenner and Robert Taft, to discuss strategy for the fall election. The use of the president's residence to conduct campaign business provoked sharp criticism in some corners of the small campus and made what had promised to be an ardent but civil contest at Columbia into one of unusual intensity and acrimony.

Nearly a quarter of a century had passed since the nation had last elected a Republican president and, as the party in power, liberals were loath to turn over the executive office to a man it believed opposed the social reforms initiated by the New Deal. The frustration of Columbia professors increased when the *New York Times*—owned and published by Columbia alumnus and trustee Arthur Hays Sulzberger—endorsed Eisenhower. Hoping to stem Republican momentum at Morningside,

Allan Nevins formed a faculty council in support of Stevenson that counted Hofstadter among its executive committee. The "Columbia Faculty Volunteers for Stevenson" went into action preparing a full-page advertisement in the *Times* designed to both support the governor and protest the paper's official endorsement. Peter Gay was in charge of soliciting funds and Hofstadter helped draft the document.[23]

As the election drew near, professors at some of the nation's best universities grew increasingly sensitive to signals that an Eisenhower victory encouraged the forces of anti-intellectualism. Columbia historian John Allen Krout remembered that "Eisenhower's failure to take a firm stand" against McCarthyism "was disquieting to a great many at Morningside." Thirty-one signatures, including those of Hofstadter, Nevins, Henry Steele Commager, and Reinhold Niebuhr adorned a letter to the *Times* admonishing the paper's endorsement of the general. At Harvard, several faculty mobilized to raise funds to defeat Jenner, while a cadre of Ivy League professors "exchanged ideas and information about McCarthy's reelection campaign" in Wisconsin. The anti-Eisenhower movement at Columbia culminated in the 16 October *Times* advertisement "We are for Stevenson because . . . ," inciting a stiff reply from acting Columbia president Grayson Kirk, who rued the aggressive partisanship of his professors and the campaigns divisive influence on his campus. "From my point of view," he complained to Nevins, "this is an ill-advised project which will be a source of difficulty and embarrassment to the University."[24]

A week later, "Columbia University faculties and staffs for Eisenhower" produced their own *Times* endorsement with 714 signatures, over twice as many as on the Stevenson ad (324). While the faculty clearly preferred Stevenson (a Columbia *Spectator* survey found that 414 of 603 professors polled supported the Illinois governor), the university's staff resented the implication of the *Times* advertisement that Columbia uniformly backed the Democratic candidate. On the morning that the Eisenhower endorsement appeared, Gay arrived at Hofstadter's apartment with a copy of the newspaper to scrutinize signatures and the two quickly realized that they were familiar with only a couple of dozen names — those serving on the faculty. Consulting the Columbia University directory, they discovered that the advertisement touting "faculty and staff" included "dieticians, building superintendents, stenographers and students, including nonmatriculating students at the School of General Studies." In reaction, they drew a distinction between the famous signatures on their petition — Daniel Bell, Robert

Merton, C. Wright Mills, Lionel Trilling—and the unrecognizable names of hundreds of students, secretaries, and support staff who opposed their political preferences. "When we said that people in the Ike ad did not count," William Leuchtenburg later recalled, "we met the rejoinder that that was curiously elitist doctrine from those who claimed to be advocates of the common man."[25]

Also curious was Hofstadter's willingness to use Columbia, or at least its name and reputation, to further the cause of a political candidate. This is precisely the kind of nonacademic activity that he felt undermined the mission of the university, and in his published work on higher education, he offered numerous examples of political pressures that compromised intellectual work. But, in this case, Hofstadter fell into the very trap that he warned against. And there was a public admonishment. In a preelection letter to the *New York Times,* Columbia professor of East Asian religions W. T. De Bary protested the use of the university's name and campus for political purposes.

> When a group of faculty members wishes to state its views . . . they have every right to do so as individuals and should not be disqualified from it by their affiliation with the university. But when any group of alumni, faculty or students, instead of working through one or another of the existing channels of political activity, chooses to make use of the Columbia campus or the name of Columbia to advance its own cause it can only be to exploit the prestige of an educational institution dedicated to an impartial search for truth. These persons are carrying the name of the university into the field of high-powered political propaganda, where no one can control the consequences of their action and political wolves will tear Columbia's reputation to pieces in order to discredit their opponents.[26]

In his 1968 address before the Columbia graduates, Hofstadter echoed De Bary's remarks. Circumstances had, of course, changed dramatically. During the Stevenson campaign the liberals were in charge at Morningside, and saw nothing wrong with using their institution to advance their ideological preferences. But the student rebellion of 1968 clearly put the professors on the defensive and they saw Columbia no longer as a dynamic force for social progress so much as a precious repository of inherited traditions.

Hofstadter's sensitivity to the fate of intellect merged with his political choices in the early fifties to redefine his scholarship. While his work for both Stevenson and the American Committee for Cultural Freedom bore little fruit, he discovered in the anti-intellectual theme a fresh strategy to comment on the egalitarian impulse that tormented talented minds. His paper "Democracy and Anti-Intellectualism in America" (*Michigan Alumnus Quarterly Review*, 1953) defined suspicion of higher learning as a political rather than pedagogical problem. In recent times, he wrote, the intellectual unfairly shouldered the blame for "creeping socialism," the "betrayal" at Yalta, and the "loss" of China. For Americans disenchanted with the New Deal, Soviet expansion, or the military stalemate in Korea, the "egg-head" served as a convenient scapegoat for what ailed the nation. The status of the thinking class had slipped to an all-time low. And Hofstadter wrote to Kenneth Stampp that the intention of the essay was as much therapeutic as explanatory—he hoped to boost the morale of American intellectuals.[27]

In the *Quarterly Review* essay Hofstadter blamed "populistic democracy" for the devaluation of higher learning and dismissed egalitarianism as "government by or through the mass man, disguised behind the mask of an easy sentimentalization of the folk. It is the idea that anything done in the name of the people is *ipso facto* legitimate." Rather than furthering the interests of the mind, democracy, Hofstadter argued, often ignored expertise in the name of suppressing privilege and preserving equality. In this way, society stacked the deck against intellect. Militant democrats—or McCarthyite demagogues—demanded "that a university ought to cater to the needs of anybody who comes out of or pretends to represent the folk, whether or not he has any real need for or interest in the use of ideas."[28]

Pushing his pointer further (and no doubt taking pleasure in the irony of the observation), Hofstadter maintained that public education historically enjoyed its most consistent support under undemocratic regimes. "Two of the greatest periods in university history," he wrote, "that of the thirteenth and fourteenth centuries and that of the German universities in the nineteenth century, occurred in societies that were not notably democratic." The foundation for the modern American university, laid from 1870 to 1910, "was for the most part an age of political and economic oligarchy" dominated by titan philanthropists who established several distinguished institutions, including the University of Chicago and Johns Hopkins, Duke, and Stanford Universities. Conversely, popular democratic figures, including Jackson, Bryan, and McCarthy, were openly hostile to intellect. Hofstadter concluded that despite several favorable trends in recent times—massive federal subsidies for higher education, a burgeoning academic job market, and increased rewards for faculty at elite institutions—the situation was bleak. "I am not optimistic enough to believe that in any calculable future the rest of society can be brought to recognize that intellectuals have their own rights and interests."[29] While postwar America elevated egalitarianism to orthodoxy, Hofstadter remained aloof and pronounced a pox on the democracy boosters.

As liberals applauded Hofstadter's labors on behalf of the intellectuals, scholars on the left read into his work a swipe at democracy and egalitarian education. After reading *Academic Freedom*, Merle Curti wrote to Hofstadter without enthusiasm,

> I find myself somehow a bit disappointed. . . . [Some] may feel that you have been a bit influenced, if inconspicuously, by the neo-conservatism that is now so pervasive in academic and non-academic circles alike. So I throw out for you to think about the suggestion that you point up a bit more the positive and constructive accomplishments in the development of . . . academic freedom . . . that you try to show more clearly and explicitly that human efforts were involved, that human judgements were also of importance; that at least on occasion personal and group interests could be, and were transcended.[30]

Curti's use of the phrase "neo-conservative" must be distinguished from its current usage. It is commonly claimed that the term was first coined by Michael Harrington in a 1973 essay "The Welfare State and Its Neoconservative Critics." In it, Harrington wrote that "the failures of the welfare state in the sixties have served as stimulus for, and rationale of, the rise of neoconservative thought in the seventies."[31] Curti's note to Hofstadter, however, indicates that the anti-intellectualism of the fifties rather than the "failures" of the welfare liberalism of the sixties explains the origins of neoconservatism. If we take a long view of neoconservatism—that is, combine both Curti's and Harrington's definitions—we are rewarded with a coherent picture of the growing conservatism of American intellectuals. In the period described by Curti, former leftists migrated to the liberal center as a reaction against the popular politics of the fifties. They moved even further to the right in the sixties, Harrington noted, as opponents of the New Left and the counterculture, groups that also prized democracy. Because Hofstadter both worked and enjoyed personal relationships with several of the men described as neoconservatives—Bell, Glazer, Irving Kristol—he has been described by some as a neoconservative himself. What we know is that he was part of a migration in the reform wing of the Democratic Party that moved to the center—but not to the right. His occupation of the political middle ground thus frustrated those on the progressive left—including Curti—who saw Hofstadter's ideological evolution as a political retreat.

If we introduce specific criteria, we learn that Hofstadter's relationship to neoconservatism is something of a mixed bag. "Neoconservatism has several components," historian Neil Jumonville writes. It is characterized by "a strong anti-Communism," it is "not sympathetic to criticism of America," it "is identified by a fear of the masses and of direct democracy," it has "a history of opposition to mass culture," and "appreciation for complexity and ambiguity in the world," and, finally, neoconservatives depend "on much of twentieth-century liberal philosophy, but are selective about it: they emphasize the meritocratic rather than the egalitarian strains."[32] And Hofstadter? He was not a strong anticommunist and certainly did not shy away from criticizing America— his books in fact featured certain tragic elements and qualities in the nation's past. Politically, in other words, he does not fit the neoconservative profile. He does, however, share what may be called a neoconservative *sensibility* that would have been described in the fifties as simply "liberalism." Hofstadter was, following Jumonville's criteria, critical of direct democracy and mass culture; he did appreciate complexity and ambiguity; and he did emphasize the meritocratic over the egalitarian. He bears, however, little relation to neoconservatism today. Its crusader mentality, devotion to Israel, and alliance with the fundamentalist Right would have left him cold. In the end, the liberal tag fits Hofstadter best. His respect for intellectual freedom, cultural latitude, and political pluralism found a home in the Democratic Party in the 1950s—and I suspect that is where he would be today (uncomfortably).

Curti's criticism of *The Development of Academic Freedom* struck Hofstadter as simplistic. There was, he believed a fundamental irony that had eluded the champions of public education: the "people" typically showed little interest in defending *democracy of the mind*. Popular rule, he wrote Curti, therefore offered no guarantee of freedom—and freedom, he insisted, was the central theme of his book. The majority routinely failed to understand or aid academic freedom, he continued, while aristocrats and conservatives often exhibited compassionate attitudes toward intellect. Perhaps this was a conservative position, he conceded to Curti, but did that make it false?[33] Hofstadter concluded by rejecting

Curti's definition of "neo-conservatism," arguing that pragmatic concerns motivated his own political instincts. Still, the labels need not obscure the point that Hofstadter's scholarship was in a state of flux and acutely sensitive to the shift from thirties radicalism to fifties liberalism.

* * *

The rise of the new conservatism played an important role in directing Hofstadter toward the social sciences. McCarthyism arose not in the wake of economic want or as a response to a disastrous military campaign, but rather in a time of abundance and on the heels of the nation's considerable contribution to the Allied victory in the Second World War. Material concerns, in other words, did not create the new conservatism — evidence again that the economic interpretations favored by Progressive historians had little to say about the postwar condition. Hofstadter's search for the social-psychological foundations of the New Right proved to be both liberating and confining. His efforts to recover a common personality type encouraged exploration into fresh areas, including status, ethnicity, and pathology, yet left him open to charges that his scholarship supported the consensus effort to read conflict out of the past.

Hofstadter's work on personality types owed a debt to the pioneering work of the Frankfurt School of Social Research, founded in 1923 and exiled at Columbia University from 1934 through the late 1940s. The Frankfurt School was a product of several important shifts in European culture and politics. The sterility of bourgeois life, collapse of democracy following the First World War, and rise of authoritarian regimes were evidence, Frankfurt scholars insisted, of a general European crisis. Add to this the popularity of relativism and one can begin to understand how the Enlightenment ideals of rationality and progress were undermined between the wars. But what kind of civilization would post-Enlightenment Europe create? For several years it seemed that the future lay in a return to less universal and more local cultural references. Nationalism, and the myths and legends that sustained it, replaced the scientific imagination with a romantic attachment to an imagined past — the ancient glories of father and mother lands. The affirmation of the irrational, Susan Buck-Morss has written, resulted in "a renewed interest in Kierkegaard, Jungian psychiatry, the novels of Hermann Hesse, the advocacy of 'culture' over civilization and 'community' over society, and even an intellectual vogue for horoscopes and magic."[34]

Initially interested in artistic and philosophical movements in Europe, Frankfurt scholars Max Horkheimer, Theodor Adorno, Erich Fromm, Friedrich Pollock, and Herbert Marcuse turned their attention to the cultural "illness" afflicting European thought and politics. Their studies on mass communication, authoritarianism, anti-Semitism, and Freudian analysis pioneered the field of critical theory that shaped Hofstadter's intellectual generation. Once in America, the Frankfurt scholars blended their interest in theoretical analysis with their host country's preference for empirical research. Adopting group interviews in studies on mass behavior, Adorno conceptualized the ambitious *The Authoritarian Personality* (1950), finding in the supposed American preference for efficiency, success, order, and stability a deep cultural compatibility with contemporary fascist regimes. It would not be long before some American scholars began to declare that a striking number of their fellow citizens — particularly in the South and Midwest — fit Adorno's profile.

Aside from developing a theoretical framework to measure mass behavior, the Frankfurt School provided Hofstadter with an exotic social scientific vocabulary that stood as an intimidating barrier to critics. Christopher Lasch noted that "*The Authoritarian Personality* had a tremendous impact on Hofstadter and other liberal intellectuals, because it showed them how to conduct political criticism in psychiatric categories, to make those categories bear the weight of political criticism. This procedure excused them from the difficult work of judgment and argumentation. Instead of arguing with opponents, they simply dismissed them on psychiatric grounds."[35]

It was also important to former American radicals that the Frankfurt School brought with it social-psychological indexes for determining political behavior. Marxism alone could not explain the explosive ideological politics of the thirties, and Frankfurt scholars convincingly emphasized the importance of culture, ethnicity, and pathology in developing popular attitudes toward state power. "For Horkheimer and Adorno," evolutionary psychologist Kevin MacDonald wrote, "the fundamental shift from the sociological to the psychological level that occurred during the 1940s was motivated by the fact that in Germany the proletariat had succumbed to fascism and in the Soviet Union socialism had not prevented the development of an authoritarian government that failed to guarantee individual autonomy."[36]

Hofstadter was favorably (but not uncritically) impressed by the Frankfurt School's pessimistic analysis of Western mass culture, and his subsequent work on populism and the radical Right selectively bear the school's imprint. In America, he concluded, authoritarian and liberal personalities clashed over a number of deep cultural issues having, in an ultimate sense, to do with the balkanization of the nation along rural-urban lines. As the country tilted toward a more secular, heterogeneous, and complex identity, the old guard could no longer count on an open appeal to racial solidarity to unite "natives" and was forced to adopt more sophisticated methods to carry its case. Combined, the curious mix of anticommunism, anti-intellectualism, and antipluralism allowed traditional constituencies to question the loyalty of the rising class while concurrently affirming their own values and traditions.

Liberalism and pluralism, of course, have their own limits of tolerance, their own tough survival instinct that can calmly (and paradoxically) silence opposition in the name of defending broadly shared but by no means universal views on race, religion, politics, culture, and economics. Hofstadter understood this and had no difficulty reconciling his commitment to a pragmatic politics with his published efforts to destabilize the groups — McCarthyites, Goldwaterites, the New Left — that threatened the liberal status quo. His distinctive brand of pluralism encouraged a cosmopolitan consensus, with New York standing as the supreme achievement, a Hapsburg-like enclave sustaining intellectual and cultural openness. The governance of this heavenly city could not be trusted to popular power, however, and the liberal mind, freed of the Progressive faith in *the people,* felt itself under siege. Mass society, of course, stood outside the gates, sometimes docile, sometimes menacing. Pluralism in American, it seemed, could only thrive as long as democracy was kept on a short leash.

Hofstadter first became interested in mass behavior when he was a young Marxist in the thirties, but this glancing introduction was given a sharper and more sophisticated focus when he began reading Max Weber. "Weber had become rather important at the time for us," remembers Daniel Bell; "it was basically Weber's influence on status politics which Marty Lipset picked up, I picked up and Dick very quickly took the lead."[37] English translations of Weber's writings first appeared in the 1930s and Hofstadter soon thereafter incorporated the German sociologist's insights on status politics into his scholarship. Weber argued that Marx's stress on materialism (what Beard had more lightly called "interests") did not offer a sufficiently complex approach to class relations, for he concluded that laborers were eager to win psychological as well as economic rewards. Weber did not dismiss consumer interests, but he believed—as did Hofstadter—that groups developed identities that were closely tied to status, prestige, and honor.

A serious student of Weber would naturally find his way to the less traveled doorstep of Karl Mannheim. In *Ideology and Utopia* (1929), the distinguished Hungarian sociologist argued that social positioning greatly influenced one's perception of the world, and that what passed as self-evident truths frequently reflected little more than particular class-based interests, values, and biases seeking legitimacy. Groups developed dogmas, Mannheim argued, as a means of expressing concerns unique to their station. The poor were attracted to utopian worldviews that promised future material or psychological relief while the powerful employed ideologies to rationalize their ambitious accumulation of resources.

In his search for a new intellectual heritage, Hofstadter read Mannheim with great interest, embracing the hypothesis that fictions (ideologies) and wish-dreams (utopias) revealed the hidden desires of both citizens and nations. Applied to America, this meant that the old political tradition had invested heavily in historical mythology to shore up its fading influence. "In our contemporary social and intellectual plight," Mannheim wrote, "it is nothing less than shocking to discover that those persons who claim to have discovered an absolute are usually the same people who also pretend to be superior to the rest." This struck a solid note of recognition for Hofstadter, who saw in the older liberalism a number of sacred absolutes—agrarianism, laissez-faire, Protestantism, nationalism, isolationism—vigorously defended by a once powerful group, a class formerly "superior to the rest." As the dominant caste declined, Mannheim noted, it engaged in a fierce struggle to regain lost status. "This cannot be done," he concluded, "without resorting to all sorts of romantic notions and myths [that] . . . distort, pervert, and conceal the meaning of the present."[38] The paternal South of U. B. Phillips and the Wasp frontier portrayed by Frederick Jackson Turner impressed Hofstadter as striking examples of reality twisted to conform to a romantic archetype of the past. These men were not merely scholars, Hofstadter concluded; they were also skillful therapists meeting the public's need to reclaim the yeoman's heroic position in the textbooks.

At Columbia several scholars applied social-psychological insights, literary criticism, and psychoanalytic theory to their work. William Leuchtenburg remembered that the intellectual climate at Morningside Heights nurtured the new approach—"We were all thinking in that direction, it was in the water." Daniel Singal wrote that Hofstadter's "Columbia colleagues proved especially influential at this juncture: Lionel Trilling, whose symbolic interpretations of literary texts suggested a similar approach to political rhetoric; C. Wright Mills, who in *White Collar* (1951) detailed the status anxieties and aspirations of the new corporate middle class; and Robert K. Merton, whose sociological concept of 'latent function' permitted an analyst to construe in rational terms behavior that at first sight appears highly irrational."[39]

The milieu of modern social theory research at Columbia culminated in a 1953–54 "University Seminar on the State" program that brought together several scholars experimenting with the concept of status. The seminar proved a perfect opportunity for Hofstadter to selectively organize the insights of Merton, Mannheim, Weber, and Adorno into an exploration of the social-psychological conditions that gave rise to McCarthyism. The informal atmosphere encouraged bold experimentation. "Unlike a campus committee that is expected to come up with recommendations," William Leuchtenburg noted, "our seminar never strove for consensus. We would take up someone's idea, or listen to a paper then weigh in with some thoughts, and, when we felt we'd spent enough time on it, move on to something else." Hofstadter's contribution to the colloquium—"Dissent and Non Conformity in the Twentieth Century"—synthesized his intensive reading in the area of symbolic analysis and applied it to the temperament of his times. His presentation scrutinized the New Right, finding two key sources of its support among traditional Wasps and second- and third-generation Catholics. The first group strove to retain its position, while the latter was still undergoing the process of Americanization and associated anticommunism with patriotism.[40] In their collective struggle to find a secure place in postwar America, these groups were psychologically exhausted, confused by the shifting scale of rank, and resentful of those constituencies whose status eclipsed their own.

Hofstadter's failure to submit the postwar Left to the same probing psychological analysis earned by the new conservatism weakened his claim to comprehensiveness. Old-stock Americans did not dismantle liberalism in 1968; rather, a younger and more eclectic constituency strongly tinctured by "rising" social groups led the assault. Abundance, station, security, and a bright future, the sixties demonstrated, could paradoxically lead to resentment and alienation. It is equally apparent that the dynamic and fluid concepts wielded by the social scientists quickly hardened, and their insights became as formulaic as the economic model favored by Progressives. When asked at the Columbia seminar how Texas oil barons fit into his analysis, Hofstadter reflexively pointed to the status thesis, insisting that East Coast envy afflicted Americans living in the vast cultural desert that lay beyond the Hudson River. His intense focus on the "irrational" glossed over the concerns of millions of Americans with legitimate questions regarding liberalism's stewardship of the state. The Korean War, threat of atomic annihilation, and disenchantment with the slow pace of racial reform rarely figured into Hofstadter's scholarship, but were among a number of important issues that shaped political attitudes in the fifties. He was by no means an uncritical observer of the New Deal state, but did believe that it served as the only productive governing philosophy among a few unpalatable alternatives, and there can be little doubt that his work served its needs.

*   *   *

"Dissent and Non Conformity in the Twentieth Century" proved to be one of Hofstadter's most durable — and controversial pieces. Published in the *American Scholar* (1955) as "The Pseudo-Conservative Revolt" and reprinted in the *New American Right* (1955), it resurfaced a decade later in *The Paranoid Style of American Politics* (1965). The essay stands as a spirited rejoinder to Far Right accusations that the reforms of the thirties undermined "traditional" American values. Hofstadter pointed out that after living with the New Deal for a generation, progressive values *were* America's values. In a manner of speaking, liberals were the new conservatives. Pseudo-conservatives, by comparison, had nothing to conserve; the genie of modernism was out of the bottle. Agrarianism, fundamentalism, and evangelicalism had all gone down with Bryan. The Pseudos were more like radicals in their bristling opposition to all the new "isms" that Americans had come to accept: urbanism, cosmopolitanism, liberalism, pluralism, internationalism, and secularism. With nothing productive to offer the nation, their opposition had to be destroyed, or at least delegitimized. Borrowing the language of the Frankfurt School — "clinical," "thematic apperception," "status," "possession," "identity," "projected," "complexes," "disorder," and, of course, "pseudo-conservative" — Hofstadter claimed that opponents of the liberal status quo suffered a kind of perversity resulting in "a profound if largely unconscious hatred of society."[41]

Intellectually, postwar scholars paid a high price defending liberalism. The marginalization of critics on the left and right contributed to the rise of the national security state and the decline of organized labor; it further offered precious little critical commentary on American militarism and nation-building. While dissent from New Deal orthodoxy may have led some extremists into an unproductive or exaggerated criticism of both state and society, it is equally true that many Americans registered honest opposition to Taft-Hartley and the containment policy (from the Left) as well as internal espionage and the growth of central authority (from the Right). The imperial presidencies that culminated in Vietnam and Watergate enjoyed the support of a generation of liberal thinkers impressed with the ideological consensus carved out during the New Deal. Confidently armed with an apparatus of scholarly terms and interpretive models supplied by the social sciences, they established the agendas and raised the questions that for nearly two decades captured the imagination of the historical profession. Scholarly initiatives and ideological preferences converged as the liberal moment aspired to orthodoxy and found in certain corners of the academy a prevailing sympathy for its expansive goals.

PART II

Engagement, 1950–1965

I know it is risky, but I still write history out of
my engagement with the present.

RICHARD HOFSTADTER, 1960

* 5 *

The Age of Reform
and Its Critics

I have the feeling that, in the philosophical sense, Hofstadter is way ahead of any living American historian, young
or old, whose work I have read, and that he will really come
into his own when America next faces a time of domestic
trouble and we once more have an immediate compulsion
to re-examine our past.

HAROLD STRAUSS TO
ALFRED A. KNOPF, 1953

The Age of Reform, Columbia historian Alan Brinkley declared thirty
years after its 1955 publication, "is the most influential book ever published on the history of twentieth-century America." It remains in our
own day a sparkling achievement in historical analysis, widely read,
provocative, and persuasive. A product of the social-psychological revolution in the postwar academy, it probed the unspoken and unconscious
ambitions of its subjects — an excursion into the Populist mind rather
than the Populist pocketbook. It was a gutsy enterprise — history without the safety net of economic causation. Elegant and iconoclastic, it
challenged not only the historiography of the reform era, but the way
historians thought and wrote about the past. Its insights were controversial, its inspiration undeniable. "To those of us who encountered
The Age of Reform in graduate school," Robert Wiebe explained, "[Hof-
stadter] more than any other writer, framed the problems, explored the
techniques, and established the model of literate inquiry that would
condition our study of the American past."[1]

The Age of Reform's focus on the illiberal side of the Populist/Progres-
sive tradition inaugurated a sea change in American historical writing.
Historians had customarily portrayed the *volk* as victims of industrialization, the human casualties of an inhumane process. In danger of de-
scending from the lofty heights of New World republicanism to Old
World proletarianism, farmers, artisans, and factory workers organized
against the great monopolies and forced their acquiescence to the regulation of transportation, finance, utilities, and corporations. These im-

99

pressive achievements — accompanied by the secret ballot, direct election of U.S. senators, and amendments in electoral laws favoring suffrage for women — encouraged historians to portray the period as a stirring rebirth of American democracy.

Hofstadter questioned all of these claims. Though he acknowledged (with perhaps too light a touch) the economic difficulties confronting small-scale farmers, he believed that Yankee reformers ultimately leveraged their grievances against the industrial state to reclaim lost status and reinforce traditional cultural privileges. Increasingly supplanted by alien ideologies, institutions, and peoples, the old stock responded by creating popular forms of power to contain the ethnic populations and captains of industry who threatened to overturn its village world.

The defensive outlook of the reform tradition cut against the grain of its earlier "radicalism." Its ill-timed connection in the 1920s with prohibitionists, creationists, and, some whispered, the Klan, recast the reputation of Progressives from one of solid social advancement to that of important ally of the fundamentalist war on modernity. Hoover's blank response to the market crash further confirmed the impotency of the tottering Yankee order and opened the door to a fresh style of reform. Under Franklin Roosevelt, the federal government emphasized vigorous intervention in the economy, and pursued policies that recognized the emerging urban-ethnic character of the United States.

In spite — or because — of its achievements, the new liberalism made powerful enemies. McCarthyism embodied the most serious threat to postwar pluralism, and Hofstadter drew historical parallels between it and the old reform tradition. He sensed in both movements hostility to the "foreign" ideologies ushered in by the last half-century of immigration. While preparing *The Age of Reform,* he apprised historian William Miller of his intention to critically evaluate liberalism as it evolved from a near exclusively Anglo-Saxon tradition to one encompassing differing ethnic perspectives. The Populist-Progressive heritage, he explained, came from a background of rural people urbanized against their will. As Yankee Protestants, they resented the rising status of Jews, Poles, and Irish, all of whom appeared to resist the values and social conservatism of the old Wasp elite. As the traditional agrarian middle class lost ground to more socially democratic and cosmopolitan interests, the tensions between the two Americas erupted in cultural conflict.[2]

Hofstadter's ethnocultural analysis aroused heated debate among economic-minded historians. Popular protest, the textbooks taught, had tamed the trusts and resurrected the promise of American liberty —

this was a success story, pure and simple. "Thanks to the triumph of Populist principles," the leading study on the subject optimistically concluded, "one may almost say that, in so far as political devices can ensure it, the people now rule."[3] The academy, of course, had much invested in the old politics. Progressive historiography arose in the Midwest, where the reformers, including Robert La Follette, Sockless Jerry Simpson, and Samuel "Golden Rule" Jones, were still recalled with affection. The University of Wisconsin personified the intellectual possibilities of the progressive idea, ensuring that the city of Madison became, in Theodore Roosevelt's words, "the laboratory of democracy." Together, town and gown produced a comprehensive reform program, including the establishment of a railroad rate commission, a civil service act, regulation of utilities, and increased taxes on corporations. The university's history department housed, at one time or another, such impressive defenders of the progressive flame as Frederick Jackson Turner, John D. Hicks, Merle Curti, and William Appleman Williams.

Hicks's influential *The Populist Revolt* (1931) stressed the striking economic inequalities between the nation's sections and the heroic efforts of Western farmers to address their grievances through democratic means. Populism may have enjoyed only limited success, he conceded, but the passage of agrarian-initiated planks a generation later by Progressives revealed the impressive legacy of farmer activism.

Hicks and Hofstadter offered the two most compelling interpretations of Populism through the 1950s, and it is a worthwhile exercise to track the ancestral taproots of their historiographical differences. Hofstadter's Jewish grandfather, Meyer, epitomized the immigrant experience: eastern European origins, furrier by trade, and settlement on the urban epicenter of New York's lower East Side. Hicks's grandfather, Eli, by contrast exhibited impressive native credentials: southern birth, midwestern pioneer, farmer, and Lincoln Republican. Hicks's mother was born in a log cabin and his father eked out a living as a small-scale agriculturist in Missouri before taking on a Methodist pastorship. Considering his impressive native credentials, it should come as no surprise that Hicks persuasively preached the virtues of the farming frontier. Like Hofstadter, he lived what he taught. Historian and agricultural specialist James C. Malin recognized among his plains states colleagues a tendency to translate their occupational resentment against the more polished eastern universities into an identification with Populism that defied temporal boundaries. "Farmers' movements and general reform movements have produced a large volume of propaganda, most of which has been accepted uncritically as history," Malin wrote. "Unfortunately, the college professor who has written in these fields has generally occupied a status which gave him a somewhat similar inferiority complex and led him to sympathize with the underdog point of view. Greenbacks, free silver, the Grange, the Alliances, Populism, the Progressive movement, and others have been treated almost invariably in a sympathetic manner that has been highly uncritical with respect to both the history of the movements themselves and their claims to constructive achievement."[4]

Hicks acknowledged the force of Malin's statement, writing in his autobiography that a congenital sympathy for the Midwest played a crucial role in shaping his historical judgments. "If in my time I overemphasized the significance of the frontier in American history and underemphasized the influence of eastern and European contributions, I came by my opinions naturally, as naturally, let us say as our urban historians come by theirs." After a brief stint teaching grade school on the Wyoming prairie, Hicks took a doctorate at the University of Wisconsin and spent his most productive scholarly years at midwestern universities before finishing his career at the University of California. His aversion to "radical" Jewish scholars is evident in a 1949 decision by the Berkeley history department to offer an appointment to Armin Rappaport. The nomination stalled until Hicks — worried that Rappaport "might have some of the ultra–left wing tendencies so common to the New York Jewish intelligentsia"—was assured of the candidate's anticommunism. Proud of his people and their traditions, Hicks summarized his life in starkly ethnocultural terms: "I, like so many others who came out of the nineteenth century, was a white Anglo-Saxon, Protestant, small-town, middle-class, midwestern American, one of those who left the country for the city. Of me and many others like me it could truthfully be said: 'You can take the boy out the country, but you can't take the country out of the boy.'"[5]

Hicks's scholarship was sustained by a generation of Wisconsin historians. Their staunchest opponents included Columbia social scientists Daniel Bell, Robert K. Merton, and Herbert H. Hyman. In the interest of clarity a few broad generalizations of the Progressive (Madison) and Anti-Progressive (Morningside) pedigrees are offered: Progressives tended to come from old-stock families; were sympathetic to the nation's rural traditions; resented McCarthy's popularity but supported mass democracy; traced their intellectual lineage to Western Europe, the Enlightenment, and Adam Smith; emphasized rational behavior as a basis for decision-making; stressed the role of economics (interest politics) in shaping political culture; and presumed that reform should be closely associated with moral behavior. Anti-Progressives tended to come from families that arrived in America after the 1880s; celebrated urban culture; blamed McCarthy's popularity on mass democracy; traced their intellectual lineage to central and eastern Europe, modernity, and Sigmund Freud; emphasized irrational behavior as a basis for decision-making; stressed the role of social and psychological needs (status politics) in shaping political culture; and presumed that reform was most effective and fair when pursued in an amoral and pragmatic manner.[6]

Both schools were critical of McCarthyism, but the social scientists — many of whom were Jewish scholars writing in the wake of Nazism — were far more sensitive to the popular origins of authoritarianism. This had not always been the case. In the thirties, intellectuals had taken their stand with the proletariat, associating the expanding influence of unions, cooperatives, and vast New Deal programs as unmistakable signs of democratic vitality. But for those who saw in the Far Right a thinly veiled anti-Semitism, McCarthy's popularity underlined an unusually retrogressive and intolerant quality in the American character. The possibility of a peoples' revolt against modernity put intellectuals on the defensive. And many, like Hofstadter, abandoned their old radicalism. In a 1953 letter to Merle Curti, Hofstadter acknowledged that he had grown more conservative over the years, and emphasized the important role of the New Deal in turning his generation toward liberalism. In a 1964 address, he went even further, confessing that his critics on the left were correct in describing *The Age of Reform* as a conservative book. It was conceived, he explained, in the satisfied social climate of postwar America, and written to defend the policies of the Roosevelt thirties.[7]

*   *   *

The Age of Reform opens with a shrewd and imaginative critique of the Populist mind. The chapter headings of this section — "The Agrarian Myth and Commercial Realities," "The Folklore of Populism," "From Pathos to Parity" — underscore the impressionistic qualities of rural reform and are indicative of Hofstadter's intent to focus on the identity and self-perception of Populism rather than its economic makeup. The rise of the metropolis, he maintained, reduced the status of the hinterlands and motivated its spirited opposition to the trusts. Populists, he conceded, no doubt experienced real economic reverses, but the essence of their protest lay in the quiet but constant recession of public affection and respect.[8]

The farmer's identity crisis straddled the dual demands of what Hofstadter defined as the "soft" and "hard" sides of Populism. The former adopted an impressionistic and sentimental attitude; it embraced the logic of agrarian superiority and fit comfortably within Turner's romantic claim that frontier ethics produced American democracy. The hard side, by comparison, stressed economic realism, limitations, and subordination to the market; it conformed to commercial circumstances while denying the farmers' preferred self-image. The jarring disconnect between the rhetoric (soft) and reality (hard) of rural life hindered the efforts of agriculturists to negotiate successfully between the bucolic vision of an idealized past and the demands of a contemporary commercial culture. Conflicted and divided against itself, the agrarian mind recoiled in confusion from the complexities of modern life.[9]

The decline of rural America, Hofstadter continued, awoke a latent anti-Semitism among the farming class. This insight proved extremely controversial, for it exposed not only the racialist thinking among reformers, but also the long-standing practice of historians to ignore the seamy side of the old liberalism. Progressive writers lavished attention on Populist achievements, Hofstadter pointed out, yet rarely explored their idiosyncrasies. Among the scholarly contributions in the field of agrarian radicalism, one found few references to the deeply ingrained provincialism that informed farmer attitudes and shaped their response to industrial-ethnic America. And no book, Hofstadter insisted, had ever investigated the anti-Semitism of rural folk.[10]

In a literal sense, he was correct — there were no major studies on the subject. But Hofstadter was not the first intellectual to comment on the connection between Populism and anti-Semitism. The talented Columbia art historian Meyer Schapiro had treated the topic in a 1938 *Partisan Review* essay — "Populist Realism." In that piece, Schapiro accused the painter Thomas Hart Benton of producing nationalist art that dismissed class and racial differences in a celebration of kitsch and Americana. Benton, Schapiro wrote, hoped "to recreate a respect for old ways, for local history and peculiarities, to win people back to native traditions." His efforts were part of an impressive body of neoagrarian sentiment advanced by such diverse personalities as Carl Sandburg, Edmund Wilson, John Steinbeck, Allen Tate, Margaret Mitchell, and James

Rorty. The allure of nativism—heightened in the face of war and economic collapse—inspired a generation of writers, poets, and painters,
but Schapiro detected in Benton's portraits a degree of artistic chauvinism that he found singularly repellent. Mass democracy seemed to be
the problem:

> Fascism draws on many streams including the traditional democratic.
> The appeal to the national sentiment should set us on guard, whatever its
> source. And when it comes as does Benton's with his conceited anti-
> intellectualism . . . his hatred of the foreign, his emphasis on the strong
> and the masculine, his uncritical and unhistorical elevation of the folk,
> his antagonism to the cities, his ignorant and violent remarks on radical-
> ism, we have good reason to doubt his professed liberalism.[11]

Quite an indictment! In his brief essay, Schapiro touched upon several
themes that preoccupied Hofstadter over the years: the connection between popular power and authoritarianism, the relationship between
folk culture and anti-intellectualism, and the transformation of the old
liberalism into the New Right. More than any of his peers, Hofstadter
made these issues central to the American story.

Several years after Schapiro's article appeared, Daniel Bell and Oscar
Handlin produced important essays that laid the foundation for Hofstadter's work on farmer radicalism. Bell's 1944 paper, "The Grass Roots
of American Jew Hatred," defined Populism as "an illustration of the
grotesque transformation of an originally progressive idea, under the
impact of modern capitalism." The grudges and grievances nursed by
the once dominant farming class, Bell added, "may well be the technique
of potential Fuehrers in achieving a mass following." Handlin's 1951
article, "American Views of the Jews at the Opening of the Twentieth
Century," placed the financial dilemma of the 1890s at the center of
Gilded Age anti-Semitism. America's preoccupation with the money
question, Handlin wrote, "fixed the tie between Jews and finance. In a
period of falling prices disaster was close at hand for a great number of
farmers who, despite mounting production saw their situation deterio-
rate steadily, particularly after the depression of 1893." Silverites looked
with suspicion at the prominence of Jewish representation at the Brus-
sels Monetary Conference and were critical of Jewish support for the
gold standard. Bryan's famous address at the 1896 Democratic national
convention—"You shall not crucify mankind upon a cross of gold!"—
underscored the economic burdens facing the farmers, but could easily

be interpreted as an effort to link Jews to the financial hardships associated with the gold standard. "What did the farmers think in the Populist areas," Handlin wrote, "while the mounting burden of debt loosened their hold on the land?" Among the farming class, "every Jewish storekeeper was in the advance guard of the new civilization, [and] bore the standard of all the dread forces that threatened their security."[12]

"American Views of the Jews" anticipated *The Age of Reform* on several fronts. It emphasized the declining status of farmers; pinpointed the time and place of rising anti-Semitism to the post–Civil War plains states; and exposed the connection between nativism and the money question. Handlin wrote that Jews were easily stereotyped as urban parasites masterminding great economic fluctuations that profited merchants and bankers but damaged the financial fortunes of the farming class. Hofstadter argued that anti-Semitism in the United States was primarily a result of the Populist perception that living standards for American Jews rose markedly during the 1880s and 1890s at the expense of agricultural interests. Jewish bankers, the farmers claimed, held all the trump cards, denying Greenbackers and free silverites the right to inflate the economy and escape from debt.[13]

Hofstadter hoped to undercut his critics (to little avail, as things turned out) by tempering his findings. He acknowledged that Know-Nothings, Anti-Masons, and the more recent interwar isolationists (the cultural Right, in other words) shared the Populist passion for conspiracy theories, and conceded that the anti-Semitic strain flashed by the People's Party was of a qualified, rather than pure content. "It would be easy to misstate the character of Populist anti-Semitism or to exaggerate its intensity," he wrote. "For Populist anti-Semitism was entirely verbal. It was a mode of expression, a rhetorical style, not a tactic or a program. It did not lead to exclusion laws, much less to riots or pogroms."[14]

Still, the sharpness of Hofstadter's attack—"a full history of modern anti-Semitism in the United States would reveal . . . its substantial Populist lineage"—troubled historians.[15] Hofstadter's best graduate students at the time, Stanley Elkins and Eric McKitrick, praised an early draft of *The Age of Reform* but had considerable reservations about its treatment of the farmers. Fresh memories of Nazism, they argued, muddied any discussion, no matter how subtle or sophisticated, of Gentile-Jewish tensions in America.

The anti-semitism. This is bad. We are afraid that you aren't analytical here—you leave yourself vulnerable & there is an over tone of unreality which is sure to bring repercussions. We feel that if *any* of this is worth mentioning at all, it deserves no more than a footnote, or at most a passing comment. . . . When one describes evidences of anti-semitism as you do, the modern reader simply cannot avoid the picture of fascism & the gas chambers. . . . The inevitable conclusion — in spite of everything — will be that populism and German fascism had much in common. One loses the sense of provincialism & naiveté of Populist anti-semitism, & what is left is the vision of brutal fascism.[16]

Another colleague close to Hofstadter at Columbia, the European historian Peter Gay, questioned *The Age of Reform*'s reliance on impressionistic rather than empirical evidence:

How inductive are you really? I presume you are presenting an empirical study. Or sure, there is intuition, the "feel" of a situation or a culture, in the piece, but fundamentally you advance one claim: that the connection of populism and anti-intellectualism is not a construct but result of investigation. But here problems arise. Let me state the question baldly: to what extent is your piece an a priori construction? That is to say, what extent do you start with an aristocratic picture of what society should be like, and then come out with your indictment of Populism? . . . As your piece now stands, its aristocratic assumptions show.[17]

Gay's friendly criticism should not obscure the fact, however, that he and other scholars valued the interpretive brilliance, impressionistic insights, and relevance of *The Age of Reform*. University of California scholar Henry Nash Smith marveled at Hofstadter's treatment of Populism and quite naturally read into it the author's purposeful probing of the New Right: "I feel . . . that your interpretation and emphasis are necessary," he wrote, "if we are to account for what seems mysterious to many people in the emergence of McCarthy and McCarran."[18]

It would be difficult to overestimate Smith's influence on Hofstadter at this time. The Depression era's uncritical celebration of democracy encouraged the creation of American studies programs in a small number of universities. By the postwar years, the programs evolved into sophisticated commentaries on American behavior. The practitioners of this genus of historical writing set out to analyze the abiding myths of the American past: agrarianism, the self-made man, the virtuous folk; and their symbols: Thomas Jefferson, Abraham Lincoln, and the yeoman farmer. The major works in this field include Smith's *Virgin Land:*

The American West as Symbol and Myth (1950), John William Ward's *Andrew Jackson: Symbol for an Age* (1955, a dissertation directed by Smith), and Marvin Meyers's *The Jacksonian Persuasion: Politics and Belief* (1957, a Hofstadter-directed dissertation).

Hofstadter found particular inspiration in Smith's *Virgin Land,* a brilliantly unconventional study of the American West that confirmed the power of popular attitudes to create an imagined past. In its graceful and penetrating analysis of the agrarian mind, the work clearly anticipated *The Age of Reform.* After reading *Virgin Land,* Hofstadter wrote Smith to affirm his admiration for what he clearly considered a landmark work in American historiography. He described the book as both beautiful and illuminating, a dazzling achievement of the historical imagination. *The Age of Reform* borrowed liberally from the language and insights of *Virgin Land*—even its chapter titles bore the imprint of the parent study. Smith explored "The South and the Myth of the Garden," Hofstadter "The Yeoman and the Myth"; Smith wrote on the "Failure of the Agrarian Utopia," Hofstadter "The Vanishing Hayseed."[19]

Virgin Land further offered Hofstadter a fresh interpretive path around a thick body of economic studies beatifying American farming. He was thus free to interpret the politics of Populism in a way fundamentally differently than if he were reading its history through a spreadsheet. Having made an uneasy—but enduring—accord with the new liberalism, it seemed important to Hofstadter to institutionalize the gains of the thirties rather than recommend a fresh round of reform. His disdain for Populism, he wrote Lee Benson at this time, was clearly a conservative reflex—the day of the radical had passed.[20]

Hofstadter's work on Populism won lavish attention from scholars, but his study of Progressivism was nearly as controversial. While he acknowledged fundamental differences in the two movements—Populism emerged from the provinces, Progressivism came from the cities— both shared a common horror of the "race" mixing of Anglo-Saxons and ethnics. Hofstadter linked the racial anxieties of Progressivism to concerns over social rank, insisting that the redistribution of money, power, and prestige made the Yankee elite fear for its status.[21] Like their Populist forebears, the middle-class leaders who directed the Progressive crusade hoped to reassert cultural supremacy over the industrial barons and ethnic populations that threatened their rule.

Historians had typically explained social rebellion in America as a reaction to declining economic fortunes, but this formula could not easily be applied to Progressivism—a cycle of civil renewal originating in an era of abundance. This is why status became central to Hof-stadter's work. If the loss of purchasing power did not create revolu-tionaries, he believed, the loss of rank did. Progressives lacked neither financial resources, opportunity, nor personal freedom, but compared to the social positioning and prestige of their parents, they perceived themselves to be in a state of decline. Sensing the public's resentment of the awesome economic powers wielded by the trusts, the reformers rushed to regain their old authority (and identity) by appealing to metro-politan fears over the rising costs of food, fuel, and rent. The urban con-sumer had come of age, and ridden the regulatory-state to power.[22]

*　　*　　*

The prestigious Walgreen Lectures delivered by Hofstadter at the Uni-versity of Chicago in 1952 (*The Age of Reform* in embryo) were curiously silent on the social welfare initiatives of the thirties. Knopf's decision to publish the manuscript encouraged Hofstadter to push the project forward chronologically in order to account for recent trends in Ameri-can liberalism. He clearly had made his peace with the new politics, and *The Age of Reform* offered a friendlier treatment of the New Deal than can be found in *The American Political Tradition*. He now juxtaposed the important achievements of the pluralist 1930s against the parochial 1920s — the last decade of the ancien regime. That era was scarred by the Scopes trial, Prohibition, the Teapot Dome scandal and the execu-tions of Sacco and Vanzetti. As the reform movement split into rural and urban wings over these and other culturally divisive issues, the old guard assumed an increasingly defensive posture. The emergence of urban cosmopolitanism, Hofstadter argued, nearly tore the country apart.[23]

On the local level, Progressives reacted to the first signs of immigrant autonomy by promoting the activities of the Klan and other "pro-American" groups. Nationally, they worked to undermine the influence of New York governor Al Smith, an Irish-Catholic opposed to the anti-drink crusade and an important political symbol for ethnic Americans. Smith's loss to Hoover in the 1928 presidential contest represented, Hofstadter argued, the last stand of the nativist tradition before the "deluge" of the New Deal. But in his eagerness to pinpoint from the electoral cycle a fundamental shift in the country's ethnopolitical pref-erences, his claims exceeded his evidence. He presumed that anti-Catholic sentiment doomed Smith's chances, ignoring the fact that probably no Democrat stood a chance of defeating the popular Hoover in that campaign. Further, his conclusion that Protestant domination continued in his own day ignored the real advances made by American Catholics since 1928. Five years after *The Age of Reform* appeared, John F. Kennedy was elected president.[24]

Hofstadter made equally questionable claims about the meaning of Franklin Roosevelt's electoral success. He praised FDR as the perfect candidate for an ethnically mixed nation — a Protestant patrician comfortable with political machines and eager to recognize his party's reliance on the new Americans. While there is no doubt a great deal of truth in this assertion, Hofstadter's claim that Roosevelt's multiethnic appeal brought him victory ignores the fact that probably no Democrat, urban or rural, would have lost in 1932. On the other hand, there is no evidence to suggest that, barring the Depression, Americans were prepared to abandon Hoover for Roosevelt.[25] One is inclined to agree with Hofstadter's critics that economic issues played a larger role in the politics of reform than his book allowed.

The cultural transition theme emphasized in Roosevelt's success is pervasive in *The Age of Reform* and places its author in a distinguished line of writers — Henry Adams, T. S. Eliot, Henry James, Sinclair Lewis — who were intellectually and emotionally sensitive to the eclipse of Anglo-Saxonism. Hofstadter's valediction for this tradition is reminiscent of F. Scott Fitzgerald's more contrite elegy to Waspdom. On the final page of *The Great Gatsby,* Fitzgerald wrote of Jay Gatsby, the westerner who lost his moral center in the East: "He had come a long way to this blue lawn and his dream must have seemed so close that he could hardly fail to grasp it. He did not know that it was already behind him, somewhere back in the vast obscurity beyond the city, where the dark fields of the republic rolled on under the night." On the final page of *The Age of Reform,* Hofstadter wrote: "In truth we may well sympathize with the Populists and with those who shared their need to believe that somewhere in the American past there was a golden age whose life was far better than our own. But actually to live in that world, actually to enjoy its cherished promise and its imagined innocence, is no longer within our power."[26]

*   *   *

Published in the autumn of 1955, *The Age of Reform* electrified the critical community. Hofstadter's attention to the mental rather than material world of the reformers offered historians innovative strategies that made reading the monograph a revelatory experience. "The book delights me not only for the freshness of its language and the subtlety of its ideas, but for the new, convincing and coherent picture which you manage to paint of these movements," Daniel Boorstin congratulated Hofstadter. "As I read your book I am continually impressed with the rigidity and unimaginativeness of the interpretations which we have been accustomed to treating as 'standard' of Populism and Progressivism." Popular reviewers agreed with Boorstin's ebullient assessment, finding immense value in the work. *New Republic* critic David Fellman declared *The Age of Reform* superior to the Progressive histories that preceded it — a "singularly brilliant book. [One] completely devoid of such historical simplicisms as the class struggle." *New York Times Book Review* contributor D. W. Brogan praised Hofstadter's felicitous style and deft handling of material: "We are always being told of the need for rethinking of the American past by American conservatives. Mr. Hofstadter has put a similar rethinking on the agenda of the liberals. And he has done it while ignoring the tradition that serious books must be dull and by illuminating his themes by a brilliant aphoristic style that really brightens and does not blind. An important and, to use a cliché, an exciting book."[27]

The most important professional review came from John D. Hicks. Though he believed Hofstadter overemphasized agrarian anti-Semitism — "My failure to brand the Populists as anti-Semites and nativists . . . worried some critics, but I think that the critics were much farther off base than I was" — lauded *The Age of Reform* as "a delightfully refreshing book. By concentrating upon what reformers thought rather than upon their political antics Hofstadter has made a unique and valuable contribution." Hicks's student, George Mowry, offered a more circumspect assessment, insisting that Hofstadter's metropolitan background tinctured his view of Populism. "One has the feeling," he wrote in the tellingly titled *Mississippi Valley Historical Review* — a journal created by midwestern scholars to break the East's monopoly on historical publications — "that the author occasionally fails to understand the agrarian mind and that he is making some of his judgments about Populism and agrarian progressivism not in terms of the conflicts of the past, but rather more fully in terms of the author's urban present." Mowry also recognized, however, the stunning presence of *The Age of Reform*, concluding that it contained "sparkling new viewpoints, insightful remarks, lively quotations, and sharply etched characterizations. This book simply demands consideration for the Pulitzer Prize."[28]

Mowry's instinct proved sound. The two judges for the 1956 history prize—Hofstadter's mentor and Columbia colleague Harry Carman, and C. Vann Woodward, an Arkansas native and specialist in southern history at Johns Hopkins University—awarded *The Age of Reform* the Pulitzer. Woodward's scholarship offered a much more sympathetic treatment of Populism than *The Age of Reform*. In light of this, and the fact that he and Hofstadter exchanged several letters over the years addressing their strong differences on the subject, it is ironic, but in keeping with Woodward's good character, generous spirit, and eye for talent, that his considerable support honored the book with the nation's preeminent award for historical writing.

Hofstadter's impressive professional achievements—a Columbia professorship, a spate of first-rate books, and a Pulitzer Prize all at the impossibly young age of thirty-nine—marked him as an important and prolific public intellectual. But controversy accompanied his success. *The Age of Reform*, its critics declared, had both minimized the hardships of agrarian life and read the McCarthy movement into the recent past. "I think [Hofstadter] is a little hard on the Populists and the Progressives," Merle Curti confided to a colleague. "Now racism was not confined to the Populists; it was endemic. The chief figures in the Immigration Restriction League were eastern academics and Brahmins and much of its literature was highly racist in character. It seems that when the young Turks revise the historical work of their predecessors they are inclined to go rather too far. Dick is to be sure too intellectually sophisticated to write his thesis without qualifications. I still think his position is as biased by his urban background and by the new conservatism as the work of older historians was biased by their rural background and traditional agrarian sympathies." Hofstadter received a taste of this criticism shortly after the book's release when Curti questioned his account of ethnic baiting among rural folk. Hofstadter admitted that anyone who read *The Age of Reform* without a background in Populist studies would be misled by his overemphasis on the anti-Semitism of the reformers. But the omission in the professional literature of Populist anti-Semitic symbolism, he concluded, was so striking that a forceful counterblow had to be made in order to correct the historical record.[29]

Curti never again raised the issue with Hofstadter, but some critics were not about to let Hofstadter off so easily.[30] William Appleman Williams, an Iowa native ideologically weaned on the high progressivism indicative of his graduate training at the University of Wisconsin, offered a more robust challenge to *The Age of Reform* than either Hicks or Curti.

In a biting review published in the *Nation,* Williams drew attention to a number of methodological weaknesses and intellectual biases in Hofstadter's work to be repeated over the years by other commentators: he avoided archival materials and relied on social scientific theories advanced by nonhistorians; he developed a priori assumptions; he was more interested in promoting a liberal ideology than writing objective history; his use of rank blurred the fact that issues of identity and power are closely intertwined and could not be neatly divided into the convenient categories of "status" and "interest."

Williams praised Hofstadter's early books as first-rate scholarship informed by a radical sensibility. But he noted a conservative strain in his recent work that "appeals to [the] New Liberalism because it explains and justifies what the liberal has been doing — and what he has not done." Apologists for the New Liberalism (what Curti and others were beginning to call neoconservatism) glossed over significant problems in American society, Williams charged, and meekly accepted the nation's burgeoning cold war commitments. Even more damning, Hofstadter's use of the status thesis cleverly marginalized both the Right and the Left, by implying that opponents of the "system" had few legitimate complaints with an efficient and socially progressive postwar liberalism.[31]

Though it may have come as no surprise that the "radical" Williams produced a sharp rebuttal to *The Age of Reform,* many of the book's most resourceful critics were liberal scholars. Woodward, for example, had grown increasingly irritated at the historical profession's treatment of Populism. While he recognized that *The Age of Reform* was not an isolated reproach of agrarian radicalism, that book placed Hofstadter in the center of a brewing debate between the defenders of interest politics and the proponents of status politics. Woodward believed that the rewriting of American history along the lines established by the social scientists favored the East, and he suggested to Hicks that the new studies betrayed a faddish quality: "I have read about the time when slavery was the root of all evil, and I myself remember a time when capitalism was the root of all evil, but I hardly expected to live to see populism fulfill the role. *Radix malorum est populism.* It seems the new key to American history."[32]

Woodward's reply to *The Age of Reform* — "The Populist Heritage and the Intellectual" (*American Scholar,* 1960) — offered a penetrating analysis of the shifting fate of the farmer's reputation among highbrows. Woodward recalled that during the Depression, scholars embraced a wide spectrum of populistic protest aimed at revising the industrial system. "In the thirties," he wrote, "intellectuals made naïve identification with farmers and workers and supported their spokesmen with enthusiasm." This generalization holds true for Hofstadter, who in 1938 planned to work at southern agricultural cooperatives in order to experience sharecropping and observe the possibilities of socialism. Hofstadter acknowledged the insightfulness of Woodward's accusation in an unpublished 1964 address in which he noted that during the 1930s, intellectuals — and he included himself — were uncritical of the working class, believing it to be morally superior to the business elite. Scholars, he continued, praised the masses as decent, honest folk, fully deserving of whatever ammunition the historical record could supply them in support of their struggle. But the McCarthy era, Hofstadter concluded, had opened a painful breach between the public and the intellectuals, and the subsequent defeats of Adlai Stevenson emphasized the depth of the divide.[33]

Prewar apologists for Populism, Woodward noted in his essay, currently found themselves "the victims of a seamy and sinister side of democracy to which they now guiltily realized they had all along tended to turn a blind or indulgent eye." He conceded the important insights yielded by the new historiography — "the consequence has been a formidable and often valuable corpus of social criticism" — but believed that the intellectuals' dim opinion of Populism distorted their view of democracy. He shrewdly drew attention as well to the geographic — and by inference ethnocultural — exceptionalism of the new school: "There are no conscious spokesmen of the West or South, but some are more or less conscious representatives of the urban East."[34]

Woodward acknowledged that the current case against Populism contained important corrections and that under the loving care of Progressive scholars the reformers had enjoyed remarkably sympathetic treatment. "The danger," he wrote, "is that under the concentrated impact of the new criticism the risk is incurred not only of blurring a historical image but of swapping an old stereotype for a new one. The old one sometimes approached the formulation that Populism is the root of all good in democracy, while the new one sometimes suggests that Populism is the root of all evil." Woodward praised Hofstadter for addressing the irrational side of Populism "in the spirit of civility and forbearance," but found in the broader critique of agrarianism, carried on by less careful scholars, strong efforts to link Populism with fascism.[35]

Woodward further discouraged scholarship that recast the Populists as proto-McCarthyites. The Columbia social scientists, he argued, had mistakenly attributed Populist strength to the Midwest, the region most receptive to the Wisconsin senator's voluble style. But these states, he pointed out, were home to the lukewarm Populism of William Jennings Bryan and had given McKinley considerable support. The South, which had largely rejected McCarthy, contained the most purely populistic sympathies in the country, and there agrarians had bravely tried to bridge the chasm between blacks and whites by creating a biracial farming coalition aimed at overcoming the undemocratic economic forces dominating the region. To suggest, as Hofstadter and others had, that southern Populists "may have been bitten by status anxiety" struck a dissonant chord with Woodward. He insisted that the agrarian legislative program "was almost obsessively economic and, as political platforms go, little more irrational than the run of the mill."[36]

Woodward sent a prepublication draft of "Populist Heritage" to Hofstadter to receive comment and perhaps give warning. The latter replied with a strong defense in words reminiscent of those he had written to Curti: historians had treated the Populists — their liberal ancestors — uncritically, and had thus followed Parrington's habit of dividing the nation into virtuous farmers and evil businessmen. In his own reply, Woodward conceded that Populism dabbled in paranoia, but he was quick to point out that it was not alone. More than a few New York newspapers shrieked that the Sherman Silver Purchase Act of 1890 meant the end of capitalism, while the persecution of anarchists and Communists by the superpatriots of the red scare era provided ample evidence of eastern anxiety. The real issue, Woodward believed, was whether the social scientists were willing to extend to agrarian radicalism the same sympathy they reserved for urban radicalism.[37]

Woodward's private correspondence with Hofstadter provides a personal context to the public skirmishes that ensued between the defenders of Populism and their opponents. The exchange is fascinating. Woodward was certain that the authoritarian personality could be found in non-Populist backgrounds: "In the McCarthy movement I believe a close study would reveal a considerable element of college-bred, established-wealth, old family industrial support." Hofstadter vigorously disagreed and noted that the typical McCarthyite was underprivileged and undereducated, lived in a small town, and subscribed to an evangelical brand of Christian worship. Nor did Hofstadter believe that *The Age of Reform* favored the elite, minimized the hardships of the farmers, or advanced the cause of neoconservatism. Nevertheless, he continued, conservatives were less given to social upheaval and to obsessing over conspiracy theories than populistic personalities. Under stress, he conceded, anyone might distrust reality, but the historical record demonstrated to his satisfaction that the masses were far more erratic as a group than their more sophisticated peers.[38]

Woodward's differences with Hofstadter were expressed with restraint, courtesy, and respect. He felt strongly, however, that the "other side"—Progressives, midwesterners, southerners—had to stand up and address the charges of the social scientists. "I . . . have long felt that an answer was required," he wrote Hicks. "I hesitated a long time to do it, because so many of our critics were long-time friends and historians with whom I have much in common in the way of tastes and sympathies. Had this not been the case, I doubtless would have been somewhat harsher in my strictures."[39]

A harsher critic did arise in Norman Pollack. An assistant professor of history at Yale University, Pollack carved out a niche in the historical profession as *The Age of Reform*'s most determined critic. In a span of five years (1960–65) he published no fewer than four articles and one book that challenged Hofstadter's work on the Peoples' Party. Pollack's most elaborate statement on the subject, *The Populist Response to Industrial America*, portrayed the farmers as radicals waging a heroic struggle against the industrial state to preserve the democratic promise of American life. If Hicks had drawn the Populists as proto-Progressives, Pollack sketched them as proto-socialists. The personal nature of his debate with Hofstadter is suggested in the titles of his articles: "Hofstadter on Populism: A Critique of 'The Age of Reform,'" and "Fear of Man: Populism, Authoritarianism, and the Historian." Lawrence Levine believed that Pollack's essays on *The Age of Reform* were "far more ideological than personal," yet remembered that Hofstadter "himself uncharacteristically fell into this mode of feeling the attack was personal." Hofstadter responded by deflecting the controversy—avoiding confrontation. When Eric McKitrick asked him if he was offended by Pollack's criticisms, McKitrick recalls, he joked, "No, of course not, it's all about me!"[40]

Pollack resurrected the familiar accusation that *The Age of Reform* ignored the profound financial problems farmers faced. In "Hofstadter on Populism," he wrote that "if Hofstadter is correct [in claiming the Populists were nascent capitalists] it follows that conditions giving rise to class feeling were themselves non existent. The result is a blanket endorsement of industrial capitalism and a consequent denial that conditions of oppression and concrete economic grievances ever existed."[41]

This argument overlooked the fact that *The Age of Reform* concentrated on the interior life of Populism rather than its economic exterior. It more provocatively, however, drew attention to the fact that the book could be read as a conservative argument in favor of an efficient business class. In any case, Hofstadter's tendency to overemphasize his insights left him vulnerable.

One of his most capable critics was David Potter, a gifted southern historian teaching at Stanford University. In a 1963 review of *The Radical Right*, an expanded edition of *The New American Right*, Potter declared that the status thesis pioneered by Hofstadter was both unscientific and intellectually biased. A historian hostile to a certain individual, idea, or political persuasion, he wrote, had only to assert that irrational psychological impulses triggered the offending party's behavior. Rational economic choices, on the other hand, automatically explained the actions of favored subjects. In other words, imprecise or shifting definitions of the terms "status" and "interest" allowed the authors of *The Radical Right* to rig the game in favor of the liberals. But the results, Potter continued, ironically played into the hands of conservatives. Industrialists had always maintained that producer radicalism — industrial strikes, agrarian coops, demands for regulation, and trust-busting — reflected an illogical assault on a corporate state that efficiently supplied goods and services to the nation. Historians labored for years, Potter concluded, to overcome this glib and self-serving characterization by the business class "only to have Hofstadter, in the *Age of Reform,* repeat essentially the same accusation, but from the vantage point of the left, rather than the right, and in the more sophisticated terminology of modern psychology."[42]

Hofstadter believed that the social sciences enlarged the historical community's vision by exposing the hidden emotional motives of historical actors. Potter's criticism, however, suggested otherwise. The status thesis, he argued, curtailed rather than encouraged debate, for it reduced behavior to uncomplicated "rational" or "irrational" categories that belied the complexity Hofstadter presumed he had introduced. The psychological duality of the social scientists had replaced the economic duality of the Progressives.

Days after reading Potter's review, Hofstadter initiated a correspondence with the Stanford historian to defend both his treatment of Populism and his use of the status thesis. While acknowledging to Potter that his review was both thoughtful and fair-minded, Hofstadter complained that it contained a common misreading of *The Age of Reform* that he wished to clear up once and for all: never in that book did he attribute the actions of the Populists to status anxiety. He insisted that the book gave a fairly straight economic account of the farmers' behavior and challenged Potter to cite any passage that suggested otherwise.[43] Potter located the passage in question:

> I am glad you wrote to me about my review, and I certainly do not want to misrepresent you in any way. . . . When we come to the point, however, of whether *The Age of Reform* attributes status anxieties to the Populists, I must say that I think it does. . . . It seems to me, *The Age of Reform* speaks very pointedly about the status anxieties of the populists and the psychological manifestations which accompanied these anxieties. In fact it seems to me that all the way from p. 7 to p. 35 this theme is built up in an effective, and I might say, convincing way. . . . I thought the argument was clinched on pp. 33–35, where I find the passage (p. 33): "Rank in society! That was the heart of the matter, for the farmer was beginning to realize acutely . . . that he was losing in status and respect. . . ." This, in short, is why it has seemed and still seems to me that *The Age of Reform* analyzes the Populists . . . in terms of status anxieties, and as I said in my review, shows these status anxieties as making the Populists suspicious and hostile, and driving them toward paranoid attitudes including anti-Semitism. As I tried to indicate in the review, I am by no means unconvinced by the argument which I think I perceive and which you say is not there. This is perhaps the irony in this exchange of letters. What I felt, in writing my review, was that the concept of status motivation is both basic and inescapable, but that it is also very tricky, and that perhaps the trickiest thing about it is that it tends to discredit any group to whom it is applied, while the concept of interest motivation or ideological motivation tends to justify those to whom it is applied.[44]

Potter's observations—repeated through the years by numerous scholars—made *The Age of Reform* a qualified triumph for Hofstadter. The caveats bothered him and he presumed that his harshest critics had simply missed the point. And perhaps they had. *The Age of Reform* is, at heart, a product of the mind rather than the archives. It is a richly symbolic book, the fruit of its author's imagination, his selective reading in the social sciences, and his reaction to McCarthyism. As the years passed and more specialized studies on Populism overturned the status thesis, Hofstadter distanced himself from *The Age of Reform*'s most provocative claims. In a 1969 letter to historian Otis Graham, he explained that the status thesis was flawed and unusable as he had tried to use it in *The Age of Reform*. He further conceded that nativism and anti-Semitism permeated American society in the 1890s and reflected the urban as well as rural mind. That he did not give attention to this fact, he acknowledged, was a serious deficiency of the book and gave its critics grounds for reproach. And yet its influence on historical writing in American could not—and cannot—be denied.[45] A brilliant, brave, and flawed masterpiece, *The Age of Reform* played a critical role in pushing historical analysis into the modern era. Psychology had entered the profession, and the Progressive penchant for self-interest would never again stand unchallenged.

Thinking about *The Age of Reform* a half century after its publication, one cannot help but notice how powerfully it speaks to the condition of our current political climate. The rise of the Christian Right in the 1970s and '80s provided a strong political base for the "values voters" that have proven important in piling up recent Republican Party majorities. Wary of the politics of morality, Hofstadter's views on populist movements have been resurrected by some historians on the left who are critical of groups like the Christian Coalition and the Promise Keepers. The painful dividing of America on issues like abortion, stem cell research, gay marriage, and intelligent design evokes the cultural wars of the 1920s when the prohibitionists fought the wets and the creationists battled the Darwinists. In the current arena of conflict, economic issues — as Hofstadter suggested in *The Age of Reform* — often take a back seat. A *New York Times* survey of the 2004 presidential election "found that a majority believed the national economy was not so good, that tax cuts had done nothing to help it and that the war in Iraq had jeopardized national security. But fully one-fifth of voters said they cared most about 'moral values.'" The long age of reform in American political culture continues.[46]

* 6 *
The Crisis of Intellect

The widespread distrust of intellectuals in America reflects
a tendency to depreciate their playfulness and distrust their
piety. Our is a society in which every form of play seems to
be accepted by the majority except the play of mind.

RICHARD HOFSTADTER, 1953

Richard Hofstadter wrote or coauthored nearly a dozen books in less
than thirty years. A prolific writer blessed with a felicitous and engaging
style, he valued the power of good prose, encouraging students to
sharpen and condense their essays with an eye toward impact and clarity. He imparted one additional piece of advice to his students: produce
at least one page of original material each day. "I write at least three
drafts of anything," he noted of his own habits. "I have a lot of second
thoughts, and I'd rather have them before the book is bound. I'll fight
right down to the galleys and sometimes even after the book is in print."
Presentation meant more to Hofstadter than a packet of facts and footnotes; and while he respected monographs generated by archival materials, his own talents tilted toward history as an artistic rather than scientific persuasion. "If one were to compare the proportion of time
given to expression with that given to research," he informed an interviewer, "my emphasis is on the first."[1]

Hofstadter's work habits were methodical and took on a momentum
born of routine that carried him through difficult periods when words
were hard to find. After collecting his first Pulitzer in 1956 for *The Age of
Reform,* Hofstadter faced the daunting challenge of producing a follow-
up. For seven years (a long time for this writer), he labored away on *Anti-
Intellectualism in American Life,* a penetrating if problematic study that
proved to be his most ambitious and least satisfying work. As a form of
therapy, *Anti-Intellectualism* delivered a magnificent blow for those who
experienced (or thought they experienced) the Eisenhower fifties as

cultural outcasts of the conservative politics, consumer pride, and shallow thinking of the great American middle class. Trembling between irritation and exposure, it recalled in certain passages the pitiless commentary of Henry Adams, and one could be excused for mistaking its broad and frequently tart social criticisms as part of *The Education of Richard Hofstadter.*

In *Anti-Intellectualism,* Hofstadter charted the progress of the American mind in a nation hostile to expertise. Speculative insights and critical commentary clashed with a consensus-seeking public drawn to pragmatic solutions and eager to make icons of the farmers, cowboys, and frontiersmen whom they believed reflected the simple and action-oriented roots of the republic. Because it so precisely exposed the majority's prejudice against intellect, *Anti-Intellectualism* is one of the most troubling criticisms of American democracy ever written. Its accusations resonate in a nation where public pressure has the power to shape college curriculums, fire controversial instructors, and force loyalty oaths upon faculty. Hofstadter made a persuasive case that the nation's uniquely democratic institutions — reinforced by the frontier, capitalism, and evangelical Protestantism — rendered it particularly vulnerable to the masses.

Exactly what constitutes anti-intellectual behavior is a matter of great debate. No doubt social training, personal histories, and private prejudices condition thinking and shape opinions on the topic. As a historian, however, Hofstadter was obliged to work within the framework of objective scholarly standards, so to avoid charges that *Anti-Intellectualism* took a particular political slant, he promised a far-ranging meditation on intellect's rocky relationship to American religion, reform, commerce, and pedagogy. A careful reading of its contents, however, reveals a less capacious offering. With post-McCarthy scores to settle, Hofstadter attacked conventional midwestern Wasp values — evangelical Protestantism, democratic politics, practical-minded business culture, and egalitarian education — for resisting the preferences of the metropolis. The new liberalism, he argued, was in danger of succumbing to the old culture. It needed a resourceful and determined advocate to make a place for the thinking class in the American imagination on par with the yeoman farmer and the self-made myth. As things stood at midcentury, Hofstadter concluded, the mind was suspect, an obnoxious rebuke to the country's egalitarian roots, and vulnerable to the whims of a volatile mass democracy.

In the contest between modernity and its opponents, *Anti-*

Intellectualism defended the political and cultural preferences of its author and thus pushed the edge of partisanship. "This work is by no means a formal history," Hofstadter candidly declared, "but largely a personal book, whose factual details are organized and dominated by my views."[2] Not, however, his views alone. Hofstadter discovered at both Columbia and the broader Morningside community a remarkably supportive environment of important thinkers equally disturbed by the rise of McCarthyism. His friends in the sociology department, C. Wright Mills and Daniel Bell, produced groundbreaking studies on the American middle class that harmonized in important ways with his own work. In *White Collar* (1951), Mills explored the psychological price Americans paid for their affluent lifestyles, identifying in the efficiency culture of the fifties a latent resentment of the managerial system. Abundance may have muted the economic issues that dominated the thirties, he noted, but a new peril provoked the middle class. Rather than abiding contentedly in the suburbs and the office parks, the American bourgeoisie chafed uncomfortably against its loss of status to the major corporate, military, educational, and governmental interests making up the "power elite." Mills, more radical than Hofstadter, held out hope that a reinvigorated critical politics might still right the situation in favor of the masses. But the unstable nature of popular power concerned Hofstadter and he cleaved to the idea that a metropolitan led democracy, operating under the useful constraints of a traditional two-party system, offered talented thinkers their best chance to deflect public passions and anti-intellectual prejudices.

Like Hofstadter, Daniel Bell rejected the crusading moralism of the thirties and produced a remarkably influential analysis of postwar America. His interpretation of the era, *The End of Ideology* (1960), stands alongside Hofstadter's *The American Political Tradition* (1948), Arthur Schlesinger, Jr.'s *The Vital Center* (1949), and Lionel Trilling's *The Liberal Imagination* (1950) as a vigorous defense of the new cosmopolitanism that praised liberal political, economic, and literary values. Much of Bell's scholarship during this period focused on the cultural origins of McCarthyism. Like Hofstadter, with whom he worked closely on *The New American Right* project, Bell observed in the defensive posture of isolationists, anti-Communist Irish, German Catholics, and other recent immigrants an eagerness to support a messianic approach to foreign policy as a show of loyalty.

While Mills and Bell investigated the sources of resentment so important to social scientists, Trilling and Reinhold Niebuhr provided a model for a new *sensitivity* to the conditions of postwar life that was critical to Hofstadter's professional development. Offended by the intellectual certainty and mechanical thinking of the Depression era, they emphasized a host of insightful analytic tools—complexity, ambiguity, paradox, tragedy—that accorded with Hofstadter's views on society.

Trilling's move to the ideological center in the late thirties anticipated the generational migration of former radicals, and his masterpiece, *The Liberal Imagination,* criticized literary champions of the old progressivism (Vernon Parrington, Theodore Dreiser), while finding greater value in the works of more nuanced and less sentimental writers (Henry James and Nathaniel Hawthorne). Like Hofstadter, Trilling saw life as a struggle and tragedy as a vitally useful guiding principle. Liberalism recognized, he maintained, the "essential imagination of variousness and possibility, which implies the awareness of complexity and difficulty." This perspective emphasized caution, conceded the imperfect nature of man, renounced the principle of social salvation, and cast a wary eye on reformers. The postwar intellectual consciousness, humbled by the Nazi death camps and the disillusionment of radical politics, sought a fundamentally different philosophical relationship with its society. It broke decisively from a "pragmatic scientific naturalism" emphasized by such thinkers as John Dewey and Sidney Hook, to offer a more chastened assessment of the human condition.[3]

Niebuhr's impassioned complaint of postwar Christian culture as too optimistic, sentimental, and self-absorbed came down forcefully on the side of a more complex and equivocal rendering of the nation's past. In *The Irony of American History* (1951), he rejected the country's commitment to liberal utopianism—faith in technology, efficiency, and material progress—as a false redemptive path. It seemed clear to him that the horror of Auschwitz represented a darker, but no less authentic, side of the scientific mentality. A disciple of Augustine and Calvin, Niebuhr conceived of intellectual work as an emotionally difficult task, in search not of perfection or the banal comfort of an affirming Christ, but rather the hard ground floor of humanity's limitations. His work rebuked the mythology of American exceptionalism (practiced by generations of historians, including Frederick Jackson Turner and Daniel Boorstin) and framed the national experience in more ambiguous and tentative terms. Concerned that liberalism cultivate a critical self-consciousness, Niebuhr, along with Trilling, Bell, Mills, and Hofstadter, formed a dynamic intellectual society in the fifties. Their certainty that the conservative tradition in America was obsolete served as a powerful bond. And they agreed that the moral regeneration impulse that ran like a disturbing tremor through the older progressivism had encouraged racism, localism, and anti-intellectualism. No self-satisfied defenders of the American dream, they sought a critical, reflective, and searching social philosophy free from the cant of frontier mythology and Horatio Alger tales. Perhaps more than any of them, Hofstadter envisioned a radically altered postwar mind. Jeffersonianism was dead. The future, he knew, belonged to metropolitanism and, he hoped, the life of the mind.

The concerns of the Claremont Avenue ghetto extended far beyond Morningside Heights. No longer the prized brain trusters who helped conceptualize the New Deal, many postwar intellectuals found it difficult to embrace the current American egalitarianism. The sharp ideological disputes of the thirties had disappeared almost too quickly, their emphasis on social conflict replaced by one of social cohesion symbolized in a middle class that aroused among some observers a mixture of both fear and fascination. Hofstadter's work during this period complimented a cottage industry of studies that dissected the lives and psychology of the American bourgeoisie. *Anti-Intellectualism* joined David Riesman's *The Lonely Crowd* (1950), David Potter's *People of Plenty* (1954), William Whyte's *The Organization Man* (1956) and John Kenneth Galbraith's *The Affluent Society* (1958) as important surveys on the character, habits, and aspirations of the American masses. These works were rich and varied exercises investigating contemporary life from a number of angles, yet they intersected in a common criticism of popular culture and popular power.

Much of this work, still read (or at least referred to) today, suffers from a thinly concealed elitism that has left it vulnerable to critics on both sides of the political spectrum. The repercussions, as historian Ellen Schrecker notes, were mixed, but, in the main, tended to emphasize the intellectual's self-defeating struggle to overcome the mass society in which he lived. "Hofstadter and his colleagues," Schrecker writes,

viewed McCarthy and his allies as populists, situating them within an anti-intellectual strand of American politics that had traditionally expressed the resentment of the unenlightened little people against the cultivated upper class. Such an interpretation cloaked considerable hostility to and suspicion of mass political action. It also delegitimized American Communism by indirectly identifying its celebration of the common man with the excesses of the far right. And it strengthened the elitism that was such an important component of the cultural criticism of the 1950s. The New York intellectuals were vociferous in their denunciations of the conformity of American life. McCarthyism, suburbia, television, tailfins, "kitsch," Communism, and nazism — they were all, in one way or another, products of mass society. Far better to leave matters of culture and politics in the hands of the educated elites, who could be counted on to maintain standards and preserve Western civilization from its enemies on both the right and the left.[4]

Hofstadter resented the fact that farmers, unions, educators, and business leaders could impose their practical choices over the theoretical preferences of the intellectuals. For this reason among others, *Anti-Intellectualism* can be read profitably as a study in self-interest, an expression of its author's quixotic concern that a healthy, pluralistic society required democracy's ready deferral to intellect.

It might be helpful to repeat that Hofstadter emerged from the thirties permanently alienated from radical politics — and that the underlying cause was a question of intellectual freedom. Reactionary leaders posing as social saviors, he argued, could easily manipulate the working-class's passion for reform. The communist movement in America, he wrote Harvey Swados in 1938, survived by enlisting the feeble-minded and promising simple solutions to the complex problems workers faced. If the revolution came, he noted, zealots would take control — and they would have no need for intellectuals.[5]

In a much more sophisticated way, *Anti-Intellectualism* updated this argument — but at the price of alienating younger scholars. Hofstadter's student Christopher Lasch noticed a high-liberal snobbery common among critics of the working class, and he complained in *The New Radicalism in America* (1965) that a sense of possession compromised the postwar professoriat and weakened its claims to objectivity. "The liberalism of the fifties and sixties," he wrote, "with its unconcealed elitism and its adulation of wealth, power and 'style,' was firmly rooted in a social fact of prime importance: the rise of the intellectuals to the status of a privileged class, fully integrated into the social organism. If the new radicalism represented the worldview of the intellectuals emergent, the liberalism of the Eisenhower-Kennedy era was the ideology of a mature class jealous of its recognized position in the social order."[6] Put another way, Lasch was describing the *status anxiety* of the postwar intellectuals.

In truth, both Hofstadter's and Lasch's generations experienced disappointing relationships with the proletariat. Graduate students went to great lengths in the thirties to identify with the labor bloc, ape its political gestures, and absorb what it assumed was a more humane and authentic value system. Hofstadter himself cultivated this fantasy, but, as he quickly came to realize, the movement belonged to the working class. Professional revolutionaries, he wrote Swados in 1940, had to experience the same hardships as the workers, and he recognized that he was neither tough enough nor intellectually capable of identifying with their situations.[7]

The New Left followed a similar pattern of romanticized identification followed by disillusionment. Understandably sympathetic to the desperate plight of blacks and the wrenching poverty experienced by rural populations, the student movement infiltrated the world of the working poor, leading to a compassionate but often uncritical evaluation of the cultural, aesthetic, and political tastes of their subjects. This situation endured as long as unions marched in solidarity with the civil rights movement and labor maintained its traditional ties to the Democratic Party. But the partnership between the workers and the students broke down in the late sixties as campus rebellions, racial integration of white neighborhoods, and counterculture efforts to push "movement" politics to the forefront of the national consciousness met with stern resistance from culturally conservative working-class constituencies. In reply, the New Left repeated the journey made by Hofstadter's generation and recast white wage earners (Nixon's silent majority of the seventies and the Reagan Democrats of the eighties) as bigots and blue-collar obstacles to reform. This pilgrimage had already begun in 1968 by the time radical Columbia graduate student Mark Naison acknowledged, "I have an almost impulsive tendency to regard working class whites — with their masculinity hangups; their love of collective violence, their intolerance . . . of personal rebellion — as the enemy."[8]

Hofstadter's own suspicion of popular action found him lagging curiously behind the political curve in post-McCarthy America. *Anti-Intellectualism* showed the scars of the academic freedom wars of the fifties but was published amid the soaring activism and grand hopes of the sixties. A disconnect of sorts was inevitable. Hofstadter's preoccupation with the privileges of the mind, while the nation teetered on the edge of a cultural revolution, suggests an introspective self-indulgence incongruous with the normally timely introductions of his best work. As a statement of contemporary commentary, the book, he conceded to his editor, had clearly missed the mark.[9]

Hofstadter's emotional involvement in the contest between intellect and egalitarianism transformed *Anti-Intellectualism* into a personal statement that taxed his physical and mental resources. Scholars close to the historian were regaled with grim reports on the book's incessant demands. He described the manuscript to Daniel Boorstin as a useless enterprise, and confessed to C. Vann Woodward that he had to force himself to write. Hofstadter's papers are littered with self-effacing commentary. But these "usual grumps" as Alfred Kazin referred to them — an expression of their author's sardonic sense of humor and innate humility — assumed a more tense and questioning attitude when he was drafting *Anti-Intellectualism.*[10]

Despite Hofstadter's concern for the American mind, the reputation of the postwar intellectual appeared in some quarters to be on the rise. While it is true that more than a few critical thinkers remained estranged from the broader culture, others, disenchanted with Marxism's failure in the West and impressed by the success of the Keynesian economy, were determined to reconcile with their society. And their embrace stood every chance of being returned. An increasingly specialized and knowledge-driven economy desperately required the expertise of the learned class and awarded practical intellect with jobs, commissions, academic positions, and seats on prestigious boards. As Richard Pells notes, "some intellectuals discovered that their talents were useful to the government, the corporations, the foundations, and the military. Economists and social scientists could function as specialists, problem solvers, advisers to policy makers, managers of crises, technicians of preindustrial society." The astonishing change in the intellectual climate caused *Partisan Review* editor Philip Rahv to observe with perhaps as much wonderment as condescension, "We are witnessing a process that might well be described as that of the *embourgeoisement* of the American intelligentsia."[11]

The role of the professional thinker varied in society. Rahv and literary critic Irving Howe secured teaching positions, but their "real" work was done outside the academy. Other scholars — Boorstin comes to mind — were eager to associate their publications with the prevailing anticommunist sentiment and produced books celebrating the particular genius of the American people. Hofstadter tried to steer a middle course, cognizant of his influential position within the historical profession yet convinced that a healthy alienation fine-tuned his critical faculties and yielded a valuable perspective denied scholars attracted to the hum of power. He knew historians who served under presidents — Kennedy advisor Arthur Schlesinger, Jr., and Johnson advisor Eric Goldman — and declared in a letter to Lasch his unwillingness to follow their lead. Hofstadter's reluctance to place himself near or be impressed by the great political personalities of his day underlined his diffident response to Goldman's 1964 invitation to serve on President Johnson's Central Group in Domestic Affairs. While he consented to have his name placed on the Central Group's roster, Hofstadter refused to reschedule a trip to Europe in order to meet with the president, and there is no evidence that he performed any work for Johnson's administration.[12]

Still, temptations in the guise of speaking engagements and book contracts lay all around. Could one simultaneously be alienated from and embraced by the academy? Whether Hofstadter managed to straddle the line between intellectual independence and the demands of academic fame as successfully as he imagined is certainly an open point of debate. It is one of the more interesting paradoxes of his life, though, that Hofstadter's self-image as a man on the margins coexisted with the insider status he enjoyed as his generation's most popular historian. In the parlance of *The American Political Tradition*'s provocative chapter titles, was Hofstadter the "Outsider as Insider" or the "Insider as Outsider?"

*   *   *

Harvey Swados resented Hofstadter's drift toward the liberal center, and it took him years to understand the deep personal dimensions of this journey. "On politics, Harvey and Dick saw things differently," Swados's wife remembers. "Harvey was up for the revolution and Dick wasn't." Hofstadter was, in some sense, an intellectual mentor to Swados — four years his senior, a radical (when they met), and a talented student of American history. When Hofstadter abandoned the Left, the act called into question a set of political and intellectual assumptions that Swados had carried since his teen years. If a part of Swados had yearned for his brother-in-law's approval, Hofstadter's rejection of radical politics would have been a sharp blow — a challenge to Swados's judgment and independence. Their political differences were brought out into the open in the autumn of 1940 after Swados, twenty at the time, informed Hofstadter of his certainty that impending revolutions in the European colonies would soon sweep away both fascism and imperialism. Hofstadter thought this was absurd, a leftist fantasy, and wrote Swados as much. In the same letter he noted that on ideological issues, the two no longer seemed to agree on anything. A friendly analysis of both men's actions might say that Hofstadter's move to the center exhibited maturity and growth while Swados's life-long commitment to the radical politics of his youth demonstrated a certain brave consistency. In any event, a permanent political breach settled over their relationship. It did not appear, however, to have completely soured their friendship — or spirited correspondence — which continued until Hofstadter's death.[13]

C. Wright Mills understood the dynamics of the Hofstadter-Swados situation as well as anyone. A warm friendship that developed between him and Hofstadter at the University of Maryland later cooled off in New York. The nature of their relationship was complex, but it is clear that Mills — like Swados — believed in the potential of radical reform in a way that Hofstadter never could. Stampp noted these differences in politics and personality in his recollection of the men he befriended at College Park in the 1940s. "Mills — I very much enjoyed him, but as a Freudian as well as a Marxist, he was always psychoanalyzing us. . . . We knew that he had a file on us, all of us — his observations about Hofstadter's family, and so on. He was always watching us to make sure that we weren't 'sellouts,' as he put it, that we didn't deviate from his radical party line. He was always suspicious of us, especially Hofstadter, that he was not passionate enough about his political feelings."[14]

Mills's radicalism emerged from a very traditional, very native context, and this may help to explain his uneven relations with Hofstadter. "For an immigrant family, a university career — status, salary, and security — signified unalloyed advance," Russell Jacoby has written. "Herein lies a critical difference between an American and an immigrant experience. Mills recalled a family past — his grandparents — of independent ranchers. Whether this was fact or fiction hardly matters, for it shaped a vision of self and world: life as an employee in an office — university, government, or publishing — did not measure up no matter the title, money, or respect." Mills, in other words, was not bred for the white-collar world he condemned in his scholarship. But Hofstadter was. For both him and his sister, education and the professions were symbols of respected social mobility and deep family pride. Hofstadter was committed from an early age to using his mind to make a living, while Mills, despite remarkable success as a popular sociologist, prized his ability to work with his hands. He built his motorcycle at a BMW factory in Germany, experimented with gardening, and displayed an unusually deft talent for photography and artisanship. In sum, Mills adopted an identity outside of his profession. He cherished his rocky relationship with the sociology department at Columbia and escaped campus commitments by living in West Nyack. Hofstadter, by contrast, emerged as a central figure in the Claremont Avenue complex that served as an important gathering place for Morningside faculty.[15]

Mills's long history with both Hofstadter (1942–62) and Swados offered him a unique perspective on the relationship between the two men, whose lives were clearly going in opposite directions politically and socially. "You keep saying you don't understand Dick," Mills wrote Swados in the late fifties,

> but of course you must, only you don't want to accept it. The brutal fact so far as his attitude with you is concerned is this: he really and truly does not give a damn what you think of him or what he does. . . . For he has achieved, with much pain in the process, but he *has* achieved a new "reference group" for his own self-image. And you are not in it. You are part of an old group — one in which he was overshadowed among friends and enemies by your sister. He wishes to forget all that and the fact is he has, he really has.[16]

Swados did not let the matter go quietly. In his contentious 1956 essay, "Be Happy, Go Liberal," he drew sharp distinctions between unrepentant radicals and their liberal protagonists, offering in the process a pointed criticism of Hofstadter's intellectual choices.

> There has been in recent years an increasing tendency on the part of certain of my contemporaries (roughly, those who were undergraduates in the Thirties) to regard international communism as one vast scheme designed solely to make them look ridiculous. Let those of us . . . who are going to be grappling with . . . radical problems in the years to come proudly call ourselves radicals, and leave the word liberal to those who claim possession of it but warp its militant tradition to fit a passive literary pattern of fashionable nuances which serve only to conceal their own utter emptiness and prostration before the status quo.[17]

Located between the ideological poles occupied by Swados and, say, Boorstin were men like Trilling, Bell, Niebuhr, and Hofstadter, too skeptical to fully embrace the democratic state, yet maneuvered by the recent past into a wary acceptance of the liberal "status quo." These men, Pells concludes with less heat than Swados did, were "no longer rebels or revolutionaries, they took refuge in ironic observation, ambivalent commentary, and occasional dissent. Perhaps given the times, little more could be demanded or achieved."[18]

Many postwar intellectuals had abandoned their youthful radicalism in order to advance what they believed to be a more constructive liberalism. But finding a political leader adept at melding liberal reform with cold war needs proved difficult. While some prominent thinkers shared Arthur Schlesinger, Jr.'s belief that the Kennedy presidency encouraged a rapprochement between government and intellect, Hofstadter hesitated, suspecting that JFK was a shallow playboy, a product of money and influence over substance. The Kennedy administration's disastrous attempt to invade Cuba in the spring of 1961 hardened this impression and reinforced Hofstadter's concern for the immediate future of the political center. In a letter to Stampp, he denounced the president's Cuba policy, insisting that it was impossible for liberals to have any politics at all as long as men like JFK represented the liberal consensus. Hofstadter's alienation is curious. That he, a self-professed liberal, should describe himself as politically alienated in an era dominated by liberal politics suggests that his need for playing the role of critic and oppositionist was a deeply ingrained part of his character that went beyond simple political choices. It speaks as well to his near obsessive concern that the Right would exploit any sign of weakness on the part of the political center.[19]

In the wake of McCarthyism and Adlai Stevenson's rejection by the American public, *Anti-Intellectualism* raised serious questions about the nature and function of popular government. "In retrospect," one colleague wrote Hofstadter, "I wonder if what you are objecting to is not so much anti-intellectualism as democracy itself. . . . What I think we are both troubled about here, basically, is not anti-intellectualism per se, but that democracy has necessarily anti-intellectual overtones, which cannot be curbed under our peculiar system of society." Hofstadter, in other words, was fighting a losing battle. *Anti-Intellectualism,* he confided to William Leuchtenburg, was the only book that grew cold on him.[20]

The intensely personal nature of the project may have had something to do with Hofstadter's difficulties. The opening essay, "Anti-Intellectualism in Our Time" — a gloss of the 1952 election — initiated an autobiographical theme that its author hewed to throughout the text. While working for the first Stevenson campaign at Columbia, Hofstadter seemed to believe that the fate of postwar liberalism hinged on the election's outcome, and writing about the event several years later stirred up powerful feelings. Stevenson is described as an unusually capable and sensitive thinker, while Eisenhower is dismissed as a mental midget with a plebeian weakness for golf, football, and Zane Grey novels. The campaign, Hofstadter believed, offered Americans an excellent opportunity to discharge their instinctive resentment of critical thinkers through political punishment. With national culture informed by the overweening egalitarianism of the radical Right, he wrote, the urbane Stevenson had no chance.[21]

It is fair to ask, however, if any candidate, perceived as an intellectual or not, could have defeated the hugely popular Eisenhower in 1952. Hofstadter clearly oversimplified the election on this score and barely even mentioned the Korean War (which does not merit a citation in the book's index), surely a more significant campaign issue than Stevenson's impressive mind. Perhaps the most revealing aspect of the 1952 contest, and one that threw cold water on the intellectuals' preferred self-image, was the way that liberalism had moved toward the center. Despite Hofstadter's characterization, Stevenson was not an intellectual, nor was he particularly progressive. He had, after all, accepted the segregationist Alabama senator John Sparkman as his running mate.

Hofstadter believed that the populism of the 1950s served as a depressing link to the agrarian anti-intellectualism of the past. In the early republic, Jacksonians created a secular theocracy, enshrining the yeoman farmer while denouncing symbols of elite authority, including the National Bank and the Supreme Court. But the age of the common man proved fleeting, as dynamic growth produced a complex society in need of experts, and in more recent times intellectuals assumed a more visible and confident profile. Brain trusters were welcomed in Washington to run New Deal programs while the hot and cold wars of the forties and fifties produced the Office of Strategic Services, the CIA, and the Rand Corporation — agencies that dealt with extremely complex issues beyond the grasp of ordinary Americans. The intellectual's growing reputation among his fellow citizens, however, proved short-lived. Kennedy's respect for the mind stressed style over substance, while the loss of capital and social control by nonspecialists, Hofstadter argued, aroused powerful feelings of envy, anxiety, and resentment.

Even on college campuses. Ironically, the forces of anti-intellectualism and ethnic prejudice could be found rather easily in the postwar academic scene — and this included Morningside Heights. "From my first day on the Columbia campus," Mark Naison remembered of his 1962 arrival, "I realized I had underestimated the university's traditionalism and exaggerated its avant-garde spirit. . . . The school's atmosphere was assimilationist and democratic. The Columbia man, whatever his background, was expected to learn the poise and emotional control of an upper-class Anglo-Saxon." In practice, cultural cleavages had a way of hardening into intellectual divisions. While the days of Jewish student quotas at the major universities had passed, Anglo-ethnic differences in historical methodology — evidenced in Wisconsin's devotion to Progressive historiography and Columbia's commitment to the social sciences — were clearly marked. "Although middle and even working-class recruits increasingly broke down the old patrician hold on the profession during the twenties and thirties," one observer has noted, "they found history less congenial than the newer social sciences. This was particularly true of Jewish scholars. For years, Selig Perlman, a professor of economics at Wisconsin, used to summon Jewish graduate students in history and warn then in a deep Yiddish accent: 'History belongs to the Anglo-Saxons. You belong in economics or sociology.'"[22]

Postwar concerns over the increasingly ethnic influence in the academy demonstrated that the American historical profession stood on the precipice of a great transformation. And the old guard did not defer without a struggle. In December 1962, as Hofstadter put the finishing touches on *Anti-Intellectualism,* Brown University historian Carl Bridenbaugh delivered a presidential address to the American Historical Association assailing the social scientific history written by scholars coming from ethnic backgrounds. As the profession moved away from its Yankee, literary roots, Bridenbaugh believed, the studies it produced became increasingly devoid of an intrinsically humanistic quality. His distress over the decline of traditional narratives broadened into a wistful longing for a passing America, the one nostalgically recalled in his address: "My childhood (a happy one and 'secure') was spent on the suburban periphery of . . . Philadelphia. . . . Although I attended city schools, on Saturdays and vacations I ranged the fields together with other boys, gathered and sold chestnuts, fished and trapped muskrats along the banks of a broad creek . . . and many summers were spent on my uncle's dairy farm in central Pennsylvania." Presumably, close contact to the agrarian paraphernalia of farms, fields, and frontiers (à la Turner) produced the necessary qualities for scholarly enterprise.[23]

Bridenbaugh agreed with *The Age of Reform*'s observation that "the United States was born in the country and has moved to the city," but he rued the coming *gesellschaft.* "It is indubitably true that physically and economically the old, comparatively stable rural society has been transformed into an unstable, urban, industrial society." He declared that the loss of ethnic homogeneity undermined national cohesiveness and produced historians lacking a fundamental sympathy or identity with the nation's traditional political, cultural, and religious institutions. "Today," he noted, "we must face the discouraging prospect that we all, teachers and pupils alike, have lost much of what [earlier generations] possessed, the priceless asset of a shared culture. . . . Furthermore, many of the younger practitioners of our craft, and those who are still apprentices, are products of lower middle-class or foreign origins, and their emotions not infrequently get in the way of historical reconstructions. They feel themselves in a very real sense outsiders on our past and feel themselves shut out." Bridenbaugh's profile of the new historical consciousness clearly applied to Hofstadter, a product of "lower middle-class or foreign origins" who employed social-scientific insights to overthrow the methodological practices favored by an earlier generation of scholars. Bridenbaugh interpreted the prewar, Progressive, gentile tradition of historical writing as fundamentally literary, humanistic and uplifting. The contemporary influence of the psychologist and the sociologist, he complained, encouraged historians to fill their monographs with "mere technical data" building into "a sort of mental cholesterol." The practitioners of the new history, he sharply concluded, failed to live up to the true ideals of the profession: "The finest historian will not be those who succumb to the dehumanizing methods of social sciences."[24]

*　　*　　*

Anti-Intellectualism presents a series of separate but interlinking essays on religious life, politics, business culture, and education. On the first, Hofstadter enumerated the "evangelical spirit"—the emotional side of American Protestantism—as illustrative of popular religion's gross disdain for intellect. If faith and the "heart" were sources of salvation, the skeptical mind was by definition sinful. Men of ideas governed the early New England plantations, but successive waves of Awakenings broke the reign of the learned clergy, preparing the ground for a hyperemotional style of religious expression. Anti-intellectualism mixed with millenarianism, Hofstadter asserted, and introduced the American fetish for conspiracy. God and country, individualism and Anglo-Saxonism were amalgamated—to question one was to oppose all. The celebration of exuberance, traditional folkways, and intuition at the expense of pluralism, cosmopolitanism, and intellect convinced Hofstadter that the modern culture war ignited in France by the Dreyfusards had now come to America. In the 1920s, Darwinism stood as the supreme evil of its day. And now it was "atheistic" communism. Fundamentalists once carried the cross for prohibition and antievolutionary laws, but in the age of ideology evangelicals responded to the complexities and uncertainties of postwar life by supporting McCarthyites, John Birchers, and Minutemen. Theirs was a revolt — and a religion — of reaction.[25]

There were, of course, political dimensions to American anti-intellectualism that stood apart from religious exuberance. Thomas Jefferson suffered under the pen of opponents who labeled the Virginian an impractical philosopher and trivialized his intellectual endeavors. To Hofstadter, this foreshadowed Stevenson's shabby treatment by the electorate and was emblematic of a perpetual suspicion of elite rule in a republic. This leveling spirit offended Hofstadter, for it tended to reinforce common passions and provoke deeply rooted prejudices. He lamented the "aristocratic" John Quincy Adams's loss of the presidency to the "democratic" Andrew Jackson as a painful symbol of the popular mind's successful assault on political talent. Arthur Schlesinger, Jr., had exalted the perspicacity of the people in *The Age of Jackson*, but Hofstadter's sympathies went instinctively to the highborn heretics and refugees of nineteenth-century democracy.

The Civil War tore apart the old Jacksonian coalition, but the new political masters in the Republican camp proved equally hostile to intellectual privilege. Strangers among their countrymen, discriminating minds lived in the shadows of the Gilded Age plutocrats or opted for an uncertain future as expatriates in European salons. Brahmin attempts to restore elite rule through civil service reform (the encouragement of expertise at the expense of patronage) frightened Americans unaccustomed to competency examinations and the meritocracy of intellect they implied. Only to Theodore Roosevelt, a Harvard "dude" equally comfortable with patricians and cowboys, did Progressives defer. Roosevelt's popularity briefly upgraded the image of the critical class, and in the name of saving the American competitive system from the trusts, he and Woodrow Wilson — a former university president — called upon the experts to preserve democracy.

Hofstadter denounced the Progressives' practical use of intellect, for in making its resources available to the state, the university sacrificed serious theoretical work for a watered-down curriculum featuring courses on citizenship and administration. The reformers' highly selective embrace of the expert followed a dismally familiar pattern. Intellectuals typically functioned under closely guarded or even oppressive conditions. Yet in times of domestic crisis — the Founding era, Progressive period, New Deal — gifted minds were allowed far greater latitude by a nation desperate for innovative solutions. During the Depression, Hofstadter noted, an unprecedented peace between the intellectuals and the public was made as the people accepted, in fact demanded, vigorous experimentation and allowed specialists to devise and administer relief agencies. For its part, intellect won a significant public relations victory by associating its talents and efforts with the great popular crusade to salvage the American economy. The president's circle of advisors included Columbia University scholars Raymond Moley, Rexford Guy Tugwell, and Adolf Berle, and optimists might be excused for thinking that a permanent bridge had been built between academics and the broader culture. But the bond did not last. The renewed opposition to intellect by the radical Right — most flagrantly exhibited in the loyalty oath preoccupation on college campuses — stunned the professors who saw McCarthyism as a depressing coda to the gains of the thirties. For those in search of historical parallels, Stevenson's loss to General Eisenhower brought to mind Adams's loss to General Jackson. The public's preference for men of action over intellect, it seemed, had never been more secure.[26]

The historically problematic relationship between critical and political classes anticipated the workers' revolt against intellectual privilege. Unions, Hofstadter declared, promoted practical agendas that emphasized winning short-term benefits rather than pushing for a radical overhaul of the industrial system. This limited vision completely contradicted the goals of the intellectuals. They looked upon organized labor as the means to socialism and social justice, and concurrently had little respect for the middle-class aspirations of most workers.[27] Pragmatic labor officials, including the powerful Samuel Gompers, were not ideologically opposed to capitalism, and aspired to the kind of white-collar propriety enjoyed by the bourgeoisie. By agreeing with the industrial barons' emphasis on practical gains over industrial experimentation, the guilds affirmed their faith in the established economic caste and those who ran it.

Anti-Intellectualism is typically regarded by historians as a reaction to the fierce anticommunism that followed the Second World War. This assessment fails, however, to explain the study's profound debt to the ideological struggles that shaped the thirties. In criticizing the cult of proletarianism — the urban equivalent of the yeoman myth — Hofstadter wrote energetically for the protection of the intellectual from the *left*. He detested party hacks and loathed demands upon the learned class to bow before the moral superiority of the working class. Hofstadter defended a separate sphere for creative thinkers, for he had no confidence in the Right (memories of Curly Byrd's University of Maryland) or Left (the polemical one-idea men defending Stalin) to champion intellect. Both political poles united in a common hostility for the social critic, and Hofstadter's evolving political sentiments came to rest in the fifties on the belief that only liberalism could nurture and defend a certain set of values consistent with intellectual freedom and cultural latitude.

Hofstadter's commitment to academic freedom piqued his long-standing interest in the politics of pedagogy, and he devoted a long section in *Anti-Intellectualism* to scrutinizing the influence of democracy in the schools. It is not an uplifting tale. Progressive education's child-centered approach, he protested, led to junk course offerings, a curriculum of self-actualization, and a culture of sports and socializing that neglected gifted children. There may have been a personal dynamic to Hofstadter's low opinion of public education. He complained to a colleague in 1951 that his son Dan struggled in school because of the content-weak progressive educational curriculum favored by New York's public system. Both Dan and his younger sister Sarah would attend private institutions in the city.[28]

In the course of defending an intellectually serious curriculum, Hofstadter unleashed a blistering attack on the egalitarian goals of the educationists that brings to mind contemporary opposition to "political correctness." "When they see a chance to introduce a new course in family living or home economics, they begin to tune the fiddles of their idealism. When they feel they are about to establish the school janitor's right to be treated with respect, they grow starry-eyed and increase their tempo. And when they are trying to assure that the location of the school toilets will be so clearly marked that the dullest child can find them, they grow dizzy with exaltation and launch into wild cadenzas about democracy and self-realization." Hofstadter put a human face on the new education, declaring that John Dewey's Progressive pedagogical theories exalting child-centered experiences over content-centered learning had greatly harmed American schools. Dewey was no anti-intellectual, Hofstadter hastened to note, but his passion for democracy in the classroom compromised the best features of the curriculum.

Rather than equip a rising immigrant class with coursework designed to promote personal autonomy through the mastery of critical thinking skills, Dewey stressed public education as a means to acculturate the new citizens into the mainstream of American life. "It is not difficult to understand the belief that a thorough grounding in Latin was not a primary need, say, of a Polish immigrant's child in Buffalo," Hofstadter noted in an autobiographical reference.[29]

The nativist undercurrent in Progressivism crippled its efforts in the classroom. The rural-urban, prohibition-wet, fundamentalism-secular divisions of Dewey's day emphasized the dangers of permitting purely speculative education to compete with more pragmatic (i.e., native) models. Rather than maintain rigorous intellectual expectations, educators became social welfare facilitators championing bottom-rung egalitarianism that prized consensus at the price of academic excellence. The quasi-religious underpinnings of the child-centered faith distressed Hofstadter, and he saw in the moral expectations of Progressive pedagogy the frightening shadow of educational fundamentalism.

*   *   *

Anti-Intellectualism won the Pulitzer Prize in the inaugural general nonfiction category and to this day remains among Hofstadter's most recognized works. It was an immediate success in the literary community, a must-read for scholars that won a substantial audience outside the academy. But this did not guarantee a warm welcome among historians. C. Vann Woodward again surfaced as a private critic, believing that Hofstadter's imprecise use of religious fundamentalism tipped the game in favor of the cosmopolitans.

> You . . . refer to "the one-hundred percent mentality"—and here I am not clear whether you are talking about the fundamentalist, the far right, or both, or whether you have shifted categories. Anyway, you say it is not only anti-intellectual but then you let go with both barrels: millennial, apocalyptic, puritanical, cynical, nationalistic, quasi-fascist, anti-foreign, anti-Semitic, anti-statist, anti-Communist, anti-liberal. Now I think you can make a case that the present-day fundamentalists, or some of them, are guilty of some of these charges, though I think you have been much more circumspect and cautious in charging this and other classes with anti-intellectualism. . . . Dick, you just can't do this. No amount of Adorno, Stouffer, Hartley, etc. will sustain it.[30]

Woodward's allusion to the Frankfurt School supported his contention that the interpretive insights promoted by the social sciences were less useful to historians than their proponents claimed. Moreover, his own intellectual heritage — southern, progressive, evangelical — suffered under the critical eye of liberal cosmopolitanism, and he hastened to defend his culture.

More public challenges were on the way. Writing in the *American Historical Review,* Arthur Bestor suggested that Hofstadter was overwhelmed by the topic, unpersuasively cramming a vast and slippery body of material into an ill-defined model of anti-intellectual activity. "What, then, is the essential subject matter of this study?" he complained. "Is it a history of the changing status and repute of the intellectual class in America? Or the history of a body of ideas? Or the history of a psychological state, compounded of suspicion and hostility? In the present book Hofstadter nowhere faces these questions." Rush Welter echoed Bestor's concerns, remarking in the *Journal of American History,* "If antagonism toward the life of the mind or toward given groups of 'intellectuals' has been prominent in American life, focusing on it as a distinct phenomenon tends nevertheless to exaggerate its importance. What Hofstadter examines was not a national commitment so much as a cluster of expressions and activities that may or may not have held the same meaning for all the men who engaged in them."[31]

Kenneth S. Lynn's penetrating review in the *Reporter* characterized both *Anti-Intellectualism* and its author's earlier studies as distressing examples of "elitism on the left." Hofstadter's work, Lynn maintained, belittled the "masses"—a task, he noted, traditionally carried out by the political Right. "For the past fifteen years Hofstadter's writings have largely consisted of an assault, steadily intensifying in severity and widening in scope, on the main historical assumptions of American liberalism." As a modern-day Mencken, Hofstadter carefully targeted "the main enemies of the American mind . . . populist democracy, the business mentality, and evangelical Protestantism — the very same unholy trinity that was described some forty years ago as Bryanism, Babbittry, and the Bible Belt."[32] What, Lynn asked, separated the "liberal" Hofstadter from the Tory champions of high culture and the ultraaesthetic advocates of the life of the mind?

Another sharp appraisal of *Anti-Intellectualism* came from an unsympathetic Daniel Boorstin. In a *Saturday Review* essay, the University of Chicago historian discounted Hofstadter's claim that the thinking class was in any sense a marginal class. "The truth is," Boorstin explained, "the

American intellectual today . . . belongs everywhere. As never before, he is welcomed in industry and in government."[33] Under the guise of cultural criticism, he continued, Hofstadter had attacked the nation's pragmatic practices while defending special privileges for intellect. Ignoring the abuse of academic freedom recently endured by scholars and the questionable coopting of mental talent to serve in the ranks of the cold war state, Boorstin emphasized accommodation rather than alienation as the central theme of contemporary intellectual life. His analysis drew attention to the fact that in the postwar period universities grew at a rate never before equaled in the history of American higher education; government lavishly funded elite institutions; and the academic job market remained impressively abundant. In measurements of physical expansion, influence, morale, and status, it was the golden age of academeme and, while Boorstin did not say so in his review, Hofstadter enjoyed its most exclusive privileges. Invitations to lecture overseas (Salzburg, London, Cambridge), generous stipends to produce reports for major foundations (the Fund for the Republic), an endowed chair at a prestigious university, requests from publishing houses, journals, and magazines to contribute essays and books, and board membership on influential organizations, including the American Committee for Cultural Freedom, were as much a part of Hofstadter's academic world as unfriendly encounters with the enemies of intellect.

Too much a product of the ideological skirmishes of the fifties to strike a truly balanced tone, *Anti-Intellectualism,* Paula Fass has written, "although occasionally brilliant, elegantly written and always interesting . . . was not really successful as history or as social commentary." Hofstadter understood this better than anyone. He described the book to Eric McKitrick as an exercise in self-exposure that failed to turn out as he intended. *Anti-Intellectualism,* he concluded, had written him more than he had written it.[34]

As the social crusades of the sixties got underway, Hofstadter recognized that the philistines on the right had company on the left. This discovery, reinforced by Columbia's near meltdown in the spring of 1968, brought him no joy. If anything, it demonstrated that intellect had even more enemies than he had imagined. Temperamentally and politically predisposed to question the nature of popular power, Hofstadter *needed* to write *Anti-Intellectualism* in order to make sense of American life in the postwar decades. It invoked the spirit of liberal skepticism and embraced the philosophy that the mind has certain needs that can never be fully appreciated — and thus fully protected — by the majority. In the end, this shadow autobiography reveals as much about its author as the society he dissects.

To dismiss Hofstadter's preoccupation with anti-intellectualism as something of a private fetish, however, would be wrong. In our own time, opposition to expertise has found a convenient touchstone in the figure of George W. Bush — described by the *Manchester Guardian* as "aggressively anti-intellectual." His presidency has resurrected the sharp division in American life between East and West, aristocracy and democracy, culture and common. Bush's constituency celebrates the president's reputation as an action-driven man, judiciously incurious about the rest of the world and drawn to make immediate "feel" decisions rather than reflective "cerebral" decisions. Correct or not, "W" claims the frontier legacies of Jackson ("Old Hickory"), Lincoln (the "Rail Splitter"), and Reagan ("The Gipper") as his own. The fact that Americans frequently handicap their presidential races as contests between the simple and the sublime touches upon a deep and powerful need within the nation's psyche. As described by Hofstadter, anti-intellectualism is the raw meat that pacifies the popular American palate.[35]

* 7 *

The Paranoid Mind

> America was the perfect subject for history. It condensed so
> much into two centuries that here was man already "in sight
> of his own end" and fascinated by his capacity for self-
> destruction. This was a comfortable thought for the
> gloomily skeptical humorist in Hofstadter. . . . The crazily
> promising yet undependable American scene gripped him
> absolutely.
>
> ALFRED KAZIN, 1978

Richard Hofstadter's scholarship offered a unique perspective into the
power of irrational politics to shape a nation. Sensitive to the firebrands
lurking on the ideological periphery, he noticed, even among the established leaders of the two-party consensus, a perpetual tilt toward political buffoonery that greased the skids of popular democracy. Toothy and
cartoonish Theodore Roosevelt stood supreme before a too easily impressed public; the empty-suited Warren G. Harding perfected the
stump speaker's talent for "spout[ing] alliterative bilge like a geyser;"
and poor Barry Goldwater's efforts to roll back the twentieth-century
welfare state earned him the unflattering sobriquet "political Grandma
Moses."[1]

Hofstadter specialized in the telling phrase, a talent for lively suggestion that cut to the heart of the matter in a few well-placed strokes. The
quality and depth of his thinking, Alfred Kazin wrote, "is an extraordinary *grace* — and makes up for anything — Amazingly adroit and *elegant*
mind." Nimble and deliberate, his thoughts moved rapidly over a wide
range of items that mixed play with purpose and blurred the line between satirical and serious. Pulitzers and professorships were balanced
by a love of Ping-Pong, bodysurfing, and mimicking everything from
presidents and dairy cows to the characters in the bedtime stories that
he read to his children. As a historian, one colleague noted, "Hofstadter
was aware of his talents — he knew that he was good," but there was
something common, sympathetic, and attractive — an absence of self-
entitlement — at his core. "I cannot say that knowing him improved

my character or changed my ideas," Irving Howe wrote of Hofstadter. "What it did was to ease my judgements and perceptions opening me to ranges of feeling I had previously not allowed myself. Perhaps it made me a little bit gentler. I suppose I'm trying to evoke a quality that can be called liberalism of spirit, a quality that seemed intrinsic to Dick Hofstadter even though I knew that with him, as with everyone else, it had to be learned."[2]

Cheerful, even-tempered, and mild-mannered, Hofstadter avoided open conflict but eagerly lampooned the self-important and the ridiculous. He excelled at pointed poetry and took a devilish delight roasting the older generation of southern historians (U. B. Phillips, E. M. Coulter, and David Potter) for the private amusement of his friend Kenneth Stampp — a member of the younger generation of historians writing on the South. A year as the Pitt Professor of American Institutions at Cambridge (1958–59) provided more targets — the aging masters, bland cuisine, and trivial traditions — at which to poke fun. "At times," wrote one interviewer, Hofstadter "fantasizes writing about each of the Presidents in a verse form dominant in his time. 'I think I can do George Washington in heroic couplet,' he muses, 'but it would be very difficult to write about FDR in the style of E. E. Cummings.'"[3]

Alert to the playful pitch of language and to the extraordinarily broad range of political attitudes that shaped American life, Hofstadter's suspicion of popular moods encouraged his interest in the "irrationality" of charismatic leaders and their constituencies. As a pluralist, he rejected the strident anticommunism that dominated public culture in the fifties and hoped the sixties might reinvigorate the "New Departure" of the New Deal. Some scholars believed, however, that Hofstadter's failure to take seriously the concerns and resentments of the Right pointed to an impartial and coldhearted analysis that tilted toward a cliché — liberal elitism. In a 1970 study of historical methodology, David Hackett Fischer accused Hofstadter of committing the *apathetic fallacy* — "treating living creatures as though they were inanimate." The error is made, Fischer argued,

> when historians are unable to empathize sufficiently with specific human subjects. Consider, for example, Richard Hofstadter's collection of essays, published as *The Paranoid Style in American Politics*. William Buckley has protested that, in the work of Hofstadter, moderate liberalism is analyzed, but radical conservatism is diagnosed. The complaint, I think, is fairly made. The thought of Barry Goldwater is no more paranoid than

the thought of Hofstadter. If Goldwater's conservatism is "fundamentalist," what shall we say of a scholar who regards other peoples' ideologies as symptoms of a personality disorder.[4]

Fischer's observations were among a number of criticisms directed at Hofstadter over the years. The status thesis brilliantly illuminated psychological sources of conflict, but *The Age of Reform*'s highly imaginative journey through the mental wreckage of Populism bothered some historians. The caveats forced Hofstadter to engage in a protracted defense of his work, a task for which he was temperamentally ill suited. His mind sparkled in a spirit of expansiveness, and while he often overplayed his insights (a creative strategy he openly acknowledged), it would be difficult to overestimate his importance as an intellectual pioneer. Leaving others to mine the libraries to verify or shake his more controversial ideas, Hofstadter aroused a certain degree of jealousy among traditionalists or, as he called them, "archive rats." Historian David Shannon wrote privately of *The Age of Reform*, "Just how much in evaluating a person's motives can we attribute to such things as anxiety over status? The idea of a status revolution is, it seems to me, useful. But . . . it is not what the sociologists are supposed to do, as I've always understood what they're supposed to do. This is not science; this is an example of what an intelligent person can do sitting in an arm chair."[5]

Forrest McDonald went public with his criticism. In a 1965 letter published in the *American Historical Review* he wrote, "May I respectfully suggest that Professor Hofstadter—who has given us a host of brilliant *interpretive* works — may be somewhat out of contact with the new breed of younger historians, those who for the past ten years or so have been doing the grubby, tedious work of digging up data and turning out the monographs." This kind of criticism meant little to Hofstadter. He understood that deduction, synthesis, and irony too nourished the historical imagination. Good, *exciting* history, after all, was something more than a dry recitation of names, dates, and facts. He allowed to a colleague, in what stands as a succinct reply to his critics, that the historical profession needed imaginative thinking more than it needed legions of historians stumbling about in distant archives.[6]

Hofstadter could afford at this point in his career to cultivate a certain autonomy from the academy. By the sixties, the sales of his books were a steady and handsome source of revenue. This monetary turnaround was quite an unexpected blessing for a scholar who once used grant money to pay the grocery bill and borrowed from his sister to finance back surgery. Hofstadter's salary in the late 1940s hovered below $5,000 (about $40,000 in today's dollars), much less, he complained to colleagues, than what he needed to live in Manhattan during the terrific price hike that followed the Second World War. As junior faculty, he worried that his monetary needs carried little weight at Columbia and that he might be eased out of the university on purely financial grounds. The prospect of a job at the University of California—more money but a radical change in lifestyle—forced Hofstadter to seriously consider leaving New York. He wrote Merle Curti of his disinclination to go to the West Coast, noting that Columbia pleased him in every respect— except financially. Did Curti know of any way a young historian could pick up extra cash?[7]

The 1948 publication of *The American Political Tradition* secured Hofstadter's place at Columbia, but the book was not an immediate financial success. Responding to its author's disappointment, Knopf editor Harold Strauss advised Hofstadter to concentrate on more reader-friendly projects in the future. "I think you are unduly pessimistic about the state of the book market and the potential salability of other books you may do. You must not judge the sales possibilities of your future books by the sales of THE AMERICAN POLITICAL TRADITION unless you persist in adhering to the essay form." Today, more than a half century after its publication, this book still sells about 10,000 copies annually. In its first year in print, however, it actually *cost* Hofstadter money. "I'm glad to see the book has earned [you] $640.54" in that period, Strauss wrote. "But counting purchases, author's alterations, and stylistic changes, you are still way in the hole to us to the tune of $1,075.32."[8]

In time, of course, *The American Political Tradition* became a major seller, and its author soon discovered other remunerative projects. A 1953 textbook deal with Prentice-Hall—a collaboration with friends Daniel Aaron and William Miller—proved to be a particularly good financial decision. There was one delicate issue—Alfred Knopf. Hofstadter was deeply involved in the writing of *The Age of Reform,* and the textbook threatened to divide his time. In a letter to Knopf, Hofstadter pointed out that his contract with the house did not literally prevent his coauthoring a textbook with a competing publisher. He obviously wanted Knopf's approval, however, and stressed both his desire to work with friends and his slight role in the project—only 50,000 words, and the more considerable use of his name. Hofstadter assured Knopf that he did not wish to jeopardize their relationship, but was eager to enter the textbook market under such favorable circumstances. Knopf put up no resistance, and *The United States: The History of a Republic* was published in 1957.[9]

By the midsixties, Hofstadter had several brisk sellers with Knopf, including *The American Political Tradition* (15,690 hardback sales, 401,000 paper, through 1965), *The Age of Reform* (9,453 hardback sales, 94,000 paper, through 1965), and *Anti-Intellectualism in American Life* (13,190 hardback sales through 1965). In what turned out to be his final Knopf contract, he agreed in 1970 to write a three-volume history of American political culture for $90,000 per volume — $425,000 per volume in today's dollars. He stood to collect $15,000 a year for seventeen years. Some at Knopf questioned the steep price, but inflation, an in-house memo noted, reduced the publisher's financial commitment each year of the contract.[10]

How did Hofstadter spend his money? The maintenance of an Upper West Side apartment and a summer home on Cape Cod were obviously two major investments; and his children attended private schools in Manhattan before matriculating to Columbia (Dan) and Princeton (Sarah). Hofstadter loved traveling, though his opportunities were limited during the first half of his life by financial considerations, an early marriage, graduate school, and beginning a career. Not until his thirties did he journey west of the Ohio River or set foot in Europe. In the fifties, however, he enjoyed long stretches of time in England and the continent — they provided a welcome break from the academic grind at home and connected him to a group of British scholars, including Jack Pole and J. H. Plumb, with whom he maintained a correspondence. Hofstadter appreciated art and, with his wife, acquired a modest collection of nineteenth-century American paintings. He was not tight with his finances, but aside from books, good wines, and travel, he had no expensive personal habits and spent little on himself. Julian Franklin, a colleague in the Columbia political science department, believed that Hofstadter's inattention to fashion (aside from the slight affectation of a beret and bow tie) might have been a response to the Depression years. "He never was a fancy dresser. I suspect that it had something to do with what all of us felt who had anything of the thirties. You had no right to finery."[11]

*   *   *

Discussing Hofstadter's financial fortunes is really just another way of measuring his success as a popular writer. As an intellectual symbol of his generation's rendezvous with the liberal zeitgeist, Hofstadter discovered a sympathetic audience for his books in postwar America. His use of the status thesis as an explanatory hypothesis, however, produced a mixed response from the academy. Caught off guard by the intensity of the debate, he began in the early sixties to reevaluate his relationship with the social sciences. It was an act of preservation. "Whatever should happen to his idea," two commentators have noted, "... he strongly believed that room should be [made] for *some* analytical category in which to take account of political behavior not directly oriented to the satisfaction of specific rational interests — and meanwhile he did not want this one too hastily thrown out." In 1963, Hofstadter produced two important essays that addressed Populism and Progressivism with more circumspection and sympathy than *The Age of Reform* had allowed. His introduction to *The Progressive Movement* included not a single word on the status aspirations of the reformers, designating rather, economic hardship as the crucial theme of the era. "The farmers, whose products had not only fed the expanding national working force but had also paid for much of the foreign capital that financed American industrialization," he concluded, "had received pathetic returns for their toils."[12]

A second, more ambitious piece introduced a republished edition of the monetary crusader William H. Harvey's *Coin's Financial School*. Hofstadter's essay, "Free Silver and the Mind of 'Coin' Harvey," criticized Populist efforts to raise crop prices by radically inflating the money supply through the coinage of "free silver." He conceded, however, that the issue attracted a wide and diverse audience beyond the farming states, declaring that Harvey's book was "a basic expression of the American popular imagination." The idea of a bimetallic economy — pairing silver with gold — was not unique to agrarians, but rather reflected "a rough popular version of a view of the matter taken by many more sophisticated contemporaries in the United States and Europe, among them distinguished economists and statesmen." What is more, Hofstadter played up the commercial crisis that radicalized the inflationists, and called for a sympathetic appraisal of their misery. "One can readily understand the fury of the inflationists, after years of deflationary monetary decisions, at being told that their proposals to raise prices were unwarranted and dishonest efforts to interfere with the course of nature. The gold advocates had taken it upon themselves to define the terms of the controversy in such a way as to make it impossible for them to be wrong."[13] By reversing his earlier emphasis on Populism's parochial character, Hofstadter both enlarged and legitimized the free silver cause. It, he now insisted, had occupied a central rather than extreme position in American political life.

Woodward thought the essay a more fair treatment of Populism than Hofstadter had produced in the past, though he believed its generous attention to Harvey's anti-Semitism skewed the overall effect. "You manage a tone of gentleness without being too patronizing," he complimented Hofstadter. "I think you maintain this tone with great balance and judiciousness until you reach the subject of anti-Semitism and there it seems to me you are inclined to bear down pretty hard on the old boy." Despite this gentle admonishment, Hofstadter's early sixties essays on popular movements pointed to a more generous reading of the history of American agrarianism than can be found in *The Age of Reform*. A decade of stiff criticism made Hofstadter sensitive to the professional consequences of his work; still he knew that he was on to something important and had no wish to deny the substantial historical gains to be gleaned by the study of "the politics of the irrational."[14]

Too, Hofstadter's interest in Populism was never more than glancing. Whatever connections may have existed between agrarian radicalism and McCarthyism no longer seemed intellectually relevant in a post-McCarthy age. Rather, a new New Right, born and bred in the nation's Sun Belt, forced a fresh appraisal of the conservative movement in America. And no one saw it coming. Among liberals it was taken for granted that the New Deal had swamped the older conservatism, encouraging its recasting as an impotent, even illegitimate ideology. Lionel Trilling's famous midcentury quip — "In the United States at this time liberalism is not only the dominant but even the sole intellectual tradition"—is updated in Dorothy Ross's observation that among Hofstadter's graduate students "our perception was very much that the liberals had won. There was nothing much to read on a conservative mind. There were conservatives around but they had no mind."[15]

In our own day, Right-bashing is still a treat for liberals. Corporate energy boosters, neoconservative imperialists, and fundamentalist holy rollers have formed a mongrel coalition ripe for caricature. But exaggeration aside, the question first posed by liberals in the fifties remains unanswered: what does the conservative mind — presumably interested in advancing hierarchy and tradition — have to offer a multicultural nation? Hofstadter may have underestimated the many layers of conservative thought, but to a remarkable degree his criticism of the Right — messianic, moralistic, wedded to Wasp privilege — are the same quills that have been tossed at Republican administrations since his death.

Perhaps there is something at the core of American conservatism that is erratic, emotional, and receptive to the moral absolutism and prosperity theology celebrated by Pentecostals and free marketers. Hofstadter may have missed a few details, but his dissection of the Right revealed its less studied tics and traits with more imagination than any scholar of his generation. Russell Kirk's classic 1953 study, *The Conservative Mind,* capably handled the ideas of elite thinkers, but Hofstadter's work recognized the popular roots of antiliberalism and thus more insightfully anticipated where the heart of twentieth-century American conservatism was heading.

The abrupt emergence of the postwar Right shocked liberals into producing highly theoretical and lightly researched investigations of the new politics. Even the most capable men associated with this school—Hofstadter, Daniel Bell, Seymour Martin Lipset—exaggerated the persecution of intellectuals while slyly drawing attention to the fragile mental makeup of their opponents. "While they correctly argued for paying attention to the ordinary people who populated the ranks of the Right," Lisa McGirr writes, "their excessively psychological interpretation distorted our understanding of American conservatism."[16] To this day, Hofstadter's treatment of popular radicalism retains a curious staying power, and readers are still charmed by the evocative phrase "paranoid style"—type it into a search engine (some half million hits appear during election seasons), and the reason for the concept's remarkable popularity becomes clear. Its impressionistic and elastic quality proves highly convenient to pundits and politicians addressing a public infatuated with conspiracy theories large and small. As long as wars, electoral intrigue, and economic inequality divide the country, the paranoid style paradigm, with its implicit search for internal enemies, will never disappear.

In fact, both sides of the political spectrum routinely appeal to Hofstadter's work as crucial to understanding the "pathology" of its opposition. Salon.com writer Michelle Goldberg's left-leaning description of a 2003 Conservative Political Action Conference as "the embodiment of what historian Richard Hofstadter once called the paranoid style of American politics," is countered on the right by Ronald Radosh's exploration of liberal bias in "Media Watch: The Paranoid Style of the *New York Times.*"[17] More broadly, liberals openly discuss the takeover of the national government by a small group of neoconservatives, Washington-area think tanks, and Fox News apparatchiks. Conservatives counter that judicial usurpation, abortion on demand, and creeping secularism are destroying the social fabric of a Christian republic. Are these examples of a "paranoid style"? Hofstadter limited his discussion to factions standing outside the American political consensus, but in recent years, both Republicans and Democrats have grown increasingly comfortable describing the beliefs and values of the other as borderline neurotic. These assessments stretch Hofstadter's idea much further than he intended. But the concept has proven too elastic to tame.

Hofstadter's work on conservative behavior drew upon crucial support from organizations critical of the Far Right. By the midfifties the Fund for the Republic, a CIA front organization financed by a $15 million endowment from the Ford Foundation, had distributed 25,000 offprints of "Pseudo-Conservative Revolt" and 1,000 copies of *Development of Academic Freedom in the United States* to civic leaders, business executives, and school superintendents. It seems almost certain that Hofstadter knew nothing of the CIA's relations with the fund. Not until the late sixties did the public become aware of CIA involvement in the Congress for Cultural Freedom and the dozens of lesser organizations committed to rallying liberal anticommunism. Hofstadter, moreover, had serious reservations about making his scholarship available to the government. In 1954, Knopf brought out a paperback edition of *The American Political Tradition* and planned to sell 7,000 copies to the State Department. Hofstadter went against his economic self-interest and protested this marketing campaign. He explained to Pat Knopf that while the book was neither unpatriotic nor subversive, its iconoclastic approach might offend conservatives in the nation's capital. He feared, he wrote, a congressional investigation of his work.[18]

The Fund for the Republic was carefully committed to distancing its programs and offices from past and present Marxists and almost certainly had no idea of Hofstadter's radical past. It did, in any case, have work for him.[19] In 1957, the American Committee for Cultural Freedom contracted the fund to conduct a study on the activities of the Far Right. An ACCF memo discussed the parameters of the project:

> It is one of the virtues of American democracy to shelter and encourage divergent beliefs, it is also one of the virtues of a secure and civilized society to tolerate the intolerant — up to a certain point. It is hard to say at precisely what point responsible members of a democratic nation must feel the need to take cognizance of the dangers posed by that small minority of their fellows to whom diversity is foul and tolerance is weakness. Perhaps the point at which a democratic citizenry must sound its

tocsin is when the intolerant band together and together try to deprive some of their countrymen of their civil liberties, employing organized effort to undermine the legal and moral foundation of democracy. The American Committee for Cultural Freedom, therefore, proposes to conduct a study of the means by which certain *extremist groups* employ slander, deceit, the distortion and falsification of historical fact, and force for the purpose of denying to others their rights under the constitution of the United States by unconstitutional means.[20]

That winter, fund (and University of Chicago) president Robert Maynard Hutchins invited Hofstadter "to prepare a memorandum along the lines suggested by the ACCF for a fee of $2,500." His task? "To set forth your current view of the significance of extremist groups — which at the moment to most of us means extremist groups of the right in American society." The following year, Hofstadter completed "The Contemporary Extreme Right Wing in the United States," a ninety-eight-page document that took the temperature of the New Right. He prefaced the study with a quote from Nietzsche condemning herd mentality: "Objection, evasion, joyous distrust, and love of irony are signs of health; everything absolute belongs to pathology."[21]

Hofstadter began with a confession, acknowledging his debt to the *Studies in Prejudice* scholars who had pioneered the field of political pathology. His use of the term "pseudo-conservative" and other clinical phrases, he noted, relied heavily on the Adorno volume. Still, he continued, *The Authoritarian Personality* was deeply flawed. Its contention that the Far Right alone among ideologies trafficked in political psychoses struck him as both implausible and unpersuasive. He encouraged a broadening of the authoritarian thesis to include the Left — but not liberalism.

Adorno's efforts to equate McCarthyism with fascism drew more criticism. While it was true, Hofstadter wrote, that some on the Far Right were sympathetic to fascism abroad, few had expressed interest in promoting fascism at home. There were, he conceded, specific connections between the prewar German and postwar American Right, including anti-Semitism, ardent nationalism, and opposition to organized labor. But there the similarities ended. While the Nazi Party in Germany was well organized, quick to resort to violence, and eager to empower the central state, the American Right had no formal program and was notably antistatist.[22]

In his published work, Hofstadter frequently accused the Right of exaggerating the nation's vulnerability to Communist infiltration. In the unpublished fund memorandum, however, he used far more moderate language. The Far Right, he wrote, was partially correct on many issues, and, he conceded, completely correct on several more. Communists had infiltrated the federal government; American foreign policy in Asia and Europe had experienced setbacks; and it was conceivable that a fresh set of conservative policies at home and abroad would have left the country no worse off. Hofstadter brushed aside the fund's ironic (considering its stated commitment to civil liberties) queries on the advisability of silencing the Right. "Are these groups necessary to the health of society?" he was asked to comment upon. "Would their elimination, either by legislation or social repression, modify the society toward or away from freedom and justice?" Hofstadter's response underscores his commitment to intellectual freedom. While he noted that, in his opinion, such groups did not contribute to the health of the nation, a healthy nation would nevertheless allow them to survive. The fund's mission, he concluded, committed it to respecting the rights of all groups, and with few exceptions the Far Right operated within the law and deserved the freedom to express its ideas under the protection of the law.[23]

*   *   *

Hofstadter had many opportunities over the years to regret these kind words. While delivering the 1962 Haynes Foundation lectures at the University of Southern California, he sarcastically declared that ultra-conservatism had "lost touch with reality. . . . We certainly cannot commit them all to mental hospitals," he winked, "but we can recognize their agitation as a kind of vocational therapy, without which they might have to be committed." Some missed the humor. The *Los Angeles Herald-Examiner*'s George Todt fired off a fierce editorial equating Hofstadter's remarks with "what [Hitler] outlined for countless innocent Jews in his Third Reich — and that's one of the reasons we fought him, exterminated him. What is the difference between Hitler placing Jews in concentration camps because they were opposed to him politically in Nazi Germany — and what Hofstadter now proposes for conservative Americans who disagree with his ultra-liberal thinking?" Nine days after Todt's column appeared, California Representative John H. Rousselot — a member of the John Birch Society — endorsed its contents in the *Appendix of the Congressional Record,* condemning "Prof. Richard Hofstadter [for his belief] that 25 million Americans who oppose radical ultra-liberal thinking and dogma should be placed in insane asylums."[24] The Sun Belt Right had just said hello to Richard Hofstadter.

West Coast conservatives emphasized a return to an America sympathetic to the social, cultural, and economic values of the older liberalism. But this was an act of self-delusion. The Sun Belt radicals were the beneficiaries of rapid migration and unprecedented economic opportunities; they abetted upheaval and redefined the conservative cause from one of security to opportunity. Right-wing redoubts mushroomed in the Southwest; their capitals in Dallas, Phoenix, and Orange County, California, were emboldened by rapid growth and close ties to energy corporations and military installations. The newly arrived "pioneers" of these boom towns liked to believe they represented a fresh generation of rugged individualists, but in truth the long-term profitability of burgeoning government defense budgets played a key role in shaping the character of the postwar West.[25]

Phoenix for example, secured several air force bases that made a tremendous impact on both the economy and culture of the Southwest. Their presence, along with Arizona's right-to-work laws, attracted Goodyear Aircraft, Consolidated Aircraft, AirResearch, Alcoa, and Motorola. California's growth was even more impressive. A climate and coastline perfect for military bases combined with unprecedented outlays of venture capital to encourage a rising jet and missile development industry. Rick Perlstein, a scholar of the New Right, notes that "New York lost 34 percent of its share of the Defense Department's procurement between 1950 and 1956; by 1965 California would have almost a quarter of the Defense Department's prime contracts and 41 percent of NASA's." Southern California in particular benefited from the state's close relationship to the Defense Department. Between 1940 and 1960 the Los Angeles metropolitan area's population nearly tripled, while the number in Orange County alone exploded from 100,000 to nearly one million.[26]

The political culture of the western tech and energy towns fluctuated between traditional conservatism and open support for the Far Right. Los Angeles is the most striking case. It contained fully one quarter of the membership of the John Birch Society and supported Barry Goldwater's 1964 presidential bid by a ratio of two to one. This New Right bore little resemblance to the economically marginalized midwesterners who had followed William Jennings Bryan on the agrarian crusades of the past. California conservatives were flush with capital, enjoyed a rising status, and had every reason to believe in a future brighter than the past. This upwardly mobile middle class exhibited little sympathy for a social welfare system that, it argued, serviced a decaying eastern infrastructure vulnerable to racial divisions, crippled by urban blight, and held hostage to the extravagant demands of organized labor.

Senator Goldwater proved an ideal lightening rod for their dissent. He denounced government subsidies, talked of rolling back the New Deal, and pressed for a more aggressive approach to Soviet imperialism. Image mattered too. A fondness for flying military jets marked the Arizona senator as a convincing symbol of the region's close ties to the defense industry and accentuated his individualism before an audience that prized personal autonomy. Predictably, the western communities that cheered on Goldwater's libertarianism aroused Hofstadter's suspicion of popular democratic movements. A self-proclaimed "conservative" coalition, the radical Right impressed Hofstadter as far less tradition-oriented than the constructive Tory governments of the past, and he refused to yield it the conservative mantle.

As the Sun Belt movement gathered momentum, Hofstadter's scholarship was in a state of flux. The 1965 publication of *The Paranoid Style* completed its author's social-psychological trilogy of the American experience, joining *The Age of Reform* and *Anti-Intellectualism* as classic defenses of postwar liberalism. His final three books, *The Progressive Historians* (1968), *The Idea of a Party System* (1969), and *America at 1750* (1971) follow more traditional methodological strategies that no doubt responded to a rapidly restructured intellectual climate. Absent in them are the clinical terminology, suspicion of popular movements, and partisan feel that characterized their author's earlier studies. The quality and insightfulness of Hofstadter's historical imagination had not changed—but the times had. "He had a very urbane mind, a quality not much appreciated in the sixties," Dorothy Ross notes. "His voice came out of the thirties and out of the McCarthyism of the fifties, and that world changed."[27]

The precise nature of that change revealed itself to Hofstadter in the 1964 presidential campaign. He believed that Goldwater's candidacy threatened to upend a liberal two-party system that chimed with the realities of an urban and ethnically mixed electorate. In June, Hofstadter composed a letter to the *New York Times* declaring that the senator's views were "not representative of the rank and file of [Republican] voters," and that he further did not "enjoy the confidence of [the party's] established national spokesman." He called upon Eisenhower—the "enemy" in *Anti-Intellectualism*—to save his party by declaring for another candidate. Hofstadter suggested Pennsylvania's patrician governor William Scranton, believing in any case that a strong statement from Eisenhower might "rally the party's moderates to challenge the Goldwater faction" and purge the organization of its radical element. "The desire for party unity is understandable," he acknowledged, "but a vigorous debate over principle and candidates will do much less damage in the long run than quiet surrender of the party to archaic notions and disastrous leadership." He concluded with a plea that "the merits of the two-party system and the need for a healthy opposition" committed Republicans and Democrats alike to follow his lead and call out Eisenhower to expel the radical candidate from the liberal kingdom.[28]

It bears repeating that Hofstadter did not classify the Goldwater movement as McCarthyism redux. The Sun Belt Right, he observed, "is something new, very new, in our politics." Goldwater's followers were drawn to conspiracy theories, blamed the nation's problems on government activism, and flirted with an authoritarian style of politics that set them apart from the milder "pseudo-conservatives" of the fifties. "Normally a major party nomination is won partly by establishing predominant popularity among its voters and partly by accommodating the other party leader," Hofstadter wrote in a preelection essay for *Partisan Review*. "Goldwater has won without doing either, but by arousing great intensity of conviction among a minority of enthusiasts, and then imposing upon this minority a tight disciplinary structure."[29]

The Goldwater candidacy caused Hofstadter to reevaluate or, in some cases, simply contradict, some of his earlier scholarly positions. *The American Political Tradition,* for example, pined for a more diverse and ideologically charged political culture. Now, in the face of a stiff challenge to the postwar consensus, Hofstadter called on Eisenhower to ignore the wishes of millions of Republicans who supported Goldwater. Intentionally or not, he was making a curious argument that pluralism could survive only in a *less* diverse, *less* ideologically tolerant environment. Under certain circumstances, of course, it may be perfectly reasonable to claim that the elimination of an extreme ideological position will ultimately preserve pluralism. But was that the case in 1964? Did Goldwater advance an extreme ideology? Did he represent a faction? A third party? He fairly won the nomination of one of the two traditional parties and, for better or worse, was the catalyst for a new consensus in American political culture that is now well into its fourth decade.

Aroused by the New Right, Hofstadter refused to give quarter. In his 1958 report to the Fund for the Republic, he recognized the naïve, provincial, and ethnocentric core of McCarthyism, believing it to be more of a traditional than revolutionary movement. He now asserted that the desert communities bred a twisted, "cult"-like version of conservatism peopled by "true believers" and "zealots." The radicals knew they could not win the campaign, he wrote in the *New York Review of Books,* but welcomed the coming electoral showdown with modern culture as a way to "express resentments."[30]

Hofstadter's campaign essays mark an important shift in his scholarship. The elitist strain noticed by critics of *Anti-Intellectualism* gave way to a growing appreciation of popular power. When it became evident that Goldwater would lose badly, Hofstadter described the public's rejection of the New Right as a healthy and happy symbol of democratic activism, an argument developed more fully in his final books. "In the ordinary course of our pragmatic, non-ideological politics, party workers are moved by the desire to find a winner. . . . If they find that they have chosen a loser, they are quick to start looking for another leader; if they see that their program is out of touch with the basic realities, they grope their way toward a new one." Consensus politics became for Hofstadter the essential ingredient to postwar liberalism. He worried that the two-party tradition was in grave danger of becoming "a kind of party-and-a-half system"—a dominant Democracy and a balkanized GOP limping from electoral defeat to electoral defeat. "Whatever may be said about the limitations of the two party system in the past, it is hard to believe that such an arrangement would be better or safer for us, especially since in this country the minor party would always be a sitting duck for the ultras and the cranks." In the interest of protecting a viable and loyal opposition, Hofstadter offered sympathy to "true" (that is, to say Nelson Rockefeller) Republicans. He steeled them for the electoral disaster that he welcomed, deplored their party's hijacking by "extremists," and welcomed them back into the fold of what he sympathetically called "the basic American consensus."[31]

Identified early in his career as a historian eager to emphasize the common qualities of the past, Hofstadter, in fact, had drawn sharp distinctions between pre– and post–New Deal America. But much had changed since *The American Political Tradition.* The New Departure was no longer quite so new; it was now the dominant postwar ideology — to defend it was by nature an act of conservation. Hofstadter hoped in 1964 to preserve an established liberalism on the verge of winning its seventh presidential election in nine contests. The Republican Party, the point should not be lost, played an important role in this arrangement. It forced Democrats to unite an ethnically diverse constituency or face defeat—as happened in the 1920s and 1950s. The impressive catholicity of the Democratic Party reached deep into the body politic, absorbed various interests, and starved radical offshoots eager to exploit the collective resentments of the people.

The consensus theme is most evident in Hofstadter's final books. His claim in *The American Political Tradition* that the nation operated under a set of common and inflexible ideological assumptions was meant as criticism. He clearly preferred a more dynamic, more openly contested political culture. But that was 1948, and it was by no means certain at that point that the reforms of the thirties would survive. Yet they did. The old liberalism gave way and Hofstadter recognized in the new politics an imperfect but constructive alternative to the Far Right and Left. The political center held a virtue that he could not deny. "Critics of our system have often said that our political life is dreary and unconstructive because the major parties, being two roughly similar coalitions of heterogeneous interests, cannot settle on clear principles or debate profound issues," Hofstadter wrote in 1964. "They have often argued that a sharper division in our party ideologies along conservative and progressive lines would serve us better. . . . It appears that we are now about to get a sharper ideological division, and keener social conflict, and they may not like it as well as they anticipated."[32]

Hofstadter's commitment to the liberal center undoubtedly contributed to the stridency of his preelection commentary. He described Goldwater's nomination as "a vital blow at the American political order," dismissed the senator's views as "unrepresentative of American thinking," and claimed that his supporters "infiltrated the party much as the Communists in their days of strength infiltrated liberal organizations in order to use them as front groups." As the election drew near, Hofstadter's commentary grew increasingly shrill, taking on a slightly manic quality. "If [Goldwater] is successful, whether elected or not, in consolidating this party coup he will have brought about a realignment of the parties that will put the democratic process in this country in jeopardy. One is loath to speculate on the consequence for the safety of the world. . . . If I am right, Goldwater owns his party for the calculable future, and if he fails this year, is likely to have another try. This is one of those moments," Hofstadter quoted William Butler Yeats, "'when / Things Fall apart; the centre cannot hold . . . / The best lack all conviction, while the worst / Are full of passionate intensity / I have never been persuaded by those who see the wave of a coming apocalypse in every wrinkle on the social surface; but it is now much easier than before to believe that America is visibly sick with a malady that may do all of us in.'" Hofstadter's colorful diagnosis of the Far Right enriched our historiography—but it told only part of the story. As his own campaign pieces demonstrated, liberals, when faced with a stiff political challenge, manifested the symptoms of their own paranoid style.[33]

Goldwater's poor performance in the autumn election electrified his opponents. "As it turned out," Hofstadter gleefully reported in a post-election essay, "Goldwater's showing was far from respectable. The vote was unmistakably cast *against him.*" The senator received only 26 million votes, 7.5 million fewer than Nixon's 1960 tally, a 22 percent drop. Hofstadter placed little significance in the fact that more than a third of the electorate supported Goldwater, reminding his readers that "under our party system even Jack the Ripper, with a major-label on him, could hope to get close to 40% of the votes." The rout of the radicals underlined both the public's rejection of ideological extremism and its commitment to the liberal mainstream. In many ways, the 1964 election was the most satisfying political experience of Richard Hofstadter's life.[34]

*   *   *

The Goldwater candidacy foreshadowed the timely publication of *The Paranoid Style in American Politics.* For several years Alfred Knopf had pressed Hofstadter to produce a major study of the Right, but other projects took precedence and he confined his criticism of ultraconservatism to a spate of provocative articles. Knopf had once warned Hofstadter that a book of essays rarely made money, and this advice proved crucial to turning *The American Political Tradition* into a more integrated work than its author intended. But the time seemed right in 1965 for Hofstadter, a distinguished historian and twice winner of the Pulitzer Prize, to republish several of his most important pieces. Moreover, the recent completion of *Anti-Intellectualism* had exhausted its author, and he was grateful to substitute existing material for original analysis. This was by no means a lesser Hofstadter book, however. The material he planned to include in the anthology, he assured Knopf, would be among the most interesting of his career.[35]

The Paranoid Style is a pioneering study in the history of political pathology. It forces us to recognize the thin line between public mood and public policy, alienation and ideology. In the clash between worldview and reality, the ultra-Right, Hofstadter argued, had a major handicap — it confused conspiracy for history. And the last few years had seen a long train of treason — both real and imagined. Soviet expansion into Eastern Europe, the "loss" of China, the Korean War, and the Rosenbergs and Hiss cases pointed to a stunning series of American reversals. Communism, it seemed certain, was on the move; enemies were everywhere. Compromise, concession, reconciliation, and rapprochement were signs of weakness, the embodiment of liberal treachery in the fantasy world of the Right.[36]

Additional problems arose, Hofstadter argued, as Wasps and ethnics broke into rival political camps. More affluent and socially mobile than its conservative predecessors, the Sun Belt Right was made up almost exclusively of white Protestants. McCarthyism, by comparison, had a significant minority of German Catholics and Irish Americans, constituencies central to its base in the old industrial Midwest. The pure racial composition of the Right concerned Hofstadter. If the party system ruptured along ethnic lines, it could take liberalism down with it — and this had nearly happened once. In the twenties, he pointed out, the Democratic Party was paralyzed between rural and urban wings. After years of fierce infighting, the cosmopolitans broke the power of the provincials, and the party emerged from its struggles a much more potent political force, in tune with the direction of demographic change.[37] Republicans, Hofstadter concluded, needed to follow this lead. Only by pluralizing its ranks could the GOP fully embrace the postwar liberal consensus and enter the mainstream of modern political life.

*   *   *

Harvey Swados read *The Paranoid Style* with great interest. The book provoked a correspondence between him and Hofstadter reminiscent of their politically charged letters in the thirties. Swados agreed that a kind of collective neurosis often gripped political actors, but he believed Hofstadter defined the paranoid style too narrowly. The Johnson administration's 1965 invasion of the Dominican Republic and expanding military commitment in Vietnam struck Swados as an irrational deployment of military power stimulated by a heightened sensitivity to cold war tensions. A clear case, he concluded, of the paranoid style among liberals.[38]

Hofstadter conceded the principle of Swados's point, noting that even Adlai Stevenson seemed ready at times to believe in the Communist "conspiracy" thesis. But the paranoid style, he continued, was an out-of-power rather than in-power phenomenon. By definition, therefore, liberals were exempt from the label and its derogatory implications. Lyndon Johnson did not suffer from the paranoid style, he wrote Swados; rather, he responded to a more mainstream anticommunism that might be self-defeating in Vietnam, and might put the United States at odds with a growing global anticolonial sentiment, but was too powerful to ignore. Rather than leading the American charge in the Dominican Republic and Southeast Asia, the president, Hofstadter argued, was a prisoner of American culture and could not—even if he had the courage—shake the crude anticommunism that guided American foreign policy.[39]

Hofstadter's selective use of the paranoid style idea brings to mind David Potter's earlier criticism of the status thesis. Like status, paranoia is a slippery concept that belies strict categorization and can be used indiscriminately to pathologize political opposition. By insisting that groups in power were, by definition, incapable of irrational behavior, Hofstadter radically oversimplified human psychology. The annals of history are filled with numerous examples of kings, presidents, emperors, and czars suffering from a variety of inner demons and delusions. On a practical level, ruling regimes can never take their authority for granted, as revolutions, plebiscites, and palace coups are ever present possibilities. In response, power has been known to purge whole populations, draw up elaborate lists of enemies, and fill its councils with pliant yes-men. In America, where the two-party system ensures hotly contested campaigns, both major parties idle in a state of apprehension—the potential for political catastrophe is never farther away than the next election.

The idea that a paranoid style influences American political culture is inescapable. Yet it must be handled with circumspection rather than mechanically applied to a single group or ideology. Always looking for the enemy on the right, Hofstadter never suspected liberalism's vulnerability to self-destruction. The Johnson administration's crusade to end poverty at home and create a New Deal in the Mekong Delta overloaded the system of liberal reform. The promise of a Great Society quickly collapsed amid the tragedy of the Vietnam War, the misery of race riots, urban violence, and a youth culture disaffected with the politics of abundance. When the consensus shattered in 1968, radicals could claim only limited credit. Rather, the politics of the party in power hastened its end.

PART III
Eclipse, 1965–1970

You have a major urban crisis. You have the alienation of the young. Still more important you have the question of race and you have a cruel and unnecessary war. And it seems to me to be a staggering parcel of questions for one society to have to tackle at one time.

RICHARD HOFSTADTER, 1970

* 8 *
Rebellion from Within

Columbia University had a way of containing within it most
of the problems in American society at large. It was a micro-
cosm. In the spring of '68, we saw a university that had for
twenty years trampled on its neighbors in Harlem, evicted
people from their homes, which was also the largest defense
contracting university. We were against the war, we were
against inequality in society, but we had in our own administration an example of what was worst about our society, and
we could confront it by confronting it right at home.

TOM HURWITZ, 2000

Our nation's intellectual history is a story of regional migrations. Sur-
veying the last century, Boston Pragmatists William James, Charles S.
Peirce, and Oliver Wendell Holmes, Jr., shaped American thought until
the emergence, about 1910, of Greenwich Village Modernists Randolph
Bourne, Emma Goldman, and John Reed. From there, ideas moved up-
town, and at midcentury New York intellectuals Lionel Trilling, Daniel
Bell, and Irving Howe wrote the essays and edited the journals that
steered sophisticated public opinion for a generation. Among America's
great institutions of learning, Columbia University is uniquely positioned
to take advantage of the cultural and educational amenities offered
by New York City—and this has made it a particularly attractive home
for intellectuals. Some stay longer than others. During Hofstadter's
many years at Morningside Heights, several of the institution's most talented American historians, including Merle Curti, Henry Steele Commager, Allan Nevins, David Herbert Donald, and Dumas Malone, left
New York for other positions. But Hofstadter thrived amid the stability
of a single residence, university, and publisher; the short ten-minute
walk from his Claremont Avenue apartment to his office at 704 Hamilton Hall offered silent though suggestive commentary on his devotion
to the metropolitan idea. "He stayed here," Fritz Stern remembered.
"He liked Columbia's unpretentious, even awkward style which paid so
little to amenities and externals and, at its best, so much to matters of
intellect."[1] Hofstadter's loyalty to the institution ran deep, and for

nearly a quarter century he lived productively in its shadow, the fortunate son of the urban cosmopolitanism his books celebrated.

Not even the most tempting offers could budge Hofstadter from Morningside Heights. These included Mills College (1948), the New School for Social Research (1949), Princeton (1950), MIT (1950 and 1969), the University of Chicago (1952 and 1954), the University of California at Berkeley (1956), Yale (1957), Harvard (joint appointment in history and education, 1958), and the Institute for Advanced Study (1967). The Harvard proposal was curious. Why offer one of the nation's most original and creative historical minds only a *half-time* position in its history department? "The American historians may have been lukewarm," former Harvard historian Arthur Schlesinger, Jr., remembered, "not so much because of any specific reservations about Hofstadter as because of their general feeling that no American historian is worthy of a Harvard appointment." Daniel Bell added that Oscar Handlin and Bernard Bailyn — among the most prominent Americanists at Harvard — may have shied away from Hofstadter because his scholarship relied on published rather than archival materials. In any case, Columbia successfully countered the Harvard offer by making Hofstadter the DeWitt Clinton Professor of American History. There were, however, more intrinsic factors working in the university's favor. Hofstadter was fiercely proud of Columbia's distinguished history department, and he knew that colleagues Lionel Trilling, Meyer Schapiro, and Herbert Weschler had turned down Harvard offers to remain in New York. The lure of Manhattan and Hofstadter's sense that Columbia students were more independent than those at Harvard were also major considerations. Comparing the pace and attitude of New York to Boston, he remarked to C. Vann Woodward that whatever shortcomings Manhattan or Columbia had, they were not dull or intellectually smug.[2]

Morningside Heights is home to an astounding collection of cultural and educational resources. Combined, Columbia, Barnard College, Union Theological Seminary, Jewish Theological Seminary, the Manhattan School of Music, International House, and the Cathedral Church of St. John the Divine make the Upper West Side an especially rich source of intellectual life. Hofstadter complemented this dynamic community, occupying a beautiful university apartment that featured high ceilings, wood floors, and French doors looking out onto the street. A double parlor for the living room had been opened up by taking out the glass doors between the two halves, thus creating a huge living space that dominated the unit. In the back of this space, but part of the same room, behind a long settee, sat Hofstadter's book-lined study. He listened to records nearly every day and kept near his desk a stereo that played the Baroque composers (Vivaldi, Monteverdi, and Bach) while he worked, and jazz and bebop (Charlie Parker, Thelonious Monk, Dizzy Gillespie, Dave Brubeck) for relaxation. "He bought very good jazz records," Dan Hofstadter remembers, "and once gave me all of his old 78's from the Thirties and Forties."[3]

A late riser, Hofstadter read the *New York Times* over breakfast before turning to his work. The telephone was a distraction, and friends were reluctant to call the apartment during his morning routine. After lunch, he walked to Columbia, where he taught, met with students, and tried to stay abreast (with the help of a personal secretary) of a heavy correspondence. Returning to Claremont Avenue in the afternoons, he frequently entertained colleagues and graduate students over drinks and conversation. In some cases, these could be wonderfully instructive exchanges. "Just before my orals," Daniel Singal recalls, "Hofstadter invited me to his apartment, handed me a gin and tonic, and proceeded to grill me for three hours on all the areas that would be covered during my exam. It was a truly amazing session: he would push me as hard as possible to see how much I knew, then carry on when I reached my limits on a particular topic, providing me with insights about American political history that I still use in my own teaching."[4]

In the evenings Hofstadter read. He subscribed to several academic journals: *William and Mary Quarterly, Political Science Quarterly,* and the *American Historical Review,* as well as the *New York Review of Books* and *Commentary.* Though he rarely engaged in archival research, he did study primary material in printed sources. He wanted to formulate his own ideas and believed that if he relied too heavily on what others had written his work would lack originality and freshness. While writing *Academic Freedom in the Age of the College,* he examined dozens of colonial sermons, and for *The Idea of a Party System* he read the political works of Bolingbroke, Burke, and Madison. His methodical work habits were completely internal, and there is little doubt that writing served an important, even therapeutic, purpose in his life. In reply to a colleague's fatigue, he allowed that his own intellectual labor evoked the physicality of a biological process. He never forced the act of creation; rather, the ideas were organic and naturally worked their way to the surface.[5]

The "West Side Kibbutz," a group of scholar-friends including Bell, Trilling, Stern, Irving Kristol, Walter Metzger, and Peter Gay, shared Hofstadter's respect for ideas. These men, Metzger remembers, were tied by common experiences and common self-doubts: "All started out as Marxists, were children of immigrants and very ambitious, the one-upsmanship that went on at some of these gatherings could be excruciating." Hofstadter enjoyed a few close friendships among historians, but he was more inclined to retreat from intimate relationships among professional thinkers. "The New York literati had taken him to their collective bosom and treated him as one of theirs," H. Stuart Hughes wrote. "Yet he never became (nor wished to become) a member of their in-group. Their high-pitched, competitive conversation was not his style." Hofstadter's emotional aloofness was a point of recognition among those who knew him well. Peter Gay's comment "He was my best friend, I don't know if I was his" is strikingly close to Michael Kazin's remark that "my father [Alfred] said that Dick was his best friend, but Dick was perhaps no one's best friend." There are, of course, many ways to reckon friendship and the satisfying exchange of human contact. In small gatherings Hofstadter displayed an impressive social flair distinguished by charm, erudition, and an effortless intellectual authority that drew others to him. "I've seen some of the best known members of the New York literary circle listen to him as though they were learning something," Columbia political scientist Julian Franklin remembered, "and people like that rarely act as if they are learning when they are at a party."[6]

The metropolis clearly nourished Hofstadter, but its intellectual pleasures were compromised by the physical demands and everyday inconveniences of living in a major urban area. "The other day," C. Wright Mills wrote in 1948, "Hofstadter figured how much time a week he spent on nonessentials like parking a car, etc., things due to the big city as such, and it came out to an unconscionable amount." The conclusion of each school year brought a much-needed holiday. Family vacations were taken in Hampton Bays and Vermont before the financial success of *The American Political Tradition,* two textbooks, and an edited set of documents permitted a more elaborate summer retreat to Wellfleet, Massachusetts, a fashionable beach colony on Cape Cod. Their home there was larger than what they could afford in Manhattan. It included a living room, six bedrooms, two baths, and a small but symbolic luxury that Hofstadter lacked at Claremont—a separate study. The area catered, as Alfred Kazin slyly put it, to "television producers, government and U.N. advisors from the social scientists and psycho-historians, professors by the dozen—all people definitely 'in.'"[7] Hofstadter's preference for writing interpretive rather than archival history freed him from exhausting the holiday months in distant libraries, and his work habits on the Cape mirrored those established in the city. He continued to work in the mornings and enjoyed the beach in the afternoons. The casual rhythm of long summer days gave way to a relaxed social scene in the evenings, when he would spend time with a number of historians, writers, artists, and poets from New York, Boston, and the Cape.

*   *   *

Columbia did not make Hofstadter, but it stimulated his intellect in a way that no other university in any other city could. This was the academic home of Dewey, Beard, Trilling, Schapiro, and Mills — self-made scholars who lacked the polished backgrounds of the eastern academic elite. In many ways a poor relation to its Ivy brethren, Columbia, with its roots in the democratic soil of a major urban area, encouraged a fertile intersection of ideas uncommon for its time. At its best, New York City sustained a variety of intellectual styles, and its penchant for pluralism surfaced time and again as the foundation upon which Hofstadter built his books. Though never a "popularizer," he could, as Merle Curti once observed, write "popular history in the *best* sense."[8] The rare combination of analytic genius and clever, even playful, prose made the release of a Hofstadter book a major literary event, and as the list of his publications grew, so did his reputation. Publishers and editors, television producers, government officials, and countless organizations regularly solicited Hofstadter for essays, appearances, commentary, or simply the use of his name. With his star rising far above the firmament occupied by most historians, he became something of a public commodity — a historian engagé.

Edward Said has defined the public intellectual as "someone whose place it is publicly to raise embarrassing questions, to confront orthodoxy and dogma (rather than produce them), to be someone who cannot easily be co-opted by government or corporations."[9] Mere popularity and a public platform, in other words, do not automatically lead to critical or consequential engagement. Hofstadter's colleagues Allan Nevins and Henry Steele Commager were prolific and important historians, but their work tended to popularize the past rather than tease out new interpretations or connect with new generations. Nevins wrote wonderfully literate prose on the Civil War era that shed remarkably little light on the racial problems of the twentieth century, and Commager's brave attempt to reinvigorate liberalism during the McCarthy era betrayed more of an activist spirit than a commitment to intellectual depth. Both failed to forge relationships with younger scholars who shared Hofstadter's skeptical opinion of the Progressive tradition.[10] In contrast to Commager and Nevins, Hofstadter successfully integrated cutting-edge insights with an informed and sensitive concern for contemporary events. He was blessed, in other words, with a remarkable ability to make the past matter.

And in the 1960s academy, little mattered more than the past. While it is true that many postwar students used the universities as mere credentialing agencies to the middle class, others consciously prized their education as an indispensable tool to fight social injustice. To do this effectively, one had to be aware of the historical roots of contemporary problems. Accordingly, during what has been described as the "Golden Age of the University," enrollments in history graduate programs trebled in size. Fewer than 400 doctorates were awarded to historians in 1960, but that number exceeded 1,000 in just ten years.[11] These newly minted Ph.D.'s represented a generation weaned on the civil rights movement, the war on poverty, and the war in Vietnam. Their demanding presence was both a surprise and a challenge for middle-age professors, for they called upon the nation's universities to trade the detachment of the lecture hall for the intensity of protest marches and public speeches.

Hofstadter was not immune to the spirit of the times. In the spring of 1965 he accepted an invitation from University of Chicago historians Walter Johnson and John Hope Franklin to participate in the march to Montgomery, a voting rights drive remembered now as one of the largest civil rights demonstrations in the nation's history. "As historians of slavery, the Civil War, and reconstruction," Johnson asserted, "we believe it is high time for the issues over which the Civil War was fought to be finally resolved. We join the march to Montgomery because we believe that the achievement of Negro voting rights will open the floodgates of freedom that will bring an end to the economic, social and political backwardness of the American South." Hofstadter defined the historians' mission — and that of the civil rights movement — more precisely. Advocates for racial justice, he explained to a reporter covering the march, "no longer believe the problem can be solved by any one remedy — voting rights, education, employment opportunities — but that all must be worked for continually."[12]

The day before the march concluded, Hofstadter flew to Atlanta and was bused to Tuskegee Institute, staying overnight in a building once segregated for white visitors. The following day, he and the other historians were driven to the outskirts of Montgomery, where they joined a group of celebrities and entertainers before merging with the main body. "We marched as historians," Kenneth Stampp remembered, "but we were also coming as individuals." Certainly their perceptions of the prospects for civil rights in the South varied. "It may be that we're reaching the end of an era," southern native C. Vann Woodward optimistically informed the press; a cautious Hofstadter countered, "I think it's more of a beginning because actually we haven't got very far yet."[13]

Despite heavy security, the professors were naturally concerned for their safety, and the tension provoked in Hofstadter a kind of mordant humor. It was a typical gesture — self-deprecation as a tool to put others at ease. Leaving Montgomery on a bus loaded with historians, he cracked to William Leuchtenburg that if segregationists firebombed their vehicle, calculating junior faculty in search of jobs and professional advancement would rejoice. Deflection aside, Hofstadter was proud of his participation that day and reconnected its larger meaning to the social justice issues he pursued in his youth. "I had the feeling that he felt liberated," James Shenton remembered, "that he was somehow getting in touch with the past."[14]

*   *   *

The turbulent mix of civil rights activism, Vietnam, and student protests was a source of great hope and great anguish in the sixties. It also challenged liberal stewardship of the state. The war was a disaster, Hofstadter wrote Harvey Swados on Christmas Day 1965, and nothing since Pearl Harbor, he continued, filled him with such a profound sense of foreboding and helplessness.[15] Vietnam undermined confidence in the government, cut deeply into Johnson's Great Society programs, and exasperated existing social tensions. To a great degree these wounds were self-inflicted. American strategists asked for public support of the war on the grounds that it represented a crucial campaign in a broader crusade to thwart international communism's threat to Western freedoms. The realities of Southeast Asian geopolitics, histories, customs, and cultures rarely counted as the anxieties of a generation of policy makers — articulated in the diplomatic language of "appeasement" and the "domino effect" — offered the more compelling if less complete lessons.

Vietnam troubled Hofstadter for personal as well as public reasons. His son, Dan, graduated from Columbia in 1966 and was eligible for induction. Eager to avoid the draft, he put his life on hold, halfheartedly pursuing what he described as "my phony history MA candidacy" at UCLA. The following year Hofstadter encouraged Dan to attend graduate school at the University of California as an alternative to military service and alerted Berkeley historian Kenneth Stampp to shepherd his son's application. Stampp was pleased to do a favor for his old Maryland colleague: "I'm glad to help Dan keep out of Mr. Johnson's War."[16]

* * *

In 1965 Fritz Stern organized a small gathering of Columbia faculty to discuss the brewing crisis in Vietnam. At odds with the current course of U.S. foreign policy, the "Stern Group"—including Hofstadter, Daniel Bell, Herbert Deane, Robert Merton, Alexander Dallin, Wolfgang Friedman, William Leuchtenburg, Henry Roberts, and David Truman—began meeting regularly at Stern's Claremont Avenue apartment to clarify their positions and await an opportunity to make their opposition known. In September, Leuchtenburg interviewed Lyndon Johnson for a study of recent congressional activity, and that solicitation opened the door for the Stern Group to draft a letter the following spring advising the president to "initiate a radical reexamination of the government's policy in Vietnam." Its authors were liberals who admired the Great Society and hoped to persuade Johnson that substantial opposition to the war existed among moderates. As intellectuals, they were eager to avoid the crude anticommunism that accompanied the nation's last Asian conflict. "We are anxious . . . about the effects of this war on the American mind and consequently on the state of our politics," the Stern Group explained. "We remember too vividly how the protracted stalemate in Korea subjected us to the scourge of McCarthyism and to a bleak period of unproductive wrangling. We fear that a prolonged commitment in Vietnam is almost certain to feed a sense of frustration in this country which will both jeopardize our liberties and encourage those forces opposed to social progress." Johnson replied one month later with a cordial seven-page letter defending his Vietnam policy.[17]

Stern spent the following academic year at Oxford and the group suspended activities. During his absence, Hofstadter continued to educate himself on a number of Vietnam-related issues; naturally the conflict's impact on Columbia University interested him most. Military and CIA recruitment on the campus led to sharp student rejoinders denouncing the institution's complicity in the war effort, prompting Hofstadter and several colleagues to direct a letter to the college's Committee on Instruction requesting that it put an end to these activities: "Novel circumstances, both within the University and in American society as a whole have resulted in an atmosphere of endemic crisis at this university." Its authors encouraged Columbia to clarify its mission as an institution founded in the spirit of academic freedom and recommit itself to serving students rather than the military. Recent undergraduate efforts to end recruitment, the letter warned (six months *before* the student uprising), reflected unmistakable "signs of conflict and anguish . . . of a wider concern: that the place and function of the universities in the large society are today acutely problematic."[18]

Stern's return briefly reenergized the group. With a nod toward George Bernard Shaw, it made plans to produce "A Model for an Intelligent Person's Guide to the Vietnam War," a pamphlet designed to lay the groundwork for a faculty-guided dialogue among the Morningside community. But the crisis that hit Columbia in April 1968 destroyed any hope of consensus. Its own ranks depleted (Dallin was appalled that police were called to campus, and he broke with Truman, the provost of the university), the Stern Group evolved into the "Stern Gang." Its mission, its founder remembers, "was to bring order and sense back to campus."[19]

The Stern Group/Gang's response to the protest culture engulfing Columbia may be interpreted as farsighted and unselfishly concerned with the preservation of a great university. By recognizing and then reacting to the most divisive points of contention between students and administrators, Hofstadter and his colleagues hoped to employ the faculty as a moderate campus presence in search of a sustaining accord. This was neither an insignificant nor unbrave position to hold. While the great antiwar protests of the era have made an indelible impression on the public consciousness and give the impression of a decade of popular activism, in the midsixties the majority of Americans (including university students) upheld the nation's military efforts in southeast Asia. "Americans supported LBJ," historian Terry Anderson reminds us. "When thirty activists at Kent State protested the bombing [campaign of North Vietnam in 1965], an angry crowd five times larger pelted them with rocks. A teach-in at Wisconsin resulted in 6,000 students signing a letter supporting the president's policy, and a fourth of the student body did the same thing at Yale. Some Michigan State professors condemned [a] teach-in on their campus as 'deliberately one-sided,' a 'rally for indoctrination,' and with the aid of students in Young Democrats and Young Americans for Freedom collected almost 16,000 signatures supporting U.S. policy."[20] One point is clear, the men involved in the Stern Group very early anticipated the corrosive effect the war would have on both their campus and their country. Their responses, considered from a friendly perspective, were designed to address the alienation of their students constructively.

But to their detractors, the measured approach of the professors appeared tepid and unlikely to result in either meaningful or timely change. This criticism irritated Hofstadter, further distancing him from a style of radical politics that he believed was increasingly out of touch with the difficult and disciplined effort of constructing useful (as opposed to merely emotionally satisfying) social commentary. Concurrently, his opinion of moderates rose, for in rejecting Goldwater had the Center not repudiated political extremism in a show of electoral support for the postwar political tradition? The Left's assault on liberalism discouraged Hofstadter, and in private correspondence, he assailed his antagonists. Philip Rahv had recently scolded liberals for signing an anti-Vietnam ad urging opponents of the war to moderate their criticism. The petition, Rahv wrote in *The New York Review of Books,* "may be a . . . maneuver on the part of Establishment liberals who wish to back away from the hard choices and severe struggles that lie ahead." Rahv's essay infuriated Hofstadter, and he complained to Harvey Swados that the antiwar ad embodied a judicious and pragmatic appeal to the middle class that went as far in condemning the war as was constructively possible. Rahv was dead wrong, he continued, to accuse "Establishment liberals" of conservative tactics, and his sentiments reflected the Left's naiveté, disregard for practical politics, and ignorance of mainstream America.[21]

In return, many on the left dismissed Hofstadter as a (neo) conservative shill for the Establishment. Intellectuals, they argued, were supposed to be creatures of the margins, living and producing in necessary tension with the broader culture. But to a remarkable degree the liberals were in power. They held seats on prestigious boards, applauded the avalanche of civil rights and Great Society legislation, held the best positions at the best universities, and deeply influenced contemporary social, political, and cultural trends. In radical quarters — and this certainly included enclaves at Columbia — Hofstadter was denounced as a "square," a "reactionary," and worse. He struggled to offer a moderate voice in an acrimonious age, but he clearly understood the limits of liberalism, even to the point of questioning its (and his own) moral position. It was easy, he wrote Swados, for him to sign antiwar petitions at

Columbia. He hated the war, Columbia hated the war, and signing cost him nothing. But his friend Irving Howe, he noted, had demonstrated a greater moral courage than he could ever muster, for he had, with great resourcefulness and humanity, devoted his life to keeping the goals and ideals of socialism alive in America.[22]

In April 1968, the *New York Times Magazine* invited Hofstadter to assess America's prospects in Vietnam — a solicitation that he initially declined. The rapid pace of current political events, he explained, rendered any statement he could make as a historian irrelevant.[23] Within a few days, however, he changed his mind. In absence of more concrete evidence, it seems likely that the 4 April assassination of Martin Luther King, Jr. (the date Hofstadter initially rejected the *Times* proposal), and its violent reverberation through American cities clinched his decision to enter the public debate. Saddened by the divisions that poisoned American society and deeply concerned with Columbia's radical incline (students began to occupy campus buildings later that month), Hofstadter prepared his article under a dark cloud.

The *Times* essay, "Uncle Sam Has Cried 'Uncle!' Before," exploded the myth of American omnipotence. Expectations for a quick victory in Vietnam, Hofstadter asserted, were unrealistic and likely, as casualties mounted, to encourage a sharp backlash against antiwar protestors, liberal professors, and any number of proscribed internal "enemies." Hofstadter plainly feared a return to the McCarthyism of the recent past, and predicted that the prolongation of the war would almost certainly bring about a reaction from the Right. In light of Nixon's "southern strategy," Reagan's massive military buildup, and various attempts by American presidents to kick the nation's "Vietnam Syndrome," Hofstadter's concerns strike the reader as prophetic. He correctly predicted the eclipse of the liberal state and forecast the return of a Protestant, property-rights persuasion that has since captured the country's political high ground.[24]

The American past, Hofstadter wrote, provided numerous examples of defeats, retrenchments, and compromises that neither crippled the nation nor prevented it from achieving a preeminent global position. In the 1790s the Washington administration swallowed Jay's Treaty rather than risk war with England, while it and later administrations paid tribute and bribes to the Barbary States of North Africa in order to maintain peaceful trade in the Mediterranean. The Founders, in other words, were sensitive to the nation's weaknesses and established a cautious and pragmatic foreign policy that served the country well in its formative years. Their legacy, Hofstadter believed, offered a compelling corrective to the imperial overreach then afflicting the nation in Vietnam.[25]

The illusion of military hegemony, Hofstadter continued, took root in the American mind in the early nineteenth century. Jackson's victory at New Orleans overshadowed an otherwise miserable American performance in the War of 1812 and served as a springboard to more successful campaigns against Native Americans and Mexicans that carried the Stars and Stripes into Florida, Texas, California, and the Southwest. The single example of United States soldiers suffering insurmountable losses — the Civil War — offered no clear challenge to prevailing impressions of military dominance. That war seemed to highlight the intriguing paradox that only American armies could defeat American armies.

The pattern of military expansion at bargain rates followed the United States into the twentieth century. The First and Second World Wars made America a global power without imposing the horrific casualty rates of the other nations involved. The Korean campaign, however, deviated from the dominant strain of American military history and became the first overseas conflict since the War of 1812 to seriously divide the nation. Still, the basic objectives in Korea — stemming the North's invasion and securing the territorial integrity of the South — were eventually met. In Vietnam, no favorable end was in sight.[26]

Hofstadter called for a sober reevaluation of American power as the nation entered into an unfamiliar age of limitations. No longer could it afford to seek military solutions to political or ideological crises, press for the total destruction of international communism, or expect to neatly solve the problems facing the free world. Belief in the omnipotence of the United State's economic and military power, he concluded, had stirred American hubris and led the country down its current troubled path. But honoring constraints did not mean isolationism, and Hofstadter advised the nation to soberly accept its responsibilities as a global leader. By recognizing well-defined limitations on when and where to commit its military assets, America would hold in reserve the preponderance of its material, political, and intellectual resources to focus on the country's domestic problems.[27]

*   *   *

The crisis in American foreign policy played a crucial role politicizing students, but the demographic revolution in higher education brought about by the baby boom and GI Bill was an even more important catalyst for change. The new "multiversity"—confirmed in the astonishing growth of California, midwestern, and Ivy League institutions—gushed operating expenditures in the billions, employed tens of thousands of faculty and staff, and colonized beyond home campuses to include agricultural and urban research stations. The age of the quaint New England liberal arts college had passed, and the serious players in academe were now empires of intellect responding less to the needs of individual students than to an increasingly knowledge-driven economy.

To its critics, the new education heralded the demise of the university as an avenue to pursue higher truths and disinterested research. Rather than standing independent of the matrix of traditional market, political, and social pressures, the multiversity threatened to overthrow the valuable role of higher learning as a necessary critic of the "system." Government, industry, business, and education, a growing number of students insisted, combined to further the nation's cold war needs. Higher learning equipped the "best and the brightest" for service in the war against international communism, made its laboratories available to weapons research, and permitted military recruitment on campuses. The unique interests of the universities, its critics concluded, were increasingly integrated into an organizational structure that inhibited academic freedom. The push toward centralization—and the image of university administrators as symbols of a monolithic, unresponsive educational bureaucracy—became a potent issue for students in the sixties.

The incorporation of academic life proved to be a source of immense frustration for undergraduates. Critical-thinking courses lost ground in the postwar decades to a technical curriculum that deemphasized faculty-student interaction and maneuvered graduates into unsatisfying career choices. To be sure, the democratization of higher education that accompanied the multiversity idea benefited millions of students in community colleges, branch campuses, and universities that did not exist before 1960. But at the elite level, grave concerns about the creeping impersonalization of educational culture took hold. At Columbia, students seeking consultation with their professors (including those in the graduate program with spouses and families) were expected to sit on the floor outside their sponsors' offices, men in jackets and ties, often referred to only by their last names. When James Banner, Jr., arrived at Morningside for graduate work, he was immediately struck by its coldness. "At Princeton, we had engaged in constant discussion with our teachers and it was exciting to see the discourse of history unfold before you. At Columbia, we rarely saw our professors in action. The place operated very much in the style of an old German university where you were on your own. It was all very cordial and all very Columbia."[28] For a generation of young Americans raised in a culture of abundance, gratification, and unprecedented opportunity to challenge the sacred, the increasingly bureaucratic character of the new education stood in stark contrast to their expectations.

The counterrevolution began in Berkeley. Barred from disseminating civil rights flyers on university grounds, some 3,000 students crowded into Sproul Plaza on 1 October 1964 to protest the institution's abridgment of their free speech rights. The administration agreed to confer with student leaders, but before the meeting could take place 500 police officers arrived on campus, further antagonizing relations between a university hierarchy concerned with asserting its authority and students angry at the obstruction of open debate at a public institution supported by their tuition dollars. An agreement between the two sides allowing a free speech zone at the campus's main entrance, leniency for protesters, and creation of a faculty-student committee to negotiate future free speech issues appeared to bring the Berkeley protest to a conclusion in a manner wholly satisfactory to the students.

Within a matter of weeks, this tentative arrangement broke down. The administration put personnel favorable to its position on the committee, which then failed to address the issues that precipitated the protest. In response, thousands of students again flooded into Sproul Plaza in a move designed to force the institution to recognize its earlier commitment to free speech at Berkeley. Once more police were brought in, this time arresting nearly 800 students who had jammed into Sproul Hall, the main administration building. Yet several thousand remained in the plaza, and the faculty condemned the use of force and threw its support on the side of the protesters. Faced with a rebellion of the professors and a student strike, the administration capitulated. Much to the distaste of conservatives sitting on the University of California Board of Regents, political demonstrations were now permitted on campus.

In January 1967 the regents got their revenge. With the prompting of newly elected governor Ronald Reagan, UC president Clark Kerr was fired. The architect of the multiversity idea, Kerr was among its first and most visible casualties. Three months later, the Berkeley faculty, still stunned by the tumult of the past three years, invited Hofstadter—the nation's leading scholar on academic freedom—to address a special convocation at Berkeley. He had long respected the University of California as a first-rate institution and had come close to joining its history department early in his career. In October 1966 he had read the Jefferson Memorial Lectures at Berkeley, and now, six months later, returned, speaking on "Academic Freedom in the University." Hofstadter took this opportunity to explore the rights and responsibilities of intellectual inquiry, the need for open debate of campus policies and the most important question facing his audience — how free is free speech on a college campus?

Hofstadter reminded his audience that instruction, rather than social reform, was the primary task of the university. Intellectual and political freedom, however, did intersect in the classroom, where students were guaranteed the right to express opinions without being penalized by individual instructors or the administration. This right, Hofstadter argued, was essential to the mission of higher education because free speech cultivated independent ideas, usefully contested bad ones, and broke neatly from the vocational side of academe. While conceding the difficulty of defining student freedoms in case-by-case scenarios, Hofstadter obviously felt more comfortable championing academic freedom for students in the classroom than in the streets.[29]

The Berkeley address concluded with a plea, revisited at the Columbia commencement, for recognition of the university as a unique institution that required unusual privileges and protections. Fragile and imperfect, it nevertheless remained the most important patron of the rights of the mind. And Hofstadter could not conceive of a single public issue — free speech, Vietnam, civil rights — worthy of prevailing upon the reputation or resources of the university to openly involve itself in political affairs. But here a fundamental problem arises. When students used campus offices for political purposes there existed a disciplinary system to monitor, regulate and, if necessary, punish their actions. But when administrators and regents politicized their institutions by bringing them into the orbit of the consumer/cold war state, no such formal oversight existed. At its best, the student movement attempted to render the universities less vulnerable to the particular needs of the military and the corporations — in its way, a commendable blow *for* academic freedom. Even if less high-minded activists used this noble mission as a subterfuge to carry out what Hofstadter described as the "politics of self-expression," the fact remains that to a great degree the universities handed them the issues.

To understand the anger and hostility that many students felt toward their professors and their universities, it might be helpful to explore their anticipation — their hopes, really — of what a reformed academic scene would look like. Young people tend to assimilate words like "justice" and "peace" in literal, concrete terms rather than metaphorically or abstractly. They *feel* these concepts more than their teachers and parents. And when their teachers and parents use the words without effect or conviction, they are disappointed, sometimes devastated. James Gilbert, a member of the faculty at Columbia's Teachers College in 1969, remembers acutely the distance between wish and reality that shaped academic attitudes among his scholastic generation.

> Much of the violence came from students who had immense respect—
> perhaps too much respect—for the University as an ideal, for professors
> as mentors, and for ideas as effective tools of civilization and culture.
> Thus, the immensity of the feeling of betrayal when everyone compromised so deeply. The war in Vietnam and the compromise of the university in pursuing that war, the failure of the intellectuals to live out their
> ideas, the cloying conservatism of institutions that refused to change,
> was intensified by the illusions that students had of their mentors. I can
> remember clearly how deeply impressed I was when, at the first Wisconsin teach-in, professors spoke in remarkable and clear and persuasive
> ways about the tragedy, the beastliness of war. And then nothing happened. It went on and on and on and that was the problem. Ultimately,
> the professors went back into their classrooms and the academy was
> proven to have no real influence. Thus the dismay; thus the anger; thus
> the need to turn against the institutions that seemed to acquiesce in the
> war because of their weakness.[30]

*   *   *

Columbia would soon have its own troubles, the result of a host of long-standing antagonisms brought into sharper relief by the war in Vietnam. In 1959 the university had joined the Institute for Defense Analysis [IDA] in compliance with the Defense Department's efforts to coordinate research among select institutions. The following year the New York legislature approved a plan for Columbia to build a gymnasium in Morningside Park. Within a few short years these seemingly unconnected decisions touched off bitter animosity among some students and faculty. Affiliation with IDA meant university complicity with America's aggressive global ambitions. And this included Vietnam. Johnson's 1965 decision to escalate the war precipitated the first teach-ins at Columbia, galvanizing debate on a number of related concerns — military recruitment on campus, submission of class rankings to draft boards and, of course, membership in IDA. The gymnasium issue grew increasingly controversial as well. It served as a catalyst for a host of problems dividing whites and blacks and, more broadly, underlined Columbia's "imperialistic" relations with the Harlem community and its own students.

The gymnasium and IDA provocations circulated in an environment poisoned by administrative neglect of student services. Hofstadter correctly noted in the wake of the rebellion that, in comparison to Berkeley, Columbia was not a repressive institution. It was an unresponsive institution.[31] During the 1966–67 academic year, the university raised nearly $60 million in fundraising—its most successful revenue-generating campaign to date. Amid this plenty, graduate programs declined in national rankings, the administration developed tougher polices on tuition payments, and the physical plant—classrooms, dormitories, Butler Library—was in a state of embarrassing deterioration. Combined, student unrest, the civil rights movement, and the Vietnam war were at the core of Columbia's protest culture.

The student movement at Morningside stirred Hofstadter's fear of popular rebellion (anti-intellectualism within the gates of Columbia itself!) and confirmed his suspicion that the liberal values of his adulthood were in danger of succumbing to a more potent radicalism. He complained to David Riesman that politics in America had very recently and very rapidly descended to a dangerously low level. It polarized people, fed off fears and discontent, destroyed older expectations of compromise and consensus building, and placed a premium on conflict as a way to express individual resentments against a monolithic "system." On specific issues, Hofstadter was in complete agreement with the students. He opposed the building of the gymnasium, denounced the presence of IDA on campus, and believed that the university's disciplinary structure (a fierce debate raged over how to punish protesting students) had to be taken out of the hands of the president's office. He further insisted that both untenured professors and undergraduates needed to assume a greater role in the governance of Columbia. He signed a faculty resolution in April 1968 that outlined his support for "the establishment of a representative commission to be elected by the faculties to propose necessary changes in the structure of the University, including the participation of junior faculty and students in decision-making."[32]

The militancy of the student Left, however, discouraged Hofstadter. He believed the young radicals took advantage of a university and a society that granted their generation unprecedented privileges and opportunities. "It seemed to me," he observed shortly after the crisis, "that the students had diagnosed very well the distinctive weakness of the academic liberal mentality, and that they had acted with corresponding ruthlessness." Correct as they were on the gymnasium and IDA, he continued, they were wrong on just about everything else — from the demand for amnesty for violent protestors to the absurd request for the right to demonstrate in buildings where classes were held. Caving in, Hofstadter insisted, meant the end of academic freedom at Columbia. In his contempt for the new radicals, he drew categorical distinctions between the serious social criticism of his youth and the leaders of the New Left. "I was raised in the 1930s, on a more severe brand of Marxism. . . . What you have, in place of revolutionaries, are clowns like Abbie Hoffman and Jerry Rubin."[33]

This censure overlooks, however, important points of continuity between the old and new radicals. As president of the University of Buffalo chapter of the National Student League, Hofstadter had both organized and participated in a number of activities that foreshadowed the student initiatives of the sixties. *Anatomy of a Movement*, a 1970 congressional report produced by the Committee on Internal Security, described the NSL as "the only militant student movement to exist in America prior to the emergence of the New Left, [it] exploited anti-war sentiment, held demonstrations and marches, and attempted physical disruption of campus activities which led to arrest, suspensions and expulsions of its members from colleges."[34] In many ways, the committee report concluded, the kind of political protest favored by Hofstadter's generation anticipated the current crop of campus radicals.

In the midst of the Columbia crisis, however, Hofstadter sensed little connection with the rebels. He wrote heatedly to Harvey Swados that the students' description of Columbia — the intellectual home of some of America's most gifted minds — as a "dead" university was contemptuous. David Herbert Donald summed up Hofstadter's frustrations during this difficult period noting that "as a liberal who criticized the liberal tradition from within, he was appalled by the growing radical, even revolutionary sentiment that he sensed among his colleagues and his students. He could never share their simplistic, moralistic approach to social problems of enormous complexity, any more than he could be attracted by their coarser rallying cries of politics." The distance that Donald described as separating Hofstadter and his students, however, was not insurmountable. Despite his belief that Columbia could not give in to the demands of those illegally occupying campus buildings (including his own), Hofstadter never lost the respect of the radicals. While some Columbia professors were the victims of violence, he escaped unscathed. After Hamilton Hall was cleared of protesters in the early morning of 30 April, he returned to his office to find a note reading "The Forces of Liberation have, at great length, decided to spare your office (because you are not one of them)."[35]

Throughout the late April confrontation, the gulf between the generations became dismayingly wide. "Red Sunday at Columbia," Alfred Kazin captured the scene, "with red flags flying from one window and the SDS militants . . . raising their fists in movie Communist salutes. Columbia's gates are barricaded, cops all over the place, students milling around. . . . Meanwhile, the Old Left (D. Bell, I. Howe, A. Kazin) are as sure as anything that all this is bad, the New Left is having a field day of gleeful dishonesty, and it is not impossible that the police will yet come in to clear the buildings of students."[36] On the other side, the apparent retreat of the intellectuals behind a misplaced reverence for academic freedom and the life of the mind filled some radicals with a sense of betrayal. Columbia graduate student Mark Naison's memoir of his orals defense illustrates the stunning disconnect between the protesters and their professors:

Fayerweather [was] occupied at the precise moment my exams began. . . . My orals board, composed of Richard Hofstadter and some equally uptight, but less renowned professors, began their questioning amidst the sounds of breaking furniture, shouts of rage and pride, fragments of falling plaster and chants of "shut it down." Every class in the building was rooted out of its routine, but my orals, whether by accident, or preference, was left more or less alone. The behavior of the faculty members was curious. They were not, as I expected, unusually hostile to me, but absolutely tickled pink at the prospect of keeping the institutional ritual alive amidst the surrounding chaos. They regarded themselves as the carriers of the light of civilization among the depredations of the strange new barbarians who had somehow exploded into their lives. Every time plaster fell on their heads they felt a strange thrill; they alone stood between America and Totalitarianism. And so it went, two and a half hours, without interruption. I sensed, during the whole awful comedy, that they were more interested in their own performances than in mine. There was no question that I would pass; the issue was; could they retain the composure to ask good questions? They did. . . . They

had, just had, to keep the ritual intact. To let no event, particularly a political one, detract from the dignity of the transmission of man's most
ancient legacy—The legacy of THE MIND. I was pretty absorbed in the
whole thing myself. I played the game by all the rules. Man, they knew
that I was for everything happening in that building, from the breaking
of the furniture to the slugging of professors, but I would express my values in measured tones, over a glass of sherry, and make a final chivalric
gesture. I would escort them out of the building. And so the final act featured Mark Naison, in a suit and tie and jive ass shoes, leading Richard
Hofstadter and Dwight Miner, equally attired, out the window of an occupied building in front of two thousand people.[37]

Naison's account, however, emphasized division at the expense of
efforts on both sides of the generational divide to find common ground.
Despite his deep disappointment, Hofstadter remained flexible
throughout the spring. "He opened his house to anyone who wanted to
talk about events," Paula Fass remembers. "These were free and open
sessions, he was very eager to understand." Even before the crisis had
played itself out, Hofstadter had written to Eric Foner of his distur-
bance over the demonstrations and asked Foner to speak to him about
what was happening at Columbia.[38] And Daniel Singal recalls an important meeting between Hofstadter and his students that took place in the
fall of 1968.

Hofstadter asked all of us who were working with him at the time and
available on campus to come by his office for an informal discussion
about the events that had closed down the university the previous
spring. . . . The meeting lasted about an hour and involved Hofstadter
posing questions to us about what our generation of students was trying
to accomplish in its radical politics. I especially recall him responding
skeptically to the notion that students might be capable of setting off a
massive uprising within society, perhaps enticing the working class to
join in. He spoke of his own experiences in the '30s, which taught him
how hard it was for the left to mobilize the American lower classes. . . .
He was also at pains to make us aware of how much he shared some of
the values of the protestors. . . . In particular he stressed how alienated
he was from the academic profession and its institutional apparatus
(which students regarded as the enemy), and he demonstrated this by
ceremoniously tossing a copy of the *Journal of American History* into the
wastebasket. . . . He liked to picture himself as something of a lone

scholar churning out his books apart from the rest of the profession, and I think it was this self-image that led him to make his dramatic gesture.[39]

Hofstadter's efforts to maintain open lines of communication were not limited to young scholars working under his direction. He rued the polarization of the faculty and worked diligently to reach a consensus among his colleagues in Hamilton and Fayerweather. "The history department," Peter Gay notes, "was essentially in line with Hofstadter's view: anti-Vietnam, anti-administration." John Mundy recalls that during the crisis Hofstadter "was a voice for moderation and pacification. Other colleagues . . . simply wrung their hands and lamented, but he kept his head admirably, and hence, as chairman of the department, I began to consult him regularly. He was invaluable." Still, others suspected that Hofstadter's efforts to understand the student rebellion were compromised by the trauma of his early political experiences. Michael Wallace, for example, believed that "a part of Hofstadter looked at the Columbia situation from a generational perspective and saw it through the focus of what transpired in the thirties with the Nazis."[40]

*　　*　　*

Before Columbia could exhale and break for the summer, one final provocation had to be hurdled — the spring graduation ceremony. In his fifteen years as president of the university, Grayson Kirk had never failed to deliver the commencement address. But the actions of his administration during the crisis made it impossible for him to go before the students. In need of a consensual figure to initiate the long and painful healing process, the university prevailed upon Hofstadter to give the remarks. He remains the only member of the faculty to be so honored. His correspondence indicates that he approached the address with some trepidation — but he never considered turning the institution down. His and Columbia's fates were intertwined. They drew strength from each other.[41]

It was, to put it mildly, an impossible situation. The administration's slow reaction and then violent response to the crisis — calling in a thousand policemen to clear campus buildings resulted in 712 arrests, more than 150 reported injuries, and nearly 400 police-brutality complaints — polarized the campus. Hofstadter believed that by agreeing to speak at the commencement he represented neither the administration nor the students. But his decision to stand on the same podium with campus officials in a cheerless exercise to keep the integrity and tradition of the academic calendar intact struck some observers as hardly impartial.

Columbia commencements are traditionally held on Low Plaza and South Field, but to avoid disruption, the university, with considerable assistance from the New York City Police Department, held the graduation in the Cathedral of St. John the Divine. The ceremony opened with the national anthem followed by the invocation and a William Byrd motet performed by the Columbia Choir. At its conclusion, Hofstadter walked to the podium to deliver his remarks The moment he spoke, nearly 300 irreconcilables stood up and left the cathedral to join some 2,000 demonstrators on the steps of Low Library for a countercommencement. Hofstadter never interrupted his address. He began on a personal note — "For a long time, Columbia University has been a part of my life"—and emphasized his attachment to the institution as an imperfect but vital symbol of academic freedom. The address steered a middle path between radicals and conservatives (undoubtedly a major reason why Hofstadter was chosen to give the address), calling for reform at Columbia while insisting that change be deliberate and disciplined. The perfect society did not exist, he cautioned, and all sides needed to take that into account as they went about assessing the future of the university.[42]

On the issue of student protests, Hofstadter predictably came down on the side of order. Students should have influence, he insisted, not authority. At its best, he continued, the university served as a fertile marketplace of ideas, and political pressures only served to cloud the primary mission of higher education. He acknowledged that Columbia's connection to IDA violated the integrity of the academy and he fairly criticized the administration for its actions in this area. The university, he insisted, should do all it could in the future to avoid entanglement in political commitments.[43]

In the nation's present crisis, he continued, universities were needed more than ever as voices of reason. At their best, they offered sanctuary to intellectual heretics wary of popular prejudices and suspicious of concentrated power. As a primary beneficiary of such protections, Hofstadter condemned the tactics of those who would destroy the system. To forcibly occupy and shut down a university, he maintained, had far-ranging and debilitating repercussions on the health of the entire society. But how was a society to quarantine itself from the radicals? In an ironic and painful twist, Hofstadter and the academy he revered faced a new and unexpected threat that came neither from the Left nor the Right, but from the children of the liberal class itself.[44]

The commencement address offered a simple, elegant, and direct reply to the recent crisis. It promised no ready solutions but communicated an important underlying truth: Columbia would go on but its future as a distinguished institution depended on the campus' reaction to the events that spring. What the university needed, Hofstadter concluded, was "stability, peace, mutual confidence."[45] This call for reconciliation occurred as the old guard scrambled to reassert its authority. Hofstadter's plea for the continuation of a civil university culture was proposed before an audience that included forty uniformed policemen and a number of plainclothes officers keeping watch over the ceremony. Their presence was more than symbolic. The year 1968 was a tragic one for representative figures; a few hours after Hofstadter spoke before the graduates, Robert Kennedy was gunned down in the Los Angeles Ambassador Hotel.

The commencement address was published in *The American Scholar* and won considerable attention. Diana Trilling remembered its emotional impact on those seated in the cathedral: "Richard Hofstadter . . . spoke about what was the point of an attack on the best thing that our society could offer us which was education. It was very moving, deeply moving, and I think I wasn't the only person who began to cry." Daniel Patrick Moynihan concurred, and complimented Hofstadter personally for producing "one of the most moving and eloquent documents of the age." The younger generation, as might be expected, had a much different impression of things. Columbia SDS member Tom Hurwitz recalled that "the senior faculty were very privileged members of the university and tended to see it in only positive terms because they loved their positions at the university. The idea of criticizing it, and the idea of looking at the whole situation, especially at Columbia, was really beyond them, because they benefited so thoroughly." Hofstadter's student John Milton Cooper echoed these remarks, arguing that his mentor's actions during this difficult period were tinged with self-interest. "Hofstadter was an extremely privileged individual and like the French aristocrats during the revolution he saw his beautiful life being challenged by the peasants. The infidels were defiling the temple; the rule of the mandarins was threatened."[46]

The spring uprising left several issues unresolved. Most immediate, a wounded administration limped into the summer as a number of student organizations geared up for fall protests. Hofstadter and several colleagues privately called upon William Peterson, chairman of the board of trustees, to press for President Kirk's resignation. "We have come to the conclusion," their petition asserted, "that Dr. Kirk's continued presidency would be grave, even perhaps a dangerous institutional liability. He has become a divisive symbol both to students and faculty, and his presence would provide far more provocation than leadership."[47] Kirk's fate was likely sealed at this point, but an expression of no confidence among key faculty did nothing to bolster his position. He resigned a few weeks before the start of the fall semester.

A second issue proved much more problematic. The fall term brought renewed agitation, including vandalism and the sporadic disruption of classes. In response, Hofstadter circulated a letter to select colleagues asking for what amounted to a faculty strike against individual students involved in activities designed to interrupt instruction. It was time, he argued, for faculty to defend themselves, their colleagues, and the students in their classes who wanted to learn. It was time, in other words, to defend academic freedom. If the professoriat did not reassert itself, it risked losing the university. He proposed withholding instruction, grades, and letters of recommendation from the agitators.[48]

His probe received an overwhelmingly positive response among senior faculty, and within days a 500-word statement on academic freedom was drafted and signed by over 800 Columbia professors. "The University as a Sanctuary of Academic Freedom" traced Hofstadter's Berkeley and Columbia addresses, calling for tougher disciplinary procedures to deal with students who prevented the meeting of classes, and upholding the university as the indispensable base of free inquiry in a troubled nation. Fritz Stern read the statement at a 10 March 1969 televised news conference, a portion of which singled out for criticism the behavior of "militant students . . . [who] have discovered the fragility of free, liberal universities; in exploiting that fragility, they are threatening to wreck the traditional purposes and values of Western universities."[49]

Stern's performance took place inside the men's faculty club, a *New York Times* photograph showing, with the exception of one smiling professor, a grim line of graying scholars in tweed and ties holding the line for the life of the mind. Outside, Students for a Democratic Society were meeting at the Sundial at the center of campus. Unfurling a red banner and singing folk songs, the small rally marked International Women's Day. Symbolically and professionally, the postwar patriarchs were in eclipse — history was pushing them aside.

After the debacle at Columbia, Hofstadter began to wonder if liberalism really could make it in America. The student movement successfully exploited the weaknesses of a university system that proved incapable of asserting its authority. It lacked a certain sensible hard edge born of confidence in its mission that suggested deeper and more troubling doubts. Hofstadter remained committed to liberalism during this difficult time, but he questioned the politics of many around him. The Columbia crisis, he explained to a colleague, forced him to realize that most liberals did not understand liberalism. They believed it was self-perpetuating, even in the face of violence. They had, he continued, no idea of the toughness and terrific effort required to sustain it against enemies and indifference. He further noted that the prevalent style of liberalism was not liberal at all. It was soft, weak, and ideologically inconsistent. Rather than serve as a kind of consensual middle ground for the majority of Americans — like the Johnson constituency of 1964 — liberals were tilting toward the left, in a sense abandoning their liberalism. If, he concluded, a group of right-wing students had occupied buildings at Columbia, the faculty would have demanded that the administration throw them out. Many liberals, Hofstadter concluded, simply did not understand that the rule of law applied to all — even ultraconservatives.[50]

The echoes of the Columbia crisis can be heard in Hofstadter's final books. They extol a consensual vision of political and intellectual life while touching upon the sense of generational purpose that Hofstadter presumed essential to the preservation of a pluralistic nation. He wrote David Riesman of his fear that a liberal democracy simply was not strong enough to survive in a secular culture. With Americans increasingly looking for meaning and self-validation outside of organized religion, politics filled a hole, but it was a hyper rather than reflective kind of politics that undermined the traditionally pragmatic and consensual foundations upon which the nation's institutions were organized.[51] Sporadic violence continued to plague Morningside for several years. Sadly, Hofstadter never lived to see the university he loved on its former footing. In the spring of 1969 he reduced his teaching commitments and moved to the East Side. An astonished observer of Columbia's self-inflicted wounds, he drew from the experience a dismal corollary to the broader decline of liberal attitudes and institutions in America.

Conflict and
Consensus — Redux

I see little point in denying that, for all its limitations, consensus as a general view of American history had certain distinct, if transitional merits.

RICHARD HOFSTADTER, 1968

Parts of each day, typically the morning and quiet hours of late evening,
found Richard Hofstadter working methodically at a cluttered desk in
his Claremont Avenue study. This creative routine served for many years
to nurture a pattern of reflection and writing that broke productively
from the constrictions of a traditional academic schedule. So ingrained,
it followed him from a winter study to a summer surf. "He was not an
easy man to vacation with," C. Vann Woodward remembered. "The
beaches tended to be strewn with bibliographical disputation, and lan-
guorous tropical mornings tended to be disturbed by the clatter of a
typewriter. He gave us all an inferiority complex—which we felt we
thoroughly deserved."[1] Mental labor calmed Hofstadter, medicated his
powerful mind, and pushed him to a remarkable level of achievement.
Publication was a life-affirming exercise. As his bibliography grew, so did
the impression of close observers that he anticipated the illness that
eventually silenced his pen. With much to say and much to lose, he discovered in the everyday act of writing history a pleasant and blind faith.

Hofstadter's professional success was never as spontaneous or smooth
as the trappings of academic stardom—appreciative reviews, sparkling dust-jacket blurbs, impressive royalties—suggested. Like any imaginative and agile thinker, he worked on several projects that never came
to fruition. Among them included a biography of Thorstein Veblen, a
history of American thought in the 1890s, and a study of Newton, Darwin, and Freud. He and Woodward agreed in 1961 to serve as coeditors
of the *Oxford History of the United States;* the first volume of that se-

ries would not appear for twenty years — more than a decade after Hofstadter's death. Predictably, the collaboration brought Alfred Knopf no joy. "The more I think over [it]," he wrote Hofstadter, "the more depressed I become. You and Vann, two of my favorites, undertaking what sounds like a magnum opus for both of you, for Oxford. What can Oxford do for you that I can't, and why should an English university press publish the two most distinguished Americans? Can you imagine your British opposite numbers doing a job like this for Yale or Harvard? The very idea brings out all the latent chauvinism that lurks in me."[2]

The prospect of overseas publication, however, appealed to Hofstadter, who saw in the venture a splendid opportunity to introduce his work to a new audience. Despite his pleasure at Knopf's issuing his books in Britain under its successful Vintage label, the idea of an independent British publication intrigued him. He cannily confided to Knopf his hope that when his next book hit the market, the house might find an English press to bring it out in Britain. This had nothing to do with sales, Hofstadter insisted; rather it was a matter of self-esteem and an author's sense of vanity. Sensitive to the needs of a bankable author's ego, Knopf helped arrange the following year for the English publication of *Anti-Intellectualism in American Life* through the firm of Jonathan Cape.[3]

Knopf's concern that his star historian might jump ship and strike up a relationship with a prestigious English university press was premature. In a highly competitive academic book market, the Oxford series foundered in a frustrating search for authors. The celebrated historians coveted by the editors, including Bernard Bailyn, Edmund S. Morgan, Norman Graebner, Arthur Schlesinger, Jr., Kenneth Stampp, David Herbert Donald, and John Morton Blum, were burdened by existing research and publication agendas that barred their participation. This inconvenient fact complicated Hofstadter's editorial chores, but he understood his colleagues' reticence. His own plans to write a long study of the Jeffersonian and Jacksonian eras for the *Oxford History* succumbed to other assignments. In place of a grand sweep of the Jeffersonian period, he published *The Idea of a Party System* (1969), a smart if less ambitious study of popular democracy in the early American republic that conformed to his personal interest in the era, rather than a survey-like assessment.[4]

Hofstadter's interest in the narrative-driven *Oxford History* marked a sharp departure from the social-psychological studies he produced in the fifties. His next major work, *The Progressive Historians: Turner, Beard,*

Parrington (1968) was his most conventionally argued book since *The American Political Tradition.* Originally conceived as a brief appraisal of Progressive literature, the study evolved into a complex interior dialogue between the author and his past. It allowed Hofstadter to clarify his thoughts on a half-century of American historiography at the precise moment that his own scholarly generation wrestled with doubt and decline. The postwar historians stood in 1968 on the same ground as the Progressives in 1938 — on the cusp of eclipse.

For years, liberal scholars had reviewed the books, critiqued the conference papers, and written the letters of recommendation of and for other liberal scholars. They — like their professional ancestors and heirs — carved out a vision of American history that accorded with their generational experiences. Hofstadter's friendliest critics included Woodward and David Potter — impeccably earnest and impressive thinkers who constructively pointed out the less tenable claims made by the social scientists. His correspondence with these men acknowledged his respect for their valued challenges to his work. First- and third-rate historians, he wrote to Potter, were easily distinguished by the manner in which they criticized their colleagues. Were they interested in drawing attention to honest differences that advanced knowledge, or did they simply hope to score points and embarrass their peers?[5] Both Woodward and Potter shared Hofstadter's appreciation of liberalism and, unlike more left-leaning critics, including William Appleman Williams and Norman Pollack, they accepted the two-party consensus as a valuable hedge against political radicalism.

The professional consensus shared by liberal scholars began to break down as the New Left arrived on the scene. This younger generation rejected liberal interpretations and assumptions in favor of a historical perspective that gave meaning to their own political and social experiences. In the process, they found few points of connection with their teachers. The liberal mind was conceived in the economic and ideological crises that defined the Depression decade — not in the material abundance of the fifties and sixties. It pointed proudly to the prosperity of Keynesian economics, progress in race relations, and the rising status of ethnic Americans as evidence of the salutary social philosophy advanced by the New Deal.

To many historians coming of age in the sixties, however, the liberal consensus served as a triumphalist ideology that legitimized American bigotry, imperialism, and economic inequality. In their search for an alternative tradition, many junior scholars felt a strong connection with the Progressive historians who, like themselves, stressed the role of conflict in the American past. "The rediscovery of poverty and racism, the commitment to civil rights for Negroes, the criticism of intervention in Cuba and Vietnam, shattered many of the assumptions of the fifties," observed radical historian Barton Bernstein. "For the Progressive historians in general," he added approvingly, "historical inquiry, as their 'new history' emphasized, should be relevant to the present." Jesse Lemisch, a young scholar then teaching at the University of Chicago, valued the Progressive achievement as well and offered a pointed criticism of the consensus school's claims to objectivity and interpretive sophistication. "Despite our pretensions to social science, we would seem to be hardly more genuinely scientific than we were fifty years ago. Many social scientists continue to draw conclusions about entire societies on examinations of the minority at the top. This approach has distorted our view and, sometimes, cut us off from past reality. Our earliest history has been seen as a period of consensus and classlessness, in part because our historians have chosen to see it that way." Hofstadter recognized the extraordinary cross-generational alliance between the two Lefts and, in returning his attention to the Progressive historians, he engaged in a fresh dialogue with their putative descendants.[6]

The New Left's commitment to enlisting history in the service of social reform reminded some liberals of the partisan use of the past that had both enlivened and marred Charles Beard's most controversial work. Hofstadter agreed that the protest culture of the sixties persuasively made the case for a return to the conflict theme, but not at the expense of the considerable interpretive advances initiated by his own generation. This became for Hofstadter something of a personal battle. He wrote a colleague in 1967 that his earlier books had been accepted both inside and out of the universities with enthusiasm and generosity. Now, he noted, junior scholars looked to make their reputations at his expense. They casually dismissed or eagerly attacked his work as part of their right of passage into the profession. The intellectual destructiveness of this act deeply troubled Hofstadter. The postwar historians introduced a healthy complexity to their field, he insisted, mainly by exploiting the interpretive insights offered by the social sciences. This rich bounty impressed him, and he regretted the younger generation's rejection of its historical fathers — even as he, in an equally sincere exercise in intellectual pruning, had rejected his own.[7]

*   *   *

The Progressive Historians is a beautifully written study that stands as a singular achievement in the fields of historiography and intellectual biography. Further, it is a contemporary document, deeply engaged with the pedagogical transition from a professor-centered model to one increasingly receptive to the demands of students. It is, even more broadly speaking, the graduate school generation of the thirties speaking to the graduate school generation of the sixties. Columbia University, with its eclectic mixture of clashing metropolitan styles and decaying physical plant, proved particularly vulnerable to the politics of protest as we have seen. The slumification of Morningside Heights, rising crime rates in the city, and confrontations between faculty and undergraduates forced Hofstadter to rethink his personal and professional commitments. The strain undoubtedly found its way into his book. "The Columbia crisis and the New Left, though nowhere mentioned," one reviewer remarked, "rise to stalk the reader from the distant dust of university and political struggles."[8]

The Progressive Historians is, of course, much more than a treatise of the times. Revisiting the conflict theme allowed Hofstadter to conclude a career-long conversation with the men who had formed his earliest historical impressions. His 1969 confession to Arthur Schlesinger, Jr., that he reacted to historians more than to history, is both instructive and refreshing in a profession that regards objectivity as its raison d'être. The bias against historiography, David Levering Lewis has written, reflected "a curious deficit in introspection . . . among professional historians, I think—a function of the inductive way we do history and of the temperamental aversion most of us develop over time to theorizing about the value of what we do." Though Hofstadter seemed never to have suffered a "deficit in introspection," he did feel the need to justify the expenditure of precious time and energy on a work of historiographical analysis. He promised himself, he wrote Schlesinger, that after finishing *The Progressive Historians* he would never again write on the topic of historiography.[9]

Despite Hofstadter's efforts to draw a clear distinction between historical and historiographical works, his own scholarship happily mixed the two. In the course of exploring the lives and cultural references of historians (Turner/Beard) or historical actors (Bryan/Goldwater), his studies consistently supported liberal metropolitanism and praised the eclipse of the older progressivism. Each of Hofstadter's books is a unique product and stands on its own, and yet the authorial concerns and interpretive assumptions connecting *The Progressive Historians* (historiography) and *The Age of Reform* (history) convey a strikingly similar thematic rendering of the past.

Reassessing Beard's generation further allowed Hofstadter to revisit material that historians had long laid to rest. "I suppose you are aware," Eric McKitrick proposed, "that everyone has lost interest in the three men you're writing about." There was truth in this tease. In an era of historical scholarship increasingly responsive to studies of race, class, and gender, the public and professional responses to *The Progressive Historians* were less than what Hofstadter customarily received. Who, after all, read Vernon Parrington anymore? Hofstadter's editor Ashbel Green remembers that Knopf anticipated the manuscript's limited appeal yet supported *The Progressive Historians* because of its author's well-regarded name. Hofstadter's talent, reputation, and felicitous style guaranteed respectable sales, but could not attract a large audience to a work of historiography. As the decade came to a close, academics grew increasingly friendly to fresher insights and more current methodologies, including computer-aided studies (quantohistory), analysis of the mind (psychohistory), and attention to the environment (ecohistory). While Hofstadter's books did not ignore the new trends — one commentator accurately described his work on the coupling of paranoia and political culture as that of "an innovator in the field of psychohistory" — neither did they, with the exception of the incomplete *America at 1750,* incorporate the burgeoning field of social history into the broader synthetic structure of his scholarship.[10]

Hofstadter was aware of the hard labor and good luck that accompanied his rapid rise in the historical profession, and on at least one occasion, he expressed concern that his best days were behind him. He admitted to McKitrick in 1960 that from time to time he skimmed through *The American Political Tradition,* proud to know that it held up well with the passage of years. Its interpretive power and literary charisma made Hofstadter question whether he would ever again write such an important and powerful book.[11] Caught in the undertow of changing intellectual currents, Hofstadter struggled in his final studies to sustain a public following. The scholarship that he produced in the fifties struck a responsive chord with a satisfied and self-assured audience sympathetic to a confident, ironic, urbane, and witty voice. More than merely capturing a mood, Hofstadter's probing criticism of popular democracy was both refreshing and useful to liberals trapped between the politics of the old populist Left and the McCarthy Right. Yet by the late sixties historical irony (and its accompanying descriptive apparatus, including ambiguity, burlesque, paradox, contradiction, and absurdity) had become — like Mencken's brand of satire in the thirties — unfashionable, a conceptual casualty to the younger generation's self-seriousness and what Hofstadter described unsympathetically as its devotion to the politics of style.

There were other factors — both professional and personal — that diminished the impact of Hofstadter's scholarship in the sixties. The popularity of the new social history encouraged tightly focused books that demanded very specialized research. Its commitment to exploring the lives of forgotten historical actors — common laborers, slaves, the poor — inaugurated a revolution in the academy friendly to microstudies of the past. The monograph, in other words, was back. And Hofstadter did not write monographic history. A master of the broad historical survey (nearly all of his books include the words "United States," "America" or "American" in the title), his publishing instincts were general rather than specialized.

Too, Hofstadter's later works lacked the freshness, originality, and bite of his early books. The demise of liberalism's most notorious political enemies likely had much to do with this. Hofstadter was a brilliant opposition writer, and in the fifties professors were on the front lines of a spirited clash with McCarthyism. Following Goldwater's defeat in 1964, however, liberalism appeared to have triumphed over its antagonists. The two books that Hofstadter completed between that date and his death — *The Progressive Historians* and *The Idea of a Party System* — are defensive in nature; they reflect their author's desire to preserve the political and cultural preferences of the postwar generation rather than strike out in fresh directions. They reveal further Hofstadter's intellectual confusion over how to respond to the New Left. Out of fear, anger, or fantasy, the Far Right inspired Hofstadter to write some of the most original studies of American political culture ever produced. The Left never provoked such a productive reaction. Hofstadter believed that liberals could reach their revolutionary-minded students and find common ground on which to strengthen the American reform tradition. In his late scholarship, he sought to instruct radicals, not — as he had conservatives — to diagnose their mental tics.

The need to reconsider the dominant historical themes of his youth buoyed Hofstadter throughout the writing of *The Progressive Historians*. He described his work as a discharging of thirty years of allegiances and second thoughts; a final engagement with ideas that he first began to explore as an undergraduate at the University of Buffalo. Nothing he'd ever written, he assured Harvey Swados, ever came so fast, so easily, and with such meaning to its author. This highly personal project, however, reached deep into the community of historians, for Hofstadter's inability to shake the Progressive legacy converged with his profession's urgent and timely impulse to revisit the theme of conflict in American history. As a result, the book stands as an eloquent testament to the achievements of the "middle" generation of twentieth-century historians, sandwiched, uncomfortably between the Old and New Lefts. "In writing something like a chapter on your own intellectual biography," Henry Nash Smith commended Hofstadter, "you are writing a chapter in the collective autobiography of a whole generation of people who work in American history and literature. And you are thus helping us to understand ourselves."[12]

*   *   *

The Progressive Historians begins with a brisk survey of historical writing in America before 1890. The impressive number of schools committed to recovering the past—nationalist, scientific, romantic, patrician— implied a wide variance of views, but this was emphatically not the case. With few exceptions, pre-Progressives shared the social and cultural values that sustained property rights, privileged Anglo-Saxon Protestantism, and championed the robust nationalism of the Civil War decades. The nation's early pastmasters, in other words, agreed that racial and economic progress were to be measured upon a common scale. Theirs was a Wasp consensus.[13]

The views of the first professional historians proved too static to survive an age of dynamic change, and by the turn of the century younger scholars from the Midwest had begun to alter the face of American historicism. Hofstadter clearly admired the Progressive challenge to the established order. Its suspicion of scientific racism, distrust of the great titans, and confidence in the efficacy of state regulation were comfortably in accord with his own views. Hofstadter recognized in their focus, energy, and commitment to change a striking and successful challenge to the status quo. Progressives wrestled the intellectual initiative away from the East, connected with an impressively large reading public, and inspired young students (including Hofstadter) with a fresh and critical style. Charles and Mary Beard's *The Rise of American Civilization* (1927) set a new standard for a work of historical synthesis, generating praise among professional historians and the public on its way to becoming a scholarly best seller. During these years, Hofstadter marveled, Beard single-handedly changed the way Americans thought about their history. And even from the darkened distance of a half century, the Progressive legacy continued to make its imprint felt upon the profession.[14]

Of the three scholars profiled in *The Progressive Historians,* Frederick Jackson Turner had the least impact on Hofstadter's intellectual development. Turner's commitment to popular action secured his reputation as the poet-historian of democracy, the author of a mythical frontier that embodied the tensions and promise of the agrarian way of life. He established, Hofstadter argued, a vision of American nationalism consistent with the character of American citizens living beyond the Appalachians. But Turner's break with the East was more apparent than real. His loyalty to the values of an older America embellished in a frontier archetype — democratic, independent, *free* — followed the well-worn path blazed by Cooper's Natty Bumpo, Melville's Ishmael, and Twain's Huck Finn. This creative recasting of the romantic revolt into a political rebellion presented Jeffersonians, Jacksonians, and Populists as more authentic Americans than the patrician or ethnic constituencies with whom they parried. Turner's failure to explore democracy's limitations, however, eroded his posthumous reputation. Hofstadter argued that a full investigation of frontier individualism revealed that anti-intellectualism, racism, violence, and vigilante justice were important — even organic — features of the western experience. The spirit of borderland democracy, he continued, unwittingly defended social Darwinism, the Ku Klux Klan, and the industrial regime while establishing an unproductive political litmus test for Republican Party presidential aspirants. In their more vacuous poses Coolidge, Hoover, and Goldwater clumsily worshiped at the alter of the western ideal, serving as spokesmen for an exhausted tradition of rugged individualism.

The fact that the frontier totem continued to resonate among serious thinkers astounded Hofstadter. Even some of the more sophisticated representatives of the New Deal, he noted, rhapsodized about the return to an agrarian paradise under government direction. They were, of course, men of a different generation, a different America. The emergence of the metropolis — and the consequent decline of Turner's influence — paralleled Hofstadter's own intellectual development. The thirties, he observed in an autobiographical passage, produced young scholars from ethnic backgrounds who were untouched by the glories and virtues of rural life.[15]

Hofstadter measured the liberties of the frontier by the intellectual and cultural latitude that western life permitted. The persistence of racism and anti-Semitism in northern cities may have caught the eye of southern scholars like Woodward, but *The Progressive Historians* accentuated the impressive level of reform energy found in the East. By comparison, the crude conditions of rural settlements inspired a unique and particularly brutal ferocity. Hofstadter accused Turner's democratic pioneer of exhibiting masculine identity hang-ups of arrogance and aggression. The killing of the Native Americans, conquest of northern Mexico, and numbing isolation of the frontier were brutal, soul-scarring realities of western life unacknowledged by Turner. His pioneers lacked the element of tragedy, for suffering and irony have no place in a story of achievement, in an epic tale of pride and celebration.[16]

Turner's robust confidence in democracy, a legacy passed down from his politically active father, Andrew Jackson Turner, compromised the intellectual possibilities of the frontier thesis. If the American West revitalized republican institutions, what was one to make of the closing of arable lands and the rise of the industrial state? Turner had little to offer on this depressing topic, but rather clutched tightly at the hope that pioneer individualism might somehow thwart the twentieth-century trend toward centralization. As a product of the reform era, Turner understood the dangers of unrestrained competitive individualism, but he presumed (with more optimism then evidence) that the yeoman ethic could arrest the growth of the interests, even after the best lands were exhausted. Powerful demographic changes, of course, spoiled Turner's vision. The crush of immigration at the century's end exasperated the prejudices of native-born Americans and intensified already existing tensions between capital and labor.

Unsurprisingly, the frontier thesis's implications for Americans of ethnic descent inspired Hofstadter's most alert criticism. The vast majority of eastern European immigrants, he pointed out — including his own paternal lineage — abandoned the countryside for the city. Were they — was he — *less* American? The most authentic Americans, he aggressively countered, resided in the East. The frontier did not produce democratic systems in the Spanish, Dutch, or French empires in North America; black suffrage in the post-Revolutionary era found a warmer reception in New England and New York than in the trans-Appalachian states; Jeffersonian democracy flourished in the cities; women's suffrage, abolitionism, prison reform, the humane treatment of the mentally ill, and the upgrading of schools were all advanced with greater care and consistency in the East.[17] And this liberal legacy survived. A dynamic and complex metropolitanism, Hofstadter concluded, encouraged recent achievements in politics, technology, commerce, and the arts that undermined Turner's shimmering faith in the spirit of frontier reform.

* * *

Charles Beard, the subject of *The Progressive Historians'* most elaborate profile, shared Turner's impeccable native credentials. The product of a provincial Ohio Valley background, his sense of national identity was firmly located in the promise of social mobility, the local customs of the tiny Indiana village in which he grew up, and the suspicion of concentrated power shared by his generation. Like Turner, Beard read his sectional allegiances into the past. His most important book, *An Economic Interpretation of the Constitution* (1913), emerged from a tradition of Populist and Progressive activism alien to historians on the East Coast. Beard accused the Constitution-makers of conspiring to limit popular rule, extending the privileges of the economic elite, and favoring eastern creditors over western debtors. That many of these same issues resurfaced during Beard's lifetime led some critics to insist that his book was less a scholarly account of the men who drafted the articles of government than a legal brief on behalf of the Progressive indictment against the industrial state. He had seized upon Turner's habit, they continued, of reading the free silver revolt, and the peoples' battles with the trusts, into a perpetual conflict pitting western producers against eastern consumers.

Hofstadter shared the critics' view and took it one step further, condemning Beard's passion — or was it paranoia? — for reading conspiracy into the past. *An Economic Interpretation* admirably captured the reform mood of the 1910s, but it also legitimized the fantasies of Progressives and by extension those of all mass movements. Beard's muckraking, Hofstadter complained, had devastating intellectual repercussions for the postwar generation of scholars, for it legitimized under the cover of objective analysis a pattern of popular anxiety that led to loyalty oaths in the fifties and the student wars of the sixties.

Hofstadter's criticisms need not obscure the fact that real points of recognition connected him and Beard. Both men drew extensively upon contemporary circumstances to bring the past alive, a strategy that ignored the historian's perennial commitment to objectivity but opened fresh avenues of exploration. This paradox intrigued Hofstadter, and he explained to Jack Pole that while writing *The Progressive Historians* he did not know exactly how to judge Beard. Obviously present-mindedness intruded upon Beard's historical work, Hofstadter conceded, and yet it was precisely the scholar's engagement with his social and political times that produced work of an intrinsically useful and relevant nature.[18]

Coupling Hofstadter and Beard as models of the historian engagé suggests other connections as well. Each produced left-of-center scholarship early in his career, yet both were later depicted as out-of-step conservatives—in Beard's case as a neopopulist isolationist, and in Hofstadter's, a consensus-affirming liberal. In fact, a latent conservatism did sustain the historical instincts of both men. During his final years, Beard revised his views on the Founders, admiring their eighteenth-century use of government as a model of a simple American republicanism that compared favorably to the powerful centralized state he saw emerging from the Second World War. Hofstadter also rethought his political commitments, moving from a youthful radicalism to a more mainstream but equally critical liberalism. His appraisal of Beard's intellectual development from muckraker to mature scholar—"to some degree he had quietly recanted"—could be accurately applied to his own progress as a thinker.[19]

The Progressive Historian's appraisal of Beard appropriately focused on the iconoclastic and remarkably influential *An Economic Interpretation* (1913). Hofstadter rejected that book's quasi-Populist claim that the urban elite overturned an essentially agrarian-democratic order. He maintained, rather, that the Founders were moderate Whigs undisturbed by the rise of popular politics in postcolonial America. Turning Beard on his head, Hofstadter argued that the abuses of the British Empire were fresh in the minds of Constitution makers who saw the Revolution as a New World rejection of centralized power. They were determined to create a *more,* not less, plural political order. Under the guidance of Madison, the Founders developed a balanced framework of government that protected majority (popular) as well as minority (elite) interests. Beard lacked, Hofstadter continued, a clear understanding of the many expressions of democratic activity and vitality, and this distorted his appraisal of the early republic. By interpreting popular action through the people's movements of the Progressive Era, he was unable to grasp the efficacy of a deferential democratic style that promoted the kind of social harmony that the revolutionary generation (and postwar liberals) hoped to achieve. The drafters of the Constitution—like the architects of the New Deal—were not directly influenced by the popular will, nor did they succumb to the temptation of trying to create a utopia; yet they crafted a liberal social order both respectful and receptive to the needs of all public interests.

In sum, Hofstadter rejected *An Economic Interpretation*'s emphasis on conflict rather than consensus. Beard had made the case too simple—"the movement for the Constitution of the United States was originated and carried through principally by four groups of personality interests ... money, public securities, manufactures, and trade and shipping."[20] This could easily be updated to suggest that a twentieth-century cultural and intellectual elite battled egalitarians for control of the country. In *Anti-Intellectualism* Hofstadter had argued as much himself, but he now dismissed this divisive theme, insisting that a certain comity and gift for compromise distinguished both proponents and opponents of the Constitution.

Since the appearance of *The American Political Tradition,* critics had described Hofstadter as a defender of the consensus idea. That work may have minimized certain divisions in the structure of American society (as a plot device to emphasize the striking philosophical changes that accompanied the New Deal), but it was nevertheless a sharply drawn portrait of political leadership. His efforts in the late sixties to address Beard's (and the New Left's) focus on conflict, however, placed Hofstadter nearer the consensus camp than anything he had written.

In his final years, Beard fiercely opposed American entry into the Second World War—a position that nearly destroyed his reputation among professional historians. "How much better it would have been for himself and the United States, and the world, if Charles A. Beard had laid down his pen forever when he published his two-volumes survey of American history!" Allan Nevins wrote Merle Curti. "He still distills the isolationist poison." Following intervention, Beard updated the conspiratorial model pioneered in *Economic Interpretation,* insisting, in two major works, that Franklin Roosevelt purposefully maneuvered the country into the killing fields of Europe and Asia. His position put him on the side of postwar ultraconservatives, and exposed to Hofstadter the central irony of Progressive thought: a once liberal ideology had devolved under the pressures of mass society into a cranky, antipluralist politics.[21]

Hofstadter had once shared Beard's reluctance to send American troops abroad. Aside from wishing in the late 1930s to see the United States join collective security arrangements to assist the Spanish Republic and Czechoslovakia, he adhered to a firm isolationist line. The single greatest danger to American neutrality, he wrote Harvey Swados in 1940, was the growing (and to him, erroneous) sentiment among his countrymen that the European Allies were fighting for freedom and democracy rather than to preserve empires and overseas markets. Like Beard, he believed that President Roosevelt conspired to bring the United States into the war against the axis powers — a point that appeared in his correspondence more than a year before the German invasion of Poland.[22]

As Hofstadter grew older, his personal recollections of this critical period underwent a gradual transformation. He argued in *The Progressive Historians* that Beard's isolationism led him to predict democracy's likely death in the United States under the centralizing pressure of a massive war. In fact, Hofstadter once shared this view. He confided to Swados in 1939 that he preferred Robert Taft — or another isolationist, anyone but an interventionist — to oversee American neutrality. He further insisted that a war would destroy the New Deal and likely preface the rise of fascism in American. Intervention in the days following Pearl Harbor did little to change his pessimistic stance, but rather convinced Hofstadter that the era of liberal reform was irretrievably over. "We assumed that [the returning veterans] would all be militarists," Kenneth Stampp remembers of his Maryland days with Hofstadter. "It was a bad guess about what G.I.'s became after the war. This was probably [C. Wright] Mills' fantasy more than the rest of us, but we all thought it was possible."[23]

It is clear that before America's entry into the Second World War, and even during that conflict, both Beard and Hofstadter were intensely critical of Roosevelt's foreign policy goals. Hofstadter's views changed due to a number of personal and intellectual transformations at work between 1945 and 1950 — the death of a spouse more politically radical than he, a growing appreciation for the New Deal, awareness that the ethnocultural background of McCarthyites suggested similarities with the midwestern isolationists of the thirties, and, much harder to discern, the impact of the Holocaust. Unfortunately, Beard's death in 1948 did not permit him — as it did his biographer — time and perspective for a more reflective appraisal of the era. But there was private charity. Hofstadter recognized an admirable, even heroic, reflex underlying Beard's isolationism. In a 1967 letter to Eric McKitrick (a World War II veteran much opposed to the America First philosophy), he discussed both the pathos and the perils of writing history with an agenda. He agreed with

McKitrick that Beard had lost his head in the fight to influence the country's foreign policy. He did insist, however, that Beard be understood within the context of his times. He lived through the Spanish-American and First World Wars and saw in the coming clash between fascism, communism, and democracy an Armageddon that could be avoided by quarantining the Western Hemisphere in a robust, republican "American continentalism." He took his responsibilities as a public intellectual seriously and wrote books to instruct his fellow citizens, and this, no doubt, merged with a moral impulse to do all that he could to keep America from entering what he was certain would be a disastrous war—disastrous, that is, for American freedoms. Beard may have lost perspective in the process, Hofstadter conceded, but his intentions were both noble and understandable.[24]

A noble man, he might have added, who made many influential friends. Alfred Knopf, a great admirer of Beard, wished that *The Progressive Historians* had handled his departed colleague more gently, and he found a way to indirectly communicate this point to Hofstadter:

> I've been looking into your book with the greatest admiration. It is always a pleasure to publish you; it always makes me proud. But thinking of Beard makes me wonder if I ever let you see my correspondence with him. If I didn't—and I fear I didn't—even though I haven't looked at it lately I have a feeling that I should have shown it to you. Whatever opinion one may hold of his writings he was one of the finest—I'm almost tempted to say noblest men I have ever known. Being with him even for a little time always had the same sort of effect on me that did Henry Mencken and in his Harvard days Felix Frankfurter.[25]

In reply, Hofstadter judiciously nodded at Knopf's sentimental appraisal of Beard (as he had Merle Curti's twenty years earlier), and agreed that Beard exhibited an impressive moral courage that he hoped his book recognized. But, he reminded Knopf, the purpose of his profile was historical criticism.[26]

*   *   *

Of the three scholars scrutinized in *The Progressive Historians,* Vernon Parrington had won the least attention among students of American historiography. Born in Aurora, Illinois, and brought to Kansas at the age of six, Parrington shared with Turner and Beard a solid middlewestern background, a schooling in the native soils of progressivism and isolationism. Virtually no published biographical material existed to provide a personal context to Parrington's professional views, and this forced Hofstadter to fly to Seattle on a rare research trip to examine the literary historian's private papers. Parrington's sprawling three-volume masterpiece, *Main Currents in American Thought* (1927), drew a compelling portrait of conflict over time between liberals (the French legacy: Jeffersonians, Jacksonians, Bryanites, Progressives) and conservatives (the British legacy: Puritanism, Federalism, Whiggery, the Robber Barons). But the dialectical nature of this work, its formulaic reliance on heroes and villains, struck Hofstadter as warmed-over Marxism. In Parrington's hands, he complained, "ideas don't develop, they only recur."[27]

Hofstadter also faulted Parrington's contention that English Whiggery and French romanticism served as exclusive sources of American liberalism. Much like Turner's Anglo frontier, the literary patterns emphasized by Parrington ignored Americans of eastern European origins in its tidy celebration of Western culture. A candid assessment of French and American institutions demonstrated to Hofstadter, however, that the Jeffersonians shared few connections with the continental physiocratic tradition. The Physiocrats, he pointed out, were not agrarian in the American sense of promoting small farming units as a precondition to democratic citizenship and constitutional liberties. Rather, they worked furiously to preserve the ancient feudal requirements that sustained prerevolutionary French society. Their commitment to the land was, in a more basic sense, a commitment to hierarchy, the Catholic church, and the continuation of a peasant class. In sum, Physiocrats were conservative aristocrats whose royalist sympathies could scarcely be more at odds with the popular politics celebrated by American farmers and their republican leaders.[28]

More problematic, for all of Parrington's shrewd insights into the literary character of American life, his analysis of the country's political culture was most noteworthy for its utter lack of sophistication. In rooting for the men in white hats, Hofstadter argued, Parrington betrayed a clear class bias that grew more obvious and less persuasive over time. It was as though representatives of the nation's conservative tradition—John Winthrop, Alexander Hamilton, the nineteenth-century Brahmin class—were, in some flawed and tragic sense, *less* American than their liberal contemporaries.

Hofstadter's criticism is both perceptive and profoundly ironic. Even as he revealed Parrington's strategy of minimizing conservative contributions, he seemed not to recognize that his own work did much the same. *The American Political Tradition* described the old liberalism as a failure; opponents of the New Deal were afflicted with status anxiety; and the politics of paranoia surely explained the rise of Barry Goldwater. Parrington was extreme, going after Federalists and Republicans; Hofstadter reserved his volleys for the "pseudo-conservatives" who strayed outside the two-party consensus. This was a difference, however, of degree rather than intent. In a 1963 essay, David Potter recognized that the status thesis contained an airtight defense of liberalism that made it as reductive as Progressive historiography. Hofstadter assumed, Potter wrote, "that when men of a given ideology (rightist in this case) display certain qualities of temperament (suspicion and intolerance), men of an opposite ideology (leftist) will display correspondingly opposite qualities of temperament (good will, tolerance)." If Potter's critique made an impression on Hofstadter, it never surfaced in his scholarship.[29]

*   *   *

The Progressive Historians concludes with a timely chapter emphasizing Hofstadter's differences with the consensus model. It is a smart piece filled with nuance and subtle second thoughts that reflect its author's dilemma: how to recognize the importance of conflict in the American past while simultaneously reaffirming his generation's considerable contributions to historical writing. Hofstadter's mixed-mindedness on the topic came through clearly in a letter to Jack Pole in which he admitted struggling mightily over what he wanted to say — and thus argued both sides of the case.[30]

Postwar intellectuals, he acknowledged in *The Progressive Historians,* had too casually combined the rise of Nazism with their own struggles against McCarthyism. The attack on academic freedom in the fifties, he continued, in something of a personal confession, produced among some scholars a sharp reaction to all forms of popular power. Daniel Boorstin's unreflective celebration of democracy in *The Genius of American Politics* (1953), was held up by Hofstadter as an example of the kind of intellectual chauvinism now so much despised by younger historians — and by himself. In a letter to Boorstin, written a few months before *The Progressive Historians* appeared, Hofstadter attempted to soften the impact of his criticism by defining it as an exercise in self-analysis. In reckoning with consensus historiography, he explained, he was much more critical now than he had been in the fifties. While he admitted that the consensus school served as a necessary corrective to the Progressive reliance on conflict, it — and by inference, Boorstin — had simply gone too far. Hofstadter warned Boorstin of his inclusion in his new book, expressing hope that they might one day meet to discuss their differences.[31]

Hofstadter backed away from the consensus model for the same reason that he rejected Progressive scholarship — its initial insights had grown stale, and new circumstances required new thinking. The student movement, assassinations of public figures, ongoing racial unrest, and debacle in Vietnam congealed in a violent attack on the postwar mind. It was now clear, Hofstadter wrote Arthur Schlesinger, Jr., that once again conflict would have to move to the center of the American story. Still, he did not wish to lose the social cohesiveness embodied in the consensus idea and he hoped to conserve liberalism as a vital force in national life. He sketched out his vision of the "good" political society in an appeal for ideological harmony. Comity, he explained, triumphed in societies where humanity, legitimacy, and existing values and cultural systems are preserved. Comity, he might have added, also permitted practical expressions of political enthusiasm and, if patiently practiced, diminished the power of a mischief-making radical Right or Left. Comity was liberalism's last hope.[32]

In important respects, *The Progressive Historians* rebuked the younger historians who challenged the ideological preferences of Hofstadter's generation. If Boorstin's work exaggerated the consensual qualities blandly handed down from one generation of Americans to the next, it seemed equally certain to Hofstadter that the New Left had adopted a parallel myth of the past — one that drew strength from reading current conditions into the lives of historical actors.[33] Rather than accentuate (or calmly accept) the differences dividing the historical profession, Hofstadter drew the attention of junior scholars to the impressive legacy of their teachers. Why, he asked, should the dazzling interpretive advances of *The Age of Reform* be lost in the adversarial culture of the sixties? At stake stood not only the reputation of a generation, but also a style of liberal scholarship that had reshaped historical writing in America.

One might have expected *The Progressive Historians* to make a powerful impression on younger historians. It was, after all, a kind of bible on the Progressive generation and it arrived in the midst of a fierce conflict-versus-consensus debate. The portrait Hofstadter drew, however, was unflattering, and of all his major works, it is the only one currently out of print. As a cautionary tale, it reminded readers that engagement and passion cloud judgment and distort historical vision. Hofstadter saw the storm clouds forming on the horizon and hoped that the rising generation of historians would assess his work with a critical—but fair-minded—attitude. He had himself experienced the inevitable cycle of professional growth and decline. In youth he embraced the Progressives and now, in his fifties, wrote history on the "wrong" side of a youth-served cultural divide. No doubt comity might heal some wounds and save some reputations. But were historians listening?

* 10 *
The Trials of Liberalism

Newsweek: You have no doubt that this is a bad time?
Hofstadter: Oh I have no doubt it's a bad time,
and it's not over yet.

RICHARD HOFSTADTER, 1970

In the closing pages of *The Progressive Historians,* Richard Hofstadter made an eloquent plea for a "vital kind of moral consensus" to sustain the American political center. His counsel to clashing interests to respect the right of principled opposition was a message teeming with self-interest. The liberal sun was setting. The radical Right, Far Left, black power movement, hippies and yippies may have stood separately in small numbers outside the political mainstream, but combined, their challenge to the two-party system could not be ignored. Deeply concerned with the fate of comity in an era of political polarization, Hofstadter produced *The Idea of a Party System: The Rise of Legitimate Opposition in the United States, 1780–1840.* The work is both a blueprint of the birth of pluralism and a provocative rejoinder to those who dismissed liberalism as a spent force in American political life. As John William Ward cogently observed in a review of its contents, "If we are dissatisfied today with party politics, *The Idea of a Party System* is a fine place to begin to think about the sources of our discontent."[1]

It is, in some respects, an unusual Hofstadter book. It lacks the bold revisionism and social-psychological insights that distinguished its author's most controversial scholarship. Published by the University of California Press (the manuscript was tied to a lecture series at Berkeley), it reads much like the kind of monographic history that Hofstadter typically avoided. Keeping in mind its 1969 publication date, one might assume that *The Idea of a Party System* was conceived in response to the political radicalism of the sixties, but its author's interest in the topic arose more than a decade earlier—probably as a reaction to McCarthyism. In a 1957 letter to Alfred Knopf, Hofstadter wrote of his interest in producing a large book on the origins of American democracy that explored the decline of deferential politics and the rise of mass politics. The project took a back seat to *Anti-Intellectualism*, was briefly slotted for the *Oxford History*, and did not resurface until the University of California's invitation to deliver the 1966 Jefferson Memorial Lectures.[2]

American society had undergone notable changes between 1957 and 1969, and so had Hofstadter's scholarship. The twin rebukes of McCarthy and Goldwater, in addition to the nation's brief embrace of the civil rights movement and the Great Society, encouraged many intellectuals to bank on the long-term prospects of the postwar liberal tradition. Hofstadter's skepticism never allowed him to go quite this far, but he did discover in the popular liberalism of the period a viable democratic alternative to political extremism. As he began working on *The Idea of a Party System,* the specter of social breakdown encouraged him to rethink his earlier criticisms of democracy. He now discovered great value in the consensual nature of American politics. And he knew that to some degree his ideological leanings found their way into his work. In a 1970 address delivered before an audience gathered to praise his work, he remarked defensively, and not completely convincingly, that *The Idea of a Party System* was not written with the intention of validating the American two-party system.[3]

Carving out liberalism's terrain in the 1940s and '50s encouraged Hofstadter to go on the attack—with uneven, but overall very exciting, repercussions on his scholarship. Defending liberalism in the 1960s, however, called for a kind of retrenchment that left Hofstadter open to charges that this once articulate critic of the American political tradition had lost his edge. He was thus delighted when informed that the Russian physicist and human rights activist Andrei Sakharov hoped to use *The Idea of a Party System* as a guide to influence political attitudes in the Soviet Union. When notified later that Sakharov dared not risk smuggling the book into the USSR, Hofstadter celebrated his return to writing "radical" history. He remarked that after years of listening to leftists accuse him of elitism, it was gratifying to have written a book that could be regarded as subversive. There is something both touching and pathetic in such a remark. It escaped Hofstadter's notice that only among the world's authoritarian governments could his work be considered "radical." In the liberal democracies, the cultural and political references that shaped his scholarship had given ground to a new generation of historians, political theorists, and literary critics dismissive of the consensus paradigm. They hoped to smash rather than save the old cannon.[4]

* * *

In *The Idea of a Party System,* Hofstadter set out to solve a long-standing historical riddle. Considering that the Founders of the American republic opposed political factions and made no provision in the Constitution for their existence, why did they then create the nation's first party system? Why, in other words, did Jefferson's generation embrace the kind of political pluralism and toleration for clashing views so notably lacking in the 1960s? And did that generation have something to teach modern liberalism's political foes? The Fathers' progress toward pluralism was an important evolutionary step in the history of opposition theory, Hofstadter argued, for it signified "a net gain in the sophistication of political thought and practice over the antiparty thought and unlegitimated or quasi-legitimated opposition that had prevailed in the Anglo-American tradition in the eighteenth century and earlier." He further praised the early republic's view of partisanship (with an eye toward the political firebombers of his own day) when he defined responsible opposition as that which contained the ability to yield an actual functioning government. Political legitimacy, he continued, rested not merely on criticism of existing policies and wildly unrealistic campaign promises, but on the sober attempts of opposition candidates to create workable alternative policies and produce effective leadership. In Hofstadter's America, the Democratic Party—winners of all but two general elections between 1932 and 1968—ruled the political roost, its "legitimate" opposition comprised of Taft, Eisenhower, and Rockefeller Republicans. While conceding that third parties and smaller factions contained a "useful agitational function" that raised "neglected grievances to the surface," Hofstadter coldly dismissed their "essentially utopian" character. Their increasingly impatient rejection of liberal positions, after all, threatened the thirty-year political accord carved out by the postwar generation.[5]

The connection between *The Idea of a Party System* and its author's troubled times can be made yet clearer. A number of daunting public issues — race, violence, war— raised serious questions about the nation's ability to both absorb dissent and reform itself through traditional political means. The consensual nature of the party system, its opponents argued, was at the heart of the problem. It stifled dissent, accommodated imperial presidencies, and largely ignored the complex problems facing black America. The bitter harvest was coming in—Vietnam, the long hot summers, and the revolt of the universities. History seemed to be leaving liberalism behind. Hofstadter fretted over the fate of American and indeed global, pluralism, a burden that made it difficult to separate commentary from scholarship. "I need hardly say," he wrote of *The Idea of a Party System,* "that I am speaking of the present as well as the past."[6]

In early America, pluralism's opponents defended the ancient idea of the Patriot King. Alexander Hamilton, the infant republic's most outspoken neomonarchist, agreed with the Tory political philosopher Henry St. John Bolingbroke that parties weakened states by encouraging rival factions. He defended the idea of a consensual leader—George Washington stood as the young nation's beau ideal statesman—capable of putting country above partisanship. Where diversity of interest bred selfishness and civil unrest, Hamilton insisted, the Patriot King harmonized the dissonant voices under his rule. But this argument struck thoughtful critics as a crude attempt to strangle legitimate opposition in the cradle. Hofstadter had little patience for the myth of the benevolent autocrat, writing that "the political foolishness inherent in the notion of a totally and consistently benign monarch was probably as strikingly evident to eighteenth-century Americans as it is to the modern reader."[7] Coming of age in an era of demagogues and dictators gave Hofstadter the historical perspective to dismiss Bolingbroke's defense of charismatic leadership. He believed that the Patriot Kings spectacularly sketched in the violent images of Stalin and Hitler (and, on a more pedestrian scale, by private tormentors Curly Byrd and Joseph McCarthy) were inherently susceptible to abuses of power. No doubt the hard fight to protect academic freedom provoked within Hofstadter a strong sense that in a time of crisis Patriot Kings could just as easily censor as sustain civil liberties.

In contrast to his critical handling of the Patriot apologists, Hofstadter wrote appreciatively of the Irish political theorist Edmund Burke. Whereas the pessimistic Bolingbroke maintained that factions were suppressible evils, the more liberal Burke declared opposition a virtue and in a series of seminal works including *Thoughts on the Cause of the Present Discontents,* he advanced persuasive arguments in favor of party principles. As the Burkean position gained strength, American statesmen continued to wrestle mightily with the concept of a loyal opposition. The notoriously thin-skinned Washington interpreted criticism of his presidential policies as an attack on the government itself and reacted with hostility to the emergence of organized dissent. His discomfort, or, as Hofstadter put it, "intellectual confusion about the problem of government and opposition," reflected the painful response of a prepluralist generation's initial confrontation with a popular faction vying for power. In 1794 Washington denounced the antiadministration Democratic Societies and, in response to public criticism over Jay's Treaty, reported to the vice-president that "meetings in opposition to the constitutional authorities [were] at all times improper and dangerous."[8]

In fact, republican self-rule appeared to be in greater jeopardy of succumbing to the party in power than from factions out of power. Absent a heritage of patriotic opposition, Federalists passed the Sedition Act of 1798 — a punitive set of laws prescribing fines and prison penalties for oral or written commentary "with intent to defame . . . or bring into contempt or disrepute" the president or members of Congress. In sum, Federalism hoped to legislate its opposition out of existence. For Hofstadter, this raw attack on the Bill of Rights bore more than a passing resemblance to the dilemma intellectuals faced in the early days of the cold war. Cast under a cloud of suspicion by cultural conservatives intent on pressing loyalty oaths upon professors, "eggheads" were among the chief targets of anticommunists. The "paranoid style" exhibited by the Right suggested other connections with Washington's generation. Federalist preoccupation with lost power culminated in a self-defeating political anxiety expressed in apocalyptic denouncements of its opposition. In the end the extreme nature of its resistance led to political extinction.

As first the targets and then beneficiaries of Federalist paranoia, the Jeffersonians paradoxically chose to follow their rival's unproductive antiparty example. Republican hubris, Hofstadter argued, led the nation into the unnecessary War of 1812 and pointed yet again to the pitfalls of a unitary governing system. Without an effective opposition to offer criticism, caution, and judgment during the long lead-up to the war, the Jeffersonian coalition lost all sense of perspective in its negotiations with Great Britain. Even more damaging, the absence of opposition enticed the new regime to betray its principles and thus lose its identity. Republicans emerged from a states' rights heritage, but after gaining office the party adopted a bristling nationalist pose supporting legislation for a national bank, federal tariff, and government-sponsored internal improvements. In effect, Jeffersonianism became indistinguishable from Federalism.[9]

Republican efforts to dissolve its opposition were famously continued by James Monroe. Unlike the unforgiving Jefferson (convinced to the core of the corrupt nature of Hamiltonianism and bitter over his shabby treatment at the hands of opposition newspaper editors), Monroe did not believe in the inherent depravity of Federalism, but rather presumed that its more liberal elements could be usefully absorbed into the Republican fold. He did, however, share Jefferson's presumption that factions were part of the poisoned political paraphernalia of the Old World and that a spirit of consensual politics — spearheaded by popular support for Republican initiatives and leadership — was destined to predominate in America. Monroe's belief in the political uniqueness of the United States blithely ignored the acrimonious party battles of the 1790s, and his goodwill tour of New England in 1817 reflected a presidency devoted to practicing symbolic acts of unitary party behavior.[10]

Despite Monroe's best efforts, the amalgamation policy he pioneered did not survive his presidency. Explosive population growth combined with relaxed suffrage requirements to produce an unusually democratic nation increasingly hostile to the deferential politics of the past. The aristocratic tone favored by the Virginia dynasty and symbolized by the congressional caucus's control of presidential candidacies was coming under increasing fire from a rising generation of western and up-country lawyers, merchants, and small-town politicians. Its chief critic, Martin Van Buren, emerged as the first important politician to unabashedly champion pluralism over privilege.[11] Van Buren's Albany Regency brought together men who hoped to crack the powerful grip on New York politics held by the aristocratic Clinton faction. In their ability to successfully straddle between Republican and Federalist camps, George Clinton and his nephew De Witt embodied the antiparty preferences held by amalgamationists. But the days of the patrician had passed, and De Witt's decision not to oppose the Regency in the 1822 gubernatorial race, followed by his death just six years later, anticipated the birth of political pluralism in America over the grave of the gentleman politician.

Van Buren devoted the most productive years of his pubic career to overthrowing Monroe's "fusion policy" and the antiparty prejudice that sustained it. He understood that without an opposition vital public issues might go unaddressed and lead to disenchantment, disillusionment, and even attempts to secede from or overthrow the government.

In the critical years bookended by the Panic of 1819 and the Civil War these concerns appeared dangerously close to coming true, as sharp fluctuations in the economy, emotionally charged religious revivals, urban riots, and heated confrontations between pro- and antislavery lobbyists unsettled the nation. By creating a political sponge to absorb dissent, Van Buren hoped to tame the forces of change unleashed by an electorate increasingly aware of its power and jealous of its privileges.

It is not difficult to understand Hofstadter's sympathy for Van Buren. He too hoped to contain popular enthusiasms within the discipline of a party structure. Van Buren's revitalization of the Democracy foreshadowed the emergence, more than a century later, of a New Deal coalition equally intent on stemming internal conflict and serving as a moderate medium for directing economic and social change. Hofstadter identified further with Van Buren's strong support for an emerging political class that reflected the changing demographic realities of American society. The Albany Regency overthrew an opposition whose chief claim to office was superior social rank. The advantages enjoyed by the plebeian men who revitalized the Democratic Party, Hofstadter noted, were "by and large, hard earned, and there was a distinct edge of class resentment in their attitude toward patrician politics."[12] A similar political revolt occurred in Hofstadter's early adulthood with the New Deal's encouragement of Americans of African and eastern European descent to assume the benefits of a more significant kind of inclusion, prosperity and political activism.

Unfortunately, Hofstadter's spirited endorsement of the two-party model prohibited a candid assessment of its deficiencies. *The Idea of a Party System*'s perceptive portraits of Madison, Monroe, and Van Buren collectively made the case that Americans benefited from living under a political arrangement that prized popular power. It failed to note, however, that parties also served as the primary instrument to choke unpopular positions. In Van Buren's day, they exerted enormous energy neutralizing critics of slavery and sought to destroy efforts to place the issue of unfree labor on the political agenda. *Real* pluralism, melding voices of southern fire-eaters and northern abolitionists to the Jacksonian-Whig concert, was precisely what Van Buren hoped to avoid. The case can be argued that without an authentic multiparty culture permitting a full airing of issues relating to sectionalism and slavery, the political crisis that splintered America in the 1860s did so with unusual force and destructiveness. A similar claim can be made for the 1960s. The public's belief that conventional political attitudes could no longer provide fresh and effective leadership must be counted as a major factor in the disillusionment, despair, and turmoil that afflicted American society in the Vietnam era.

*   *   *

As the 1960s came to a close, the theme of violence — assassinations, campus rebellions, Weathermen bombers — permeated the culture. Accordingly, in the spring of 1968, the *New York Times Magazine* invited Hofstadter, Hannah Arendt, Clifford Geertz, Paul Goodman, Michael Harrington, David Riesman, and C. Vann Woodward to contribute original essays on the topic "Is America by Nature a Violent Society?" Hofstadter's brief piece — produced days after the murder of Dr. Martin Luther King — saw more darkness than light. He lashed out at "the feebleness of our efforts at gun control" and the ease with which "any zealot, any maniac" could purchase a firearm. He pinpointed the locus of conflict in the American past to the labor movement's pained struggle for recognition, and more recently to racial clashes culminating in the desperate eruption of urban ghettoes. Disturbed by New Left posturing, and concerned with the fate of pluralism in a political system crippled by sharp ideological divisions, Hofstadter saw little promise for a peaceful society. Quoting from D. H. Lawrence, he concluded that "the sacred rights of American manhood" to arm oneself led to a deeper and more ominous truth — "the essential American soul is hard, isolate, stoic and a killer."[13]

The popularity of the *Times* essay led Hofstadter to a deeper engagement with the topic of violence. He devoted part of a sabbatical year (1968–69) trying out his ideas on the lecture circuit with gratifying results. Their success encouraged him to pursue the subject in a more substantial way, and he generously invited Columbia doctoral candidate Michael Wallace to collaborate on a documentary history of American violence. Their Knopf contract called for Hofstadter "to be responsible for selecting final items, writing a general introduction essay of 8–10,000 words [and] writing brief headnotes for each item." In reality, Wallace wrote the headnotes and performed all the research. Hofstadter saw that he was rewarded accordingly. By contract, Wallace received a $4,000 advance — $1,500 more than Hofstadter's, whose name and introductory essay Knopf coveted.[14]

*   *   *

Hofstadter and Wallace had been on opposing sides during the Columbia crisis. It was Wallace's key that opened Fayerweather Hall—the history building—to the protesters, and the violence project reconnected Hofstadter with a talented young scholar who appeared to have damaged his professional prospects in the Columbia bust. "I think," Wallace remembers of their collaboration, "that Hofstadter wanted to rehabilitate me by association." Reconciliation proved difficult, however, for Hofstadter intended his introduction—"Reflections on Violence in the United States"—to explore the destructive side of the new radicalism. The mystique of violence that seduced intellectuals and radicals alike fascinated him, he wrote Wallace, and he was drawn to understand its power and attraction.[15] He never presumed that the various expressions of movement politics were strong enough individually to destroy liberalism, but did suspect (correctly) that if sufficiently provoked by the Left, middle-America would turn right.

The revolt of the universities struck Hofstadter as a particularly inexplicable phenomenon. His students enjoyed unprecedented educational opportunities, experienced less overt racism or ethnic prejudice than previous generations, and received the material benefits of an affluent society. Their protest appeared irrational. Clashing intellectual styles further alienated Hofstadter from his young critics. He believed in the use of irony to shed light on the confusing and often absurd episodes of the past. This struck many younger scholars as a strategy of careful detachment or evasion—imposing an artificial sense of "complexity" as a means of avoiding or rationalizing away conflict. Hofstadter explored this generational division in his introduction to *American Violence,* causing a spirited exchange with Wallace that resulted in the latter writing a separate essay on the subject for the *American Scholar.* Hofstadter's introduction, Wallace complained, accentuated left-wing violence while playing down conflict initiated by the Right. Hofstadter's credentials as an opponent of ultraconservatism, however, were too well known to let the accusation stand. He informed Wallace of his long opposition to right-wing violence in all its populistic forms and emphasized that his initial venture into the topic—"The Pseudo-Conservative Revolt"—had appeared in print fifteen years earlier. Consequently, he had little to say to the Far Right, but hoped his piece might connect with open minds on the left.[16]

Hofstadter's introduction to *American Violence* denied the nation's youth culture the moral high ground it believed it earned in a decade of protest. The students who shut down Columbia (including Wallace) seemed to Hofstadter remarkably oblivious of their responsibility in promoting a bloody showdown with police. "When strikers sit down in a factory, or when a group of students seizes a university building, or when pacifists throw themselves on the ground before a convoy of army trucks," he wrote, "they have, however, non-violently, used force." Claiming a superior ethical position, he continued in a private communication, allowed the Left to slyly dismiss the humanity of its enemies — a dark tactic carried out in the past by dark regimes. The Nazis, he noted, used this strategy against the Jews and now his students were doing the same by attacking a monolithic "system" and slandering police officers as fascist "pigs."[17]

Hofstadter's interest in the protest culture celebrated by the Left did not alter his impression that violence in America exhibited a clear conservative bias. The most destructive forms of social rebellion, he insisted, were closely linked to declines in status. When legal protections could no longer sustain the advantages of "The American, the Southern, the white Protestant, or simply the established middle-class way of life and morals," terror became an acceptable tactic for majorities to maintain authority. Class conflicts, Hofstadter noted, emphasized economic grievances, but frequently reflected more vivid ethnocultural tensions. The pace of organized aggression escalated in the 1830s, he wrote, because of a sharp rise in immigration, the growth of cities, and simmering tensions between abolitionists and proponents of slavery. As traditional Anglo-American structures changed, whites resented the erosion of their privileges and were amenable to strategic forms of violence to preserve standing and perpetuate the traditional Protestant, property-rights rhythms of national life.[18]

Hofstadter had, of course, covered this ground many times before. Again, he puts the Nazi analogy into play. Close observers of European fascism, the Minutemen, southern white opposition to the civil rights movement, and the rantings of George Wallace, he wrote, would have no trouble recognizing that violence in the twentieth century exhibited a pronounced right-wing bias. The record on this score was so clear and so well understood, he continued, that no further documentation was necessary. Rather, fresh areas of exploration on the conflict theme pointed to an appraisal of recent activities on the left. Historically, radicals emphasized a commitment to nonviolence, and that made the new style of protest a challenge to place within the context of the American past. It also called into question the actions of their liberal apologists.[19]

Liberalism's cordial tolerance of violence greatly discouraged Hofstadter. "He despised the *New York Review of Books* for running Andrew Kopkind's inflammatory articles and printing a diagram of how to make a molotov cocktail," Dan Hofstadter remembers. "He vowed never to write for that magazine." He further denounced the current crop of radicals as representative of a therapeutic society more interested in self-actualization and immediate gratification than constructive change. Tom Hayden's shrill cry for "two, three, many Chicago's" remained in Hofstadter's thoughts, and he believed it quite conceivable that a culture of authoritarianism might follow hard on the heels of liberalism's retreat. In reply to student veterans of the Columbia bust who demanded that the New Left drop legal forms of protest and pursue victory in the streets, Hofstadter excitedly warned that such intemperate talk would recall for some listeners "the promises of Mussolini."[20]

The bonding of violence and celebrity aroused Hofstadter's sharpest rejoinder. He believed that establishment critics shrewdly (and cynically) structured their confrontations for maximum exposure. Radicals, he argued, had discovered television and gleefully baited police lines in anticipation of the volatile guerilla-theater they knew they could provoke. The innocence claimed by the protestors, Hofstadter continued, was a sham, nothing more than a dishonest attempt to disguise self-indulgence as a youthful virtue. In correspondence, Wallace objected to Hofstadter's remarks, but his letter did not stand as the final word. Radicals, Hofstadter fired back, were naïve to think that they could incite law enforcement officials without repercussions. On this score, he informed Wallace, he meant every bit of the condescension his coauthor thought he detected in his comments. Hofstadter ended with an assessment — and appraisal — of Wallace's intellectual leanings that ironically aligned with conservative criticism of his own work: Wallace indulged the Left and would never forgive the Right if it engaged in the same behavior.[21]

Hofstadter's central and almost obsessive concern — the eclipse of liberal democratic politics — came true, and for him it had deep personal repercussions. After 1968 the academy/life-of-the-mind idea defended in so many of his books expired. In the final sentence of *American Violence*'s introduction, he again found meaning in Yeats's haunting prophecy, quoting, "The nation seems to slouch onward into its uncertain future like some huge inarticulate beast, too much attainted by wounds and ailments to be robust, but too strong and resourceful to succumb." Wallace wondered if his cocontributor had not produced a prelude that offered too little faith in the future. Hofstadter thought the matter over and acknowledged that his thinking about the fate of the country changed almost daily, and that recent insecurities and uncertainties no doubt colored his opinion. Perhaps, he conceded to Wallace, his essay was too dark, too pessimistic.[22]

*　　*　　*

Alfred Kazin wrote of himself and Hofstadter, "We had been formed by the Great Depression, but Hofstadter was a secret conservative in a radical period. The times caught up with him." While working on the violence project, Wallace counseled Hofstadter to drop the term "Negro" in his introduction in favor of the more contemporary "black." And when John Milton Cooper advanced to doctoral candidacy, Hofstadter suggested that he write a dissertation incorporating statistical analysis — not because he knew anything about it, but rather because "quanto history" appeared to be on the verge of revolutionizing historical work. Hofstadter hoped to meet the culture half-way — even to the point of self-censorship. He believed hostility to traditional forms of patriotic expression had turned the American flag into a symbol of ultranationalism, and asked his publisher at Harper & Row to rethink its heavy use of the stars and stripes in the illustration of his textbook *A People and a Nation.* More visceral and frustrating encounters followed. After referring to the Nazi-Soviet pact in a public lecture at San Francisco State University, Hofstadter was shouted off the stage. "He was mystified," Robert Dallek recalls. "It was as if he had invented this historical fact. He was deeply disturbed by the irrationality of the Left."[23]

Hofstadter's involvement in racial issues proved equally problematic. He refused in 1968 to sign a statement condemning the Oakland Police Department's use of violence against the Black Panthers, because he disagreed with the petition's reference to the Panthers as "political prisoners"—a designation he also refused Columbia's student rebels. He took a more active role supporting the author and activist Eldridge Cleaver, injured in a shoot-out between the police and the Panthers. Hofstadter contributed money to Cleaver's defense fund and wrote to Henry Kerr, the chairman of the California Adult Authority, in praise of *Soul on Ice* and to suggest that its author's incarceration may have resulted from an effort by the Bay Area police to target the Black Panther Party. His commitment to racial justice, however, did not preclude serious concerns over the balkanization of the academic curriculum along racial lines. It was obvious, he allowed to a colleague at Spelman College, that more courses in black history were needed. But he was concerned that the demand to have black professors teach black studies would divide academic departments and erode standards — all in the name of racial politics.[24]

In 1969 Angela Davis, an African American assistant professor of philosophy at UCLA, faced dismissal by the regents for her membership in the Communist Party. Just two years earlier, Hofstadter had read a special convocation address at Berkeley drawing attention to the privileges and responsibilities of faculty governance and free speech. On the strength of this lecture, University of California professor Paul Goodman called upon him to support both Davis and efforts to unionize the faculty: "You thought that out of the crisis at that time might come a progressive fulfillment of the longer term trends towards the establishment of academic freedom and faculty autonomy." Hofstadter endorsed Davis without hesitation, agreeing that the university's actions were a clear violation of academic freedom. The issue of unionization he found more complex. Concerns over the ability of educators to protect academic freedom — Columbia's faculty remained bitterly divided over the events of 1968 — compelled Hofstadter to back away from the issue of mobilization, confessing to Goodman that he was unsure about where he stood on the issue of faculty unions for university professors.[25]

The question of professional autonomy hit Hofstadter particularly hard in 1969 when junior scholars urged the American Historical Association (AHA) to pass a resolution condemning United States involvement in Vietnam. AHA membership had quadrupled over the previous two decades, and the proposed resolution symbolized the emergence of a fresh generation of historians at odds with the liberal preferences of their mentors. The distinguished Princeton Europeanist and AHA president-elect, R. R. Palmer, summed up the resolution issue as an institutional self-identity crisis: "Are we activists or academics? Is our Association a trade union or a learned society?"[26] Hofstadter shared Palmer's concerns, and he believed that by publicly denouncing the Vietnam War the association was in danger of becoming a political organization.

New Left scholars underlined the seriousness of the Vietnam plank by supporting for the association's presidency an opposition candidate who would represent their views. Ironically, the only other contested election in the organization's history had occurred in 1944 when Hofstadter joined Kenneth Stampp's and Frank Freidel's revolt against the candidacy of Carlton J. H. Hayes over what amounted to a foreign policy issue — the former ambassador's alleged support for Franco's Spain. Prior to the 1969 conference, Hofstadter directed a form letter to "American Historical Association Colleagues" urging their attendance at the business meeting in order to put down the young Turks. The meeting, he wrote, would likely be packed by a small caucus of agitators looking to politicize the association by putting on record its opposition to the war. His efforts, he informed Daniel Boorstin, were designed to prevent a minority of disgruntled younger faculty from turning the AHA into a political society.[27]

Hofstadter's letter succeeded. The typically low turnout at the annual business meeting (only 116 voting members had attended the year before) swelled to over fourteen hundred. The majority voted against the antiwar resolution and elected Palmer AHA president (opposition candidate Staughton Lynd received nearly 30 percent of the vote). Significantly, they also voted to reduce the power of the business meeting in an effort to protect the association's council from future takeover bids. This was accomplished by a modification to the AHA constitution decreeing that forthcoming disputes between the business meeting (a potential source of New Left power) and the council (retained by the old guard) appeal to the membership as a whole for resolution. Presumably the majority of the 18,000 AHA members could be counted on to side with the "establishment" over the younger scholars. "I know that there were some," Palmer candidly observed in his presidential address, "who think that in obtaining those amendments the Council was acting defensively, that it was afraid of a take-over by some small unspecified group, generally supposed to be far to the left, or that it was protecting its own oligarchic freedom of action by appeal to a large uninformed or apathetic electorate."[28]

The AHA battle painfully evoked for Hofstadter the broader generational struggle in American society between the New Left and its liberal fathers. Dismayed by the ideological divisions that weakened the nation, Hofstadter completed *The Idea of a Party System* — a study praising pluralism — even as he worked to maintain the unitary political culture of the association. The urgent pace and uncertain direction of political activism forced him further to the Right than he would have liked and, combined with illness, taxed both his patience and his physical resources. "Dick looking very old and tired," Kazin confided to his journal in the autumn of 1968. "Much talk of Columbia. Dick is right in principle, of course, but how funny it all comes out to see our generation the custodians of law and order?" As the decade wound down, Hofstadter became increasingly convinced that the days of liberal men controlling liberal agendas had passed. He considered himself finished with politics.[29]

* 11 *

A World Full

Columbia was filled with Giants. That was a day of giants,
and that day has passed.

JAMES BANNER, JR., 2002

Any attempt to assess Richard Hofstadter's contribution to American historical writing must contend with the sad fact that he died at the relatively young age of 54. As the author of several important books, Hofstadter compiled a distinguished bibliography that suggested a long lifework of scholarship; his legacy, however, rests largely on the accomplishments of a young man. Accolades aside, a mere twenty-seven years separated the appearance of *Social Darwinism* (1944) and the posthumous printing of *America at 1750* (1971). By comparison, a generations-spanning sixty-one years bookends Arthur Schlesinger, Jr.'s *Orestes A. Brownson* (1939) and the autobiographical *A Life in the 20th Century* (2000). Hofstadter did not live to write his memoirs, appear on cable television, or provide authoritative sound bites to the flourishing "public intellectual" trade. Healthy until his early thirties, he suffered a back ailment in 1947 that foreshadowed a series of orthopedic discomforts, compounded by bursitis, knee problems, a weak digestive system, and finally the leukemia that took his life.

The psychological toll exacted from these and other physical setbacks was considerable, and the dark moods that shadowed Hofstadter's achievements were rooted in a chain of cruel and life-altering concessions to loss. H. Stuart Hughes suggested that the early deaths of his mother and first wife forced the meaning of mortality before Hofstadter, sharpening his sensitivity to the schedule and fate of his work. "Hence his need for a supporting cast of loyal friends, his pessimism, his ideological caution, his insistence on protecting his working time and

222

his privacy—plus his hypochondria. Dick was forever developing symptoms of one or another ailment. . . . In retrospect I believe he feared all along that he was destined to die young."[1]

There is a pitiable consistency in the premature death of a man who encountered the notable transitions and responsibilities of life in relative youth. Hofstadter graduated from college and married at twenty, took a Ph.D. at twenty-five, was widowed with an infant child at twenty-eight, won his first Pulitzer at thirty-nine, and became Columbia University's De Witt Clinton Professor of American History at forth-three. His publication record pointed to an equally dazzling story of early successes, and it was agreed upon by supporters and critics alike that studies of singular analytical quality and literary craftsmanship dripped from his pen with intimidating regularity. A careful evaluation of Hofstadter's résumé suggests that as health concerns jeopardized his ambitions, an economization of resources became necessary. He rarely contributed original essays for historical journals, preferring to place sections of forthcoming volumes in popular periodicals, including *Harper's Magazine, American Heritage,* and *American Scholar.* Reviews were also a strain on stamina, and he composed only seven in the 1960s after churning out nearly eighty between 1937 and 1957. By comparison, C. Vann Woodward, eight years Hofstadter's senior but still within the same peer category, completed thirty-nine reviews in the sixties, but no manuscripts other than edited works and a collection of essays. Books were the alpha and omega of Hofstadter's publishing world, and he authored or coauthored seven monographs between 1944 and 1965, an extraordinary rate of one every three years. This pace actually increased during his illness, and between 1965 and 1970 he completed three additional studies—an astonishing record or one every twenty months. In the tense, purposeful years of his body's decline, Hofstadter exhibited a dynamic and fierce determination to endure and create.

In need of an environment supportive of his changing physical needs, Hofstadter reevaluated his relationship with Columbia and seriously considered leaving New York. "I am not at all in my element," he complained of the grinding lifestyle that characterized the city. "The pressure—the sheer physical pressure is exhausting." And in the wake of what some at Morningside referred to as the "recent unpleasantness" (that is, the student occupation of university buildings), Hofstadter found himself strangely alienated from a campus he loved. The enemies of the university, he wrote J. H. Plumb, slept in its dormitories and attended his classes. It was, he confessed, a painful, dispiriting place to be.

Still, he found it impossible to turn away. In 1969, the Massachusetts Institute of Technology aggressively courted Hofstadter, hoping to make him the university's first Elizabeth and James Killian Professor. He resisted, citing scholarly concerns. As he got older, he wrote one MIT official, the need to balance an ambitious publication schedule against the reality of diminishing years increasingly entered his thoughts. The move to Boston would prove disruptive, require too much effort, and remove him from a familiar, comfortable work environment.[2] In the end, there really was no choice. He simply could not leave New York.

Columbia College dean Carl Hovde understood precisely Hofstadter's decision to remain in Manhattan during this difficult period:

> He told me that he was seriously considering a position at another university. I asked him what our chances were of keeping him, and he replied that there was a large difficulty in that — there was, he said, nothing more he wanted for himself. His frustrations with New York City life were common knowledge among his friends, and this was the impulse which lay beneath his thought. In the long run it was not the administrators who kept him here, energetic though we were; more it was the close friends and colleagues who spoke to him at length about it; and most of all it was himself. He stayed because on examination he saw how deep his roots were here, and he decided that he wished to leave them in this turbulent but interesting earth.[3]

The "interesting earth" of the city provided Hofstadter with vibrant and familiar examples of the pluralism celebrated in his work. "Columbia has a very special intellectual quality which was part of the medium in which he moved," remembered Julian Franklin. "That intellectual quality also impressed him. It was something he wanted to live up to."[4]

To remain in the city amid the pressures of campus politics and declining health, Hofstadter reduced his commitments to the university. He made plans in 1968 to withdraw from the faculty of the college and soon thereafter reached an agreement calling for a leave of graduate instruction every other semester. His stated reason for this break — the Columbia University band's infrequent but highly annoying 5:30 A.M. performances of "We Own New York" — seems thin. Rather, a number of unfortunate circumstances forced Hofstadter to reassess his commitments. Among them can be counted the slumification of New York City. Garbage strikes, escalating crime rates, and the deterioration of civic services encroached upon the Morningside-Harlem area and sapped the morale of its residents. New York, Hofstadter complained to Jack Pole in 1968, was a pigpen. A more personal episode, however, may have cinched matters. Hofstadter's wife was the victim of a gunpoint robbery in the elevator of the couple's Claremont Avenue apartment building, after which he emphasized in correspondence his eagerness to abandon the West Side for a more secure residence. With its star historian struggling to find a suitable New York situation, Columbia was compelled to ask itself how far it would go to retain Hofstadter. Concerned that the two-time Pulitzer winner and only member of the faculty to give the college's commencement address might leave, the university completed Hofstadter's separation from Morningside Heights by placing him and his family in a subsidized apartment on Park Avenue.[5]

The move anticipated deeper changes for Hofstadter and more permanent endings. Projects, interviews, and speaking engagements were conceptualized, granted, and contracted with a generosity that belied the grave circumstances of his physical condition. He concealed the seriousness of his illness from friends and colleagues and threw himself into commitments he could not possibly keep. During the last months of his life, for example, Hofstadter served as the vice president of the Organization of American Historians. His August 1970 letter to its executive secretary discussed plans for the OAH's upcoming spring conference, and concluded with his determination to fulfill the responsibilities of his office — which included moving up to the presidency of the organization the following year. Two weeks later, C. Vann Woodward informed the executive secretary: "Dick Hofstadter's wife . . . asked me to write you about his condition. This must be confidential but I am very much afraid he will never get well and will not be able to conduct any further business of his office with the Organization. At present he is gravely ill and may not have long to live." The following month — less then three weeks before his death — Hofstadter resigned the vice presidency of the OAH.[6]

Undoubtedly the routine of long-standing work habits served an important therapeutic purpose that brought a certain relief to Hofstadter and his family. While close friends were alarmed by his rapidly failing health — "I am greatly distressed about his condition and share your concern," Woodward wrote to Irving Howe — Hofstadter pushed the implications of his illness away. He stoically informed Harvey Swados a scant three months before his death that he expected to nurse his ailments for another twenty or thirty years. Rather than submit to a disappearing act, Hofstadter remained incredibly active; his self-protective pessimism, capacity for hilarity amid ingrained sadness, and openness to friendship encouraged society and stimulation rather than silence and self-pity. He fought hard against his fate and bravely feigned control of his future.[7]

*　　*　　*

The crack-up of the postwar liberal tradition paralleled Hofstadter's personal health crisis and provoked his final reflections. In the summer of 1970, *Newsweek* asked a number of distinguished American historians to comment on their bitterly divided country. "The six contributors," *Newsweek* announced, "are men of widely divergent backgrounds and points of view. Two are men of the Left: Eugene D. Genovese and Staughton Lynd. Two are centrist liberals: Richard Hofstadter and Arthur M. Schlesinger Jr. And two are, relatively speaking, conservatives: Andrew Hacker and Daniel J. Boorstin." Too ill to produce a written analysis, Hofstadter sat for an interview with the magazine's editors. His remarks, by turns sharp, thoughtful, and angry, focused on the spiritual and vocational rootlessness of young Americans.

The failure of the churches and the universities to command their traditional respect, Hofstadter believed, undermined social cohesiveness and fueled the youth culture's rebellion. As children of the Depression era, he continued, his generation scrambled early in life to earn livings, build families, and develop careers. The world their children inherited — more affluent, secular, and atomistic — operated from different, less tradition-based values. "Students keep saying that they don't know why they are here," he complained. "They are less disposed than they used to be to keep order partly because the sense that they are leading a purposeful life is gone." In place of vocation, he continued, students filled the existentialist void with political protest, confusing self-expression with serious social criticism. Wounded by the youth culture's scattered assault on the "establishment" and certain that New Left anti-intellectualism invited a strong right-wing backlash, Hofstadter held out little hope for the future. "I can't see much that is positive coming out of this period. If I get around to writing a general history of the recent past, I'm going to call the chapter on the '60s 'The Age of Rubbish.'"[8]

Despite these choice remarks, Hofstadter found much to value in the sixties. "He was very buoyed by the Civil Rights Movement, greatly admired Dr. King, and marched in Selma," Dan Hofstadter remembers.

"My father was quite attracted by the Kennedy clan—with reservations I'm sure. He even liked the Beatles and went to see a Hard Days Night! The Sixties an age of rubbish? Perhaps the Year 1968—the Tet Offensive, the rise of New Left posturing, etc. Remember that by this time he was dying, and that this must have colored his views."[9]

To find fresh meaning in his work, a new approach would have to be worked up. *The Progressive Historians'* affirmation of postwar liberalism could not win a substantial audience in a divided nation. Hofstadter's early scholarship struck a pleasing note precisely because it offered something more vital and instructive than traditional monographic history. From *Social Darwinism* and *The American Political Tradition* to *The Age of Reform* and *Anti-Intellectualism,* Hofstadter wrote the memoir of twentieth-century American liberalism. His work powerfully influenced a nation forced by the Depression and the Second World War to abandon the ideological baggage of its forefathers. The country had to learn *why* the new liberalism was necessary—and *how* its history led to this moment. Now, that moment was passing.

In contrast to these earlier studies, *The Progressive Historians* was a personal book—brilliant, felicitous, and learned, but more interior and thus less accessible to nonacademics. It was a painful insight for its author. Intellectual life in America had gotten to the point, Hofstadter explained to Ashbel Green in 1968, where he felt he could no longer connect with his audience. Frustrated with the reception of his recent work and facing an uncertain future, he embarked upon an ambitious and life-affirming endeavor, a three-volume history of American political culture from 1750 to the near present. Postwar scholars had pushed historical inquiry into original areas and no one had attempted to produce a general history that accounted for their findings. The historiographical advances forged in the monographic revolution that followed the war were increasingly called into question by younger scholars, and it struck Hofstadter as important to record the achievements of the older group—not merely for the sake of posterity, but rather to emphasize those aspects of the New Deal coalition that were still fresh, constructive, and worth commemorating.[10]

The new project drew Hofstadter curiously close to a fading style of historicism. The age of the gifted generalist had passed, and it was rapidly becoming something of an article of faith that a single study, no matter how ambitious or thorough, could capture anything more than a fragment of an era. The emergence of novel fields of inquiry—gender, sexuality, environmentalism, and race—infused academe with fruitful sources of investigation while simultaneously working against synthetic treatments of the past. As one looks beyond the postwar generation of scholars, no succeeding cohort has spoken as confidently of a single American voice or representative American mind. Dorothy Ross underlined the generational implications of Hofstadter's decision to produce a multivolume history in her observation that "it is very revealing of his life-span and the profession in that life-span, that at the end he still obviously thought in terms of capstone works, believing that this is the way a historian consummates a life's work." Christopher Lasch defended Hofstadter on this score, arguing that the studies written by his own generation lacked a compelling narrative focus. "People say, 'Well, it's no longer possible to write the kind of synthetic history that Hofstadter did. The genre has played itself out. We know too much. There's too much specialized knowledge.' There's some truth in that, but it's still a cop-out, which reflects a refusal or failure of academic historians to write for the general reader."[11] Hofstadter would have undoubtedly agreed with Lasch. He conceived, after all, of the three-volume work as a product for both the public and the ages — the last liberal history.

Hofstadter's decision to undertake a massive project requiring eighteen years, just eighteen months before his death, suggests that the would-be opus served psychologically to evade the implications of his illness. Unable to maintain a full schedule at Columbia, the presence of a scholarly Shangri-la allowed Hofstadter to back away from his customary duties without directly naming the cause. Like *The American Political Tradition* — begun during Felice Swados's fatal illness — *America at 1750* played a humane role for its author, providing for a close continuation of familiar patterns of work and leisure while accommodating, with a minimum of compromises, Hofstadter's intellectual routine.

The financial implications of the project — in particular the need for research and secretarial assistance over a period of nearly two decades — were immense, and Hofstadter was eager to strike an advantageous commercial deal. During the years he anticipated working on the book, he explained in a project proposal, he planned to teach only half-time at Columbia. Royalties and speaking fees, he continued, would not be enough to meet both his living expenses and research needs. Fifty thousand dollars, he estimated, would just about cover costs. As his thoughts on the manuscript crystallized in the spring of 1969, Hofstadter considered leaving Knopf. He informed Oxford University Press editor Byron S. Hollinshead — very much courting Hofstadter — that his attachment to Knopf had weakened because of what he considered slack promotion of his recent books. Oxford, however, had competition. Atlantic–Little Brown publishers were eager to produce Hofstadter's "big American history" and offered $225,000 as an advance against the earnings. In the end, however, Hofstadter returned to Knopf, signing an agreement dated 9 January 1970 (some two months *after* his leukemia was diagnosed) that promised to pay $15,000 each year between 1970 and 1987 for a total compensation of $270,000 — $1.3 million in today's dollars. The contract committed Hofstadter to producing a book every six years, to be completed December 1975, 1981, and 1987.[12]

For one year, Hofstadter worked on his grand history — a meditation on the American condition at the tail end of the colonial period. The steady mental activity kept him busy while serving an important curative function. "This was Dick's way of shaking his fist at what was happening to him," Green remembers, and Hughes believed "there was in [the final book] a desperate effort to keep alive." As his resources diminished, Hofstadter reluctantly pushed aside the main text and began writing an introduction — a sign that what he had completed was publishable. With his time exceedingly precious, he maintained a generous correspondence throughout the summer of 1970, acknowledging the scholarship of others even as his own remained incomplete. An August letter to Jack Pole doted on his friend's publishing options, emphasized how well his own work was coming, and gave only the lightest hint of his failing health. As the fall approached, he considered offering graduate instruction, but the academic calendar now ceased to have meaning. Working up until his strength gave out — "I've never had the slightest trouble with my *will*," he remarked at the end — Richard Hofstadter died in New York on 24 October.[13]

*   *   *

The long prologue to the intended first volume was published in 1971 as *America at 1750*. This coda continued its author's enduring fascination with the steep contradictions that shaped the country's past and gave direction to its future. The horrors of slavery and white indentured servitude paradoxically coexisted alongside a pluralistic, Protestant ethic. The result? A nation torn between morality and materialism. Too much of the former — as in Puritan New England — resulted in religious persecution, intellectual chauvinism, and a crippling cultural exclusivity. A proper mix of the latter — as in the famously open Quaker colony of Pennsylvania — promoted social toleration and economic prosperity.

In none of the colonies did the breakdown of the old monarchical order immediately lead to a more humane worldview. Yet the abuse of the impoverished in early New England eventually gave way to a remarkable middle-class mobility that underlined the fundamental irony of American history: a land of racism, injustice, and broken dreams simultaneously offered hope, opportunity, and redemption. Despite the slave trade and indentured status of a significant percentage of whites, the metropolitan centers of North America had unwittingly created a social and economic structure that favored egalitarianism. As the first nation in history formed under the ascendant influences of Protestantism, capitalism, and nationalism, Hofstadter concluded, the United States combined a passion for reform with an underlying impulse toward reaction.[14]

Hofstadter's need to make sense of postwar America prompted his interest in the colonial period. The sixties forged a sweeping challenge to the prevailing culture, and he believed that a thorough reinvestigation of the past could yield valuable insights to nurse the country through its present crisis. Social cohesiveness proved depressingly elusive in an age of identity politics, and it seemed worthwhile to recover the common interests that made the nation. The book further reflected its author's darkening mood and dawning realization of his own end. In a brief ten-page span relating to the Atlantic slave trade, Hofstadter made twenty-one references to death, and the pitch of the book is one of declension, displacement, and loss. The desperate spilling of European populations to North America, stunted lives of unfree laborers, and eclipse of established faiths by fresher spiritual sects form the core of his story. "It is a safe guess," Stanley Elkins and Eric McKitrick have written, "that no general work purporting to be a history of early America ever opened so somber a tableau as that which emerges from the initial chapters of this one."[15]

We see in this study an empathy for the historical actor that is largely absent in Hofstadter's earlier books, an ability to identify, as he never had before, with the fates of his routinely luckless pioneers. "*America at 1750* showed Hofstadter in a new role," Paula Fass wrote, "not as a social critic but as a tragic philosopher for whom history was less a model for future behavior than an illustration of the human condition." Jack Pole explained that "the sadness and sense of cost that pervades Dick's last book may have been to some extent reflections of his pessimism about himself, but they convey a sense of concern for the experience of the past for its own sake which seemed to me to belong to the true historian in him above and beyond the historical critic or contemporary commentator."[16] Finally, James Banner, Jr., believed the work pointed toward a new historiographical path illuminated by Hofstadter's sober response to the misfortunes of his subjects.

> America at 1750 is a more important work in Dick's corpus of writings than has been recognized. In it, he began to write of the difficulties of settling the United States; he's writing about the pain and terror and the harrowing cost and the suffering that it took to set up this society, and I don't know of anyone else who has ventured this insight anywhere. I do think he had come to an appreciation that creating a nation such as his own was not simply a matter of having battles over ideology or working out the implications of liberalism and the like. Instead, there were other dimensions to creating American society and creating American history that had to be captured. There's a clear note in that book that he had come to an appreciation of the toll that it took to create the United States. That is the book's distinctiveness, and it's truly fresh.[17]

Hofstadter modeled *America at 1750* after *England in 1815*, the first volume of Elie Halévy's impressive history of the English people in the nineteenth century. That book's grand thematic sweep — politics, labor, economy, religion, and culture — anticipated the eclectic nature of his new work. In it, Hofstadter emphasized the unusual degree of diversity colonists found in British North America. Swedes, Scots, Germans, Jews, Welsh, Irish, Finns, and French peopled the empire and distinguished particular settlements as havens for religious, political, and intellectual pluralism. Deeply impressed by historical irony, he delighted in the paradox that despite the power of Protestant individualism and capitalist accumulation, western European immigrants largely retained their clannish customs in the New World. Minority sectarian groups, including Swiss Mennonites and German Dunkers, coexisted in peace with Lutherans and Moravians, while Scotch-Irish settlers lived uninhibited lives on the frontier. Only in New England, Hofstadter noted, did British colonists manage to retain the character of the initial émigrés. The Scotch-Irish Presbyterians of Worcester complained of having to support the Puritan ministry and attempted in the 1730s to create a new township building in order to establish a separate church. As this structure neared completion, neighboring Anglos showed their contempt for religious independence by destroying it. New England preserved its homogenous character, Hofstadter shrewdly observed, only through violence.[18]

The tension between toleration and exile found a parallel in recent American history. A succeeding wave of European colonists (1890–1920) pressed Mediterranean and eastern European peoples into contact with the ruling Wasp majority. The ensuing power struggle between urban and rural, ethnic and Anglo, underlined the clash of contesting cultural traditions. *America at 1750* reminded readers that this competition did not begin with the more recent migrations; rather, the promise and perils of pluralism were present at the dawn of America's history.

The most moving chapters of *America at 1750* explore the brutal world of forced labor in British North America. A doleful chapter on white indentures exposed the folly of the Horatio Alger myth that prudence, thrift, and effort ensured social mobility, human dignity, and financial security. Most white servants, Hofstadter noted, never lived to reach their terms of freedom. While textbooks typically presumed that the impressive growth of the colonial economy justified a celebratory narrative, Hofstadter argued that labor's failures and humiliations demanded a more sensitive and balanced judgment. "If we consider the whole span of time over which English indentured servitude prevailed," he came to the crux of the matter, "its heavy tolls and death is the reality that stands out."[19] Personal freedom and material advantage advanced in imperfect, staccato waves and established an equally mixed legacy for future generations. The nation proved to be both a beacon and a burden to immigrants, offering educational, political, and economic opportunities, yet demonstrating a tenacious commitment to the older liberalism that barred ethnic Americans from traditional sources of power.

Chapters on the slave trade and black servitude comprise an informed sensitivity to the peculiar anguish of the black experience while curiously denying the survival of African cultural folkways in the New World. Hofstadter's belief that the barbarity of chattel servitude destroyed African identities relied on an older interpretation of black history. In *An American Dilemma* (1962) Gunnar Myrdal insisted that "in practically all its divergences, American Negro culture is not something independent of general American culture." A year later, Nathan Glazer and Daniel Patrick Moynihan wrote that "the Negro is only an American, and nothing else. He has no values and culture to guard and protect." In fact, the trend of scholarship in the 1970s emphasized the successful transmission of African customs, folkways, and cultures into mainland North America. "Upon the hard rock of racial, social, and economic exploitation and injustice," Hofstadter student Lawrence Levine wrote in his groundbreaking study *Black Culture and Black Consciousness: Afro-American Folk Thought from Slavery to Freedom* (1977), "black Americans forged and nurtured a culture: they formed and maintained kinship networks, made love, raised and socialized children, built a religion, and created a rich expressive culture in which they articulated their feelings and hopes and dreams." Enlivened by the civil rights movement and the fresh promise of the "New Social History," scholars increasingly detected in the music, humor, and oral patterns of slaves a sustaining cultural connection with Africa that continued to inform the black experience in contemporary times.[20]

If Hofstadter's assessment of American slavery is any indication of his broader historiographical allegiances, one might question his role in a postsixties academy. Political and intellectual history interested his generation, but these fields were losing ground, replaced by a devotion to a new conceptual rubric broadly categorized as social history. "In many ways," Fass wrote, "Hofstadter . . . by 1970, had become a kind of institution, a figure fully honored but no longer central to the dynamic impulses of the craft now seeking out other methods such as quantification, increasingly devoted to monographic studies, and whose younger practitioners expressed their own deep commitments to the subjects of inquiry (the working class, women, blacks). Hofstadter had foreseen the transience of his own influence in *The Progressive Historians*. It would have saddened but not surprised him." Robert Dallek believes that respect for the complexity of the human experience motivated Hofstadter during this difficult period. "I think that what was at work there was not a lack of understanding or compassion, rather he saw the new history as a kind of sentimentalism that did not lead you on to any new intellectual ground. He saw it as a cliché in a liberal environment to dwell on the suffering of these groups. He wanted to find out what was fresh about them." In *America at 1750,* Hofstadter continued his late career turning away from the social sciences and moved toward an unmistakably humanistic approach. The great proprietors, military figures, and commercial agents are relegated to a peripheral position in a study respectfully sympathetic to society's forgotten.[21]

One can readily imagine Hofstadter's grand narrative connecting with interested lay readers (certainly the major commercial publishing houses did, and bid accordingly). His inattention, however, to the type of narrowly conceived social history increasingly written by professional scholars threatened to distance him from the guild. His talent for producing popular history, his financial independence from classroom teaching, and his ebbing commitments at Columbia were symbols of autonomy. Most scholars feel beholden to a purely academic audience and defer to the specialized interests of dissertation committees and university presses. From the perspective of publishers, of course, it is the academics who are overly beholden to their own special interests. Hofstadter occupied two publishing spheres — general and professional — and, at his best, won over both camps. This balance shifted in the late sixties as *The Progressive Historians* and *The Idea of a Party System* failed to find audiences beyond campus walls. Hofstadter envisioned the multivolume history as a bridge to span the fragmentation of recent historiographical trends and present a synthetic account of the past that would be in line with the political values of an appreciative — and aging — postwar generation.

*   *   *

On a warm, cloudy day in late October a memorial service was held for Hofstadter at Columbia University's St. Paul's Chapel. C. Vann Woodward's moving tribute to his departed friend — "what might first appear to be a chronic melancholia really masked a mischievous wit and a marvelous gift for spotting the absurd" — anticipated a steady stream of condolences from across the country. President Nixon, historians, university officials, high school teachers, publishers, and students alike felt compelled to offer their regrets. "My sympathy to the Hofstadter family," began one letter, "from an obscure elementary teacher who never met the gentleman but thoroughly admired his work." Another reads, "To me he was the man who demystified our history in the *American Political Tradition,* the man whose book (which I read as a high school student) touched the roots of American life so vitally that it gave me my first sense that historical writing could sometimes be literature." A few days after Hofstadter's death, WCBS television aired an evening editorial commemorating his legacy. It was subsequently inserted into the *Congressional Record.* The memorial reads in part,

> Richard Hofstadter . . . was not just a student of the past. His great skill was unraveling the skeins that tie the present to the past, that make history relevant to our time.
>
> What most occupied Professor Hofstadter's interest recently was

America's history of violence, a subject much studied in these terrible times of political assassinations, urban rioting and campus bombings. And to this subject, Dr. Hofstadter was able to bring a perspective that is enlightening, and, in some ways, encouraging. . . .

The present danger with violence from the Far Left, he argued, is not the violence itself, but the backlash it can bring from the conservative majority of Americans who might support a government committed to political repression.

But Professor Hofstadter did not leave us with such a gloomy prophecy. For in the closing words of his essay, he argued optimistically that the strength of our political system can continue to overcome its afflictions.[22]

Even in death, Hofstadter served as a consensual figure for a nation reeling from internal discord. A postwar generation that came to know American history through Hofstadter's books turned to his final reflections for resolve and relief.

The least impressive tribute came from the most visible source — the *New York Times* obituary. Commencing with a workmanlike "One of the leading historians of American affairs . . . ," the piece drew extensively from Richard Kostelanetz's recent profile of Hofstadter in *Master Minds: Portraits of Contemporary American Artists and Intellectuals* (1969).[23] While the notice provided a reasonably complete outline of Hofstadter's many professional accomplishments, it utterly failed to recover the inner qualities of the man. Such tepid praise as "Dr. Hofstadter was . . . a man of regular habits, scrupulous discipline and insulated temperament [who] moved through life with a contained methodicalness that might [have] dull[ed] a less lively intelligence," offended those close to the departed scholar. Lionel Trilling submitted a rebuttal to the *Times* editor:

> Although it is unusual to write in comment on an obituary article, as an old friend of the late Richard Hofstadter and on behalf of those members of the Columbia University faculty for whom he was an especially cherished colleague I feel the necessity of correcting the misleading description of him which was quoted in your notice of his death of Oct. 25. Richard Hofstadter was anything but an "almost nondescript man," or limited in "social flair," or of an "insulated temperament." On the contrary, he was one of the most clearly defined persons I have ever known; he was an enchanting companion, often memorably funny; he was notable for his openness not alone to ideas but also to people of all kinds.

I hope that those who were acquainted with Richard Hofstadter only through his writing will ignore the strangely grudging quality of the obituary notice and heed the photograph which accompanied it, so accurate in its indication of this remarkable man's grace and charm and luminosity of spirit.[24]

Trilling referred to a photograph taken by Dwight D. Webb. Mouth in the formative stage of purposeful motion, intelligent eyes, widow's peak obscured by the "long" hair that had replaced a functional close cut, head tilted in soft animation, a three-quarter-inch shadow between the curvature at the hollow of the neck and the collar of a loose shirt (a visible concession to the disease that took his life). Here, Hofstadter appeared both formidable and fragile.

The dispute between the *Times* tribute and its detractors is revealing. Hofstadter deftly cultivated a sense of marginalization that merged easily with an inner reserve or, as he once put it, an encompassing inner despair.[25] Above all, he sought a careful detachment in order to preserve his emotional and intellectual resources. The subject of several interviews and personal profiles, Hofstadter never spoke of his childhood in Buffalo, nor did he discuss — even with those close to him — his brief membership in the Communist Party. He conveyed different impressions to different audiences and, to some of his students, the respectful but flat *Times* piece seemed a fair assessment of their distinguished but distant professor. To intimates, however, it slighted the charismatic mind suddenly and cruelly removed from their midst. Both groups had it right, of course, and Hofstadter would have perhaps preferred it this way.

There may have been a touch of effort and even self-defense in his attachment to the margins, but the outsider status came naturally enough. Half Protestant and half Jewish from the interior city of Buffalo, Hofstadter did not share the physical and linguistic characteristics that served as cultural imprints among his friends in the Upper West Side Kibbutz. The cosmopolitanism of Manhattan blurred the sharp ethnic distinctions commonly made in the nation's hinterland, and Hofstadter's identity was perhaps not as secure as Trilling had imagined. Linda Kerber remembered her inability as a Columbia graduate student to "read the signs of ethnicity if they were unaccompanied by a New York accent." When the Kaddish was recited at Hofstadter's memorial service, she writes, "I was surprised and moved to tears."[26] What did Hofstadter gain from the confusion? Perspective. The product of a freshly urbanized, postimmigrant nation, he was determined to make American history both relevant and responsive to the liberal state. His skepticism of popular passions and commitment to the political center troubled some scholars and sealed his estrangement from both the Left and the Right. But one is hard-pressed to name another historian of the postwar period who engaged such a diverse and democratic readership. In an age of paralytic specialization, Hofstadter wrote predominately for the public, contributing books of such erudition and consequence that they remain in our own day symbols of the artistry and influence that historical writing can achieve.

Notes

Introduction

1. See, for example, Lewis Lapham's "Tentacles of Rage: The Republican Propaganda Mill, a Brief History," *Harper's* (September 2004), 31–41; and Peter Beinart's "Death Rattle: What Richard Hofstadter Teaches Us about Ralph Nader," *New Republic* (8 March 2004), 6. In the latter piece, Beinart quotes from Hofstadter's *The Age of Reform*—"Third parties are like bees, once they have stung, they die"—to criticize Ralph Nader's second presidential campaign. Beinart writes, "On election night 2000, Nader boasted, 'Tomorrow, the Green Party will emerge as the third-largest party in America, the fastest growing party, and the best party in its democratic spirit.' On election night 2004, the Green Party may be essentially defunct, along with the man who once led it. Somewhere, Hofstadter is smiling."

2. Edward Hallett Carr, *What Is History* (New York, 1961), 54; Hofstadter to Jack Pole, 24 January 1968, JPP.

3. Nevins to Curti, 19 June 1942, MCP; Hofstadter quoted in Richard Kostelanetz, *Master Minds: Portraits of Contemporary American Artists and Intellectuals* (New York, 1969), 168.

4. Dan Hofstadter correspondence with author; Metzger, *Richard Hofstadter Project*, OHRO; Hofstadter, *The American Political Tradition: And the Men Who Made It* (New York, 1989 edition), 271; Hofstadter, *The Age of Reform: From Bryan to FDR* (New York, 1955), 77–82; Hofstadter, "Some Comments on Goldwater," *Partisan Review* (Fall 1964), 591. Colleagues frequently advised Hofstadter to resist overstating his arguments. Given the Roosevelt chapter to read in draft form, Howard K. Beale suggested a thorough revision. Beale to Hofstadter, 6 February 1948, box 1, RHP. On the subject of Populist anti-Semitism, Merle Curti, Kenneth Stampp, Eric McKitrick, Stanley Elkins, and Lee Benson—among others—shared serious reservations about Hofstadter's treatment of the farmers.

5. Hughes, *Richard Hofstadter Project*, OHRO; Hofstadter and Leuchtenburg correspondence with author.

6. Hofstadter correspondence with author; James Banner, Jr., interview with author. Stanley Elkins and Eric McKitrick wrote "meeting Richard Hofstadter face to face . . . one was astonished. The absence of personal contentiousness or of self-assertiveness in the man accorded not at all with the most striking quality in the writing: the assurance of a mind that is on top of its subject and delights in itself." Elkins and McKitrick, eds., *The Hofstadter Aegis: A Memorial* (New York, 1974), 307–8.

7. Hofstadter to Riesman, internal evidence suggests 1955, DRP.

8. Paula Fass interview with author. Fass worked closely with Beatrice K. Hofstadter preparing the unfinished manuscript for *America at 1750: A Social Portrait,* for publication. In 1960, Hofstadter directed an interviewer to the one book he wrote without Kevitt's assistance. "Let me show you the difference between the original and paperback editions of *Social Darwinism.* The chance came to bring it out in paper. We made — I say 'we' because I get a tremendous amount of editorial criticism from my wife — some seven or eight hundred changes nearly all of them purely stylistic." "Interview: Richard Hofstadter," by David Hawke, *History* 3 (1960), 138.

9. Irving Howe, *A Margin of Hope: An Intellectual Autobiography* (New York, 1982), 322.

10. Hofstadter correspondence with author.

11. Elkins and McKitrick, eds., *Hofstadter Aegis,* viii.

12. Bell quoted in Richard Gillam, "Richard Hofstadter and C. Wright Mills," *American Scholar* (Winter 1977–78), 74.

13. Lionel Trilling, *The Liberal Imagination* (New York, 1950), ix; Hofstadter, *American Political Tradition,* xxxiii.

Chapter 1

1. Adams quoted in Alex Zwerdling, *Improvised Europeans: American Literary Expatriates and the Siege of London* (New York, 1998), 337, note 6.

2. "My first conscious awareness of the possibility of something called ethnic history," Columbia historian James Shenton observed, "was the result of conversations with Hofstadter." Shenton interview with author.

3. Frederick Jackson Turner, *The Frontier in American History* (New York, 1920), 277–78.

4. Theodore Hamerow, *Reflections on History and Historians* (Madison, 1987), 44.

5. Michael Krause and Davis Joyce, *The Writing of American History* (Norman, 1985), 145.

6. The primary names associated with the social gospel include Jane Addams and Washington Gladden; literary realism emerged as a potent force for reform in the work of Frank Norris, Jack London, and Theodore Dreiser, while William James, Charles Peirce, and Oliver Wendell Holmes were the most original Pragmatists.

7. Douglas Hofstadter interview with author. *Hof* means "court," *stadter* refers to an urban dweller, a reference, perhaps, to Krakow's close proximity. Hofstadter spelled his mother's name Katherine, others in the family spell it Catherine. Hofstadter to Kenneth Stampp, 5 May 1952, KSP.

8. Samuel Hofstadter to Robert Hofstadter, 29 March 1967, box 4, RHP; Susan

Stout Baker, *Radical Beginnings: Richard Hofstadter and the 1930s* (Westport, 1985), 4–6; Gay interview with author.

9. Mark Goldman, *High Hopes: The Rise and Decline of Buffalo, New York* (Albany, 1983), 168.

10. Ibid., 212; Selig Adler and Thomas Connolly, *From Ararat to Suburbia: The History of the Jewish Community of Buffalo* (Philadelphia, 1960), 163, 172, 185–86; Baker, *Radical Beginnings*, 11.

11. H. Stuart Hughes, *Gentleman Rebel: The Memoirs of H. Stuart Hughes* (New York, 1990), 245.

12. Hofstadter correspondence with author; Baker, *Radical Beginnings*, 11.

13. Kostelanetz, *Master Minds*, 167–68; Felice Swados, "Prologue," 27, HSP. This is a sketch of Felice Swados's never completed second novel. As a work of fiction, its contents must be approached carefully. Its familiarity with Hofstadter's early life and the circumstances of his mother's death are indisputable.

14. Baker, *Radical Beginnings*, 7.

15. Hofstadter's University of Buffalo transcripts include his high school record; *Buffalo Blurb*, 10 June "1953"; *Buffalo Evening News*, 29 June 1933; *The Chronicle*, 1933 Senior Yearbook, Fosdick-Masten Park High School. Fosdick-Masten Park alumni include the Columbia University economist Rexford Tugwell and Robert E. Schmidt—better known as "Buffalo Bob" of the *Howdy Doody Show*.

16. Hofstadter correspondence with author.

17. *Buffalo Bee,* 1 November 1935; Gay interview with author.

18. Adler and Connolly, *From Ararat to Suburbia*, 239–41; Alan M. Wald, *The New York Intellectuals: The Rise and Decline of the Anti-Stalinist Left from the 1930s to the 1980s* (Chapel Hill, 1987), 334; Dr. Richard Plotz, Bette Swados, and Daniel Bell interviews with author.

19. Hofstadter to Harvey Swados, internal evidence suggests 1937, HSP. "Felice was very intellectual," Hofstadter's University of Maryland colleague Kenneth Stampp remembers, "and very much in her own writing, and very radical and sort of making sure that Dick didn't stray from his radicalism." Kenneth Stampp, *Historian of Slavery, the Civil War, and Reconstruction, University of California, Berkeley, 1946–1983,* University History Series (Berkeley, 1996), 104.

20. Alfred Kazin, *Starting Out in the Thirties* (New York, 1965), 99.

21. Elizabeth Early, *Richard Hofstadter Project*, OHRO; Kazin, *New York Jew*, 16.

22. Felice Swados to Harvey Swados, 9 May 1939, HSP.

23. Hofstadter to Harvey Swados, 10 November 1938, HSP

24. *House of Fury* was republished in 1948 under the title *Reform School Girl* with Canadian model and figure skater Mary Collins on the cover. A clean copy of this edition can fetch over a thousand dollars. For a review see the *New York Times,* 2 November 1941.

25. After completing a doctorate at Harvard, Farber studied in Germany under Edmund Husserl and later founded the *Journal of Philosophy and Phenomenological Research;* an organ devoted to perpetuating Husserl's influence in America; Hawke, "Interview: Richard Hofstadter," 140–41. In interviews for this book, Peter Gay and Jack Pole stressed Hofstadter's respect for Pratt.

26. Charles and Mary Beard, *The Rise of American Civilization: The Industrial Era* (New York, 1927), 480; Julius Pratt, *Expansionists of 1898* (Baltimore, 1936), 234.

27. Pratt, *Expansionists of 1898*, 3.

28. Pratt's influence is clearly evident in Hofstadter's 1952 essay "Manifest Destiny and the Philippines." In it, Hofstadter wrote that "since Julius W. Pratt published his *Expansionists of 1898* . . . it has been obvious that any interpretation of America's entry upon the paths of imperialism in the nineties in terms of rational economic motives would not fit the facts." Richard Hofstadter, "Manifest Destiny and the Philippines," in *America in Crisis: Fourteen Crucial Episodes in American History,* ed. Daniel Aaron (New York, 1952), 197.

29. *Buffalo Bee,* 25 October 1935; *Buffalo Bee,* 12 April 1935.

30. *Buffalo Bee,* 15 November 1935; Richard Hofstadter to Robert Kahn, 15 August 1968, box 27, RHP.

31. Baker, *Radical Beginnings,* 50; Beard and Beard, *Rise of American Civilization,* 54; Richard Hofstadter, "The Tariff and Homestead Issues in the Republican Campaign of 1860" (Senior Thesis, University of Buffalo, 1936), 1, box 31, RHP.

32. Ibid., 24.

33. Hofstadter correspondence with author.

34. For Samuel Hofstadter's obituary see the *New York Times* 12 July 1970.

35. Hofstadter to Farber, 30 July 1936 and Farber to Hofstadter, 5 August 1936, MFP.

36. Felice Swados to Harvey Swados, 5 March 1936, HSP.

37. Kazin, *New York Jew,* 17; Hofstadter to Harvey Swados, internal evidence suggests 1937, HSP; Felice Swados to Harvey Swados, 20 June 1937. Alfred Kazin wrote of Felice's professional circle "there was a curiously pretentious show of intellectual 'guilt' around the *Time-Fortune* offices, an unnecessary need to show oneself pure and uncorrupted. Professional liberals . . . liked to think that their gifts were misused and exploited; grumbling about the boss made them feel that their wine had not yet turned into Luce's corporate vinegar. There was an affected moral uncomfortableness to liberal and left intellectuals who worked for Luce, a readiness to suffer." Kazin, *Starting Out in the Thirties,* 111.

38. Hofstadter to "Fred," internal evidence suggests fall 1936, HSP; Hofstadter to Aaron, Rivie, and Harvey Swados, 24 January 1937, HSP.

39. Harry J. Carman, untitled ms, HCP; Hofstadter to Carman, 19 March 1946, HCP; Shenton interview with author. Carman's first wife died in 1943, two years before Felice Swados's death. His relationship with Hofstadter may have been deepened because of this.

40. Hofstadter to Harvey Swados, 9 February 1938, HSP.

41. Ibid. Felice Swados to Harvey Swados, 6 May 1940, HSP. Hofstadter preferred not to use his middle name, a practice that caused some confusion. The 1934 University of Buffalo yearbook listed him as Richard L. Hofstadter, while a memorial service held shortly after his death recorded his name as Richard F. Hofstadter, box 19, RHP. To complicate matters, Hofstadter's last name was often misspelled — sometimes by himself as a joke. Merle Curti could not help but confuse the Knopf Fellowship award committee with his solemn promise that "of all the graduate students

I have taught Hofstaeder is the best." Curti to Alfred A. Knopf, 20 April 1945, AAKP. On Columbia's relationship to Jewish scholars and students see Robert A. Mc-Caughey, *Stand Columbia: A History of Columbia University in the City of New York, 1754–2004* (New York, 2003), 256–76; and Harold Weschler, *The Qualified Student: A History of Selective College Admission in America, 1870–1970* (New York, 1977). George Mosse, *Confronting History: A Memoir* (Madison, 2000), 119.

42. Hofstadter to Harvey Swados, 15 April 1939; Kostelanetz, *Master Minds*, 169; Kostelanetz to Hofstadter, 15 January 1968, box 5, RHP; Shenton interview with author. Dan Hofstadter adds, "I recall my father mentioning anti-Semitism only once, in relation to his difficulties in getting a job at Columbia after he received his doctorate. He later came to the conclusion, he told me, that anti-Semitism had played no role in his failure to obtain an appointment." Dan Hofstadter correspondence with author.

43. Richard Hofstadter, "The Southeastern Cotton Tenants under the AAA, 1933–1935" (MA thesis, Columbia University, 1938), 19–23.

44. Ibid., 42, 98.

45. David L. Carlton, "Merle Curti," in *Twentieth-Century American Historians,* ed. Clyde N. Wilson (Detroit, 1983), 132.

46. Hofstadter to Fred Kersner, 26 November 1954, MCP; Hicks to Curti, 19 September 1961, MCP.

47. Hofstadter to Parrington, Jr., 22 September 1967, box 7, RHP.

48. Richard Hofstadter, "Parrington and the Jeffersonian Tradition," *Journal of the History of Ideas* (October 1941), 392–93.

49. Ibid., 396–400.

50. Hofstadter to Harvey Swados, internal evidence suggests fall 1936, HSP.

51. Kenneth Stampp interview with author; Hofstadter to Harvey Swados, October 1938, HSP.

52. Hofstadter to Harvey Swados, October 1938 and 16 February 1939, HSP; Stampp interview with author; Alfred Kazin, *Richard Hofstadter Project,* OHRO.

53. Felice Swados to Harvey Swados, 6 May 1940, HSP.

54. Hofstadter to Harvey Swados, 9 October 1939 and 16 December 1940, HSP.

55. Hofstadter to Harvey Swados, 16 December 1940, HSP.

56. Hofstadter to "Chums," May 1941, HSP; Hofstadter to Harvey Swados, 25 November 1939, HSP.

57. Eric Foner, "Introduction" to Richard Hofstadter's *Social Darwinism in American Thought* (Boston, 1992),xii–xiii. Foner met Hofstadter in 1962 and recalls that "with a certain amount of embarrassment" Hofstadter related his regret at taking Foner's father's position two decades earlier. Foner interview with author.

58. Hofstadter to Swados, 10 October 1939, HSP.

Chapter 2

1. Richard Hofstadter, *New York Review of Books* (23 January 1964), 12; Felice Swados to Harvey Swados, 2 June 1940, HSP.

2. Hofstadter, 1955 author's note reprinted in *Social Darwinism in American*

Thought, 1860–1915 (Boston, 1992), xxix. For a discussion of *Social Darwinism*'s debt to Progressive thought see David W. Noble, "The Reconstruction of Progress: Charles Beard, Richard Hofstadter, and Postwar Historical Thought," in *Recasting America: Culture and Politics in Cold War America,* ed. Lary May (Chicago, 1989), 61–74.

3. Hofstadter, *Social Darwinism in American Thought, 1860–1915* (Philadelphia, 1944), 18.

4. Ibid., 25.

5. Ibid., 37.

6. Ibid., 90.

7. Ibid., 53, 65, italics added.

8. Louis Menand, *The Metaphysical Club: A Story of Ideas in America* (New York, 2001), xi–xii; Hofstadter, *Social Darwinism* (1944), 107.

9. Hofstadter, *Social Darwinism* (1944), 145; Hofstadter, "The Great Depression and American History: A Personal Footnote," box 36, RHP. This is an unpublished lecture given in 1964. A brief document, it is the closest thing to an intellectual testimony that Hofstadter wrote. In it, he discussed the influence of Buffalo, the Depression, and the New Deal on his thinking. Most valuable are Hofstadter's summaries of his books, which, he acknowledged, were creatures of their environment.

10. Hofstadter, *Social Darwinism* (1944), 153. "Strong," Hofstadter wrote, had an "uncanny capacity" to make social Darwinism consistent with "the prejudices of rural Protestant America."

11. Hofstadter to Kazin, internal evidence suggests 1943, AKP. "Hofstadter," Kazin wrote, "liked to mock my fascination with Henry Adams by quoting Adams's insane hatred of Jews, especially immigrant Jews." Kazin, *New York Jew,* 14.

12. Hofstadter to Swados, November 1940, HSP.

13. The *New York Times,* 21 January 1945. Jones's description of Hofstadter's writing style — "compact, lucid, informed, vigorous" — is remarkably similar to David Potter's unpublished assessment, made over twenty years later — "clean, flexible, muscular, relaxed." David Potter, marginalia of advanced proofs, *Progressive Historians: Turner, Beard, Parrington,* DPP; for Billington's remarks see *Mississippi Valley Historical Review* (December 1944), 458–59; and for Lowenberg's, the *American Historical Review* (July 1945), 820–21; Albert G. Keller quoted in Robert C. Bannister, *Social Darwinism: Science and Myth in Anglo-American Thought* (Philadelphia, 1979), 5.

14. Hofstadter, "Great Depression and American History"; Bannister, *Social Darwinism,* 5–8; Eric Foner, introduction to Hofstadter, *Social Darwinism* (Boston, 1992), xx.

15. Kostelanetz, *Master Minds,* 169; George H. Callcott, *A History of the University of Maryland* (Baltimore, 1966), 314.

16. Kenneth Stampp interview with author; Callcott, *History of the University of Maryland,* 314.

17. Hofstadter to Henry Steele Commager, 30 December 1942, HSCP; Stampp to William B. Hesseltine, 9 September 1942, WBHP; Hofstadter to Swados, 19 August 1943, HSP; Early, *Richard Hofstadter Project,* OHRO.

18. Gewehr to Beale, 17 August 1942 and 17 April 1946, HKBP.

19. Bogue interview with author.

20. Freidel, *Richard Hofstadter Project,* OHRO; Stampp to Hesseltine, 14 December 1942, WBHP; Stampp, *Historian of Slavery,* 100; Richard Hofstadter, "The Quality of a Publisher," in *Portrait of a Publisher, 1915–1965* (New York, 1965), vol. 2, 217.

21. Hofstadter to Swados, 15 July 1943 and 19 August 1943, HSP; Dan Hofstadter correspondence with author; Freidel, *Richard Hofstadter Project,* OHRO; Kostelanetz, *Master Minds,* 169. James Shenton served in the military from 1943 to 1946 and recalled Hofstadter's interest in his experiences during these years. "It was almost as if he was trying to fill in what he didn't have." Shenton interview with author.

22. Hofstadter to Harvey Swados, 19 August 1943, HSP; Stampp interview with author; Freidel, *Richard Hofstadter Project,* OHRO.

23. Callcott, *History of the University of Maryland,* 336; Kathryn Mills and Pamela Mills, eds., *C. Wright Mills: Letters and Autobiographical Writings* (Berkeley, 2000), 70.

24. Hofstadter to Harvey Swados, 19 August 1943, HSP.

25. Krout to Hofstadter, 10 October 1944, box 20, RHP.

26. Hofstadter to Curti, 25 April 1944, MCP; Hofstadter to Stampp, 4 August 1944, KSP; Felice Swados to Kenneth and Kay Stampp, 4 December 1944, KSP; Hofstadter to Commager, 15 April 1945, HSCP.

27. Stampp to Hesseltine, 13 December 1944, WBHP; Hofstadter to Stampp, December 1944, KSP; Earnest P. Lindley and Edward Weintal, "How We Dealt with Spain," *Harper's Magazine* (December 1943), 23–33.

28. Hofstadter to Stampp, December 1944, KSP.

29. Stampp to Hesseltine, 13 December 1944, WBHP.

30. Hofstadter to Stampp, December 1944, KSP. "Things got kind of nasty," Stampp recalled some forty years after the event. "Frank and I wrote a letter to Hofstadter saying, 'well, we know you're dying to go back to Columbia, Hayes is there,' and Hofstadter wrote an indignant letter back saying, 'what kind of friends are you?' I eventually wrote an apologetic letter to Hofstadter about it." Stampp, *Historian of Slavery,* 112.

31. Shenton interview with author. Dan Hofstadter recalled of his father, "There was a certain brave uncharitableness that he lacked, to his cost, I think." Dan Hofstadter correspondence with author.

32. *American Historical Review* (April 1950), 662–64. Many years later, Hofstadter did sign a letter of protest against conditions in Spain. In 1969, the Franco regime banished eighteen prominent intellectuals to remote villages around the nation, and a number of American thinkers addressed a note of objection to United Nations Secretary-General U Thant. It reads in part, "This random seizure of some of Spain's most respected intellectuals as well as arrests of hundreds of students and workers is an unpleasant reminder of the early days of Nazi Germany and the totalitarian Spain of thirty years ago." *New York Review of Books,* 27 March 1969, 46.

33. Hofstadter, "William Leggett: Spokesman of Jacksonian Democracy," *Political Science Quarterly* (December 1943), 582–85.

34. Ibid., 586.

35. Ibid., 589.

36. Ibid., 593; Fox to Hofstadter, 17 January 1944, c.c. box 1, RHP; Woodward to Hofstadter, 30 April 1963, CVWP.

37. Hofstadter, "U. B. Phillips and the Plantation Legend," *Journal of Negro History* (April 1944), 109–10.

38. C. Vann Woodward, *Thinking Back: The Perils of Writing History* (Baton Rouge, 1986), 15–16, 41.

39. Hofstadter to Stampp, April 1945; Hofstadter *Portrait of a Publisher,* 2:217. In a letter supporting Hofstadter's application, Harry Carman stated that "at Columbia we rate him as the ablest of the younger generation working in the field of American intellectual history. His ability of literary craftsmanship is . . . outstanding." Henry Steele Commager concurred—"of all our graduate students in the last five or six years, Hofstadter is the ablest. . . . I feel confident that he is going to do many important things in the field of history and especially intellectual history." Carman to Alfred A. Knopf, 16 April 1945, AAKP; Commager to Alfred A. Knopf, 4 May 1945, AAKP. Knopf graduated from Columbia and cultivated friendships with many of its faculty, several of whose work he published. Hofstadter not only wrote books for the house, but also steered several Columbia students Knopf's way.

40. Knopf reader's report (B. Smith), 14 May 1945, AAKP; Hofstadter, *Portrait of a Publisher,* 2:218.

41. Dallek interview with author; see several letters from Hofstadter to Stampp during the spring and summer of 1945, KSP.

42. Commager to Curti, 19 February 1945, HSCP; [Illegible name] to Beatrice Hofstadter, 25 October 1970, box 18, RHP.

43. Kostelanetz, *Master Minds,* 169; Hawke, "Interview: Richard Hofstadter," 139–40.

44. Curti to Hofstadter, 21 September 1970, MCP. Hofstadter student Daniel J. Singal wrote, "With his firm ties to his family, university, publisher, and urban local, it is striking how rooted Hofstadter became for a supposedly rootless modern intellectual. I suspect that this secure personality and professional life was essential in enabling him to sustain his critical stance toward American society." I find much value in Singal's insight, yet believe that Hofstadter's self-image as a "rootless modern intellectual" was also sustained by his periodic depressions, sense of emotional detachment, and personal aloofness. Temperamentally, in other words, he was well equipped to criticize the exuberance of postwar American society from an "outsider" position. Certainly Columbia and its environs were critical to shaping Hofstadter's work, yet I am also mindful of James Shenton's remark that "Dick lived in his head." Daniel Joseph Singal, "Beyond Consensus: Richard Hofstadter and American Historiography," *American Historical Review* (October 1984), 983, note 14. Shenton interview with author.

Chapter 3

1. The books I refer to are Goldman's *Rendezvous with Destiny: A History of Modern American Reform* (New York, 1952); Schlesinger, Jr.'s *The Age of Jackson* (Boston, 1945); and Woodward's *Origins of the New South, 1877–1913* (Baton Rouge, 1951).

2. Knopf to Hofstadter, 22 December 1947, AAKP; Strauss to Hofstadter, 18 December 1947, AAKP.

3. Hofstadter, *American Political Tradition*, xxxiii, xxxvi; Document 1377.6, AAKP.

4. Hofstadter to Strauss, 30 December 1947 and 22 January 1948, AAKP; Strauss to Hofstadter, 9 January 1948, AAKP.

5. Hofstadter to Strauss, 25 March 1948, AAKP; Strauss to Hofstadter, 29 March 1948, AAKP.

6. David M. Potter, *People of Plenty: Economic Abundance and the American Character* (Chicago, 1954).

7. John Higham, "Changing Paradigms: The Collapse of Consensus History," *American Historical Review* (September 1989), 464–65.

8. Bell interview with author; Kostelanetz, *Master Minds*, 168; Hicks to Sontag, 29 November 1947, JHP.

9. Hofstadter to Curti, internal evidence suggests spring 1948, MCP. The book's dust jacket reads, in part, "It is unorthodox; it will outrage many people; but no one will deny the authority of its arguments, the happy disenchantment of its mood, or the edged and sparkling irony of its style." On the social milieu from which Hofstadter's book emerged see Christopher Lasch's foreword to *American Political Tradition*, ix.

10. Fass interview with author; Hawke, "Interview: Richard Hofstadter," 140. The American politicians who graced the pages of Mencken's *Prejudices* — Lincoln, both Roosevelts, Wilson, and Bryan — all appear in *The American Political Tradition*. Kenneth Lynn perceptively remarked in 1963 that "*The American Political Tradition* . . . might have more appropriately been called *Prejudices: First Series*." Kenneth Lynn, *Reporter* (4 July 1963), 38.

11. Casey Blake and Christopher Phelps, "History as Social Criticism: Conversations with Christopher Lasch," *Journal of American History* (March 1994), 1317.

12. David Greenberg, "Richard Hofstadter's Tradition," *Atlantic Monthly* (November 1998), 134.

13. Lewis Mumford, "The Corruption of Liberalism," *New Republic* (29 April 1940), 568, 572–73.

14. Schlesinger, Jr., *Age of Jackson*, 263.

15. Bray Hammond, "Public Policy and National Banks," *Journal of Economic History* (May 1946), 83–84; Hofstadter, *American Political Tradition*, 466.

16. Schlesinger wrote that Hofstadter and his colleagues made a cottage industry of attacking his Progressive interpretation of the period: "For a time *The Age of Jackson* became a designated target for Columbia faculty and graduate students, with Hofstadter, Richard B. Morris, Lee Benson, Edward Pessen and the historian of economic thought Joseph Dorfman organizing the attack. Columbia seminars, I was told, were devoted to meticulous exposures of Schlesinger's fallacies." Arthur Schlesinger, Jr., *A Life in the 20th Century: Innocent Beginnings, 1917–1950* (Boston, 2000), 364.

17. Hofstadter, *American Political Tradition*, 204.

18. Strauss to Alfred A. Knopf, 6 June 1947, AAKP.

19. Hofstadter, *American Political Tradition*, 298.

20. Beale to Hofstadter, 6 February 1948, and Hofstadter to Beale, 11 February 1948, box 1, RHP. Hofstadter later admitted that he had been too critical of TR and that as a writer influenced by the reforms of the 1930s, he saw progressivism as tepid

and conservative by comparison. Hofstadter, "The Great Depression and American History," box 36, RHP.

21. Pole correspondence with author. Hofstadter, *American Political Tradition*, 428–29.

22. Lauraine Vaughn to Beatrice Hofstadter, 26 October 1970, box 18, RHP.

23. Pole, "Richard Hofstadter," in *Clio's Favorites: Leading Historians of the United States, 1945–2000*, ed. Robert Allen Rutland (Columbia, MO, 2000), 72; Eliot Janeway, *Saturday Review of Literature* (9 October 1948), 19.

24. Woodward, *Mississippi Valley Historical Review* (March 1949), 682; Schlesinger, Jr., *American Historical Review* (April 1949), 613.

25. Perry Miller, *Nation* (16 October 1948), 440.

26. Hofstadter to Harold Strauss, 19 April 1948, AAKP; Curti to Hofstadter, 15 April 1948, AAKP.

27. Hofstadter to Knopf, 16 October 1948, AAKP.

28. Rawick to Merle Curti, 28 February 1955, MCP; O'Brien to Buhle, 11 June 1967, RAP; Foner quoted in (Columbia) *University Review*, 7 April 1974.

29. Foner, Gay, and Banner, Jr., interviews with author.

30. Gilbert correspondence with author.

31. Shenton interview with author.

32. Ross and Cooper interviews with author. Hofstadter once remarked to a seminar that he served as primary advisor to some forty "active" students. As in most graduate programs, the majority never finished. David Strauss interview with author.

33. The two books that I am aware Hofstadter blurbed for are Marvin Meyers's *The Jacksonian Persuasion: Politics and Belief* (Stanford, 1957) and Christopher Lasch's *The New Radicalism in America, 1889–1963: The Intellectual as Social Type* (New York, 1965). Wallace and Ross interviews with author.

34. Lane interview with author.

35. Ross and Lane interviews with author.

36. Lane interview with author.

37. Shenton, Ross, Banner, Jr., interviews with author. Gerald L. Fetner, *Immersed in Great Affairs: Allan Nevins and the Heroic Age of American History* (Albany, 2004), 9. On the intellectual differences between Nevins and Hofstadter see 5–6.

38. Hofstadter to McKitrick, 8 September 1960, EMP.

39. Elkins interview with author; Donald's review is in the *American Historical Review* (July 1960), 922. For Hofstadter's influence on Elkins see Benjamin DeMott, "Rediscovering Complexity," *Atlantic Monthly* (September 1988), 72. Like Elkins, Hofstadter student David Strauss met with a favorable reply to an unusual entreaty. After finishing undergraduate work at Amherst, Strauss taught for two years in France and returned to America intrigued with the French image of America — a topic he hoped to pursue at Columbia. "Hofstadter simply astounded me," Strauss remembered, "by taking on the project." He later learned of Hofstadter's regard for France — his love of French cuisine, interest in Sartre and de Beauvoir, and "passion for French culture." Strauss interview with author.

40. McKitrick to Hofstadter, 17 October 1957, EMP.

41. Levine interview with author.

42. Singal correspondence with author.

43. McKitrick to Ashbel Green, 21 November 1973, EMP.

Chapter 4

1. Hofstadter, "History and the Social Sciences," 364–65.

2. Bell interview with author.

3. David Hollinger, *Science, Jews, and Secular Culture: Studies in Mid-Twentieth-Century American Intellectual History* (Princeton, 1996), 25, 136.

4. Dorothy Ross, "The New and Newer Histories: Social Theory and Historiography in an 'American Key,'" in *Imagined Histories: American Historians Interpret the Past,* ed. Gordon Wood and Anthony Molho (Princeton, 1998), 85; Turner quoted in Peter Novick, *That Noble Dream: The 'Objectivity Question' and the American Historical Profession* (Cambridge, 1988), 90.

5. Richard Hofstadter, "Turner and the Frontier Myth," *American Scholar* (October 1949), 435; Richard Hofstadter, "Beard and the Constitution: The History of an Idea," *American Quarterly* (Fall 1950).

6. Hofstadter, "Turner and the Frontier Myth," 435.

7. Hofstadter to Curti, internal evidence suggests 1948, MCP.

8. Kirkendall to Curti as quoted in Novick, *That Noble Dream,* 346. Gay's remark can be found in *International Encyclopedia of the Social Sciences,* ed. David L. Sill, 18:311 (New York, 1979).

9. Leuchtenburg interview with author. It may be more accurate to say that Hofstadter's distrust of the mass mind originated in his revolt against the Communist Party in the thirties and was reinforced in the McCarthy years. Freidel, *Richard Hofstadter Project,* OHRO.

10. Hofstadter to Edward Elkind, 13 January 1960, box 34, RHP.

11. Hofstadter to Kenneth Stampp, 26 April 1950, KSP; Hofstadter to Bridenbaugh, 9 November 1950, KSP.

12. Hofstadter to Merle Curti, 31 January 1949, MCP.

13. Shenton interview with author.

14. Eric Bentley, *Thirty Years of Treason: Excerpts from Hearings before the House Committee on Un-American Activities, 1938–1968* (New York, 1971), 601–6.

15. Hofstadter to Curti, internal evidence suggests February or March 1951, MCP.

16. Richard Hofstadter and C. DeWitt Hardy, *The Development and Scope of Higher Education in the United States* (New York, 1952), 107, note 5; 110.

17. Ibid., 121. Stringfellow Bar, *New Republic* (6 April 1953), 29.

18. Richard Hofstadter and Walter P. Metzger, *The Development of Academic Freedom in the United States* (New York, 1955), xiii.

19. Ibid. 209, 223.

20. Roger Geiger quoted in Richard Hofstadter, *Academic Freedom in the Age of the College* (New Brunswick, 1996), xvii.

21. Frances Stoner Saunders, *The Cultural Cold War: The CIA and the World of Arts and Letters* (New York, 1999), 1.

22. Sol Stein to Richard Hofstadter, Nathan Glazer, Irwin Ross, Melvin Arnold,

Daniel Bell, internal evidence suggests 1953, ACCFP; Daniel Bell to Messrs. Hook, Farrell, Pitzele, Beichman, Stein, 14 January 1954, ACCFP.

23. James Shenton interview with author.

24. Travis Beale Jacobs, *Eisenhower and Columbia* (New York, 2001), 289–91; *New York Times,* 16 October 1952.

25. Ibid., 298. Leuchtenburg interview with author.

26. *New York Times,* 17 October 1952.

27. Hofstadter to Stampp, internal evidence suggests March-July 1954, KSP.

28. Richard Hofstadter, "Democracy and Anti-Intellectualism in America," *Michigan Alumnus Quarterly Review* (Summer 1953), 286.

29. Ibid., 286, 295.

30. Curti to Hofstadter, 20 November 1953, box 34, RHP.

31. Michael Harrington, "The Welfare State and Its Neoconservative Critics," *Dissent* (Fall 1973), 435.

32. Neil Jumonville, *Critical Crossings: The New York Intellectuals in Postwar America* (Berkeley, 1991), 237–38.

33. Hofstadter to Curti, December 1955, MCP.

34. Susan Buck-Morss, *The Origin of Negative Dialectics: Theodore W. Adorno, Walter Benjamin, and the Frankfurt Institute* (New York, 1977), 7.

35. Blake and Phelps, "History as Social Criticism: Conversations with Christopher Lasch," 1317–18.

36. Kevin MacDonald, *The Culture of Critique: An Evolutionary Analysis of Jewish Involvement in Twentieth-Century Intellectual and Political Movements* (Connecticut, 1998), 159.

37. Bell interview with author.

38. Karl Mannheim, *Ideology and Utopia: An Introduction to the Sociology of Knowledge* (New York, 1958 reprint), 87.

39. Leuchtenburg interview with author; Singal, "Beyond Consensus," 986.

40. Leuchtenburg correspondence with author; University Seminar on the State, box 24, RHP.

41. Richard Hofstadter, "The Pseudo-Conservative Revolt," *American Scholar* (Winter 1954–55), 9.

Chapter 5

1. Alan Brinkley, "Richard Hofstadter's *The Age of Reform:* A Reconsideration," *Reviews in American History* (September 1985), 462. Robert M. Collins's "The Originality Trap — Richard Hofstadter on Populism," *Journal of American History* (June 1989), 150–67, joins Brinkley's essay as the most insightful evaluations of *The Age of Reform.* Robert Wiebe, "Views But No Vista," *Progressive* 33 (1969), 47.

2. Hofstadter to Miller, internal evidence suggests 1952, box 6, RHP.

3. John D. Hicks, *The Populist Revolt: A History of the Farmers' Alliance and the People's Party* (Minneapolis-St. Paul, 1931), 422.

4. Ibid. For Hicks's survey of the grievances of the farmers, see pp. 54–95, and on

their contribution, pp. 404–23. For a review of the historiography of Populism from 1890 to 1930, see James C. Malin, "Notes on the Literature of Populism," *Kansas Historical Quarterly* (February 1932), 160–64. Lee Benson introduced Hofstadter to Malin's work—a series of perceptive essays on agricultural policy in America that stand among the earliest attempts to explore the Populist mind. Eschewing a simple economic approach, Malin probed the "emotional connotations" of the family farm and the impact of urbanization and centralized planning among farmers. His insistence that "too many resentments were accumulated and every additional grievance added to the probability of revolt on the part of rural America, the last stronghold of nineteenth-century individualism" anticipated Hofstadter's own observations on the subject. Malin, "Mobility and History: Reflections on the Agricultural Policies on the United States in Relation to a Mechanized World," *Agricultural History* (October 1943), 183, 186–87, 178. Benson interview with author.

5. John D. Hicks, *My Life with History: An Autobiography* (Lincoln, 1968), 2, 61, viii. On the Rappaport hire, Hicks is quoted in Novick, *That Noble Dream,* 330.

6. For the intellectual heritage of the Progressives and Anti-Progressives see Michael Paul Rogin, *The Intellectuals and McCarthy: The Radical Specter* (Cambridge, 1967), 9–31; and Novick, *That Noble Dream,* 322–48.

7. Hofstadter to Curti, internal evidence suggests December 1953, MCP; Hofstadter, "The Great Depression and American History," box 36, RHP.

8. Hofstadter, *Age of Reform,* 33.

9. The conceptualization of Populism along nontraditional (i.e., noneconomic) lines was advanced not only by Hofstadter but also by his talented research assistant, Eric McKitrick, a midwesterner who came to Columbia after serving in the army. Notes for *Age of Reform* in the Hofstadter Papers indicate that McKitrick performed a substantial investigation into the internal "guilt" and "catharsis" that Populism wrestled with as it combated the trusts. Box 25, RHP.

10. Hofstadter, *Age of Reform,* 61.

11. Meyer Schapiro, "Populist Realism," *Partisan Review* (January 1958), 56–57.

12. Daniel Bell, "The Grass Roots of American Jew Hatred," *Jewish Frontier* (June 1944), 15–20; Oscar Handlin, "American Views of the Jews at the Opening of the Twentieth Century," *American Jewish Historical Society* (June 1951), 332, 342–43.

13. Handlin, "American Views of the Jews," 344; Hofstadter, *Age of Reform,* 80.

14. Hofstadter, *Age of Reform,* 80.

15. Ibid., 81.

16. Elkins and McKitrick to Hofstadter, comment on second draft of "Age of Reform," September 1954, EMP. Hofstadter remarked to an interviewer near the end of his life, "If I had known what an imbecile fuss would be raised about my having mentioned the occasional anti-Semitic rhetoric among the Populists, I would either have dropped it as not worth the trouble or else spent even more time than I did clarifying what I was saying." Kostelanetz, *Master Minds,* 167.

17. Gay to Hofstadter, internal evidence suggests 1954, box 3, RHP.

18. Smith to Hofstadter, 15 July 1954, HNSP. As Hofstadter completed *Age of Reform* in the summer of 1954, McCarthyism was reaching its apex. Peter Gay spent

time that summer with the Hofstadters at Hampton Bay and recalls that "Dick interrupted his writing only to watch the Army-McCarthy hearings." Gay correspondence with author.

19. Hofstadter to Smith, internal evidence suggests 1950, HNSP.

20. Hofstadter to Benson, internal evidence suggests 1951, box 1, RHP.

21. Hofstadter, *Age of Reform,* 134–35.

22. Ibid., 171.

23. Hofstadter to Alfred A. Knopf, 19 February 1952, and Knopf to Hofstadter, 25 April 1952, AAKP. Hofstadter, *Age of Reform,* 294.

24. Hofstadter, *Age of Reform,* 300. Kennedy's political success caused Hofstadter to alter his views. He had written in *Age of Reform* that Smith's Catholicism cost him the election. But in a 1960 essay (drafted, Peter Gay notes, to forward Kennedy's candidacy) he recanted. "Only recently William E. Bohn, writing in the *New Leader,* said of Smith: 'He was defeated for the worst of reasons — because he was a Catholic.' Absurd as it is, this notion has been too seldom challenged in public discussion. A little thoughtful attention to the history of the 1920's will convince almost any student that there was not a Democrat alive, Protestant or Catholic, who could have beaten Hoover in 1928. The overwhelming character of Hoover's victory should itself suggest to us that the religious issue may not have been decisive." Hofstadter, "Could a Protestant Have Beaten Hoover in 1928?" *Reporter* (17 March 1960), 31. Gay interview with author.

25. Hofstadter, *Age of Reform,* 301.

26. Ibid., 328. F. Scott Fitzgerald, *The Great Gatsby* (New York, 1925), 182. Both Fitzgerald and Hofstadter were interested in the decline of Victorian moral codes — this theme informed *Gatsby* as well as *Age of Reform.* That Fitzgerald's novel may have influenced or reinforced Hofstadter's thinking on the subject is not inconceivable. Hofstadter admired Fitzgerald's work and in 1951 — as he began writing *Age of Reform* — he produced a sympathetic essay on Fitzgerald. Hofstadter, "The Fitzgerald Revival," *Progressive* (April 1951), 34–35.

27. Boorstin to Hofstadter, 4 November 1955, c.c., box 1, RHP; Fellman, "History in the Round," *New Republic* (October 1955), 20; Brogan, "Fifty Years of Dreams, Protests, and Achievement," *New York Times Book Review* (October 1955), 7.

28. Hicks, *My Life with History,* 147; John Hicks, "Politics in Pattern," *Saturday Review* (22 October 1955), 12. The review satisfied Hofstadter, who wrote to Kenneth Stampp of his relief that Hicks had not attacked his book in print. Hofstadter to Stampp, 23 October 1955, KSP; Mowry, *Mississippi Valley Historical Review* (March 1956), 769.

29. Curti to Howard K. Beale, 27 November 1955, HKBP; Hofstadter to Curti, 17 January 1956, MCP.

30. Neil Basen kindly allowed me to read the notes from his 1993 interview with Curti.

31. Williams, "The Age of Reforming History," *Nation* (30 June 1956), 552–54. On the ideological differences separating Hofstadter and Williams see Paul Buhle and Edward Rice-Maximin, *William Appleman Williams: The Tragedy of Empire* (New York, 1995), 119–24.

32. Woodward to Hicks, 14 June 1957, CVWP.

33. Woodward, "The Populist Heritage and the Intellectual," *American Scholar* 29 (1960), 56; Hofstadter, "The Great Depression and American History," box 36, RHP.

34. Woodward, "Populist Heritage," 56, 58.

35. Ibid., 59.

36. Ibid., 63.

37. Hofstadter to Woodward, internal evidence suggests 1959, box 9, RHP; Hofstadter to Woodward, 15 May 1959, CVWP; Woodward, "Populist Heritage," 72.

38. Woodward to Hofstadter, 22 May 1959, and Hofstadter to Woodward, 30 May 1959, CVWP.

39. Woodward to Hicks, 4 January 1960, CVWP. "Woodward once confided to me that he felt able to criticise Dick's views after Dick's death only because he had made these criticisms in discussions with Dick," notes Jack Pole. "Otherwise, Vann's sense of the loyalty owed to friendship would have foreclosed such comment. It throws light both on the quality of the friendship and perhaps on the Southern concept of a gentleman." Pole correspondence with author.

40. Pollack's works on the topic include "Hofstadter on Populism: A Critique of 'The Age of Reform,'" *Journal of Southern History* (November 1960), 478–500; "The Myth of Populist Anti-Semitism," *American Historical Review* (October 1962), 76–80; "Fear of Man: Populism, Authoritarianism, and the Historian," *Agricultural History* (April 1965), 59–67; *The Populist Response to Industrial America: Midwestern Populist Thought* (Cambridge, 1962). Levine correspondence with author; McKitrick interview with author.

41. Pollack, "Hofstadter on Populism," 486–88.

42. David Potter, "The Politics of Status," *New Leader* (24 June 1963), 26.

43. Hofstadter to Potter, 2 July 1963, DPP.

44. Potter to Hofstadter, 8 July 1963, DPP.

45. Hofstadter to Graham, 31 July 1969, box 4, RHP.

46. *New York Times,* 4 November 2004. For an excellent study of how Hofstadter's insights on mass behavior continue to illuminate our understanding of populist movements see Michael Kazin, "Hofstadter Lives: Political Culture and Temperament in the Work of an American Historian," *Reviews in American History* (June 1999), 334–48.

Chapter 6

1. Foner interview with author; Hawke, "Interview: Richard Hofstadter," 137–39.

2. Richard Hofstadter, *Anti-Intellectualism in American Life* (New York, 1963), viii.

3. Trilling, *The Liberal Imagination,* xv; Jumonville, *Critical Crossings,* 126.

4. Ellen Schrecker, *Many Are the Crimes: McCarthyism in America* (Princeton, 1998), 410–11.

5. Hofstadter to Swados, October 1938, HSP.

6. Lasch, *The New Radicalism,* 316.

7. Hofstadter to Swados, 16 December 1940, HSP.

8. Naison to Paul Buhle, 21 October 1969, RAP.

9. Hofstadter to Ashbel Green, 2 July 1969, AAKP.

10. Hofstadter to Boorstin, 19 June 1962, DBP; Hofstadter to Woodward, internal evidence suggests July 1962, CVWP; Kazin to Hofstadter, 20 October 1955, c.c. box 1, RHP.

11. Richard H. Pells, *The Liberal Mind in a Conservative Age* (New York, 1985), 120; Rahv is quoted in Russell Jacoby, *The Last Intellectuals: American Culture in the Age of Academe* (New York, 1987), 76.

12. Hofstadter to Lasch, 9 October 1964, box 6, RHP. In May 1979, Lasch attended a White House dinner at which President Carter encouraged him and other intellectuals to discuss their views on what ailed American society. Lasch attended despite his reservations, as he put it, "about the folly of intellectuals' setting themselves up as advisers to men of power." Lasch quoted in Daniel Horowitz, *The Anxieties of Affluence: Critiques of American Consumer Culture, 1939–1979* (Amherst, 2004), 243. H. Stuart Hughes remarked that Hofstadter "would not have been awed in the slightest by the political leaders who impressed me." Hughes, *Gentleman Rebel,* 246. On Hofstadter's nearly nonexistent relationship with LBJ's Central Group in Domestic Affairs, see Goldman to Hofstadter, 9 March 1964, and Hofstadter to Goldman, 11 March 1964, EGP.

13. Bette Swados interview with author; Hofstadter to Swados, 3 October 1940, and Hofstadter to Swados, 16 December 1940, HSP.

14. Stampp, *Historian of Slavery,* 110.

15. Jacoby, *Last Intellectuals,* 92.

16. Mills to Swados, 13 February 1957, HSP.

17. Swados, "Be Happy, Go Liberal," *Anvil* (Winter 1956), 14.

18. Pells, *Liberal Mind,* 121.

19. Hughes, *Richard Hofstadter Project,* OHRO; Hofstadter to Stampp, 8 May 1961, KSP.

20. David Herbert Donald to Hofstadter, 10 June 1963, RHP; Leuchtenburg to author.

21. Hofstadter, *Anti-Intellectualism,* 3–4.

22. Mark D. Naison, *White Boy: A Memoir* (Philadelphia, 2002), 33–34; J. Anthony Lukas, *New York Times Magazine* (12 March 1972), 40.

23. Carl Bridenbaugh, "The Great Mutation," *American Historical Review* (January 1963), 317. Jack Rakove suggested that Harvard's appointment of Bernard Bailyn, a Jewish historian working in American colonial history, might have provoked Bridenbaugh's remarks. Rakove, "Bernard Bailyn," in *Clio's Favorites,* 9, note 8. Kenneth Stampp noted of Bridenbaugh's address, "It was a terrible speech. . . . Oh, it didn't surprise me very much. There was a streak of anti-Semitism in Bridenbaugh. . . . He went to Dartmouth as an undergrad, he was a Ph.D. at Harvard and loved Harvard, and wanted desperately to go back to Harvard some day. The disappointment of his life was that he never did." Stampp, *Historian of Slavery,* 169, 161. In Bridenbaugh's defense, Jack Pole wrote, "Yes, Carl Bridenbaugh was a social snob, but he did have an eye for quality, which overrode ethnic prejudices where they may have existed. I do not think of him as anti-Semitic; on the contrary, he took pride in having led the opening up of institutions like Berkeley and in having

helped to promote Jewish scholars like Joe Levenson." Pole correspondence with author.

24. Bridenbaugh, "Great Mutation," 320, 322–23. Although he was certainly one of the "practitioners of the new history" that concerned Bridenbaugh, Hofstadter's use of the social sciences was highly selective and extremely dependent upon literary expression. Peter Gay observed that "Bridenbaugh's indirect attack on Dick was particularly ill-advised because Dick was a *stylist.*" Gay correspondence with author.

25. Hofstadter, *Anti-Intellectualism,* 55–56.

26. The cultural repercussions of the Jackson-Adams contests are explored in John William Ward's *Andrew Jackson: Symbol for an Age* (Oxford, 1955), a study familiar to Hofstadter. In a pivotal chapter, "The Plowman and the Professor," Ward wrote, "One of the factors in Jackson's success seems to have been that the people believed that their will had been thwarted in the election of 1824. Another was that, running against an ex-Harvard professor, Jackson embodied a rejection of the intellectual. The followers of Adams could never bring themselves to believe that the American people in selecting a President could spurn a trained diplomatist and statesman like John Quincy Adams and embrace a man so eminently unqualified by background as Andrew Jackson" (64).

27. Hofstadter had practical, if only very limited, experience with labor issues. "He had participated as a picket in one of the steel strikes of the 1930s," Kenneth Stampp noted. Stampp, *Historian of Slavery,* 101.

28. Hofstadter to Kenneth Stampp, 16 February and 20 April 1951, KSP.

29. Hofstadter, *Anti-Intellectualism,* 340, 337. Hofstadter took three units of Latin at Fosdick-Masten Park High School in Buffalo, as well as a life-adjustment course in elementary cookery. Richard Hofstadter Transcripts, SUNY Buffalo. Hofstadter student Paula Fass argued in a 1989 study that her mentor had it backward and that a *lack* of confidence in democracy undermined public education. "Richard Hofstadter described the substitution of a concern with life adjustment for a commitment to learning as anti-intellectual. If this was the result of developments in American education in the early twentieth-century, it was less a by-product of a too exuberant democratic enthusiasm, as Hofstadter suggests, than of an inadequate faith in democracy. In the full flush of victory at the opening of the schools to a new democratic constituency, educators restricted the access of that constituency to the education for which they had come by predefining them as not fully able to benefit from its best resources." Paula Fass, *Outside In: Minorities and the Transformation of American Education* (Oxford, 1989), 70–71.

30. Woodward to Hofstadter, 11 May 1962, CVWP. Woodward believed that in *Anti-Intellectualism,* Hofstadter had used the term "fundamentalist" with too little historical context: "The man who clings to fundamentalism today is bound to be something of an odd ball and his oddness undoubtedly manifests itself in other ways, including many of the unpleasant traits you attribute to him. But being a fundamentalist before the twentieth century was, I should guess, 'normal' for the vast majority of Catholics and Jews as well as Protestants."

31. *American Historical Review* (July 1965), 1119; *Journal of American History* (December 1964), 482.

32. Kenneth S. Lynn, "Elitism on the Left," *Reporter* (4 July 1963), 37–39.

33. Daniel J. Boorstin, "The Split-Level Tower," *Saturday Review of Literature* (1 June 1963), 20.

34. Fass, "Richard Hofstadter," *Twentieth-Century American Historians,* 222. Hofstadter to McKitrick, internal evidence suggests 1962–63. After learning that *Anti-Intellectualism* had been awarded the Pulitzer in general nonfiction, Hofstadter told Eric Foner, "I don't deserve it. I did the first time, but not for this book." Foner correspondence with author.

35. *Manchester Guardian,* 2 September 2003; Todd Gitlin, "The Renaissance of Anti-Intellectualism," *Chronicle of Higher Education* (8 December 2000), B7.

Chapter 7

1. Hofstadter, "The Available Man: Warren Gamaliel Harding," *New York Review of Books* (3 June 1965), 12; Hofstadter, "Goldwater and His Party," *Encounter* (October 1964), 8.

2. Kazin, 4 April 1968, Journal 23, AKJ; Dan Hofstadter correspondence with author; Eric McKitrick interview with author; Irving Howe, *A Margin of Hope: An Intellectual Biography* (New York, 1982), 323.

3. Hofstadter to Stampp, 1 February 1952, KSP; Hofstadter to Alfred Kazin, 15 December 1958, AKP; Kostelanetz, *Master Minds,* 177.

4. David Hackett Fischer, *Historians' Fallacies: Toward a Logic of Historical Thought* (New York, 1970), 193, 195.

5. Hughes, *Gentleman Rebel,* 246; Shannon to Merle Curti, 15 December 1955, MCP.

6. McDonald, *American Historical Review* (October 1965), 402; Hofstadter to William Hixon, 23 September 1969, box 4, RHP.

7. Hofstadter to Stampp, 12 October 1946, KSP; Hofstadter to Curti, internal evidence suggests 1948, MCP.

8. Strauss to Hofstadter, 19 March 1949 and 1 July 1949, RHP; Ashbel Green interview with author. In today's dollars, Strauss's 1949 figures — $640 and $1,075 — come out to $4,950 and $8,300.

9. Hofstadter to Knopf, 15 July 1953, AAKP.

10. Document 1377.4, AAKP. Hofstadter drew additional income delivering public lectures. Late in his career, he earned between $1,000 and $1,500 per address — minus a one-third cut to his agent. In today's dollars, each lecture would gross between $5,300 and $8,000. Hofstadter to Richard Fulton, 12 August 1968, box 2, RHP.

11. Franklin to Beatrice Hofstadter, 28 February 1971, box 18, RHP.

12. Elkins and McKitrick, eds., *Hofstadter Aegis,* 339; Hofstadter, ed., *The Progressive Moment, 1900–1915* (New Jersey, 1963), 2.

13. W. H. Harvey, *Coin's Financial School,* with an introduction by Richard Hofstadter (Cambridge, 1963), 5, 48. The last quote in this paragraph, not included in the 1963 essay, can be found in a revised edition included in Hofstadter's *The Paranoid Style in American Politics* (New York, 1965), 287, note 4.

14. Harvey, *Coin's Financial School,* 66; Woodward to Hofstadter, 9 April 1963, CVWP; Elkins and McKitrick, *Hofstadter Aegis,* 337.

15. Lionel Trilling, *The Liberal Imagination: Essays on Literature and Society* (New York, 1950), ix; Ross interview with author.

16. McGirr, *Suburban Warriors: The Origins of the New American Right* (Princeton, 2001), 7.

17. Goldberg's essay, "Shock Troops for Bush," can be found at http://www.salon.com/news/feature/2003/02/04cpac/index.html; for Radosh's, see http://hnn.us/articles/613.html.

18. Robert M. Hutchins to Hofstadter, 5 July 1955, box 5, RHP; statistical information on the fund's support of "Pseudo-Conservative Revolt" and *Academic Freedom* can be found in Hofstadter's FBI file. For discussions of this subject see Christopher Lasch's essay "The Cultural Cold War: A Short History of the Congress for Cultural Freedom," in *Towards a New Past: Dissenting Essays in American History,* ed. Barton Bernstein (New York, 1967), 322–59; Peter Coleman, *The Liberal Conspiracy: The Congress for Cultural Freedom and the Struggle for the Mind of Postwar Europe* (New York, 1989); and Saunders, *The Cultural Cold War.* Hofstadter to Pat Knopf, 4 March 1954, AAKP.

19. Several notable intellectuals wrote for the Fund for the Republic, including Andrew Hacker, Adolf Berle, and Gunnar Myrdal. Hofstadter's uncle, Justice Samuel Hofstadter, produced "The Fifth Amendment and the Immunity Act of 1954" for the fund.

20. American Committee for Cultural Freedom to the Fund for the Republic, internal evidence suggests 1957, box 3, ACCFP.

21. Hallock Hoffman to Hofstadter, 9 December 1957, and Hofstadter to Hoffman, 26 November 1958, box 24, RHP; Hofstadter, "Prefatory Note for Essay on Radical Right for Fund for the Republic," box 36, RHP.

22. Hofstadter, "The Contemporary Extreme Right Wing in the United States: A Memorandum," box 24, RHP.

23. Hofstadter, "Prefatory Note," RHP; Hoffman to Hofstadter, 9 December 1957, box 24, RHP; Hofstadter, "Contemporary Extreme Right Wing," RHP.

24. *Los Angeles Herald-Examiner,* 26 March 1962; *Congressional Record-Appendix,* A2618, 4 April 1962.

25. Gerald D. Nash, *The American West Transformed: The Impact of the Second World War* (Bloomington, 1985).

26. Rick Perlstein, *Before the Storm: Barry Goldwater and the Unmaking of the American Consensus* (New York, 2001), 124.

27. Ross interview with author.

28. *New York Times,* 16 June 1964.

29. Hofstadter, "Some Comments on Goldwater," *Partisan Review* (Fall 1964), 590.

30. Hofstadter, "A Long View: Goldwater in History," *New York Review of Books* (8 October 1964), 18.

31. Ibid., 18, 20

32. Hofstadter, "Goldwater & His Party: The True Believer and the Radical Right," *Encounter* (October 1964), 4. "The achievement of the Democratic party over the past thirty years," Hofstadter wrote, "has been testimony to the effectiveness of the consensual ethos."

33. Hofstadter, "Goldwater and His Party," 3, 6–10, 13. Hofstadter was not the only liberal drawn to Yeats's "The Second Coming." Arthur Schlesinger, Jr.'s 1949 book, *The Vital Center,* opens with a stanza of the poem. In more recent times, conservatives have laid claim to "The Second Coming"—see the opening page (and note the title) of Robert H. Bork's *Slouching Towards Gomorrah: Modern Liberalism and American Decline* (New York, 1996). In a chapter on "The Decline of Intellect," Bork quotes approvingly from Hofstadter's *Anti-Intellectualism.*

34. Hofstadter, "The Goldwater Debacle," *Encounter* (January, 1965), 66.

35. Hofstadter to Knopf, 11 June 1964, AAKP.

36. Hofstadter, *The Paranoid Style in American Politics: And Other Essays* (New York, 1965), 29.

37. Ibid., 78.

38. Hofstadter to Swados, 25 December 1965, HSP.

39. Ibid.

Chapter 8

1. Curti, Commager, and Nevins grew up in the Midwest. Donald and Malone were southerners. Stern's comments are in the *Columbia Daily Spectator,* 29 October 1970.

2. Schlesinger, Jr., *Richard Hofstadter Project,* OHRO; Bell interview with author; Hofstadter to Woodward, 20 February 1959, CVWP.

3. Dan Hofstadter correspondence with author.

4. Singal correspondence with author.

5. William Leuchtenburg interview with author.

6. Metzger, Gay, and Kazin interviews with author; Hughes, *Gentleman Rebel,* 245; Franklin to Beatrice K. Hofstadter, 28 February 1971, box 18, RHP. Arthur Schlesinger, Jr., noted a world-weary attitude in Hofstadter—"I think he had a lot of friends, but in retrospect I think he was protecting himself and hoarding his energies." Schlesinger, Jr., *Richard Hofstadter Project,* OHRO.

7. Hofstadter to Kazin, 6 May 1959, AKP; Kazin, *New York Jew,* 237.

8. Curti to Hofstadter, 14 April 1948, MCP.

9. Edward Said, *Representations of the Intellectual* (New York, 1994), 11.

10. Commager's biographer writes "two historians of the talent of Commager and [his son-in-law Christopher] Lasch might have been expected to get along well and talk incessantly. Neither was the case. As a student at Columbia, Lasch had been drawn to Leuchtenburg and Hofstadter instead of Commager. Lasch had been introduced to history as a youth by Morison and Commager's *Growth of the American Republic,* but as a graduate student, while he admired Commager's vigorous public writing, he found him too Parringtonian in his uncritical admiration of liberals and the liberal tradition. 'As far as I could see,' Lasch explained, 'Commager had no interest even in replying to its critics [on the left]—which didn't leave us much to talk about." Neil Jumonville, *Henry Steele Commager: Midcentury Liberalism and the History of the Future* (Chapel Hill, 1999), 161.

11. Louis Menand, quoted in Thomas Bender, Philip M. Katz, Colin Palmer, and

the Committee on Graduate Education of the American Historical Association, *The Education for Historians for the Twentieth-Century* (Urbana, 2004), 6.

12. *New York Times,* 23 March 1965; *Atlanta Constitution,* 25 March 1965.

13. Stampp interview with author; *Atlanta Constitution,* 25 March 1965.

14. Leuchtenburg and Shenton interviews with author.

15. Hofstadter to Swados, 25 December 1965, HSP.

16. Dan Hofstadter to Swados, December 1966, HSP; Stampp to Richard Hofstadter, 28 August 1967, HSP.

17. Leuchtenburg and Stern interviews with author; Hofstadter et al. to Lyndon Johnson, 18 May 1966, box 2, RHP; Lyndon Johnson to Daniel Bell, 16 June 1966, box 2, RHP.

18. Hofstadter et al. to the Committee on Instruction, 3 October 1967, box 2, RHP.

19. Stern interview with author.

20. Terry Anderson, *The Movement and the Sixties: Protest in America from Greensboro to Wounded Knee* (Oxford, 1995), 126.

21. Philip Rahv, "Left Face," *New York Review of Books* (12 October 1967), 10; Hofstadter to Swados, 9 November 1967, HSP.

22. Hofstadter to Swados, 8 August 1967, HSP.

23. Hofstadter to Mitchell Lovitas, 4 April 1968, box 26, RHP.

24. The author's title, "Peace Without Victory: The American Problem," was changed without Hofstadter's authorization. Jane Slater to M. J. Casey, 3 June 1968, box 2, RHP.

25. Hofstadter, "Uncle Sam Has Cried 'Uncle!' Before," *New York Times Magazine* (19 May 1968), 121.

26. Ibid., 124.

27. Ibid., 125.

28. Banner, Jr., interview with author.

29. *Daily Californian,* 1 May 1967.

30. Gilbert correspondence with author.

31. Hofstadter to Roger Kahn, 15 August 1968, box 27, RHP.

32. Hofstadter to Riesman, 25 October 1968, c.c. box 1, RHP; Hofstadter, *Columbia Crisis,* OHRO; Resolutions for the meeting of the faculties, 30 April 1968, box 27, RHP.

33. Hofstadter, *Columbia Crisis,* ORHO; Hofstadter to Swados, 7 June 1968, HSP; Hofstadter, "Spirit of '70," *Newsweek* (6 July 1970), 22.

34. *Anatomy of a Revolution: Students for a Democratic Society: A Report by the Committee on Internal Security,* House of Representatives, 91st Congress, 2nd session (Washington, 1970), 6.

35. Hofstadter to Swados, 7 June 1968, HSP; Donald, *Commentary,* March 1972, 90; The Forces of Liberation to Professor Hofstadter, internal evidence suggests 1968, box 27, RHP.

36. Kazin, 28 April 1968, Journal 23, AKJ.

37. Naison to Paul Buhle, internal evidence indicates April 1968, box 2, RAP. Naison was later nearly expelled from Columbia due to his participation in a protest-

related fistfight outside Philosophy Hall. Hofstadter and several other letter writers persuaded the university to reconsider its decision. Naison, *White Boy,* 113–14. Hofstadter's flexibility with students is evident in the following exchange between Naison and Buhle: "Some fairly exciting things are beginning to happen here with radical history. There is a better than 50-50 chance that we will be allowed to teach our seminar for credit on the history of American radicalism. Richard Hofstadter, of all people, has begun to feel guilty about the 'alienation' of young historians, and has supported our scheme." Naison to Buhle, spring 1968, box 2, RAP.

38. Fass correspondence with author; Hofstadter to Foner, 10 May 1968, box 3, RHP.

39. Singal correspondence with author.

40. Gay and Wallace interviews with author; Mundy correspondence with author.

41. Hofstadter to Swados, 7 June 1968.

42. Jerry L. Avorn, Andrew Crane, Mark Jaffe, Oren Rout, Paul Starr, Michael Stern, and Robert Stulberg, *University in Revolt: A History of the Columbia Crisis* (London, 1968), 281; Hofstadter, "The 214th Columbia University Commencement Address," *American Scholar* 37 (1968), 583, 588. The year after his address, Hofstadter emphasized his debt to Columbia by dedicating *The Idea of a Party System* to "the Columbia Historians."

43. Hofstadter, "Commencement Address," 588, 585, 586.

44. Ibid., 586.

45. Ibid., 588.

46. Trilling and Hurwitz quoted in Joseph Dorman, *Arguing the World: The New York Intellectuals in Their Own Words* (New York, 2000), 155, 153; Moynihan to Hofstadter, 14 October 1968, c.c. box 1, RHP; Cooper interview with author.

47. Hofstadter, Peter Kenen, Poly Karp Kusch, Robert Merton, Fritz Stern, Cheves Walling to William Peterson, Chairman of the Board, Columbia University Trustees, 17 July 1968, box 7, RHP.

48. Hofstadter to Colleagues, 5 March 1969, box 3, RHP.

49. *New York Times,* 11 March 1969.

50. Hofstadter to Marvin Opler, internal evidence suggests 1968, box 6, RHP.

51. Hofstadter to Riesman, 25 February 1969, c.c. box 1, RHP.

Chapter 9

1. C. Vann Woodward, *The Future of the Past* (Oxford, 1989), 352.

2. See "Books Dropped" files in boxes 31 and 35, RHP. *The Oxford History* produced its first volume in 1982 — Robert Middlekauff's *The Glorious Cause: The American Revolution, 1763–1789.* In the editor's introduction, Woodward wrote, "In the earliest stages of planning the *Oxford History,* the editor had the enormously valuable collaboration of Richard Hofstadter, who originally served as coeditor. His death was a deeply felt personal loss as well as a grave loss to this series. His inestimable contributions to the present work are gratefully acknowledged. Over time some changes have been made in the authors of volumes, but the general conception and plan for

the series retain the character fixed in the original collaboration" (xvi). Knopf to Hofstadter, 3 May 1961, AAKP.

3. Hofstadter to Knopf, 5 May 1961, AAKP.

4. Hofstadter to Woodward, 21 June 1960, December 1961, and 7 October 1963, CVWP. Hofstadter's book on the early republic was never written. Stanley Elkins and Eric McKitrick agreed to produce the Jeffersonian era study for the Oxford series but became so immersed in the history of Federalism that they published a separate book with Oxford in 1993 — *The Age of Federalism: The Early American Republic, 1788–1800*. The book is dedicated "To the Memory of Richard Hofstadter." McKitrick interview with author.

5. Hofstadter to Potter, 12 July 1963, DPP.

6. Bernstein, ed., *Towards a New Past*, ix, v, 4.

7. Hofstadter to Jack Pole, internal evidence suggests 1967, JPP. Between 1941 and 1950, Hofstadter produced four essays sharply critical of Parrington, Phillips, Turner, and Beard.

8. Robert Sklar, "Historians: Simple-Minded and Complex," *Nation* (November 1968), 533–34. *Progressive Historians,* David Herbert Donald wrote, "exhibited how a want of scholarly detachment undermined the historical world of Turner, Beard, and Parrington. When the radical student movement shook the foundations of his beloved Columbia University, [Hofstadter] had still further reason to reconsider the social responsibilities of the historian." *Commentary* (March 1972), 90.

9. Hofstadter to Schlesinger, Jr., March 1969, c.c. box 1, RHP; Lewis, "From Eurocentrism to Polycentrism," in *Historians and Race: Autobiography and the Writing of History,* ed. Paul A. Cimbala and Robert F. Himmelberg (Bloomington, 1996), 68.

10. Hofstadter quoting McKitrick to C. Vann Woodward, 18 April 1968, box 13, CVWP; Green interview with author. Marion J. Morton, *The Terrors of Ideological Politics: Liberal Historians in a Conservative Mood* (Cleveland, 1972), 109. I am not suggesting that Hofstadter avoided newer methodological approaches. He served late in his career, for example, as a knowledgeable commentator on a panel assessing the work of the noted psychologist Erik Erikson. His remarks were published in the *Journal of American Psychiatry* (September 1965), 250–53. Rather, he came to these fields late in life and they were never to make more than a modest imprint on his scholarship.

11. Hofstadter to McKitrick, internal evidence suggests 1960, EMP.

12. Hofstadter to Swados, 24 October 1967; Smith to Hofstadter, 3 December 1968, HNSP.

13. Richard Hofstadter, *The Progressive Historians: Turner, Beard, Parrington* (New York, 1968), 27.

14. Ibid., 299.

15. Ibid., 93.

16. Ibid., 104.

17. Ibid., 130.

18. Hofstadter to Pole, 24 January 1968, JPP.

19. Hofstadter, *Progressive Historians,* 222.

20. Charles A. Beard, *An Economic Interpretation of the Constitution of the United States* (rev. ed., New York, 1935), 24.

21. Nevins to Curti, 7 March 1947, MCP. See Beard's *American Foreign Policy in the Making: 1932–1940* (New Haven, 1946); and *President Roosevelt and the Coming of War* (New Haven, 1948); Hofstadter, *Progressive Historians,* 341.

22. Hofstadter to Swados, January 1938 and 20 January 1940, HSP.

23. Hofstadter, *Progressive Historians,* 327–29; Hofstadter to Swados, 2 September 1939 and 20 January 1938, HSP; Stampp interview with author; Stampp, *Historian of Slavery,* 103.

24. Hofstadter to McKitrick, internal evidence suggests 1967, EMP.

25. Knopf to Hofstadter, 4 October 1969, AAKP.

26. Hofstadter to Knopf, 9 October 1969, AAKP.

27. Hofstadter, *Progressive Historians,* 400.

28. Ibid., 427.

29. Potter, "The Politics of Status," 27.

30. Hofstadter to Pole, 9 February 1968, JPP.

31. Hofstadter, *Progressive Historians,* 448–50. Hofstadter to Boorstin, 27 June 1968, DBP. "Hofstadter," John Milton Cooper notes, "hated being lumped in the consensus camp. He enjoyed setting his seminars after Boorstin's book, *The Genius of American Politics.* It never occurred to those of us in the seminar to compare him with Boorstin." Cooper interview with author. For contemporary statements on this theme see John Leo, "American Historians Shift Emphasis to Conflict," *New York Times* (2 January 1969); C. Vann Woodward, "Wild in the Stacks," *New York Review of Books* (1 August 1968), 8–12; Daniel J. Boorstin, "The New Barbarians," *Esquire* (October 1968), 159–62, 260–64; and Irwin Unger, "The 'New Left' and American History: Some Recent Trends in United States Historiography," *American Historical Review* (July 1967), 1237–63.

32. Hofstadter to Schlesinger, Jr., 1 March 1969, c.c. box 1, RHP.; Hofstadter *Progressive Historians,* 454. The comity theme permeates Hofstadter's 1969 book, *The Idea of a Party System,* the genesis of which was delivered at the University of California Berkeley in the autumn of 1966—the year Hofstadter began writing *Progressive Historians.* It seems certain that both books—on the surface very different projects—were in fact products of a similar private rebellion on Hofstadter's part against the tide of sixties radicalism.

33. Hofstadter, *Progressive Historians,* 451.

Chapter 10

1. Hofstadter, *Progressive Historians,* 454; Ward, *Virginia Quarterly Review* (Winter 1970), 176.

2. Hofstadter to Knopf, 15 December 1957, AAKP. Hofstadter's lectures were collectively titled "Jeffersonian Democracy and Political Parties—Notes on the Intellectual History of the Virginia Dynasty."

3. Hofstadter, Van Am Award Speech, 5 May 1970, box 23, RHP.

4. Ibid.

5. Richard Hofstadter, *The Idea of a Party System: The Rise of Legitimate Opposition in the United States, 1780–1840* (Berkeley, 1969), xii, 4–5.

6. Ibid., 7.

7. Ibid., 20.

8. Ibid., 99, 95. Hofstadter admired Burke's moderate political views before a radicalized Enlightenment that culminated in regicide, terror, and the military despotism of the French Revolution. Burke's emphasis on restraint, morality, and tradition, moreover, struck a pleasing note among postwar liberals who denied that the American Right was conservative at all.

9. Ibid., 170–71.

10. Ibid., 196.

11. Ibid., 213.

12. Ibid., 241.

13. Hofstadter et al., "Is America by Nature a Violent Society?" *New York Times Magazine* (April 1968), 24–25, 111–14. Hofstadter borrowed from D. H. Lawrence's *Studies in Classic American Literature* (New York, 1972 edition), 62.

14. Hofstadter to Richard Fulton, 13 November 1968, box 2, RHP; "Reader on American Violence," box 6, RHP; Wallace interview with author.

15. Wallace interview with author; Hofstadter to Wallace, 16 August 1969, box 9, RHP; "Interview with Mike Wallace," conducted by Ellen Noonan, *Radical History Review* (Winter 2001), 52. In 1969, Bernard Bailyn informed Hofstadter that Harvard was considering Wallace for an appointment but had concerns about his political activities. Hofstadter responded paternally. He acknowledged, without going into detail, Wallace's role in the turmoil at Columbia, but emphasized his recent marriage (attended by Hofstadter) and desire for professional advancement as signs of maturity and stability. Hofstadter to Bailyn, 17 December 1969, box 9 RHP.

16. Wallace, "The Uses of Violence in American History," *American Scholar* (Winter 1970–71), 81–102; Hofstadter to Wallace, 26 June 1969, box 9, RHP.

17. Hofstadter and Wallace, eds., *American Violence: A Documentary History* (New York, 1970), 9. Hofstadter to James Banner, Jr., 29 August 1969, box 1, RHP.

18. Hofstadter and Wallace, *American Violence,* 11.

19. Ibid., 29.

20. Dan Hofstadter correspondence with author; Hofstadter and Wallace, eds., *American Violence,* 30.

21. Hofstadter and Wallace, *American Violence,* 39; Hofstadter to Wallace, 16 August 1969, box 9, RHP.

22. Hofstadter and Wallace, *American Violence,* 43; Hofstadter to Wallace, 16 August 1969, box 9, RHP. Hofstadter's pessimism was perhaps, in part, a reflection of dire health concerns. He died of leukemia five days before *American Violence* was published.

23. Kazin, *New York Jew,* 15; Wallace, Cooper, Dallek interviews with author; Hofstadter to Daniel Ryan, 24 November 1969, box 4, RHP.

24. Hofstadter to Elizabeth Sutherland, 16 April 1968, box 2, RHP; Hofstadter to Melvin Drimmer, 31 January 1969, box 3, RHP.

25. Goodman to Hofstadter, 24 October 1969, c.c. box 1, RHP; Hofstadter to Goodman, 3 November 1969, c.c. box 1, RHP.

26. R. R. Palmer, "The American Historical Association in 1970," *American Historical Review* (February 1971), 1.

27. Hofstadter to Boorstin, 31 December 1969, DBP. Hofstadter also worked during this period to keep the Columbia history department depoliticized. "After the police 'bust,' the history graduate students demanded a meeting with the faculty," remembers department chairman John Mundy. "What I planned to ask of them was what the faculty would do about examinations, dissertation defenses, etc. In a telephone call the night before, Richard Hofstadter remarked that the students instead wanted to have the faculty join them in condemning the Vietnam War and the university's complicity in that and other 'crimes.' We agreed that, however suitable that was for individual members, it was not the business of the department." Mundy correspondence with author.

28. Palmer, "The American Historical Association," 3.

29. Kazin, 6 September 1968, Journal 23, AKJ; Hofstadter stated that he was through with politics in a letter to Walter Johnson, 1 April 1970, box 5, RHP.

Chapter 11

1. Hughes, *Gentleman Rebel,* 246.

2. *Columbia Daily Spectator,* 26 October 1970; Hofstadter to Jerome B. Wiesner, 13 November 1969, box 9, RHP.

3. "Professor Richard F. [*sic*] Hofstadter in Memoriam," by Carl F. Hovde, Dean of Columbia College, 29 October 1970, box 19, RHP

4. Franklin to Beatrice K. Hofstadter, 28 February 1971, box 18, RHP.

5. Andrew Cordier to Hofstadter, 27 June 1969, box 2, RHP; Hofstadter to Jack Pole, 9 February 1968, JPP; Hofstadter to Detlev Vagts, 25 March 1969, box 9, RHP; William Leuchtenburg interview with author.

6. Hofstadter to Thomas D. Clark, 19 August 1970, box 18, RHP; Woodward to Clark, 4 September 1970, OAHRP; Hofstadter to David Potter, 7 October 1970, OAHRP. Four months after receiving Hofstadter's resignation, OAH president David Potter himself died of cancer.

7. Woodward to Howe, 15 June 1970, CVWP; Hofstadter to Swados, 18 July 1970, HSP.

8. "The Spirit of '70: Six Historians Reflect on What Ails the American Spirit," *Newsweek* (6 July 1970), 3, 21, 23.

9. Hofstadter correspondence with author.

10. Hofstadter to Green, 17 July 1968, box 4, RHP; "Proposal for a Three-Volume History of American Political Culture," 14 May 1969, box 1, RHP.

11. Ross interview with author; Blake and Phelps, "Conversations with Christopher Lasch," 1318–19.

12. "Proposal for Three-Volume History," box 1, RHP; Hofstadter to Hollinshead, 24 April 1969, box 4, RHP; Peter Davison to Hofstadter, September 1969, box 2, RHP; Memo, internal evidence suggests 1969, box 1, RHP.

13. Green interview with author; Hughes, *Richard Hofstadter Project,* OHRO; Hofstadter to Pole, 5 August 1970, JPP; Kazin, *New York Jew,* 15. During these difficult months, Hofstadter made himself available to his students. Shortly before he died, he wrote enthusiastically to William Hixson of his eagerness to read the conclusion of his dissertation. Hofstadter to Hixson, 15 August 1970, WHP.

14. Hofstadter, *America at 1750: A Social Portrait* (New York, 1971), 35, 143.

15. Elkins and McKitrick, eds., *Hofstadter Aegis,* 363.

16. Fass, in *Twentieth-Century American Historians,* ed. Wilson, 228; Jack Pole correspondence with author.

17. Banner, Jr., interview with author.

18. Hofstadter, *America at 1750,* 27.

19. Ibid., 62.

20. Lawrence Levine, *Black Culture and Black Consciousness: Afro-American Folk Thought from Slavery to Freedom* (Oxford, 1977), 442–43, xi.

21. Fass, in *Twentieth-Century American Historians,* ed. Wilson, 228; Dallek interview with author.

22. *Congressional Record,* 16 November 1970, House 37431.

23. Alden Whitman, *New York Times,* 25 October 1970. Hofstadter presented to Kostelanetz — a former Columbia graduate student — the image of a dispassionate historian intently focused on his craft. While this portrait did not disclose the full complexity of its subject, it communicated quite a bit. Pleased with the sketch, Hofstadter wrote Kostelanetz that the austerity, self-protective habits, and devotion to work attributed to him produced an image and an effect that he recognized and liked. Hofstadter to Kostelanetz, 30 September 1968, box 5, RHP.

24. Trilling, *New York Times,* 5 November 1970.

25. Hofstadter to Kenneth Stampp, December 1944, KSP.

26. Linda Kerber, *Toward an Intellectual History of Women* (Chapel Hill, 1997), 6.

In Search of Richard Hofstadter

I should say that I think of him all the time. He would have enjoyed Watergate, Reagan's 'Morning in America,' and other dramas that called for a Mencken. But where is he now that we need him.

PETER GAY, 2003

I was introduced to the work of Richard Hofstadter in 1988, producing a brief review of *The Idea of a Party System* for a summer history course. I was particularly impressed with Hofstadter's deft handling of Martin Van Buren — a mysterious figure to me brought to life in swift and illuminating strokes: "Van Buren typified the spirit of the amiable county courthouse lawyer translated to politics." And, like many of Hofstadter's readers, I was easily charmed by his lucid, telling sentences. From there I discovered *The American Political Tradition* and still vividly recall the pleasure of reading it during my breaks at the Catholic hospital where I washed dishes. It appealed as much to my sense of humor as to my sense of the past — insightfully irreverent, by turns comical and persuasive; a young man's book perhaps best read in youth.

Some years later, a graduate professor of mine remarked that while stationed in Korea during the war, he enthusiastically read all three volumes of Vernon Parrington's *Main Currents in American Thought*. He was convinced, he smiled, that its sharply drawn portraits of important personalities offered the last word on American history. What else did one need to read? *The American Political Tradition* had the same impact on me (I now smile). Every November the Planned Parenthood affiliate of Dayton, Ohio, held a giant book sale at the Montgomery County Fairgrounds. And each year I picked up a copy or two of *The American Political Tradition* to give to friends. Tangible proof, I suppose, of professional aspirations.

In graduate school I read all of Hofstadter's books, my interest in historiography persistent enough to persuade my teachers to indulge my interest in texts long since superseded by fresher approaches or simply more contemporary preferences. One professor—a specialist in Populism—turned me loose on *The Age of Reform* with a mixture of admiration and trepidation. Two words in our conversation still stand out: "brilliant" and "wrong."

I happily discovered during these years some of the excellent used bookstores that adorned large universities. Browsing the aisles of Dawn Treader or Books in General in Ann Arbor, Michigan, or the legendary Paul's Books in Madison, Wisconsin, one got a sense of Hofstadter's professional fortunes. Copies of his early studies, *Social Darwinism* and *The American Political Tradition,* as well as the student-friendly *America at 1750,* could be found with little difficulty. His later books, however, appeared less frequently; *The Progressive Historians* and *American Violence* bearing the author's dreaded code for commercial irrelevancy — "O/P," out of print. Reading Hofstadter during these years opened my eyes to the impact of environment on a historian. His books always struck me as particular to a time and place completely alien from my own 1970s midwestern origins; and yet there was a timeless quality about them that I found intriguing and attractive.

The decision to write this book led me to a number of institutions holding Hofstadter papers, but it also directed me to several cities, universities, and homes familiar to my subject. Sensitive to physical environment, I hoped to get a sense (admittedly imperfect and no doubt colored by my own impressions) of the important spaces in his life. Hofstadter made this task easy, for with the exception of an extended stay in England, working summers at Wellfleet, and three years in College Park, he lived his entire life in two cities — Buffalo and New York. The former retains the feel of an immigrant or, to use more contemporary language, a multicultural, city. Synagogues and Orthodox churches coexist with Baptist and Presbyterian congregations, and Buffalo's South Side still shows evidence of the Polish American population pioneered by people like Emil Hofstadter nearly a century earlier.

Much of Richard Hofstadter's Buffalo — circa 1916–1936 — no longer exists or is so radically altered as to defy recognition. His childhood home on Welmont Place has disappeared to make way for a Wendy's fast-food restaurant and low-income housing. Its ethnic composition has changed too. What was once a German American neighborhood is now peopled mainly by African Americans. For years, Hofstadter's father owned a furrier shop on 36 West Huron Street in the city's downtown area near the lakeshore, but it was destroyed some time ago to make room for a municipal parking lot. Other markers have survived. Fosdick-Masten Park High School is still in the business of educating young minds — now as a City Honors School. Each spring it celebrates its famous alumnus by holding the Richard Hofstadter Competition for Historical Writing. Four miles to the northeast, Rockwell Hall continues to dominate the layout of the old University of Buffalo — its importance was diminished, however, following the 1970s removal of the main campus from the city to the suburbs. The large Swados house at 453 Richmond Avenue also stands. In it, Hofstadter nursed his terminally ill wife for nearly a year and wrote the first chapters of *The American Political Tradition*.

Unsurprisingly, one gets no sense of Hofstadter's presence at the University of Maryland, his first postdoctorate position. The physical plant has long outgrown its modest prewar appearance when the grounds — a plantation until 1858 — consisted of little more than a few columned buildings surrounded by fields. The intellectually and socially sleepy campus held no interest for Hofstadter, a commuter who preferred the city and took the D.C. bus in each day.

A more revealing image is gleaned among the sand and surf at Wellfleet, the upper Cape Cod summer home that Hofstadter and his family occupied for several years. In his journal, Alfred Kazin provided a memorable description of its redemptive natural environment: "Wellfleet, delightful walk through the woods to the water this morning. . . . The blackened grasses and rushes, cast-off work gloves, dismembered hulls of boats. Here is the end of the land and the approach of the beach. But how clean the Cape always is" (Kazin, 4 August 1953, Journal 23, AKJ). Following Hofstadter's death, his Gull Pond Road property was sold and three houses currently occupy the tract. The largest belonged to the historian; its placid surroundings and interesting seasonal neighbors of beach-going professors struck just the right note, and provided an important balance to the bustle of Manhattan. Though altered by development since last visited by Hofstadter in 1970, Wellfleet retains much of the intimacy and seclusion that were important sources of strength to its visitors.

One block west of Columbia University sits Claremont Avenue, a faculty magnet whose apartment buildings were erected nearly a century ago. Hofstadter lived here from 1947 to 1969. These efficient units are practical and elegant. No lawn to mow, no car to maintain, just minutes from Butler Library; their convenience suggests Hofstadter's need to be near the people, ideas, and books that kept his searching intellect in a state of constant activity. Entering, as Hofstadter did, the University at Broadway at 116th, one crosses nearly the length of the campus to reach Fayerweather Hall, the fabled home of Columbia's graduate history faculty. Hofstadter never kept an office there. His long habitation near the top of Hamilton is emblematic of both his commitment to Columbia College and his self-image as a detached thinker in the midst, but still apart, from the collectivity.

The archival material available to scholars working on Hofstadter is voluminous — and heavily concentrated on the East Coast. The best place to begin is the extraordinarily rich Hofstadter file in the Harvey Swados Papers at the University of Massachusetts Amherst. This series contains dozens of letters written by Hofstadter to Swados dating from 1936 to 1970. The collection is by turns funny, volatile, and touchingly sincere. It comprises a series of set-pieces on Depression-era New York City, private squabbles between Hofstadter, his first wife, and in-laws, and the insecurities of a generation deeply concerned and deeply pessimistic about its chances in a world broken by fascism and war. The communications trace Hofstadter's formative intellectual and political experiences in a relaxed and unguarded forum that offers a unique perspective on this critical period in the history of the American Left.

A significantly larger but less concentrated collection is the Richard Hofstadter Papers at Columbia University's Rare Book and Manuscript Library. The sheer volume is intimidating — 47 boxes, 19,200 items — but the bulk of the materials relate to the last few years of Hofstadter's life and the collection is particularly weak on the thirties and forties. No archivist himself, Hofstadter showed little interest in the systematic preservation or cataloging of his correspondence. While Harvey Swados appears to have saved all of Hofstadter's letters, for example, only a handful of his own survive. What remains — university and professional communications, boxes of research materials — offers a better sense of the minutia of academic life than the remarkable quality of Hofstadter's mind.

But there are gems for the patient researcher. These include revealing exchanges with two generations of historians and social scientists. The list itself is staggering — Bernard Bailyn, Daniel Bell, Daniel Boorstin, Henry Steele Commager, Merle Curti, Eric Foner, Peter Gay, C. Wright Mills, Allan Nevins, David Riesman, Arthur Schlesinger (Sr.

and Jr.), C. Vann Woodward — and reads like a who's who of twentieth-century American historiography. The cumulative impact of these and other letters clarifies the concerns, debates, and interpretive differences uniting and dividing the postwar historical profession. Information that could never be recognized in a single or perhaps even in a dozen documents — Hofstadter's evolving appreciation of liberalism, his dawning awareness of his physical decline, and his sense of American history as one of tragedy and limitations — comes through over time.

The Hofstadter and Swados Papers form the core of open archival materials, but they are selective and researchers are fortunate that a number of important scholars have made their correspondence available. The Merle Curti Papers at the State Historical Society of Wisconsin contain some three dozen Hofstadter letters written between 1943 and 1968. They attest to Hofstadter's growing professional confidence and address the ideological differences that were a source of tension in his relationship with Curti. The C. Vann Woodward Papers at Yale University contain a smaller collection of Hofstadter-related items than one finds in Madison, but they are of a more intimate nature. Gossipy appraisals of the projects and reputations of peers, and several letters that respond directly to Hofstadter's work on Populism and the paranoid mind highlight their exchange. The poignant ethnocultural drama in the meeting between, as Woodward put it, "the Arkansas-bred, Georgia-Carolina educated provincial and the cosmopolitan city bred intellectual," provides a magnificent backdrop to their relationship (Woodward, *Thinking Back*, 41).

The largest private collection of Hofstadter letters (over a hundred) belongs to Kenneth Stampp in Berkeley, California. Dating primarily from the 1940s and the 1950s ("By the early sixties," Stampp noted, "Dick and I began using the telephone"), they constitute a crucial link between the Swados and Hofstadter Papers. The correspondence describes the early professional insecurities of two young men who quickly became giants in their fields. It touches as well upon several delicate matters, including Felice's death and Hofstadter's determination to rebuild his life in New York.

Eric McKitrick's papers in Manhattan are another excellent source in private hands. Though not as extensive as the Stampp collection (McKitrick and Hofstadter worked together at Columbia for a decade; most of their communications were oral), Hofstadter's correspondence with perhaps his favorite student accentuates his playful side. He obviously felt relaxed and expansive with McKitrick, and his reflections on the quality and reception of his work in these pages offer valuable self-assessments.

Finally, the Alfred Kazin Papers and Journals at the New York Public Library, and the Alfred A. Knopf Papers at the University of Texas at Austin deserve mention. Michael Kazin observed in an interview that Hofstadter and his father "played to each other's strengths and filled in each other's gaps," a case of the detached historian finding a pungent companion in the emotional literary critic. Alfred Kazin's thoughts on Hofstadter are recorded in several of his published works; the most revealing is *Starting Out in the Thirties* (1965), a personal history of the Depression decade that introduced the reader to "John" (RH)—"the most charming man I had ever met" (100) and "Harriet" (Felice). Coupled with the Swados Papers, Kazin's published and unpublished memoirs are the best source we have of Hofstadter's first years in New York. The Knopf collection, by contrast, is obviously professional in nature. Charting the progress of Hofstadter's manuscripts (both those completed and some only conceptualized) and the in-house assessments of his projects, it makes compelling reading. Too, one is rightly reminded of the commercial interests at stake, and the papers contain information regarding royalties, contracts, and Knopf's treatment of its authors.

I could not imagine undertaking this project without interviewing the important people in Hofstadter's life. How could one write about his teaching without talking to those whom he taught? And how could one claim even a spare understanding of his interior qualities without listening to the stories and observations of those who lived and worked with him? I was also aware, however, of the inherent difficulties in recording memories. I quickly learned to weigh oral responses against each other and against what archival and published materials could and could not verify. While approaching oral evidence with a healthy discretion, I had to grant that Hofstadter was a complex personality, perhaps in the end, too elusive to gather more than an approximation of his motives.

Without such conversations, the hidden history of these years would be lost. Stampp's and James Shenton's recollections of Hofstadter's deconversion from the Left add a powerful coda to the ideological journey of a generation of former radicals. And John Milton Cooper's memory of sitting outside 704 Hamilton Hall while he and a friend tried to guess their professor's ethnicity illuminates the identity "issue" that accompanied Hofstadter. Dan and Sarah Hofstadter offered helpful if conflicting impressions of their father—the consequence, one might suppose, of having different mothers compounded by a nine-year age gap. Dan (the elder) remembers a careful and distant man, emotionally complex with a distinct streak of melancholia. Sarah cites a more present figure, sharing the chores of child rearing and playfully attuned to the needs of a young girl. The diversity of description, instead of clouding the overall portrait, hints at the tensions in Hofstadter's life.

The Richard Hofstadter Project is part of the incomparable collection of materials located at the Oral History Research Office at Columbia University. Taped in 1973, these conversations, mainly with colleagues, provide a friendly depiction of Hofstadter, shedding light upon his intellectual influences: "I think the base point of his work was a skepticism with the enthusiasm of the 1930s"; or touching upon deeper personal currents: "[He was] . . . a natural clown in the sense of a background of sadness" (Hughes, Richard Hofstadter Project, OHRO). These tapes are best used as character sketches, for there is very little critical analysis of Hofstadter's scholarship. The *Project* contains only nine interviews, and the absence of several important observers— Woodward, Shenton, Stampp, William Leuchtenburg, Merle Curti, Lionel Trilling, Fritz Stern, Peter Gay—makes it an incomplete series. Still, its existence along with the institution's stewardship of the papers solidifies Columbia's claim as the main archive of Hofstadter materials.

Though Hofstadter never sat for extensive discussions of his life or work, four published interviews of varying quality exist. Taken in chronological order, "A Historian's View of the Mass Media: An Interview with Richard Hofstadter" (*Senior Scholastic*, 1957) clarifies Hofstadter's views on electronic media, pedagogy, and the popular portrayal of history. David Hawke's "Interview: Richard Hofstadter" (*History* 3 [1960]) has long served scholars seeking background information on Hofstadter's early works and influences. *Under Pressure: The Writer in Society: Eastern Europe and the USA* (1965) contains a few comments by Hofstadter on the intellectual's relationship to society and makes an eloquent plea for the useful alienation of the thinking class. Richard Kostelanetz's portrait of Hofstadter in *Master Minds* (1969), though not in the strict sense an interview, also deserves inclusion. It is a breezy, witty, and fascinating late reference to the man and his life. We are invited to smile at the absentminded professor's amiable professional embarrassments: "[I am] reaching the age when I black out on book titles all the time. I can't produce references spontaneously." We nod respectfully at his chilly working space: "His office . . . is large, sparsely adorned except for forbiddingly high history-stocked bookcases and a large lithograph of Joseph Pulitzer against the institutional light yellow wall." And we pay homage to his commitment to the life of the mind: "His body may go downtown . . . but his mind stays at Columbia" (173, 175, 171).

We do not have Hofstadter's reflections, nor do we know if he would have written them, or, if so, in what form. Woodward chose a modest venue, the Walter Lynwood Fleming Lectures in Southern History; Schlesinger, Jr., is producing an ambitious multivolume summary of his life. Shards of autobiography perforate Hofstadter's published works, and the final chapter of *The Progressive Historians* can be read as an extended defense of the intellectual choices he felt compelled to make. An unpublished Hofstadter address of great value to anyone working seriously on twentieth-century historiography is "The Great Depression and American History: A Personal Footnote" (1964; located in box 36 of the RHP), a sweeping overview of the historical circumstances that influenced Hofstadter's books.

Four biographical essays are of particular interest. Schlesinger, Jr.'s cogent profile in *Pastmasters* (1969) offers an appreciative but balanced appraisal of its subject's liberal spirit and is an excellent place to begin. The Festschrift essay "Richard Hofstadter: A Progress," written by Stanley Elkins and Eric McKitrick for *The Hofstadter Aegis* (1974), is filled with shrewd observations by men who knew Hofstadter well. Paula Fass's profile of Hofstadter in *Twentieth-Century American Historians* (1983) is attentive to her mentor's shortcomings but is fully appreciative of his special intellectual gifts and remarkable contributions. Jack Pole's more recent essay in *Clio's Favorites* (2000) weaves together life and work, accentuating the connection between Hofstadter's unique personal qualities and brilliant historical skills.

Christopher Lasch, Eric Foner, Daniel Singal (all Hofstadter students), and Alan Brinkley have contributed valuable summaries of Hofstadter's most important books. Lasch's 1973 foreword to *The American Political Tradition* emphasizes the intellectual exhaustion of Progressive historiography and the determination of postwar historians to replace a narrative of nostalgia with sobriety and realism. Singal's 1984 essay "Beyond Consensus: Richard Hofstadter and American Historiography" argues that Hofstadter's experiments with a variety of methodological styles are indicative of an open and protean thinker inaccurately characterized in recent years as a conservative. Brinkley's 1985 article "Richard Hofstadter's *The Age of Reform:* A Reconsideration" helpfully places that controversial book in the cultural context of its time and offers a candid analysis of both the work and its critics. Foner's 1992 introduction to a revised edition of *Social Darwinism* explores Hofstadter's early professional struggles and the intellectual milieu that produced his stunning dissertation.

I have drawn on several biographies of American historians and social scientists familiar to Hofstadter and the ideological controversies that defined his era. Among the most helpful were Howard Brick's *Daniel Bell and the Decline of Intellectual Radicalism,* Neil Jumonville's *Henry Steele Commager: Midcentury Liberalism and the History of the Present,* and John Roper's *C. Vann Woodward: Southerner.* I owe a special debt to Susan Stout Baker's *Radical Beginnings: Richard Hofstadter and the 1930s* (1985), the first work to make extensive use of the Harvey Swados Papers and explore the youthful leftist politics of her subject. Baker's book is informed by interviews with several figures, including Alfred Kazin, Julius Pratt, and David Riesman, who are not available to future biographers.

I have not attempted to offer a comprehensive list of Hofstadter studies. That would include many other names and many other titles, and these can be found elsewhere in these pages. This brief essay, rather, offers a sense of the important scholarship available on Hofstadter and speaks as well to my considerable debt to those who have gone before me.

Sources

Archives

AAKP   Alfred A. Knopf Papers (the Harry Ransom Center for the Humanities, the University of Texas at Austin)

ACCFP   American Committee for Cultural Freedom Papers (the Tamiment Library and Robert F. Wagner Archives, New York University)

ALCIA   American Labor Conference on International Affairs (the Tamiment Library and Robert F. Wagner Archives, New York University)

AKJ   Alfred Kazin Journals (the Berg Collection, New York Public Library)

AKP   Alfred Kazin Papers (the Berg Collection, New York Public Library)

ASJP   Arthur Schlesinger, Jr., Papers (the John Fitzgerald Kennedy Library, Boston, Massachusetts)

CLP   Christopher Lasch Papers (Rush Rhees Library, University of Rochester)

CVWP   C. Vann Woodward Papers (Yale University Library)

CWMP   C. Wright Mills Papers (the Barker Texas History Center, the University of Texas at Austin)

DBP   Daniel Boorstin Papers (the Library of Congress)

DBPT   Daniel Bell Papers (the Tamiment Library and Robert F. Wagner Archives, New York University)

DPP   David Potter Papers (Stanford University Library)

DRP   David Riesman Papers (Harvard University Library)

EGP   Eric Goldman Papers (the Library of Congress)

EMP   Eric McKitrick Papers (private collection)

HCP   Harry Carman Papers (Columbia University Rare Book and Manuscript Library)

HKBP   Howard K. Beale Papers (State Historical Society of Wisconsin)

HNSP   Henry Nash Smith Papers (Bancroft Library, the University of California at Berkeley)

HSCP	Henry Steele Commager Papers (Amherst College Library)
HSP	Harvey Swados Papers (W. E. B. Du Bois Library, University of Massachusetts Amherst)
KSP	Kenneth Stampp Papers (private collection)
JHP	John Hicks Papers (Bancroft Library, the University of California at Berkeley)
JPP	Jack Pole Papers (private collection)
JPPB	Julius Pratt Papers (Buffalo Historical Society)
MCP	Merle Curti Papers (State Historical Society of Wisconsin)
MFP	Marvin Farber Papers (State University of New York at Buffalo)
OAHRP	Organization of American Historians Records Papers (Indiana University, Purdue University at Indianapolis)
OHRO	Oral History Research Office (Columbia University)
RAP	Radical America Papers (State Historical Society of Wisconsin)
RHP	Richard Hofstadter Papers (Columbia University Rare Book and Manuscript Library)
WHP	William B. Hixson, Jr., Papers (private collection)
WBHP	William B. Hesseltine Papers (State Historical Society of Wisconsin)

Interviews and Correspondence

Eric McKitrick, phone interview, 27 May 2000.
William Leuchtenburg, Chapel Hill, NC, 17 June 2000.
Sarah Hofstadter, Oakland, CA, 22 August 2000; San Francisco, CA, 18 March 2004.
Kenneth Stampp, Berkeley, CA, 23 August 2000.
Walter Metzger, New York, NY, 4 December 2000.
Bette Swados, New York, NY, 5 December 2000.
Michael Wallace, New York, NY, 12 December 2000.
Eric Foner, New York, NY, 13 December 2000.
Peter Gay, New York, NY, 10 January 2001; 13 December 2002.
Fritz Stern, New York, NY, 10 January 2001.
Margaret Beattie Bogue, Madison, WI, 8 March 2001.
John Milton Cooper, Madison, WI, 9 March 2001.
Dan Hofstadter, correspondence, 31 March 2001.
Richard Plotz, phone interview, 6 April 2001.
Douglas Hofstadter, phone interview, 16 April 2001.
Paul Buhle, correspondence, 21 April 2001.
Daniel Bell, Cambridge, MA, 7 May 2001.
Stanley Elkins, Northampton, MA, 8 May 2001.
Jack Pole, Oxford, England, 19 May 2001.
Lee Benson, phone interview, 26 August 2001.
Ann Lane, Charlottesville, VA, 7 September 2001.
Dorothy Ross, Washington, DC, 22 September 2001.
James P. Shenton, Wayne, NJ, 28 September 2001.

Lawrence Levine, Washington, DC, 19 October 2001.
Ashbel Green, New York, NY, 12 December 2001.
Daniel Singal, correspondence, 26 March 2002; 21 May 2004.
Paula Fass, phone interview, 3 April 2002.
James Banner, Jr., Washington, DC, 24 June 2002.
Robert Dallek, Washington, DC, 23 July 2002.
Michael Kazin, phone interview, 23 September 2002.
William B. Hixson Jr., phone interview, 15 April 2003.
David Strauss, phone interview, 29 April 2003.
Edwin G. Burrows, phone interview, 27 May 2003.
John Mundy, correspondence, 20 June 2003.
David Burner, correspondence, 11 May 2004.
James Gilbert, correspondence, 28 May 2004.

Students of Richard Hofstadter

During Hofstadter's tenure at Columbia, the history department operated very informally in regard to mentoring graduate students. Many of the following students completed doctorates under Hofstadter, though some took courses or seminars with him but wrote dissertations for William Leuchtenburg, Eric McKitrick, and David Rothman.

1954   Paul Allen Carter, "The Decline and Revival of the Social Gospel: Social and Political Liberalism in American Protestant Churches, 1920–1940."

1956   Wilson Smith, "Moral Philosophers in Northern Society: Studies of Academic Men and Public Affairs, 1830–1860."

   Marvin Meyers, "The Jacksonian Persuasion."

1959   Stanley Elkins, "Slavery: A Problem in American Institutional and Intellectual Life."

1960   Eric McKitrick, "Andrew Johnson and the Reconstruction."

1961   Christopher Lasch, "Revolution and Democracy: The Russian Revolution and the Crisis of American Liberalism, 1917–1919."

1962   Lawrence W. Levine, "William Jennings Bryan: The Last Decade, 1915–1925."

1963   Robert Dallek, "Roosevelt's Ambassador: The Public Career of William E. Dodd

1965   David Burner, "The Democratic Party in Transition, 1918–1928."

   Dorothy Ross, "G. Stanley Hall, 1844–1895: Aspects of Science and Culture in the Nineteenth Century."

   Thomas R. West, "Discipline and Energy: The Machine in American Literature, 1918–1941."

1966   Otis Graham, "The Old Progressive and the New Deal: A Study of the Modern Reform Tradition."

James S. McLachan, "The Education of the Rich: Origin and Development of the Private Prep School."

Richard Weiss, "The American Myth of Success, 1865 to the Present: A Study in Popular Thought."

1968   James M. Banner, Jr., "To the Hartford Convention: Chapters in the History of Massachusetts Federalism, 1800–1815."

John Milton Cooper, Jr., "The Vanity of Power: American Isolationism and the First World War, 1914–1917."

Carol S. Gruber, "Mars and Minerva: World War I and the American Academic Man."

Linda K. Kerber, "The Federalist Mind: Rhetoric and Ideology in the Assessment of Jeffersonian America."

Ann J. Lane, "The Brownsville Affair: National Crisis and Black Reaction."

David Strauss, "Anti-Americanism and the Defense of France: An Analysis of French Travel Reports, 1917–1960."

John J. Turner, Jr., "New York in Presidential Politics, 1789–1804."

1969   Eric Foner, "Free Soil, Free Labor, Free Men: The Ideology of the Republican Party before the Civil War."

William B. Hixson, "Moorfield Storey and the Abolitionist Tradition."

1970   Perry Goldman, "The Republic of Virtue and Other Essays on the Politics of the Early National Period."

1971   Regina Morantz, "'Democracy' and 'Republic' in American ideology, 1787–1840."

1973   Edwin G. Burrows, "Albert Gallatin and the Political Economy of Republicanism."

Michael Wallace, "Ideologies of Party in the Ante-bellum Republic."

1974   Paula Fass, "The Fruits of Transition: American Youth in the 1920s."

1976   Daniel J. Singal, "The Development of Modernism: Intellectual Life in the South, 1919–1941."

Index

Aaron, Daniel, 145
academic freedom, 70–71, 78, 81, 180, 186
Academic Freedom in the Age of the College (Hofstadter), 165
Adams, Henry, 3, 34–35, 110, 121
Adams, Herbert Baxter, 5, 74–75
Adams, John Quincy, 135, 136
Adorno, Theodor, 90, 138, 151
Affluent Society, The (Galbraith), 124
Age of Jackson, The (Schlesinger), xxi, 57
Age of Reform, The (Hofstadter): content of, 99–119; criticism of, 99–119; 144–48 passim; genesis of, 79; and historical scholarship, its relation to other works of, 154, 193, 227; and midwestern populism, xvi; Pulitzer Prize awarded for, 120; style of, 15, 205; and the University of Wisconsin, its intellectual incongruity with, 74
agrarian bias in historiography, xiv, 23–24, 45, 92, 103
America at 1750 (Hofstadter), 154, 193, 228, 229–33
American Dilemma, An (Myrdal), 232
American Historical Association (AHA), 42–44, 53
American Negro Slavery (Phillips), 46

American Political Tradition and the Men Who Made It, The (Hofstadter): content of, xvi, xix, xxii, 49–65, 200, 204; and historical scholarship, its relation to other works of, 73, 122, 190, 227; and Hofstadter's career, 145–46, 150, 166; and Hofstadter's changed thinking about, 155–57; Hofstadter's esteem for, 193; and Progressive thought, 72; reputation of, xiii; the writing of, 41, 48, 158, 228
American Violence (Hofstadter et al.), 215, 217
Anderson, Terry, 171
Andrew Jackson: Symbol for an Age (Ward), 108
Anglo-Saxonism, 35, 60, 100, 110, 133–34, 195. *See also* Wasp historiography
anti-intellectualism, 79–83, 120–41 passim
Anti-Intellectualism in American Life (Hofstadter): content of, 120–41 passim; and Eisenhower, 154; elitist strain of, 156; genesis of, 79; and historical scholarship, its relation to other works of, 227; its publication in England, 189; sales of, 146; and the

Great Gatsby, The (Fitzgerald), 110
Green, Ashbel, 193, 227, 229
Greenberg, David, 56
Growth of American Thought, The (Curti), 22

Hacker, Andrew, 226
Hadas, Moses, 65
Halévy, Elie, 231
Hamilton, Alexander, xxi, 203, 210
Hammond, Bray, 57
Handlin, Oscar, 105–6, 164
Harding, Warren G., 142
Hardy, C. DeWitt, 79
Harrington, Michael, 87, 214
Harvey, William H., 147–48
Hawthorne, Nathaniel, 123
Hayden, Tom, 217
Hayes, Carlton J. H., 42–44, 68, 220
Hesse, Hermann, 89
Hesseltine, William, 42–43
Hicks, John D., 53, 101, 111, 112, 116
Hicks, Myra, 22
Higham, John, 53, 101–2
Higher Education: A Documentary History (Hofstadter and Smith), 79
Hill, Katherine. *See* Hofstadter, Katherine
Hill, Richard, 7
History of the United States from the Discovery of the American Continent (Bancroft), 5
Hitler, Adolph, xvii, 56, 152, 210
Hoffman, Abbie, 180
Hofstadter, Benjamin, 8
Hofstadter, Betty, 9
Hofstadter, Dan: birth of, 4; as a child, 49, 137; education of, 137, 146, 169–70; and the military draft, 169–70; recollections of his father, Richard, xvi, xvii, xix, 9, 39, 165, 217, 226–27; recollections of Samuel Hofstadter, 17
Hofstadter, Douglas, 7
Hofstadter, Emil, 7–8, 9–10, 13, 17
Hofstadter, Emma, 7
Hofstadter, Felice (née Swados), xviii,

10, 11–14, 18–19, 20, 24–26, 29, 41–43, 48–49, 228
Hofstadter, Katherine (née Hill), 7, 9
Hofstadter, Meyer, 7–8, 101
Hofstadter, Richard: and academic freedom, 70–71, 78, 81, 180, 186, 218; vs. agrarian bias in historiography, xiv, 23–24, 45, 92, 113; and the American Historical Association (AHA), his dispute with, 42–44; ancestry of, 7; and anti-intellectualism, 79–83, 86–87; and anti-Semitism, 20–21, 35, 38, 103–19 passim, 148; vs. Beard's (Charles) historiography, 16–17, 76, 198–202; and the Central Intelligence Agency (CIA), 82, 150; at Columbia University, on the faculty, 48–49, 65–71, 163–87 passim, 223–26; and "comity" between conservatives and liberals, xxii, 205–6; and the Communist Party, 24–27, 29, 77–78, 236; as a consensus historian, 50–51, 53–54, 200, 204–6, 237; and consensus politics, 156–60, 187; and conservatism, xxi–xxiii, 40, 50, 60, 66, 94, 123–24, 148–50; death of, xiv, 222; and education, his criticism of, 79–82, 137–38; and ethnic diversity, his recognition of, 7, 16–17, 53–54, 100, 108, 110, 159, 231–32; family life of, xviii–xix, 8–26 passim; financial status of, 144–46; Frankfurt School's influence on, 89–90, 94, 139; and Barry Goldwater, 142, 153–58; health of, 40, 222–26; hypochondria of, xvi, 223; and immigration, his recognition of its importance, 17; as an intellectual opposed to egalitarianism, 120–41 passim; Jewish background of, xv, xviii, 8–9, 12–13, 20–21, 38, 53, 73–74, 101–3; journalistic activities of, 48–49; vs. William Leggett, 44–46; and liberalism, xiii–xv, xx–xxiii, 28, 33, 44–45, 148, 187, 207–21 passim; and the liberal consensus, 190–206 passim; his first marriage, 18; his second marriage,

Rousselot, John H., 152
Rubenstein, Lewis, 9
Rubin, Jerry, 180

Said, Edward, 167
Sakharov, Andrei, 208
Sandberg, Carl, 54, 104
Schachtman, Max, 25
Schapiro, Meyer, xx, 104–5, 164, 167
Schkolnick, Meyer. *See* Merton,
    Robert K.
Schlesinger, Arthur, Jr.: and American
    culture, his effect upon, xiv, xxi; his-
    torical scholarship of, xxi, 50, 56, 57–
    58, 122, 135, 189, 222, 226; and Hof-
    stadter, 192, 205; on Hofstadter's
    offer from Harvard University, 164;
    on Hofstadter's *The American Politi-
    cal Tradition,* 63, memoirs of, 222
Schlesinger, Arthur, Sr., 44
Schrecker, Ellen, 124
Shannon, David, 144
Shaw, George Bernard, 171
Shenton, James, 21, 44, 66, 68, 78, 169
Shotwell, James T., 74
Sillman, Benjamin, 47
Simpson, Jerry, 101
Singal, Daniel, 70–71, 92, 165, 182
*Slavery: A Problem in American Institu-
    tional and Intellectual Life* (Elkins), 69
Smith, Adam, 102–3
Smith, Al, xx, 109
Smith, Henry Nash, 107–8, 195
Smith, Wilson, 79
social Darwinism, 15, 29–37
*Social Darwinism in American Thought,
    1860–1915* (Hofstadter), xix, 26, 29–
    37 passim, 49, 59, 72, 227
Sontag, Raymond, 53
Soul on Ice (Cleaver), 218
Sparkman, John, 132
Spencer, Herbert, 30–31, 36
Stalin, Joseph, 25, 56, 210
Stampp, Kenneth: and Hofstadter, his
    professional association with, 37–43,
    189, 220; and Hofstadter, his recol-
    lections of, 25, 129, 201; Hofstadter's

correspondence with, 47–49 passim,
    86, 131, 143, 170
Stanton, Guy, 43
status thesis, 94, 108–11, 117–18, 144
Stein, Sol, 83
Steinbeck, John, 104
Stern, Fritz, 163, 165, 170–71
Stern Group, 170–72
Stevenson, Adlai, 84, 86, 131–32, 135, 136,
    159
Stimson, Henry, xxi
Strauss, Harold, 51–52, 59
Strong, Josiah, 34
student rebellions of the 1960s, 176–87,
    214–18
Studies in Prejudice (Adorno et al.), 151
Sulzberger, Arthur Hays, 83
Sumner, William Graham, 31–32, 35, 36
Swados, Aaron, 11–12, 13, 18, 19
Swados, Felice. *See* Hofstadter, Felice
Swados, Harvey: and Hofstadter, famil-
    ial connection with, 9, 13; and Hof-
    stadter, intellectual differences with,
    128–30, 159–60; Hofstadter's corre-
    spondence with, 20–27 passim, 35–
    39 passim, 77, 125, 126, 159–60, 169,
    172, 195, 201, 225; marriage of, 49; as
    a novelist, 9
Swados, Israel, 11

Taft, Robert, 83, 201
Tate, Allen, 104
Thorndike, Lynn, 74
*Thoughts on the Cause of the Present Dis-
    contents* (Burke), 210
Todt, George, 152
Trilling, Diana, 185
Trilling, Lionel: at Columbia University,
    12, 65, 164, 165, 167; on conservative
    ideas, xxii, 148; and Hofstadter, fa-
    milial connection with, 12; and Hof-
    stadter, his influence upon, 12, 49,
    93; and Hofstadter, his recollections
    of, 235–36; importance of, 73, 163;
    and liberalism, 122–23, 148; as a mod-
    erate, 122–23, 130; and Stevenson's
    presidential bid, 85